International Relations and Scientific Progress:
Structural Realism Reconsidered

International Relations and Scientific Progress: Structural Realism Reconsidered

PATRICK JAMES

The Ohio State University Press

Columbus

Library of Congress Cataloging-in-Publication Data

James, Patrick, 1957–
  International relations and scientific progress : structural realism
reconsidered / Patrick James.
      p. cm.
Includes bibliographical references and index.
  ISBN 0-8142-0900-9 (hbk. : alk. paper) -- ISBN 0-8142-5095-5 (pbk. :
alk. paper)
  1. International relations--Philosophy.   2. World politics. 3.
Realism. I. Title.
  JZ1307 .J36 2002
  327.1'01--dc21
                                                2001006963

Cover design by Diane Hall.
Printed by Thomson-Shore

The paper used in this publication meets the minimum requirements of the
American National Standard for Information Sciences— Permanence of Paper
for Printed Library Materials. ANSI Z39.48- 1992.

9 8 7 6 5 4 3 2 1

To the memory of Maurice "The Rocket" Richard

CONTENTS

LIST OF FIGURES

LIST OF TABLES

ACKNOWLEDGMENTS

Several people read either all or part of this book at various stages of its development. I would like to thank Mark Brawley, Mario Bunge, Raymond Cohen, Ray Dacey, Charles F. Doran, Andrew J. Enterline, Yale H. Ferguson, Annette Freyberg-Inan, Ewan Harrison, K. J. Holsti, Carolyn C. James, Arie Kacowicz, Korina Kagan, Stuart J. Kaufman, James Keeley, Richard W. Mansbach, Manus I. Midlarsky, John R. Oneal, Galia Press-Barnathan, J. L. Richardson, Gerald Schneider, Sasson Sofer, James Wirtz, and the late Murray Wolfson for their helpful commentaries. None of these fine scholars, of course, is to blame for the shortcomings or errors that may be found in this book.

I also am very grateful to Barb Marvick, Joyce Wray, and Cindy Stuve for assistance with word processing and to Dan Merriman and Yasemin Akbaba for their work as research assistants.

Among those who have helped me with this work, one person stands out. Without Michael Brecher's help, I believe this book simply would not exist. He offered encouragement throughout the process, read the entire manuscript on several occasions, and offered a vast range of insights that have made this a much better work than it would have been otherwise. For this, and the many other fine things he has done for me in his long and distinguished career, I always shall be grateful.

Several institutions offered assistance to me in the completion of this work. Iowa State University supported this project at every stage of its development. I completed various parts of the work while visiting Utah State University as the Milton R. Merrill Chair of Political Science and the Hebrew University of Jerusalem as Lady Davis Professor of International Relations. To all of these excellent institutions I am most grateful.

My life at home is a happy distraction from academe. Carolyn James has supported me at every stage of this project and in so many other ways. To her I owe so much that it is hard to find the right words. My family, and especially Carolyn and Ben, is the foundation for whatever success I enjoy.

This book is dedicated to the memory of Maurice "The Rocket" Richard, one of the finest hockey players of the last century. My book goes somewhat against the direction of current thinking within the discipline of international relations, which tends to see both realism and system-level analysis—the main themes of my book—as being rather behind the times. The Rocket, who had a dedication to excellence that remains unrivaled in his sport, went against the grain a lot of the time and produced some memorable results. Thus I dedicate this work in memory of the unceasing effort and sometimes contrary nature of this extraordinary man.

Patrick James, Columbia, Missouri, January 2002

Part 1

Theorizing about International Relations

. . . [Professor] Pangloss sometimes said to Candide: "All events are linked up in this best of all possible worlds; for, if you had not been expelled from the noble castle, by hard kicks in your backside for love of Mademoiselle Cunegonde, if you had not been clapped into the Inquisition, if you had not wandered about America on foot, if you had not stuck your sword into the Baron, if you had not lost all your sheep from the land of Eldorado, you would not be eating candied citrons and pistachios here."

"'Tis well said," replied Candide, "but we must cultivate our gardens."
—Voltaire, *Candide*

CHAPTER ONE

The Realist Tradition and System-Level Theory

1. Purpose, Rationale, and Plan of Work

1.1 Why Create a System-Level Theory?

Can a theory that grants pride of place to the structure of the international system be used to explain a wide and interesting range of events in world politics? This book seeks to answer that question affirmatively from a realist point of view. The lineage of political realism, the traditional but increasingly embattled approach toward the study of international politics, can be traced from the philosophies of Kautilya, Mencius, Thucydides, Machiavelli, and Hobbes to any number of exponents in the twentieth century.[1] Such theorizing currently is out of favor among students of international politics as the result of what appears to be the failure of structural realism (or neorealism), by far the most prominent system-level theory over the last two decades, on any number of fronts.[2] The most prominent shortcoming, perhaps, is a perceived failure by structural realism to anticipate the ending of the Cold War and its dramatic aftermath throughout Eastern Europe.

While subsequent chapters will discuss many of the complaints directed against structural analysis in general and neorealism in particular, the argument pursued by this book is not the prevailing one, namely, that realism should be discarded in favor of theories that focus on the characteristics and internal politics of either states or international institutions. The current embrace by international relations of reductionism, most notably a virtual fixation over the last decade on democracy as the answer to the world's problems, seems too optimistic and out of touch with enduring truths.

Like Candide in the epigraph to part 1 of this book, we would be wise to tend the intellectual garden rather than trust, as did Professor Pangloss, to good fortune that is expected to arise in some form or another. Pangloss's description is one of dynamic complexity and interdependence, but Candide's response suggests that the knowledge required for action forces some degree of simplification. Thus, in this book, system-level theorizing is put forward as the potential answer to the questions raised by dynamic complexity.

The overall argument of this book is that, with appropriate revisions, structural realist theory can compete effectively in the new millennium and even reclaim its primacy in the field of international relations.

1.2 Plan of Work

This book will unfold in three parts. It moves from meta-theoretical concerns about international relations[3] through theory at a general level and finishes with conclusions and future directions.

Part 1 focuses on theorizing about world politics at a general level. It introduces and develops major concepts (chapters 1 and 2) and assesses the meaning of progress in the discipline of international relations (chapter 3). This section culminates in creation of the scientific research enterprise, a new concept in the philosophy of science with greater potential for application than thus far has occurred.

Part 2 reviews structural realism within the context of a scientific research enterprise and identifies the lack of connection between the theory and research that links capability-based indicators to conflict, crisis, and war in the international system (chapters 4 and 5). The overall purpose of part 2 is to make the case for elaboration of structural realism by showing that, at least in principle, a system-level theory based on structure could have great unrealized explanatory potential that could overcome incoherent development within the study of international politics.

Part 3 sums up the work and explores new directions. Implications for future research are discussed, most notably as related to empirical testing of an elaborated version of structural realism. The new theory might just as easily be called system-based realism, but self-designated continuity with structural realist theorizing suggests that its name should be Elaborated Structural Realism, or ESR for short (chapter 6).

This latter point draws attention to one limitation of the work as a whole: empirical testing will await the sequel to this study (James 2002a). At that point, extensive empirical analysis will be used to obtain a compelling judgment about whether an elaborated version of structural realism can explain and predict aspects of both international crises and foreign policy crises.[4]

Several tasks are carried out in the remaining sections of this chapter. The next section describes the realist tradition in brief, from its origins to contemporary manifestations in neorealism and neotraditionalism. This discussion brings out the vast range of ideas with some connection to realism, from the economistic reasoning of neorealists to the undiluted return to power politics advocated by neotraditionalists. In the third section, an overview of international politics in the twentieth century and beyond is used to suggest an approach toward understanding rapid change and complexity, namely, system-level theory. Section 4 offers a detailed justification for continued development of system-level theory on the basis of both the properties of systems and units and general principles behind theory building. This discussion also addresses objections that might be raised to renewed system-level theorizing. The chapter's fifth and final section reviews what has been accomplished and outlines the next set of steps in theorizing about world politics: a more detailed treatment of (a) system-level theory and the concepts of international system and structure; (b) realism and structural realism; and (c) international conflict, crisis, and war.

2. The Realist Tradition in International Theory

Many volumes have been devoted to the subject of political realism, so the point of this review is not to have the "last word" or even to evaluate such a vast body of knowledge. Instead, the purpose of this brief excursion into intellectual history is to place the further development of structural realism in a long-range context: the realist tradition in international politics.

Any discussion of the realist tradition finds a natural point of departure in Thompson's (1980, 1994) overview of international theory from classic to modern times. As Thompson (1994) points out, international theory can "bring order and meaning to otherwise-disparate bodies of information" and "produce new knowledge by virtue of the questions it asks" (22). These are the goals of realism, which seeks to understand the history of international relations through a sustained focus on the concept of power. Classic texts such as Thucydides' *Peloponnesian War*, Sun Tzu's *The Art of War*, Machiavelli's *Prince*, and Clausewitz's *On War* attempted to derive wisdom about policy from philosophy and the experience of history (Handel 1992). In each instance the underlying problem—how to survive in an anarchical world of rivalry and power seeking—remains the same. The problem of international war is immanent because the struggle for power is fundamental to human nature. For a realist this statement is considered to be valid for historical systems such as ancient Greece or Renaissance Italy, the world today, and even the future.

Realism, which originated in antiquity, experienced a series of challenges in the twentieth century to its vision of international relations. It would be an exaggeration to describe the scholarship of the period after World War I as some kind of idealist "monolith," for it certainly featured considerable diversity, but for the most part it rejected the power politics that was receiving the blame for the Great War of 1914 to 1918. Thus the period between World Wars I and II presented the first great challenge to realism. But the common view of the interwar era as one of idealist legalism versus more pragmatic realism is simplistic and inaccurate. Rather than the liberal idealism of Woodrow Wilson, embodied in the Fourteen Points and subsequent legal scholarship, the major intellectual development of the time might be seen as the "scientific movement" (Kahler 1997). *A Study of War*, Wright's (1942) systematic, even monumental, attempt to describe and explain the history of war from almost every imaginable angle, seemed likely to draw interest toward interdisciplinary research and aggregate data. *A Study of War* conveyed a world much more complex than that of realism, which had tended toward a one-dimensional focus on power politics. In sum, a return to realpolitik in the discipline of international relations seemed most unlikely, based on the impressive achievements of this tour de force and widespread dissatisfaction with past practices.

Yet political realism did come back into favor after the failure of appeasement in the 1930s, the trauma of World War II, and the onset of the Cold War (Kahler 1997: 26l; Knutsen 1997). Realism regained prominence after dictatorship and war had left much of the world in ruins. This intellectual approach seemed on target in blaming war on the evil side of human nature and the resulting quest for power. In particular, the failure of leaders in the interwar period to balance against the rising power of Germany, Italy, and Japan, along with the widely perceived failure of the League of Nations, discredited alternative approaches toward political practice. The most prominent treatment of these issues is found in Carr's ([1940] 2001) *Twenty Years' Crisis, 1919–1939*, which communicated disapproval of interwar diplomacy from an authoritative, realist point of view. In sum, the need to deal with "power politics" seemed obvious as the United States and the USSR began to eye each other across a chasm of suspicion.

Over half a century after its publication, *Politics among Nations* (Morgenthau 1948) still stands as the exemplar of twentieth-century realism. It became the most common basic textbook in the field of international relations for over two decades and had an immense influence on every subsequent research agenda in the field. Realism claimed as adherents the overwhelming majority of influential scholars in the era after World War II. Important contributors to the realist dialogue (some of whom started writing before the period just noted) included Raymond Aron, E. H. Carr, John Herz, George F. Kennan, Henry A. Kissinger, Reinhold Niebuhr, Frederick L. Schuman, Nicholas J. Spykman, Robert Strausz-Hupé, Inis Claude, and Arnold Wolfers.[5] Interpretation of diplomatic history and philosophical debates about policy among realists occupied center stage for many years.

Challenges to realism in more recent decades have occurred at two levels: method and theory. Inspired by systematic approaches from disciplines such as psychology and sociology, behavioral scientists in the 1960s rejected realism's emphasis on history and philosophy and opted for new methods. They searched for patterns in aggregate data about war and many other international events (Russett 1972). Although this research focused overwhelmingly on variables consistent with the realist tradition, such as the distribution of capabilities among great powers and how that related (in various forms) to the outbreak of war (Singer, Bremer, and Stuckey 1972, 1979; Bueno de Mesquita 1980b; Zinnes 1980a, 1980b; Nicholson 1989), it represented an important break from the past. Behavioral research disputed the seamless web of philosophizing combined with anecdotal evidence from diplomatic history that had characterized traditional realism. By creating a higher standard of evidence, behaviorists (defined inclusively) set the stage for more direct criticism of realism as a guide to theory and policy.

Only a few years later, critics started a frontal assault on realism as a theory. This debate went far beyond methods and focused instead on the primacy of states and power politics as fundamental concepts in explaining international relations (Haas 1958, 1964). The idea of interdependence gained prominence and stimulated research on international organizations in general and the politics of economic issues in particular as alternatives to the realist agenda of interstate relations and security policy (Young 1969; Keohane and Nye 1972, 1977; Jacobson 1978, 1984).

With the appearance of *Theory of International Politics* (Waltz 1979), intellectual currents shifted again. Waltz's "structural realism" focused on the system level in holistic terms; rather than offering advice on the management of power politics in international relations, his exposition searched for regularities in behavior among great powers. On the basis of a market metaphor, with great powers seen as similar to oligopolistic firms, Waltz (1979, 1986) concluded that states would seek to balance against attempts at hegemony and that wars could be expected to occur. This vision of international politics stood as a rejection of traditional, unit-level realism's emphasis on the individual decision maker, as well as the rising tide of institutional analysis (Keohane 1984).

While a more detailed review of structural realism and its critics will take place in chapters 4 and 5, it is sufficient for present purposes to say that the weight of opinion over the last decade has moved against Waltz's theory. This also is true of realism in general. "Neotraditional" realism, which emphasizes power seeking and foreign policy analysis rather than security maximization and the impact of structure, is found wanting as well (Vasquez 1997, 1998; Freyberg-Inan 2001). Efforts toward synthesis that bring together aspects of neotraditional and structural realism are a natural reaction. An interesting example is "dynamic differentials theory," which combines "power differentials, polarity, and declining power trends into one cohesive logic" (Copeland 2000a: 3; see also Copeland 1997). Still, even the best informed observers assert that realist paradigm is "degenerating" (Legro and Moravcsik 1999; see also Legro and Moravcsik 1998). At the beginning of a new millennium, it would be fair to say that the realist tradition is at or near a low point in its long history.

International theory is undergoing a sustained crisis. Neither realists nor critics, for example, anticipated the sweeping nature and rapidity of changes in Eastern Europe a decade ago. Realism is widely regarded as beyond salvation, but, after a reading of the critics, it is far from obvious what should be put in its place (Vasquez 1998). Under such conditions it is reasonable to step back and ask whether an *elaborated* version of structural realism might be able to fill the void: in other words, to sustain the basic contribution of realism and neorealism alike, which is to explain continuity in foreign policy and international relations while also coping with events such as crises and other sources of turmoil. The next section will begin to make the case that international politics in the twentieth century (and even beyond) can be explained, at least in principle, by a system-level theory with some connection to the realist tradition. Rapid change and complexity may imply the need for system-level theory now more than ever. In other words, it is essential that we not lose sight of continuity while confronted with a high volume of developments that may, in the fullness of time, lack staying power.

3. International Politics in the Twentieth Century and Beyond: An Approach toward Rapid Change and Complexity

In thinking about how the system's structure might affect either international politics in general or conflict in particular, the most important thing to recognize about the last century is the rapid pace of change and the resulting enhanced level of complexity. Global politics barely existed in 1900. Regional affairs tended to stay that way, although the empires of Britain, France, Belgium, Germany, the Netherlands, Portugal, Spain, and the United States created some intercontinental relationships. (The international system itself might be dated back to European expansion, from approximately 1500 onward [Bull and Watson 1984: 425].) Actors such as Japan, the United States, and China, which later rose to the forefront of conflict, crisis, and war in the twentieth century, had little or no involvement in the politics of Europe, the central subsystem. Similarly, events on that continent had only an indirect and gradual impact on the rest of the world, manifested by colonial rivalry. Exceptions such as the Anglo-Dutch wars of the seventeenth century and the war of the American Revolution in the eighteenth century—where combat extended from North America to India—stand out against a backdrop in which cooperation and conflict usually occurred between and among contiguous entities. The global network of communications, which today can bring a revolution in Poland, Romania, or the former Soviet Union into hundreds of millions of living rooms, did not exist. Given the impact of air travel, radio, television, and other innovations, it would not be an exaggeration to say that the previous century witnessed the beginning of global politics and that the concept of "globalization" enters into every contemporary debate over policy (O'Meara et al. 2000; Langhorne 2001).

All of the far-reaching changes in international relations during the twentieth century are connected in some way with the expanded range of contacts among individuals, interest groups, governments, and transnational organizations (Rosenau 1990, 1997; Ferguson and Mansbach 1996). Consider the words of Brown (1988), from over a decade ago, with regard to the emergence of "polyarchy," a situation of "many communities, spheres of influence, hegemonic imperiums, interdependencies, trans-state loyalties—some of which overlap, some of which are concentric, some of which are substantially congruent—that exhibits no clearly dominant axis of alignment and antagonism and has no central steering group or agency" (242). These observations create a challenge to system-level, realist theorizing because governance is held to exist in various forms and at different levels, with transnational actors and allegiances being involved (e.g., ethnicity and religion—see Stack 1981, 1986; Gurr 1993, 2000; Fox 2000a, 2000b, 2000c; Kaufman 2001; Saideman 2001; Sislin and Pearson 2001). The test for an elaborated version of structural realism would be to show that anarchy, state centrism, and related characteristics can provide the basis for a more compelling account of the international system than either polyarchy or related approaches.

Developments in a given state, geographic region, or issue area have become much more likely to affect the decisions and behavior of actors in widespread locations and with seemingly different concerns. This trend may be summed up in the idea of interdependence (Young 1969; Keohane and Nye 1977, 1987, 1989, 2000a, 2000b). Improvements in transportation and communication, which gained momentum throughout the twentieth century, ensure that causal linkages will increase in speed and complexity. As a result, effects are likely to register more widely and quickly than ever before. Bull and Watson (1984) noted that "the most striking feature of the global international society of today is the extent to which the states of Asia and Africa have embraced such basic elements of European international society as the sovereign state, the rules of international law, the procedures and conventions of diplomacy and international organization" (333). "It is a truism," as Wesson (1990) observed, "that we are carried breathtakingly forward by the achievements of science and engineering, at a seemingly ever-quickening pace, in directions unknown" (110). Crawford (1991) pointed toward a range of new global forces: "the nuclear and information 'revolutions,' the evolution of an integrated international food system, a dramatic increase in cross-border pollution and the globalization of production and investment, to name but a few" (438). Clark (1997) added that globalization seems to be "a continuing, if periodically accelerating, aspect of the twentieth century as a whole" (19). Sandler (1997) summed all of this up in terms of "global challenges" that defy traditional ways of thinking. Taken together, the increasing speed and volume of interaction point toward greater interconnectedness and complexity on a worldwide basis.

Both intuition and summary data at the global level indeed do confirm that the international politics of the new millennium are more complex by an order of magnitude than in the past. Consider the range of issues that produce conflict in a given era as a fundamental indicator of the international system's complexity: A compilation from Holsti (1991b: 307) makes it possible to compute the degree of concentration on issues that have generated conflict for respective periods since 1648. The widely accepted index of concentration developed by Ray and Singer (1973) can be used to estimate the extent to which conflict is produced by one issue versus many. A score of 1.0 means that all conflict derives from one issue, while 0 indicates a precisely equal share for all issues.[6] The concentration scores for the periods identified by Holsti are as follows: 1648–1714, 0.24; 1715–1814, 0.26; 1815–1914, 0.19; 1918–1941, 0.11; 1945–1989, 0.07. Thus the scores seem to suggest that issues producing conflict at the international level have become more diverse, although it is interesting to note the relatively modest scores for even the seventeenth and eighteenth centuries.

Among the twenty issues raised in the period since 1945, none accounts for more than 9 percent of the overall distribution, although territory, strategic territory, and boundaries, if combined into the more general category explored by Vasquez (1993; see also Huth 1996), would yield 18 percent. The issues and percentage shares for the period from 1945 to 1989, as identified by Holsti (1991b: 307), are as follows: territory, 8; strategic territory, 7; territory (boundary), 3; national liberation/state creation, 9; national unification/consolidation, 6; secession/state creation, 2; commerce/navigation, 1; commerce/resources, 3; protect nationals/commercial interests abroad, 3; protect ethnic confreres, 3; ethnic/religious irredenta, 4; defend/support ally, 5; ideological liberation, 4; government composition, 9; maintain integrity of state/empire, 9; enforce treaty terms, 2; maintain regional dominance, 2; state/regime survival, 7; autonomy, 2; and balance of power, 1. (The percentages do not add up to 100 because Holsti excludes issues that account for less than 1 percent of those in the period.) In terms of the number of issues represented and the lack of any that predominate, the previous century—and especially the period since World War II—appears to be the most complex so far. Of course, it is possible to combine these categories—for example, something like "territory," "influence," and "other" might come to mind—but, upon closer inspection, the range of substantive issues would stand out nonetheless.

The potential for issue linkage, along with the range of expertise that might become necessary to manage foreign policy, increases qualitatively because of the expanded agenda. It also is interesting to note subsets of issues in this list, such as ethnic/religious irredenta, that normally are associated with nonstate actors. Even more striking is the contrast between the diverse set of issues and the usual characterization of the Cold War bipolar era as one of relative simplicity (Waltz 1979). Perhaps the simple-looking structure described by Waltz had greater resilience than even he imagined, given its ability to contain such an array of substantive conflicts.

Since rapid change, a higher volume of interaction, and greater complexity are uncontroversial among respective schools of thought (however defined) on international politics, it is not necessary to present more systematic and detailed data on these subjects. If the years after 1989 had been included in the preceding calculations, in all likelihood the more unconventional items on the list would account for an even higher percentage of the cases. The sense of awe in the face of so much cumulative change over a brief interval of world history is summed up well by Mansbach (1996): "[W]e might be pardoned for wondering whether our theories are relevant to an era of failed states, warring tribal and ethnic identities, hot money, environmental catastrophe, massive popular mobilization and participation, and the immobilisme of governments everywhere. Neither neorealism nor neoliberalism (nor any other perspective) provides a Kuhnian paradigm for global politics, whatever their adherents might claim" (91). Even Holsti (1996), a persistent defender of traditional scholarship on international politics against various perceived forms of extremism,[7] expresses concern for the current state of theory: "Key analytical concepts such as balances of power, hegemony, alliances, deterrence, power projection, and a whole range of geopolitical ideas also derive from the European and Cold War experiences. Their relevance to most post-1945 wars is highly problematic" (14).

When juxtaposed with the list of security issues introduced by Mansbach a moment ago, Holsti's list of concepts derived from Cold War realpolitik seems rather outdated, a point of which he also is aware (Holsti 1996). Thus, from one point of view, which sees the world as simply beyond the reach of realist theory, it may be time to "start all over again."[8]

Perhaps the furthest departure from the existing edifice of theory is the concept of "turbulence," which Rosenau (1990, 1997) uses to summarize the high complexity and dynamism of contemporary world politics. A basic question arises: Are anomalies more pervasive than recurrent patterns and discontinuities more prominent than continuities? Rosenau (1990: 66, 5) concludes that world politics is about to enter—or perhaps already has reached—a state of unpredictability, with the concept of turbulence referring to simultaneous changes in the basic "parameters" of the system. The resulting bifurcation of the international system produces a parallel and viable world of transnational and subnational actors alongside the traditional interactions among states. Young (1999) introduces the concept of a "global civil society" (9), consisting of professional associations, interest groups, corporations, and other nonstate actors, that exists alongside the traditional interstate system. While no reason exists to believe that "states are on their way out as centers of power and authority," evidence shows that "a second social system is growing up around the society of states, a system that is coming to form a part of the social environment within which regimes operate" (9). Thus one response to rapid change and increasing complexity, as per Young and Rosenau, is to analyze state-centric and transnational relations separately, with the ultimate goal being to specify an overall network of effects.

More than just the end of the Cold War is at work in encouraging such a fundamental change in outlook (Rosenau 1997): "The information revolution and other technological dynamics are major stimulants, but so is the breakdown of trust, the shrinking of distances, the globalization of economies, the explosive proliferation of organizations, the fragmentation of groups and the integration of regions, the surge of democratic practices and the spread of fundamentalism, the cessation of intense enmities and the revival of historic animosities—all of which in turn provoke further reactions that add to the complexity" (7). Thus "to treat the established frameworks as the baseline from which the balance between change and continuity should be assessed amounts to a procedure that seems bound to hinder thinking afresh" (9). Instead, established boundaries for theorizing, referring to both an explicit interstate orientation and the underlying assumption that the system is in equilibrium, should be replaced with the "Frontier," a concept that represents the new and wider political space within which governance can be investigated under turbulent conditions (4, 9). The process of "fragmegration," for example, refers to simultaneous integration and fragmentation of political systems (Rosenau 1988, 1990). Global and instantaneous communications coexist with the resurgence of parochial, ethnolinguistic identities; these forces combine to threaten conventional ideas about state centrism and citizenship in fundamental ways.

Rosenau, Mansbach (see also Ferguson and Mansbach 1991, 1996), and numerous other critics ranging from feminists to constructivists (Tickner 1992; Adler 1997) oppose what might be labeled "incrementalism" in further efforts to theorize about world politics.[9] Why build, it might be asked, on an obsolete foundation, at the system level or otherwise?

Despite the pace and volume of change, seemingly revolutionary differences from the recent past, and even a sense that the world already may be on the road to unpredictability, the basic belief underlying this investigation is that *political interactions produce patterns that can be detected by systematic research.* Outcomes in world politics result from behavior with a purpose, even if the results do not always correspond to the intentions of the actors.[10] Events, as noted by Niou, Ordeshook, and Rose (1989), "follow from the actions of people pursuing their goals in a world constrained by limited resources, innovative skill, and the actions of others" (3). A degree of competition over resources and security is rooted in the international system, meaning that regularities should be detected across time and geographic locations (Booth 1987: 61). It is most constructive to probe for connections based on such properties because much of what happens at the international level may be explained without resort to specific characteristics of situations or actors. The fact that events occur more rapidly than in the past does not alter the unchanging content of political behavior: the pursuit of goals selected by actors on the basis of their identity (i.e., power status) within the context of a system (Gilpin 1981).[11] With that assumption intact, even the multitude and diversity of developments spanning the twentieth century and the new millennium can become intelligible, at least in principle.

Based on the above-noted line of reasoning, the present investigation adopts a deductive-nomological approach toward the development of theory (Hempel 1965: 337, 374; Nicholson 1989: 19). In the tradition of social scientific research, probabilistic linkages are expected to emerge for classes of events (Frankel 1988: 2). Each explanation derived in that manner constitutes a potential prediction because the appearance of certain conditions will increase the likelihood of associated effects.[12] The resulting position on causal relations is summed up by Krathwohl's (1987: 218, 221; see also Brecher 1993; Bunge 1996: 31) notion of a contributing cause: while it "increases the probability that the effect will occur," a contributing cause is neither a necessary nor a sufficient condition (221). This cautious outlook is especially appropriate regarding linkages that involve the international system and its processes. Given the length of the causal chain that might connect an individual event to a system-level trait, constant conjunction almost certainly can be ruled out.

With regard to international conflict in general, or important subsets of events such as crisis or war, the most appropriate approach toward theory is to focus on units, both on an individual basis and collectively, as components of a system. Questions arise about the experiences of units *and* systems: Given information about a unit's characteristics or position in the international system, what is its probable degree of involvement in strife? For example, would knowledge about traits such as the type of government or geographic position of a state be useful in explaining its activity in conflict, crisis, and war? Alternatively, on the basis of the composition of the system (possibly referring to the distribution of wealth or variation in political organization), how much conflict should be expected in the aggregate? Does the distribution of military capabilities, to cite one possibility, have any connection to the conflict prone-ness of states in a region? Many other questions could be posed about states and systems, and it will be argued that, while both are important, theorizing should begin at the system level for a wide variety of reasons.

4. Properties of Systems and Units

4.1 Presenting the Case for System-Level Theory

Two basic alternatives exist for attempting to explain international politics in the complicated twentieth century and beyond: focusing on individual units or on the system level composed of those units.[13] The first approach entails exploring how a system is affected by interactions within and among its units. Foreign pol-icy is traced outward from the actor to its environment, with resulting incre-mental or possibly more dramatic changes in the latter. Some studies of this type focus on how policy is made under both ordinary and crisis conditions.[14] Others examine the role of national attributes in determining the actions directed by governments toward the international system.[15] The second option is to examine the system's impact on its units, with the latter normally referring to states. From this point of view, more enduring aspects of the system, most notably the con-straints imposed by structure, shape interactions. Processes develop, in turn, either within or beyond the conditions that permit the system to persist in equi-librium (Brecher and Ben Yehuda 1985; Brecher and James 1986).[16]

Among students of international politics, it is an accepted principle that causes and effects operate in both directions (Frankel 1981: 233; Stoll 1987: 387; Domke 1988: 2; Almond 1990: 284; Brown 1991: 217–18; Carlsnaes 1992: 256, 260). The basic differences focus on relative importance; what deserves priority in causal ordering among elements at each level? The issue, of course, is where to start, not whether to leave either unit or system out of cau-sation. Gilpin's (1981: 12; see also Doran 1991) exposition on political change is instructive. A system leaves a state of equilibrium when differential rates of growth in capabilities among its units result in a redistribution of capabilities. Disequilibrium ensues, with eventual resolution of a system-level crisis produc-ing a new order that, in turn, conditions subsequent interactions. Thus Gilpin's unit-system linkage is interactive, as opposed to unidirectional.

What, then, is the appropriate starting point for a general investigation of international conflict? Without delving into the controversy over exactly what these terms might represent in one theory or another, is it better to begin with the "trees" or the "forest"?

For several reasons it will be argued that system-level theory, with a primary focus on the impact of structure on processes of interaction, should receive priority as the point of departure for analysis of international politics in the twentieth century and beyond. The reasons concern (a) issues pertaining to respective properties of systems and units and (b) aspects related to theory building at a more general level. Each set of reasons for a system-level orientation will be presented in turn, followed by responses to some obvious objections that might be raised along the way. This is necessary because attacks on system-level approaches have been so extreme and pervasive that it is appropriate to justify carefully any further significant investment of time in such theorizing.[17]

Unit-level complexity, asymmetry of impact, the greater range of system effects, and relative durability of influence are properties that encourage the choice of system over unit as the point of departure for theorizing. First, the complexity of the unit level makes it extremely difficult to trace the cumulative effects of foreign policy on global and regional systems. Second, impact is asymmetric—while all actors operate within the same international system, individual units (or, for that matter, coalitions) will be working at cross-purposes in terms of foreign policy. Third, the range of effects is greater for the system than those generated by any set of actors. Finally, the system's influence is more durable than that of its units either alone or in various combinations. Each of these properties of systems and units will be described in turn.

Given that the components and processes of the international system appear to be more diverse, complicated, and interconnected than at any other time in history, pursuit of the unit-level option appears problematic from the outset. This task is daunting even if the meaning of a significant unit remains highly conventional: over 190 states possess nominal status as sovereign entities. (The smaller subset of great powers could be cited as a more feasible option, perhaps, but this effectively regresses back to Waltz's [1979] system-level model cast in terms of an oligopoly of power.) Global, regional, and national networks of communication have expanded the observed and potential volume of interaction dramatically (Jacobson 1984; Keohane and Nye 1977, 1987, 1989, 2000a, 2000b). While some events have more comprehensive effects than others, the *opportunity* for global impact is increasing with time. The modern state must cope with rapid and basic change along multiple dimensions; the world financial crises of October 1987 and the summer of 1998 and the third Russian Revolution in 1991 are prominent examples within the economic and political domains, respectively.

Regardless of an actor's position, policy must anticipate and deal with many more issues than in the past. Overpopulation, environmental decay, and mounting debt affect all states and nonstate actors, either directly or through intermediaries (Sandler 1997). Governments remain accountable for the protection of territorial sovereignty and national prosperity, but the range of concerns falling within each of these general designations continues to expand. Transnational, subnational, and supranational actors further complicate the formulation and implementation of national policy in a fast-paced world (Ferguson and Mansbach 1996; Rosenau 1997). The events of September 11, 2001 and their aftermath reinforce this point dramatically.

All things considered, the actors in world politics are more numerous than ever before, and each exists in a situation more complex than that of decades, and especially centuries, past. These long-term developments suggest that general explanations based on unit-level factors will be progressively *more* difficult to derive and sustain. As system components proliferate and become more diverse, with a high rate of change in social, economic, and political terms, it is more promising to look toward the system as a prior source of explanation for processes. Put differently, the advantages of studying any system in these terms increase, relatively speaking, with its size and internal complexity. The international system is no exception.

Consider the metaphor of the "billiard balls" as applied to international politics in the modern state system. Among political realists, this is a convenient way of emphasizing that "[a]ll the units of the system behave essentially in the same manner" (Wolfers 1962: 82). The metaphor can be extended to summarize the linkage of the system to its units (Wolfers 1962: 82; Mansbach and Vasquez 1981: 3; Krasner 1982a: 498, 1982b). The billiard table, which constitutes a closed and stable environment for interaction, sets boundaries for the classic, state-centered system. The billiard balls, both impenetrable and functionally interchangeable, represent sovereign states. They collide with each other in ways that may be anticipated to some degree but with results that are more difficult to predict in recent times. The basic nature of the system, however, is competitive and relatively impervious to large-scale change.

Within the preceding Eurocentric vision of world politics, foreign policy analysis could focus on a few great powers—no more than a dozen throughout the history of the modern states system—and patterns of interaction among them largely determined outcomes in international relations. This relatively simple (if not always fully predictable) system emerged from the ashes of the Thirty Years' War. After the Treaty of Westphalia in 1648, foreign policy in the great capitals shaped the affairs of the continent and gradually extended European influence around the globe.[18] Causal inferences from the unit to the system remained a viable alternative to system-level theorizing. More than just chance accounts for the fact that realist tracts focused almost exclusively on policy formulation and implementation until well into the twentieth century. Theorizing focused on foreign policy from a prescriptive point of view, while systemwide conceptualization probably received marginal attention because it seemed to have comparatively little pragmatic importance. After all, system-level evolution in terms of capability distribution and like matters could not rival short-term machinations in foreign policy with respect to implications for the near future.

From today's vantage point, the billiard table looks rather crowded and complicated. Perhaps more than a dozen significant units must be monitored, and the most important ones sometimes vary from one issue to the next. It also is obvious that states no longer are the only components that matter, especially in the realm of political economy, but also with respect to security issues (to the extent that these areas can be distinguished at all). The actions of multinational corporations and terrorist groups serve as well-established examples in each respective domain (Vernon 1977; Mickolus, Sandler, and Murdock 1989; James and Mitchell 1995).[19] Given the extension of interstate rivalry into space, which started with the superpowers during the Cold War, even the physical limitations of the international system may change.

Some things, however, appear to be the same.[20] Anarchy and coercion persist (Waltz 1979, 1986, 1991, 1993, 1995, 1997). States possess a virtual monopoly on full-scale military force, the most extreme means of influence. To cite a prominent example of the continuing importance of states, consider the forces behind the most dramatic change in world politics since 1945: disintegration of the network of authoritarian regimes in Eastern Europe. This development can be traced clearly to the Soviet Union, which experienced a transformation in both foreign and domestic policy after the ascent of Mikhail Gorbachev to national leadership. While democratization, ideology, and transnational actors (such as members of the international financial network and epistemic communities) may have influenced the Soviet General Secretary's decision to pursue reform, change nevertheless emanated from the center of a powerful state seeking to compete effectively under conditions of anarchy.[21]

Furthermore, the international system still operates within limits. Although the system is complex and includes more units than in the past, structure still can be identified. Thus the effects of the system on its units are more likely to be intelligible than those in the opposite direction if the goal is to identify patterns in the aggregate. This point is made at a more general level by Bunge (1996): "One of the philosophical myths that has hindered the scientific treatment of social problems is the belief that the study of a system, such as a society, is necessarily more difficult than that of its components" (83). A key reason for choice of the system as a point of departure for theorizing in the present context is the *existence of many types of regularities at the systemic rather than component level*: averages, ratios, and other aggregate properties are more meaningful for systems and also happen to be more stable than the traits of components.[22]

Important knowledge can be gathered through the use of simulated international systems; two recent examples will be used to illustrate this point. Simon and Starr (1996: 286–87; see also Simon and Starr 2000) use a simulation model to assess how units in search of both internal and external security will function under conditions of anarchy. A ten-actor system produces subtleties in the effects of a bipolar distribution of capabilities: it provides the highest average gain in *domestic* security for both major and minor powers, which is consistent with the standard argument about bipolarity and stability. But Simon and Starr find that, with respect to *international* security, this holds true only for minor powers. Kadera's (1998; see also Kadera 2001) simulation model of the spread of war within and across regions, which varies the "barriers" and "transmission mechanisms" faced by states, suggests that the "complete elimination of war in conflict-prone regions such as the Middle East appears to be an overly optimistic and impractical policy goal" (384). Taken together, these simulation studies and others suggest that unit-level characteristics such as resource allocation and threat perception, along with system-level traits like the degree of permeability across regional systems, will interact with each other and combine to form overall patterns.

Since significant causal forces operate in each direction—that is, for units and systems—both sets of dynamic relations must be acknowledged. However, intuition suggests that the structure of the international system will have more of an ongoing impact on its components than the reverse. Although individuals, states, and transnational actors contribute to a system's evolution, over the course of decades the constituents still confront many of the same features. Even the more dynamic elements of what later will be identified with structure—alliances, relative capabilities, and the like—rarely change as rapidly as officials in government, national business cycles, and other unit-level characteristics. While that difference does not establish a greater ongoing impact for structure, all other things being equal, it suggests a higher likelihood.

More specifically, there is an asymmetry of motivation to consider, which leads into the second reason to begin with system-level theorizing. The international system is not "trying" to achieve any specific goals, such as eliminating certain states or creating others; instead, it conditions interactions among all of the actors within its boundaries. "[E]ssential rules" of a system will hold regardless of the labeling of actors (Kaplan 1957: 63). Balance of power and policies aimed at its preservation are to be expected (Morgenthau and Thompson 1985: 187). This is different from saying that norms are constructed and followed self-consciously by collectivities, as in the case of social constructivism (Wendt 1999); instead, the international system of anarchy serves as a selection mechanism. Failure to balance effectively is expected to result in loss of capabilities or even destruction of the state itself. Viewed through that lens, all systems give the appearance of resisting hegemony, whether referring to efforts by Louis XIV, modern Japan, or others. Thus a world empire, where the system and one of its units become coterminous, is regarded as only a remote possibility because of tendencies toward countervailing power.[23]

Today's global system, which appears to be led by a transnational oligopoly of trading states and their international institutions, is not really an exception to this point. Countervailing power and fracturing of supramajorities are not always to be expected immediately. The media in major Western states, most notably the United States, already are full of "Sinoanxiety," and no proof exists that the coalition of leading states always will remain intact. For such reasons it is better to assume that the conflict, crisis, and war between organized groups that have been going on for multiple millennia are likely to continue in some form than that the world will be transformed in the near future into a global Kantian community.

Gilpin (1981: 86) also considers structure to be of fundamental importance in conditioning foreign policy for all states, while Ruggie (1989)—in an exposition that is largely critical of system-level theory as it has developed—notes that it "imparts organization, disposing and constraining effects, on domains of social discourse and action" (21; see also Ruggie 1986). (The idea that structure can either impede or facilitate communication goes back at least as far as the systems analysis of Rosecrance [1963] and even Kaplan [1957].) Actors within an international system, by contrast, may attempt to achieve different and sometimes clashing goals, whether the focus is global, regional, or otherwise. Some of these aims will result in policies intended to produce change, while others will result in efforts to preserve all or part of the existing operation of the system. The most obvious example of clashing goals would pertain to the territorial status quo, with Israel/Palestine and the dispute between France and Germany over Alsace/Lorraine as just two prominent examples that could be cited.

Regardless of the difficulty sometimes encountered in identifying the full range of goals pursued by states, it is clear that variation exists among them. Unless the sum of the forces produced as a result of those goals exceeds a threshold for system-level change, evolution rather than revolution is to be expected, and structure will continue to condition interactions.

Individual states, aside from a few temporary anomalies such as Napoleonic France and Germany under Hitler, cannot match the system's global range of effects. While some units are capable of exerting influence virtually anywhere, such as Great Britain in the "balancer" role from 1815 to 1914, the United States and the USSR from 1945 to 1989, and the United States alone since that era, this occurs neither constantly nor uniformly around the world. A state will be more active at some times than others, and its geographic focus and ultimate goals, or "grand stratgegy," also may vary (Tillema 1991; Brawley 1993, 1999; Desch 1993). Consider, by comparison, the dispersion of capabilities among units as one possible way of representing structure. The distribution of capabilities (regardless of the exact way in which it is measured) affects world politics in an ongoing and systemwide—if not always straightforward—manner (Waltz 1979).[24] Thus unit-level approaches may be more suited to account for *behavior* than for *effects*.

Even the most erstwhile critics of realist theory and "power politics" acknowledge the importance of capability-based variables such as the number of great powers in comparing the propensity of international systems toward conflict, crisis, and war. This remains true even as would-be linkages are debated fiercely and often without any decisive resolution (Vasquez 1993, 1998; Geller and Singer 1998). Any effort to elaborate structural realism should include an attempt to resolve these differences through specification of scope conditions.

Durability of influence provides another reason to begin the process of theorizing at the level of the system. National policies can change quickly, resulting in effects on the system that are not sustained. Consider, for example, relations between the superpowers over the last two decades of the USSR's existence. In the early 1970s, détente created a wave of optimism. President Richard M. Nixon, a prominent "Cold Warrior," visited Moscow and signed the Strategic Arms Limitation Treaty (SALT I) with the USSR. A decade later, the Soviet invasion of Afghanistan, references to an "evil empire," and the downing of a South Korean airliner by a Soviet fighter in 1983 symbolized an apparently irreversible decline in superpower relations. Yet only a few years onward, journalists and scholars joined together to observe the demise of the Soviet Union and announce the end of the Cold War.

This example of fluctuating policies and perceptions of them should serve as a warning that the impact of the system on international politics is likely to be more sustained and less subject to rapid fluctuation and misperception than that of any actor or combination of them. (It also is a reminder that actors have discretion in spite of structural imperatives.) After all, during the period from détente to the end of the 1980s, when all of the above-noted changes took place, the United States and the USSR remained alone at the apex of states, at least in military terms and most notably with regard to nuclear second-strike capabilities. Despite gyrations in foreign policy that resulted from shifting attitudes and motivations within the two leading capitals, this duopoly of capabilities (or power bipolarity), complete with spheres of influence, continued to confront members of the international polity.[25] The constant system-level effect in the era concerned is a competition for spheres of influence.

Consider, with a focus on the U.S.-Soviet rivalry that dominated world politics for almost half a century, the extraordinary events witnessed by the world since 1945. International crises erupted around the globe, with the Truman Doctrine (1947), Berlin Deadline (1958–1959), Cuban Missile Crisis (1962), Prague Spring (1968), Entebbe Raid (1976), Fall of Amin (1978–1979), Cambodia Peace Conference (1989–1990), Kashmir III: India/Pakistan Nuclear Crisis (1990), Yugoslavia I: Croatia and Slovenia Crisis (1991–1992), and North Korea Nuclear Crisis (1993–1994) as only a few prominent examples (Brecher, Wilkenfeld et al. 1988; Brecher and Wilkenfeld 1989, 1997). Some intense conflicts have escalated to interstate war, including the Korean War (1950–1953), Vietnam War (1965–1975), Second Kashmir War (1965), Six Day War (1967), October—Yom Kippur War (1973), Russo-Afghanistan War (1979–1989), Iran-Iraq War (1980–1988), and Gulf War (1990–1991) (Small and Singer 1982: 59).[26] Military technology, especially in the realm of nuclear weapons and delivery systems, improved at a disturbing rate. Generations of leaders, from Winston Churchill to Ronald Reagan, moved across the international stage. Empires disappeared, and a level of collective consciousness emerged among developing states.

Along with such memorable events, the duopoly of military capabilities that arose at the end of World War II—commonly understood as the essence of the system's structure (i.e., power bipolarity)—persisted until at least the beginning of the 1990s. Thus it is wise to take a skeptical view toward supposed system transformation; the urge to see a "New World Order" every time a major change occurs or to perceive each development as unique (McClosky 1962: 189) should be resisted in order to maintain some perspective.[27] The impact of prominent events in particular may be misunderstood in their immediate aftermath; for example, did Neville Chamberlain's announcement of "peace in Our time" really mean an end to interstate rivalry and the ultimate triumph of international law? Events soon after proved that it did not.

To sum up, durability of impact can be added to the three preceding reasons—complexity of the unit level, asymmetry of impact, and range of effects—to argue in favor of renewed priority on system- over unit-level theorizing as a point of departure. This approach ultimately should give the advantage to an elaborated structural realism over alternative theories because of an enhanced ability to deal with both continuity and change.

4.2 Theory Building

Two aspects related to theory building in more general terms also point toward the system level: (a) basic principles underlying construction of scientific models favor a choice of the system, and (b) the bias toward explanations cast at the dyadic level needs to be addressed through a more comprehensive gathering of evidence about international conflict.

To begin, in building a model of any kind, it is best to add complications only when necessary (Nicholson 1989: 16). If a wide range of interactions can be explained without resorting to the naturally more intricate and mercurial unit level, that is good in principle (Keohane 1982: 328). Of course, "from a purely systemic point of view, situations of strategic interdependence do not have determinate solutions" (Keohane 1989: 63). A theory centered on the system, however, can narrow the range of feasible outcomes and greatly facilitate the process of explanation (Niou et al. 1989: 31). The nature of the limits encountered by such a theory may suggest the relevant nonsystemic factors that, in turn, find a place within a treatment of unit-level behavior. For a realist exposition, such factors presumably would refer to capabilities in some way or another.

Over the past decade the most successful line of research on conflict, crisis, and war has focused on the characteristics of dyads composed of states. It has been more successful than research conducted at either the state or system level (Geller and Singer 1998: 68, 113; Vasquez 2000b: 381). (The increasing relative frequency of civil conflict, often with foreign intervention, is a separate matter.) The most sustained and prominent results are that aspects of domestic political economy and democratic status impose constraints on escalation of conflict to war (Russett 1990, 1993). Dyads made up of democratic states, in fact, appear virtually invulnerable to the temptation of war, at least on the basis of aggregate data analysis in the last decade (Levy 1988, 1989; Ray 1995; Geller and Singer 1998). The apparently confirming results from several hundred single-equation regression models of democracy and peace have affected the distribution of intellectual resources dramatically, with an increasing number of studies investigating the war propensity of dyads in terms of the characteristics of states within them.[28]

Results from dyadic research designs on interstate conflict, crisis, and war appear impressive in comparison to system-level treatments, which so far in response have offered only general assertions about international politics and foreign policy (Waltz 1979, 1986; see also Freeman and Job 1979: 136). Hypotheses that power balancing will take place and war will occur become increasingly less interesting in contrast to high rates of predictive success for important, specific events like the outcomes of crises and disputes (Bueno de Mesquita 1981b; James 1988; Bueno de Mesquita and Lalman 1988, 1992; Bremer 1992, 1993). Levy (1995) sums up the recent trend effectively: "Over the last decade there has been a significant shift in the quantitative empirical study of international conflict, driven largely by the increasing recognition that structural systemic models are theoretically incomplete and empirically unable to account for much of the variance in the outbreak or expansion of international disputes and wars" (219). Kahler (1997) also notes the "decline of system-level theory" in an overall sense, beginning with dependency theory and neoliberalism and continuing because of the failure of structural realism "to develop a convincing research program at this level of analysis" (43). Holsti (1998) goes a step beyond the observations of Levy and Kahler to cite a more fundamental problem: "System-oriented theories simply ignore the personal sources of policy: the logic of the international system forces statespersons, whether saints, sinners, or bullies, to behave within strict limits imposed by the external environment. . . . [E]lements of free will and choice in these approaches were minimal" (21). Thus the disappointing empirical performance noted a moment ago may be traced to the determinism that pervaded system-level theories. For at least two reasons, however, it is inappropriate to infer from the recent primacy and success of systematic, dyadic research on war in particular that system-oriented theory should continue to receive marginal attention.

First, dyadic models are not well equipped to answer many important questions. Aggregate patterns are unlikely to be explained by an examination of the properties of dyads (Schelling 1978: 14). The frequency, intensity, and other properties of conflict at a regional or global level can be understood only in terms of system-oriented theory. Thus the observations by Levy from a moment ago are subject to inherent and important limitations: dyadic theorizing seems to be outperforming structural analysis, but the competition *excludes areas to which actor-based models cannot be applied in principle.* Properties such as the crisis proneness of the international system, to cite just one example, cannot be inferred from the traits of individual actors; this point, of course, is as old as the idea of the individualistic fallacy. Furthermore, the "incomplete" structural systemic model—to use the term introduced by Levy—may be even better across the board than dyadic counterparts when more fully developed.

Second, dyadic treatments currently enjoy an advantage in explaining specific events, such as the escalation of a dyadic conflict to war, because system-level theories invariably have been put forward without a relatively complete model of state behavior. Unit-system linkage is essential for a theory cast at the level of the system to compete effectively in accounting for the traits of individual events while maintaining the unique ability to explain properties at a higher level of aggregation. As even Waltz (1993) concedes, "[F]oreign policy behavior can be explained only by a conjunction of external and internal conditions," and structure therefore takes on the role of a "permissive" cause (79). Thus the holistic development of system-level theory as it exists so far, rather than an inherent nature, stands in the way of improvement.

Intellectual bias at a more general level provides a final justification for renewed emphasis on system-level theory. Can the reality of international politics be represented properly through an accumulation of dyads?[29] Any system of size N will have $N(N-1)/2$ dyads but will also feature $N(N-1)(N-2)/6$ triads and many other subsets that just as easily could be aggregated and subsequently granted centrality in the creation of meaning shared by a given set of actors. The reason that the dyad continues to provide the focus for research on conflict, crisis, and war is not that it is such an obvious organizing principle for reality. Instead, its simplicity as a unit of analysis and the sustained ability of several variables (contiguity and political regime being two prominent examples) to produce significant coefficients combine to guarantee that virtually any dyadic model will explain enough variance in one or more forms of interstate behavior to get published.[30] While dyadic findings may tell an important part of the story, the nature of international relations as an unfolding system makes it certain that deeper understanding will remain elusive.

Consider an alternative way of constructing reality, with a shift in priorities away from the path of least resistance. The claim that the interstate dyad is the fundamental unit of interaction is not supported, for example, by everyday experience; it is more likely to be the *normal form of contact* than the *basis for perception of reality*. It is highly improbable that the actors in world politics see the world in terms of an assembly of dyads composed of states; instead, it is more realistic to infer that each pairwise experience is interpreted and reacted to within some greater frame of reference. Individual state-to-state relations are important, but it is very unlikely that leaders rely on algorithms that tell them to (a) focus seriatim on dyadic relationships, (b) assess the status of each in turn, and (c) add that information to an accumulating sense of reality. A more integrated view of the world, influenced significantly by an actor's overall place in the international system, is likely to affect behavior across dyads.

Perhaps all of this can be said more directly: the whole of international relations or global politics is more than the sum of its dyads. It is understandable that the relative simplicity and manipulability of the dyad encourage aggregate research on this unit of analysis, and the approach is not without its advantages in coming to grips with the properties of specific interactions. It seems inappropriate, however, for the dyad to become established as the effective representation of how processes unfold within world politics. As Onuf (1995: 53) observes in a discussion of levels of analysis, such seemingly innocuous choices have pervasive effects on overall understanding. The relentless pursuit of dyadic "truth" through more data gathering and increasingly sophisticated statistical methods would seem to be inherently self-limiting.[31] Two historical instances will be used to illustrate this point.

Consider first the familiar story of the outbreak of World War I in the context of the preceding argument about dyads. It is possible to identify patterns of communication within and across the Triple Alliance and Triple Entente as war approached during July and early August of 1914. More specifically, the proportion of communication in allied and adversarial dyads increased and decreased, respectively, as the crisis moved forward. The data suggest that, as crisis interactions intensify, communication shifts in a relative sense toward intra-alliance affirmation of views between friendly dyads (Holsti 1972). The negative implications for crisis management are obvious.

While on the surface it would appear that the preceding story encourages a dyadic interpretation of communication in international crises and other events, this would be an oversimplification for at least two reasons. First, the meaningful division is by *coalition*, not on the basis of each individual pair of states; dyads can be classified as either hostile or friendly, and communication-related properties then are identified. Second, every pairwise communication entails third-party effects; the cable traffic between London and Paris, Vienna and Berlin, or any other pair of capitals during the crisis will reveal numerous allusions to what is (or might be) going on in still other places. Thus the Great War developed as something beyond an explanation based on a mere aggregation of great power dyads.

Another example—perhaps a better one because it spans almost a century—is conveyed through an overview of British diplomatic concerns in Europe and the Near East in the post-Napoleonic era up to the early twentieth century. As Jervis (1979: 214) observes, the components of a system are interconnected:

> Events in one area influence other areas. Changes in the relations between two states lead to alterations in the relations between other states. One minor example can stand for many: British relations with Persia in the nineteenth and early twentieth century depended in part on British relations with France. During the Napoleonic wars, France was Britain's main enemy, Russia therefore had to be courted, and Russian encroachments on Persia—which would threaten India—had to be ignored. When relations with France improved, relations with Russia deteriorated, and Britain came to Persia's support. With the beginning of the twentieth century, Germany became Britain's chief concern, giving England a major incentive to establish good relations with Russia. To this end she first agreed to divide Persia into spheres of influence and then tolerated Russian violations of the agreement.

This summary of British interests over many decades reveals that, in every dyad, concerns extended beyond the agenda of issues within the immediate pairing. The analysis could be continued further: at no point, for example, are either empire-related concerns in regions other than the Near East (such as the colonies in Africa) or domestic security issues (like the Irish question) factored into the discussion. For such reasons it may be unwise to focus too narrowly on a given dyad even when the goal is to understand relations between precisely that pair of states.

Although the preceding examples are just two from among the vast array of narratives available in international history, the general principle should be evident and relatively uncontroversial: many pairwise interactions include a range of considerations that go substantially beyond the actors immediately involved. When pairs of states seem to be concerned overwhelmingly with each other, such as Syria and Israel or Brazil and Argentina, factors outside of the immediate dyad still influence its evolution and impact on the rest of the world. Even the near-fixation that India and Pakistan have had on each other for years on end is influenced by considerations related to their status within the South Asian Association for Regional Cooperation; India, in particular, is anxious to limit the perception that it seeks hegemony in the region (James 1990b) and also worries about China. Thus even the most compelling micro-micro linkages can prove misleading if viewed outside the context of a full range of connections that include those emanating from the system level.

4.3 Objections to System-Level Theorizing and Responses

While objections might be raised to the reasons just presented for renewed priority on system-level theorizing, only a few salient possibilities will be addressed at this point. A more detailed treatment of the virtues and vices of structural realism in particular will appear in chapter 5, so it seems appropriate at this point to confront a few basic arguments that might be put forward against the utility of any theory cast at the level of the international system. The points to be addressed are concerned, respectively, with the accuracy of preceding assertions about the advantages of system- over unit-level theory and general aspects of theory building.

Are system structures really more pervasive, consistent, enduring, and important in their effects as compared to units? Consider a prominent historical example that might be raised in objection to these claims: the rapid collapse of the USSR in 1991 as one of the "poles" in bipolarity, which Waltz (1979), the creator of structural realism, virtually had ruled out as a possibility for perhaps as long as a century into the future (quoted in Mansbach 1996: 91). While Mansbach (1996) is correct in pointing out that the USSR, a prominent unit of the international system, disappeared quite rapidly and unexpectedly in 1991, a passage from Waltz (1979) can be used to bring out some important nuances in the argument over system-level theory: "Who is more likely to be around 100 years from now—the United States, the Soviet Union, France, Egypt,

Thailand, and Uganda? Or Ford, IBM, Shell, Unilever, and Massey-Ferguson? I would bet on the states, perhaps even on Uganda" (95). For at least two reasons, these observations make it possible to derive an interpretation of the USSR's passing that is more favorable toward system-level theory in general and perhaps even realism in particular.[32]

First, the demise of a given unit, no matter how prominent, should not be equated with the end of the structure of the international system itself. As Waltz (1979) claims, the weight of historical experience suggests that the majority of states around in the late 1970s (or today) *are* likely to outlast even the most successful transnational actors, such as multinational corporations—what matters is that a system of states persists. Furthermore, is the Soviet Union really gone? If the reference is to a militarily powerful, economically inefficient state with a vast population and the potential to follow a dictatorial leadership (of either the left or the right), then the changes of the last dozen or so years are at best superficial. Viewed from a distance, a decade or so after the heady events of 1990–1991, the USSR might be regarded as "downsizing" or "rightsizing" in today's parlance—that is, adjusting its physical boundaries and regime type to a wide range of pressures from multiple directions. Moreover, this is not the first time that the Eurasian Bear has experienced fundamental change and remained a key player in international politics (Watson 1992: 302): earlier in the twentieth century, Tsarist Russia lost significant territory, experienced a revolution, and changed its name as a country, yet the resulting entity, the USSR, remained a member of the system of states. Within a generation, the Soviet Union's capabilities in both absolute and relative terms greatly exceeded those of the regime that its leaders had overthrown. Even to say that Russia is no longer a "pole" in the international system reveals a bias toward short-term thinking. As Motyl (1999) points out, while Russia "may be weak militarily [this] does not mean that a Russian empire cannot reemerge by other means—stealthily, even unintentionally" (158). This remains true in spite of drastically reduced economic output and a demoralized army, among other problems. The Depression-era United States, for example, with an isolationist foreign policy, the Dust Bowl, and visible political extremism, might have been written off in similar terms.

To reinforce and extend the preceding point, a comparison might be made between the end of the Soviet Union and the demise of the British Empire in the aftermath of World War II. Great Britain experienced major change in territorial expanse and even a shift in identity; while the country's name did not change, its former self-designated role as the preeminent colonial power disappeared (in all likelihood) forever. Britain, in spite of all this, remained within the states system and continued as a prominent member, with former colonies being integrated into the Commonwealth. In sum, very powerful actors can either transform or disappear and the system of states can still persist.[33]

Second, the argument that the USSR's exit from the system is an example of a unit-level development exerting systemwide impact, which might naturally be accompanied by the idea that structure itself may have disappeared, is at best a partial truth. While some controversy exists, and the relative impact of internal and external factors may never be known for sure, it is certain that system-based effects played a significant role in the fate of the USSR (Wohlforth 1995). Rivalry with the United States and its much wealthier coalition definitely contributed to the internal pressures that ended the communist "reign of error"; Bueno de Mesquita and Lalman (1992), among others, point to "slow erosion of the Soviet ability to compete simultaneously on the dimensions of guns and butter, and a gradual alteration of Soviet political institutions" (249). Even domestic mismanagement can be blamed to some degree on system-level forces, which caused both human and material resources to be allocated in nonproductive ways within an extremely militarized and inefficient infrastructure.[34]

With these factors in mind, an assertion that the end of the USSR constitutes a micro-level event that led to a macro-level transformation is at least partially misleading; to place this development in proper context it is important to look further back within the causal chain and allow for the sustained and probably crucial role of system-level, rivalry-based effects.[35] The rapid demise of the USSR exacerbated the usual tendency to overestimate the relative impact of proximate causes, so it is especially important in such a case to disobey intuition and look for the most fundamental reasons behind change. (Of course, it would be reasonable for critics of system-based and other forms of realism to put forward the argument that the case is an important manifestation of the long-term erosion of the "state" as an actor.) This advice becomes even more relevant when the demise of the Cold War or any other surprising development needs to be put in perspective because international relations lacks a "standard for evaluating theories in response to major events" (Wohlforth 1998: 651). Such events will be complex and will produce evidence that is multifaceted in implications. The Cold War in particular had a contingent nature, and it is reasonable to ask whether, if its outcome had been anticipated in full, the series of events leading up to the end of the Soviet system could have occurred at all (669). Thus it is not clear that the inability of a system-level theory such as structural realism to predict the end of the Cold War should be regarded as a serious failure. Instead, the unanticipated transformation of Eastern Europe might be viewed as encouragement for theorizing that includes a unit-system linkage.[36] Such theorizing might at least provide a reasonable "postdiction" of the end of the Cold War and perhaps an improved ability to predict important changes in the future.

With regard to the second set of reasons for making the system level a priority, which focuses on general principles of theory building, Blalock (1989) argues against the position taken so far on the appropriate point of departure: "Once a complex and more inclusive theory has been formulated, it may then be simplified" (21). Erroneous components presumably can be identified and eliminated through statistical testing. The implications of such a process for the theory as a *whole,* however, are unclear. It is not obvious how to proceed when at least some parts of the overall framework have been found to be questionable; what if measurement error or a more subtle threat to inference produces either false-negative or false-positive results (Cook and Campbell 1979)? Furthermore, models built inductively through data analysis must confront the "dark and troubling fact that among those alternatives there may be many which would pass the same statistical test quite as well, or even better, and which would also square with well-established substantive knowledge about the domain" (Glymour et al. 1987: 8). A more reliable approach is to deduce propositions from a logically consistent set of axioms (Brodbeck 1962), reassess the theory on the basis of its ongoing performance, and refine it as needed.

Despite the advantages offered by a system-oriented approach, what about the possibility of diminishing returns from application of any framework at that level? The call for "more attention to domestic politics, and its links to international politics," however, may constitute rejection of a specific *kind* of structural realist theory that focuses almost exclusively on major warfare (Keohane and Nye 1989: 267).[37] Elaboration of the system level of explanation remains the principal option in spite of the influence that domestic factors undoubtedly have on foreign policy. While certain forms of system-oriented analysis appear to be exhausted, that does not rule out the success of a more comprehensive theory, which even critics such as Keohane and Nye (1987: 742; 1989: 258) find implicitly interesting when presented in the form of the international regime concept.[38] Thus elaboration of structural realist theory can be pursued in recognition that a simpler explanation is preferred per se *and* as a foundation for more complex arguments.

5. Conclusions

Several tasks have been accomplished so far. The purpose, rationale, and plan of work are clear. This book is committed to reassessment of structural realism toward the ultimate goal of obtaining a viable system-level theory. The intellectual lineage of an elaborated structural realism has been established through an overview of the realist tradition in international relations. Properties of international politics in the twentieth century, most notably rapid change and heightened complexity, have been outlined. The recommended approach toward coping with this world of greater speed and complications is development of system-level theory, which offers a range of advantages over the unit level under such conditions.

A series of steps in theorizing about world politics follows naturally from those already taken. The meaning of system-level theory in international relations needs to be explored in further depth. This process entails development of the concepts of international system and structure. Since an Elaborated Structural Realism (ESR) would follow in the realist tradition and attempts to build on

Waltz's (1979) foundation in particular, the axiomatic basis for each type of theorizing needs to be established rigorously. Finally, international conflict, crisis, and war, the empirical range in which structural realism is presumed to operate, must be defined. Each of these tasks will be carried out in chapter 2.

CHAPTER TWO

International Systems, Structural Realism, and Conflict in World Politics

1. Further Work on Concept Formation

This chapter builds on identification of the realist tradition and system-level theory as the two "pillars" of the investigation as a whole. Work now continues on concept formation with regard to international system and structure, realism and neorealism, and international conflict, crisis, and war. These areas are important to both eventual development and testing of an elaborated structural realism and more immediate concerns related to theorizing about international relations. An overview of how work is to proceed in each area will be provided in turn.

While system-level theory is recommended for international relations, it is essential to specify what this would entail in practice. It is not enough to say, for example, that something more encompassing than the dyadic level in isolation is needed to make progress in theorizing. Thus the important concept of *systemism* is introduced as an alternative to the extremes of holism and individualism as a point of departure for analysis of international relations. Systemism means a commitment to understanding a system in terms of functional relationships, as opposed to a "black box" or some form of reductionism, which result from holism and individualism, respectively (Bunge 1996). (Each of the preceding terms will be explained in some detail.) Basic concepts within system-level theory, referring to the international system and its structure, must be defined. This includes a review of previous concept formation and choice of definitions. The definitions of international system and structure that emerge from assessment of prior concept formation are intended to create the maximum potential for eventual elaboration of structural realism as a theory in terms of description, explanation, and prediction of macro and micro processes.

System-level theory, as advocated in the previous chapter, will be brought together with realism to produce the foundation for an elaborated structural realism. In particular, structural realism is reinvigorated to seek a wider range of goals than this theory either accomplished or articulated at or near its outset. While the realist tradition has been described in a general way, it is essential to establish the meaning of realism and structural realism more rigorously to provide the basis for elaboration. Thus the axioms for both realist and structural realist theory are identified in order to provide a solid foundation for development of structural realism.

International conflict is the basic domain for structural realist theory. Thus international conflict, along with its principal variants of crisis and war, must be identified in a way that facilitates the study of both events and the series of actions that occur within them. Definitions for conflict, crisis, and war are essential to permit the evaluation of empirical work based on structural realism that appears in chapter 5.

All of this work on concept formation is essential for a range of immediate and later purposes. It will be carried out in the sections of this chapter. In section 2, systemism is put forward as an approach to theorizing. Consistent with that priority, international system and structure are defined. Section 3 presents the axiomatic bases for realism and structural realism, respectively. The fourth section defines international conflict, crisis, and war. Section 5, the chapter's conclusion, reiterates what has been accomplished and introduces the next chapter, which addresses the meaning of scientific progress in the study of international relations.

2. The International System and Its Structure

2.1 Systemism, Theorizing, and Concept Formation

While system-level theory has been presented so far as the preferred option for international relations, it is helpful to place that argument in a wider context. Specific reasons related to theory construction and the properties of international relations have been used to justify the system as a point of departure for theorizing, but some additional arguments, which are both more general and interconnected, will be put forward in favor of systemism as the foundation for the ontology of an elaborated structural realism. These arguments are that (a) systemism is the most likely solution to the ongoing problems that result from adoption of either holism or individualism; (b) systemic analysis seems to be the basis for success in widely divergent disciplinary settings; and (c) the popular puzzle metaphor (Kuhn 1962; Zinnes 1980a, 1980b; Most and Starr 1989; Vasquez 1993; Siverson 1996), while useful for thinking about some specific empirical problems, is inappropriate because it fails to identify the importance of the system as a point of origin for theorizing. After systemism is introduced as a concept, each of the three preceding arguments will be presented in turn.

Systemism is advocated by Bunge (1996) as a way of thinking about the world. In principle, it can be applied to any aspect of social life: "The alternative to both individualism and holism is systemism, since it accounts for both individual and system and, in particular, for individual agency and social structure. Indeed, systemism postulates that everything is a system or a component of one. And it models every system as a triple (composition, environment, structure), or CES for short, so it encompasses the valid features of its rivals" (264). From the standpoint of systemism, the choice between unit and system is, as Brecher (1999: 299) termed it, a "flawed dichotomy." A useful theory must deal with both systems and units in some way. The question, of course, is how best to proceed.

Figure 2.1
Comparing Social and Literary Systems

a. Functional Relations in a Social System

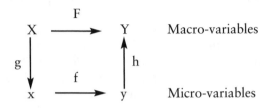

Source: Bunge (1996: 149).

b. A Scheme of the Literary System

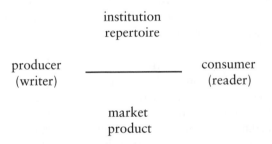

Source: Even-Zohar (1990c: 31).

Figure 2.1a presents Bunge's (1996: 149) vision, based on systemism, of functional relations in a social system. (Figure 2.1b will be discussed at a later point in this chapter.) It traces the full range of effects that might be encountered in any such system, which includes both micro and macro variables. (Upper- and lower-case letters refer to macro- and micro-level variables, respectively.) The logically possible connections are micro-micro, micro-macro, macro-macro, and macro-micro. The essence of systemism is to get away from holism, individualism, and other mindsets that convey only part of the picture of a working system. Macro variables may have an impact upon each other, as in the case of X affecting Y, with the functional form—perhaps linear in some instances and more complex in others—represented by F. The same is true at the micro level, as in the case of x having an impact upon y through function f. These linkages represent the limits of theorizing for holism and individualism, in that order. Systemism, by contrast, allows for both micro-micro and macro-macro connections. Furthermore, systemism recognizes that effects also can move *across* levels. Thus the macro-micro linkage of X to x through function g also appears in the figure, as does the micro-macro connection from y to Y on the basis of function h. Thus the linkages that appear in figure 2.1a are sufficient to exhaust the logical possibilities; many others, such as a direct connection from x to Y (or, for that matter, from Y to x) also could be added to an ever more complex model.

Consider the incomplete pictures offered by individualism and holism in comparison to systemism. Individualism focuses on $y = f(x)$, or micro-level processes. This specification is incomplete because it is possible for a causal chain to be traced further back and at a different level altogether. What about (a) the prior effect of X on x, expressed as function g, and (b) the direct impact of X on Y through function F? Each of these connections is left out of individualism, which cannot incorporate macro-level processes explicitly into its unit-centered vision of the system.

Holism, by contrast, begins at the macro level and stays there. It focuses explicitly on system properties alone and treats all else as a "black box." The other processes already noted, which transmit effects from X to Y indirectly, are not incorporated into theorizing. Thus $Y = F(X)$, a relationship based only on macro variables, becomes the whole story. This is the story of systems analysis as traditionally defined.

One example from each side of the macro-micro "fence" should be sufficient to reveal the negative implications of both individualism and holism for the development of international theory. The democratic peace and structural realism bring out two sides of the same fundamental problem. In each instance, only one of the four preceding kinds of linkage is developed in any systematic way. The others, if they appear at all, are relegated to passing references.[1]

Consider first an exegesis of the democratic peace, a theory that normally is put forward in terms of micro-micro connections and that clearly follows in the tradition of individualism as defined above.[2] Let x_d be the level of autocracy of a regime and y_d be its warlikeness. (In such instances the subscript "d" is used to identify the particular variables included in the democratic peace and the critique that follows.) In this instance, f_d is presumed to be some monotonically increasing function: that is, increasing levels of democracy are identified with a greater disposition toward peace. Systematic testing of this hypothesis on data from the post-Napoleonic era (and even the few studies on earlier settings) seems to offer uniform support, to a degree that stimulates continuing references to a "law" or paradigm shift (Levy 1989; Ray 1999).

What, however, can be gleaned from the democratic peace theory with respect to connections between variables at the macro level? Even if y_d is a positive function of x_d, that does not mean that the same will hold for $Y_d = F(X_d)$. Consider just one possible complication: What if the existence of a dictatorship with contending status (defined, for the moment, as a great power with the potential and possibly the desire to aim for hegemony) is the driving force behind pacific interdemocratic approaches toward problem solving? One illustration might be the creation of NATO in response to a widely perceived Soviet threat. What if the existence of such an effect, which could be described as macro-micro (i.e., $X_d \longrightarrow x_d$), is prior and even crucial to any micro-micro properties that have been observed for democratic states within the international system? If that is true, then the functional relationship of x_d to y_d could be completely different from what seems to have been confirmed over the course of decades. Autocracy and warlikeness as a micro-micro connection could be an artifact of a macro-micro linkage that is invariant over the standard testing period: in other words, no era exists in which the democracies have not confronted at least one major and potentially threatening nondemocratic power, so the importance of this factor remains beyond proper estimation.

This point can be highlighted by a comparison with the natural sciences. Boyle's law for gases is $pv = k$, where p is pressure exerted by a gas, v is the volume of its container, and k is a constant that holds for a given temperature.[3] If a laboratory conducted a series of experiments at a given temperature, T', the result of each trial would be an estimate of k', for the constant value. This conclusion would change quickly, however, with trials at different temperatures because it is known that the value of the constant will vary under such conditions. In the language of systemism, the macro variable, temperature, affects the mapping of the micro variables, pressure and volume, onto each other. The parallel with the preceding argument about democracy and peace becomes straightforward: the "law" about democracies being peaceful with each other may work at the micro level as long as crucial macro variables stay within certain boundaries. One possible macro-level complication, noted already, is the ongoing existence of at least one threatening nondemocratic state. This could be the equivalent of temperature in the example just introduced; in fact, the situation is more difficult for the democratic peace because so many other macro variables might cause the existing pattern to change if they left some range of values. This possibility should give pause to any endorsement of the democratic peace—an isolated micro-micro connection—as the foundation for understanding of international relations from a systemist's point of view.

Still further complications emerge for the democratic peace. Macro-macro connections, whether consisting of regime type and interstate conflict or other combinations of variables, also are absent. The reason for this gap is the same one that Waltz (1979: 18–37) cited with respect to the Leninist theory of imperialism: both the democratic peace and imperialism have been articulated as reductionist (or individualist) theories; to use the language of systemism once again, each focuses on micro-micro linkages and cannot cope well with the full range of connections that must be developed to understand a working system. Thus the democratic peace stands as an isolated island of individualist theory rather than an integrated set of answers to basic questions about the international system.

Structural realism as articulated by Waltz (1979, 1986) illustrates the problem that is at the other extreme from individualism, namely, holism. (This point is ironic because Waltz [1979] is most emphatic in pointing out the problems associated with reductionism and previously set a trend in the field with his three-level framework [Waltz 1959].) Waltz (1979: 161–93) links the structure of the international system, defined in terms of the number of great powers under anarchy, with propensity toward highly destructive war. The main contrast is between international systems with two versus three or more great powers; the former are preferred to the latter for reasons that Waltz (1964, 1979) sees as permanent and compelling, such as the relative simplicity of conflict management through spheres of influence. Thus, for Waltz, the key macro variables are Y_w, the warlikeness of the system, and X_w, the number of great powers defined by the categories of bipolar and multipolar. Y_w is expected to be an increasing (actually, step-level) function of X_w. Waltz explicitly eschews all but this and a few other macro-macro linkages, asserting that structural realism claims to be a theory of international politics rather than foreign policy. Thus it includes neither micro-micro nor hybrid linkages.[4]

From the standpoint of systemism, theories like the democratic peace and structural realism are inherently self-limiting. It is important to leave room in any theory for the full range of connections that appear in figure 2.1a. A theory must incorporate macro-macro and micro-micro connections, as in holism and individualism, respectively, along with the hybrid macro-micro and micro-macro linkages. At the very least it must explain why it is legitimate for one or more of these categories to be held constant; otherwise, threats to inference such as those that confront the democratic peace and structural realism are likely to emerge once again.

Without going too far afield, it is interesting to note that systemism, while not articulated in quite the same way as in Bunge (1996), already has demonstrated its value in other disciplines. Consider an example that is selected deliberately because of its distance from international relations: "polysystem theory" in comparative literature (Even-Zohar 1990a, 1990b, 1990c, 1997).

Figure 2.1b shows a scheme of the "literary system," defined as the "network of relations that is hypothesized to obtain between a number of activities called 'literary' and consequently these activities themselves observed via that network" (Even-Zohar 1990b: 28). While figure 2.1b does not include the kinds of causal relations that appear explicitly in figure 2.1a, it is feasible to identify parallels with a social system as described previously in terms of the four logically possible kinds of connections between macro and micro variables. Consider the following summary by Even-Zohar (1990b) of the framework depicted by figure 2.1b:

> It suffices to recognize that it is the *interdependencies* between these factors which allow[s] them to function in the first place. Thus, a CONSUMER [upper-case in the original for each instance] may "consume" a PRODUCT produced by a PRODUCER, but in order for the "product" (such as "text") to be generated, a common REPERTOIRE must exist, whose usability is determined by some INSTITUTION. A MARKET must exist where such a

good can be transmitted. None of the factors enumerated can be described to function in isolation, and the kind of relations that may be detected run across all possible axes of the scheme. (34)

The preceding paragraph can easily be put into the language of systemism. Micro-micro relations presumably would consist of transmission of texts from writers to readers. At the macro-micro level, a repertoire, which "designates the aggregate of rules and materials which govern both the making and use of any given product" (39–40), creates a systemic context for written products. At the macro-macro level, the repertoire is said to depend on an institution, defined as "the aggregate of factors involved with the maintenance of literature as a socio-cultural activity" (37). The final linkage is macro-micro: a market, meaning "the aggregate of factors involved with the selling and buying of literary products and with the promotion of types of consumption" (38), permits the transmission of products (Even-Zohar 1990b: 34–40). Although nothing is said in this exposition by Even-Zohar about micro-macro linkages, their potential is implicit in the assertion that relations may be detected "across all possible axes of the scheme" (34). To cite just one example, Even-Zohar (1990c: 19–26) notes elsewhere that the repertoire could be either altered incrementally or transformed by creation of an especially important text.

Instead of being seen as a definitive treatment of issues that arise in a rather different discipline, the preceding discussion is put forward to illustrate what can be achieved through systemic analysis. Rather than thinking strictly in terms of the reader/writer (i.e., micro-micro) or repertoire/institution (macro-macro) connections, Even-Zohar's literary system encourages a more comprehensive approach toward the development and dissemination of ideas.[5]

Successful application of systemism to the field of comparative literature is especially instructive because, at least on the basis of intuition, international relations would appear to be more of a "hard" social science. In other words, comparative literature would seem to stand closer than international relations to the humanities, yet even in this "soft" social science, systemism proves useful to the advancement of knowledge. An outlook based on systemism may be crucial in achieving the full potential of *any* theoretical approach, as opposed to missing opportunities as a result of pursuing either individualism or holism. In the case of international relations and many other disciplines as well, systemism can help to build theory more effectively than either of the preceding alternatives, which in turn increases its credibility as an approach toward social scientific problem solving.

For international relations the implications of the preceding series of arguments are crucial with respect to building theories: *the standard metaphor of puzzle solving encourages a suboptimal approach toward understanding a complex social system.* While the idea of treating international relations (and especially the central problem of the causes of war) as a puzzle to be solved finds wide and seemingly expanding support (Zinnes 1980a, 1980b; Most and

Starr 1989: 74–75, 90–91; Vasquez 1993; Siverson 1996), it seems misplaced from a systemist's point of view. As will become apparent, the problems that arise from puzzle solving as a point of departure derive from the path dependence of theorizing and the fundamental difference this makes in what ultimately can be achieved.

In the solving of a jigsaw puzzle, the choice of strategy and tactics will not affect the ultimate result of putting the pieces together; instead, some approaches simply will yield faster results than others. Therefore, unless time is limited or some kind of competition is involved, it does not matter where work begins. Some will start off by selecting pieces of a particular color or perhaps those along the border of the puzzle and will go from there, putting together different sectors in varying orders. It also will not matter whether "dyads" or larger subsets are used in searching for pieces that fit together. The end result, regardless of strategy or tactics, is the same in each instance: a full picture that is identical to all others of its kind.

Forays into systemism in general and the example of comparative literature in particular raise serious doubts about whether starting points and overall strategies and tactics for the study of international relations are analogous to those of puzzle solving. From the standpoint of systemism, the point of entry matters a great deal because theorizing is a path-dependent enterprise. It is possible and even probable that an individualist theory, consisting strictly of micro-micro linkages, will produce an incomplete and even distorted picture of international relations. A holistic theory, which includes only macro-macro connections, also is unlikely to result in an accurate representation. By comparison, a point of departure based on systemism necessarily builds in the need to confront all four types of logical connections between and within the micro and macro levels. It encourages, from the very beginning, comparative analysis of potential linkages of all kinds rather than a "flawed dichotomy" (Brecher 1999: 217) that favors one level over another at the outset and discourages or even closes off development of a more comprehensive theory.

With these thoughts in mind, it is time to move on to the task of defining the international system. This will be carried out in a way that encourages a comprehensive approach toward theorizing, from conventional (macro-macro and micro-micro) connections to hybrid (macro-micro and micro-macro) linkages.

2.2 Defining the International System

What is an international system? This concept, like others central to the field of international relations, elicits multiple associations. Table 2.1 contains a selection of alternative definitions of the international system that date back to the initial era of influence for systems theory in the social sciences.[6] The definitions can be placed into a few general (and certainly overlapping) categories on the basis of relative emphasis: (a) interaction based, (b) stability based, (c) combined interaction-structure, (d) consequence oriented, and (e) systemist.

Table 2.1
Defining the International System

Category	Source	Definition
1. interaction-based	Kaplan 1957: 4	a set of variables so related, in contradistinction to its environment, that describable behavioral regularities characterize the internal relationships of the variables to each other and the external relationships of the set of individual variables to combinations of external variables.
	McClelland 1966: 20, 21	an expanded version of the notion of two actors-in-interaction. A view of the whole phenomenon is involved. The outmost boundaries of international relations are suggested if we imagine *all* of the exchanges, transactions, contacts, flows of information, and actions of every kind going on at this moment of time between and among the separately constituted societies of the world. . . . The international system is meant to encompass all interactions, in full scope.
	Bull 1977: 9–10	when two or more states have sufficient contact between them, and have sufficient impact on one another's decisions, to cause them to behave—at least in some measure—as parts of a whole.
	Ray 1980: 37	an aggregation of social entities that share a common fate or are sufficiently interdependent to have the actions of some consistently affect the behavior and fate of the rest.
	Frankel 1988: 160	a collection of independent political entities which interact with considerable frequency and according to regularized processes.
	K. Holsti 1988: 23	any collection of independent political entities—tribes, city-states, nations, or empires—that interact with considerable frequency and according to regularized processes.
2. stability-based	Rosencrance 1963: 220–221	comprised of four mechanistic elements. . . . (1) a source of disturbance or disruption (an input); (2) a regulator which undergoes certain

Table 2.1 continued

Category	Source	Definition
		changes as a result of the disturbing influence; (3) a Table or list of environmental constraints which translate the state of the disturbance and the state of the regulator into (4) outcomes.
	Gilpin 1981: 26	aggregation of diverse entities united by regular interaction according to a form of control.
	Doran 1989: 83	defined by configurational and temporal limits and, therefore, static.
3. combined inter-action-structure	Young 1968b: 6	a group of actors standing in characteristic relationships to each other (structure), interacting on the basis of recognizable patterns (processes), and subject to various contextual limitations.
	Waltz 1979: 79	a system is composed of a structure and interacting units.
4. consequence-oriented	Jervis 1979: 212	the term more usefully applies when two conditions are met: (1) one cannot infer the outcomes from the attributes and behavior of the actors; and (2) interconnections are present with the result that changes in some parts of the system produces changes in other parts—these conditions lead to a major characteristic of systems: the consequences of behavior are often not expected or intended by the actors.
	Gaddis 1987: 217	interconnections between units and the collective behavior of the system as a whole differs from the expectations and priorities of the individual units that make it up.
5. systemist	Brecher and Ben Yehuda 1985: 17	a set of actors who are situated in a configuration of power (*structure*), are involved in regular patterns of interaction (*process*), are separate from other units by boundaries set by a given *issue*, and are constrained in and from outside the system (*environment*).

Kaplan (1957), McClelland (1966), Bull (1977), Ray (1980), Frankel (1988), and Holsti (1988) offer interaction-based definitions.[7] Each emphasizes interactions, along with interdependence and regularities in behavior, in different measures. The definitions of Rosecrance (1963), Gilpin (1981), and Doran (1989) share some similarities with those just listed but can be described more accurately as stability based. Each introduces a homeostatic element; interactions are essential to the notion of an international system, but so is the idea of stability or limits on what happens within its boundaries. Young (1968b) and Waltz (1979) offer combined interaction-structure definitions. Each includes the idea of structure to complement process in a system, while Young goes a step beyond and mentions context as well. Jervis (1979) and Gaddis (1987) are consequence oriented. They stress the idea of unintended consequences: a system exists when those in it can neither fully predict nor control the results of their actions. This is a more exact and useful way of saying that "the whole is greater than the sum of its parts." In other words, the essence of a system is that it operates beyond the full control of any of its units.

What do the preceding ideas from the last four decades of thinking about international systems mean when taken together? It is interesting to note that, while points of emphasis and level of detail may vary, blatant contradictions are not in evidence. Some sense exists that regular interactions are most central to identification of a system, with stability, structure, and unintended consequences being important further strands of development.

From the standpoint of systemism, each of the definitions discussed so far is valuable in identifying a range of features, but all remain incomplete. The definition by Brecher and Ben Yehuda (1985), which has been left till last because it most effectively meets the needs of the present study, represents a point of culmination in thinking about international systems.

Figure 2.2 extends the definition from Brecher and Ben Yehuda (1985) through a diagrammatic exposition. It will be presented at this point in general terms and applied more thoroughly in subsequent chapters when its components, such as structure and actors, are developed in greater detail. The basic idea of the overview that follows is to explain how an international system functions in the way made familiar by systemism. The examples used to highlight the respective linkages, it should be noted, are taken from a range of theories and thereby illustrate the comprehensiveness and adaptability of international system as a concept.

Note that the international system in the figure includes composition, environment, and structure, as advocated by systemism. The system's components and environment, as represented by the arrows near the top of the figure, influence each other. The best way to explain how this works is to start off with the input from the environment and follow the process through to the end, at which the system generates output for the environment.

For a given international system, either cumulative effects or sudden shocks from the external environment can effect change in structure.[8] Two examples involving the United States in relation to different regional systems are helpful here. Over the course of two decades, economic assistance and arms transfers from the United States turned Israel from a fledgling state into the preeminent power within the Middle East (Brecher 1980). More rapid change occurred in the power structure of Southeast Asia as a result of the United States' disengagement from the Vietnam War in the early 1970s. South Vietnam disappeared in 1975, with China and the newly united Vietnam squaring off as the major powers in the region and experiencing a series of international crises (Brecher and Wilkenfeld 1997: 158–64).

Figure 2.2
The International System: Composition, Environment and Structure

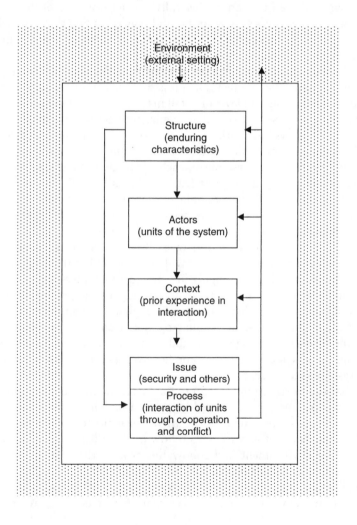

Structure, which consists of relatively enduring characteristics that have some potential to influence the decisions of rational actors, is most fundamental and appears at the beginning of the series of linkages within the system itself. In the case of structural realism and associated approaches, structure consists of the distribution of capabilities (leaving aside its representation through one or more indicators). In the generic international system appearing in the figure, however, other possibilities, such as norms or attitudes, also could be incorporated. Using the language of systemism, structure would be analogous to X from figure 2.1a; it is a macro variable.

Structure is expected to influence actors, the units of the system. They can, either individually or collectively, represent macro or micro variables. As individuals or in subsets of the whole, actors provide the basis for deriving micro variables; when considered collectively, actors can be used to generate macro variables. Examples include, respectively, the absolute capabilities of a given state and the number of great powers in the system.

Since one of the basic ideas behind system-based analysis is that rational units are expected to take structure into account when making decisions, this connection within the figure is straightforward and represents one possible macro-micro connection (i.e., $X \longrightarrow x$ from figure 2.1a), where X_s = structure and x_f = foreign policy for one or more states and $X_s \longrightarrow x_f$. The figure reveals that structure also is expected to have some direct impact upon process, without mediation through decisions and resulting behavior by actors. This connection will be explored more directly in short order when issue and process are described.

Actors, while influenced by structure, also act in context. This is understood by intuition but can be developed more systematically within any given theoretical approach. An obvious example that might be cited is prior experience in conflict, whereby actors create the context for their further interaction. States that have been involved in many prior conflicts, crises, or wars are likely to perceive each other differently than those who have no such record. Thus an action that might be seen as neutral or friendly in one context might elsewhere be regarded as cause for concern ("What are they up to now?"). From the standpoint of systemism, this connection could be articulated as a micro-micro connection (i.e., $x \longrightarrow y$ from figure 2.1a), where x_e is prior experiences between a subset of actors within the system and y_i is interpretations of statements or actions by those included, with $x_e \longrightarrow y_i$.

Issue and process appear together in the figure. In a traditional realist vision, one issue—the struggle for power—stands above all others. Put differently, the competition might be viewed as a pattern of behavior common to all real issues. Regardless of how realism might be represented, other theories would be inclined to see less of a hierarchy and to allow for multiple issues with the potential for trade-offs in bargaining. Still other approaches, closer to realism, might be inclined to grant power or related considerations pride of place in intense conflicts, such as international crises, but not otherwise. An elaborated structural realism would be in the latter camp, with an emphasis on security seeking that might, in turn, permit the pursuit of a much wider range of goals once some satisfactory level of "safety" had been achieved. Consider the following potential micro-macro linkage as one example (i.e., y $\longrightarrow$ Y from figure 2.1a): let y_f equal high versus low politics and Y_c equal conflict versus cooperation, with high (low) politics leading to conflict (cooperation), or y_f $\longrightarrow$ Y_c.

Also identified in the figure is a connection, identified in passing a moment ago, that goes directly from structure to process. This macro-macro linkage bears some resemblance to the idea of unintended consequences as put forward by Jervis (1979) and Gaddis (1987) in definitions of an international system from table 2.1. Structure may condition process directly and produce results that no actor in particular had pursued: that is, emergent properties at the aggregate level. One idea of this kind is manifested in the argument linking polarity to war, regardless of which specific configuration—bipolarity, multipolarity, or anything else, for that matter—is advocated. This can be represented as a macro-macro connection (i.e., X $\longrightarrow$ Y from figure 2.1a): X_g is the number of great powers, Y_g is the amount of war in the system, and X_g $\longrightarrow$ Y_g. These macro variables are posited to show various connections as the result of behavior. Actors, in other words, must cope with being in either a bipolar or a multipolar setting, and their actions are more or less likely, depending on where they are situated, to result in war. To link this influence with the idea of unintended consequences developed by Jervis (1979) and endorsed by Gaddis (1987), Miller (1995), and others, the actors in a multipolar system, according to advocates of bipolarity, will be more likely to end up in general war because their behavior—whatever its specific intention—contributes in an overall way to the tendency of that system toward self-destruction.

Processes unfold and then reverberate throughout and beyond the system, as represented by the series of arrows on the right side of figure 2.2. The context for interaction for a given set of actors may be altered as a result of experiences with some form of cooperation or conflict or even elements of both at or around the same time. Actors can even change as a result of some process; to take the most extreme example, an actor may exit the system as a result of losing a war. The structure of the system itself can shift as a result of a process of interaction. If a war is lost decisively by one or more great powers, they can exit that subset and, as a result, at least one basic aspect of the distribution of capabilities will become different. Finally, even the environment beyond a system can be affected by some process within it. For example, suppose that a major war occurs and a formerly regional power develops as one with wider importance as a result of the outcome. If the environment in this example is understood to be the global system, that can be altered as the new great power becomes active beyond its previous limits.

Figure 2.2, to reiterate, takes the idea of an international system as put forward by Brecher and Ben Yehuda (1985) and develops it in the context of systemism. Its ability to be presented in that manner constitutes the first of five advantages that the definition has to offer as a foundation for further development of system-level theory.

First, as just noted, the definition is neither holistic nor individualistic. By including actors, structure, process, issue, context, and environment, the definition creates the potential to explore micro-micro, macro-macro, and hybrid (i.e., macro-micro and micro-macro) connections.

Second, the definition provided by Brecher and Ben Yehuda (1985) is at least as comprehensive as any of the others that appear in table 2.1 and more useful for later operational purposes. Its six components, ranging from actors to environment, provide a thorough formation of the concept of an international system. Compare this with other definitions from the table: the early example of Kaplan (1957) makes no reference to actors, structure, or an issue, while the later option provided by Frankel (1988) includes only actors, processes, and boundaries. The definition from Brecher and Ben Yehuda also is preferred to those, such as the one offered by Gaddis (1987), that focus on the international system as a whole greater than the sum of its parts but without enumerating attributes. Thus the definition is useful as a foundation for unit-system linkage because it entails neither reductionism nor holism.

Third, and more specifically, structure is separated from process, which facilitates the designation of roles for variables in this study and others cast at the system level. Structure ultimately is granted a conditioning role, with processes understood as effects. Properties of conflict, crisis, and war, such as substantive outcome, frequency of cases experienced by individual states, and the distribution of these events over time, can be connected with various configurations among elements of structure. Of course, the definition of structure also permits a theory to be set up with conditioning effects in the opposite direction, from issues and processes to structure. It does not entail a commitment to any form of system-based determinism.

Fourth, the definition sets boundaries for a system explicitly, with membership determined by proximity, status, or both. While more precise limits for regions as subsystems might be subject to disagreement, it is clear in principle that such margins exist (Maoz 1997; Kacowicz 1998; Gleditsch and Ward 2000).[9] The external configuration of capabilities, to cite one possibility, could play the role of environment (Cantori and Spiegel 1970: 25). As noted earlier, the obvious exception to this rule is the limiting case of the global system, for which context and environment effectively coincide.

Fifth, and finally, the definition from Brecher and Ben Yehuda (1985) is consistent with structural realism as a theoretical approach with the potential for elaboration and greater explanatory power. (This will become apparent in the following subsection.) Waltz's (1979) definition of an international system refers only to a structure and interacting units. While the definitions do not contradict each other, the concept formation of Brecher and Ben Yehuda allows for a more inclusive treatment of how the effects of structure are transmitted to interacting units.

2.3 Defining System Structure

Although *structure* is a term with a range of meanings in social scientific theorizing, it still is possible to provide a definition with analytical value and general relevance. A natural point of departure is provided by the following demarcation of social structure: "In its most general sense, social structure consists of all those relatively stable features of a social system which an acting unit would be prudent to take into account if it wishes to make rational decisions in interacting with others" (Johnson 1985: 787). This description could apply to a subnational group, an individual state, or the international polity.[10] In one instance the most relevant aspect of structure might be the hierarchy within a labor union, while in another it could refer to the sharing of power among levels of government as described in a state's constitution. Units also might vary from one case to the next, ranging from individuals to centers of government.

Despite its generality, this definition introduces themes that recur in the social sciences, most notably international relations. Self-interest among units and stability of ostensibly structural attributes play central roles in various system-level expositions. By contrast, rapidly changing aspects of a system, along with internal characteristics of its units, are excluded. Sayer's (1984: 87) analysis provides an example of the prominent role played by durability and rationality in virtually all delineations of structure. Enduring social structures "lock their occupants into situations which they cannot unilaterally change"(87) but still permit movement "between existing positions"(87). (For example, an employee may switch from one firm [or even industry] to another, but the market persists as an economic structure.) Thus the fundamental issues related to applied structural analysis are identification of a threshold for rapid change and setting boundaries for the units.

Within international relations theory, however, this is about where agreement on structure ends (Ray 1980: 37; Singer 1989: 4). Concept formation that is useful in application requires a reassessment of the range of meanings already attached to the structure of the international system. As the definitions listed in table 2.2 reveal, the term can mean a number of things. A brief review of developments since the advent of systems theory in the social sciences four decades ago should be sufficient to bring out the main points of similarity and difference with regard to structure as a concept.[11] Three kinds of definition can be identified: (a) actor taxonomy based; (b) subsystem linkage oriented; and (c) relationship and stratification based, with (i) exclusive and (ii) inclusive variants.

Kaplan's (1957) initial effort toward definition of structure focused on identifying types of actors. McClelland (1966) followed by emphasizing subsystem linkages. Neither of these definitions, however, seems to have influenced those that appeared later in any obvious way. Young's (1968b) definition, which introduced relationships among actors and the stratification of power, is the first in a series with similar properties. Definitions since then are similar to Young's concept formation in varying degrees and can be divided into two groups, exclusive and inclusive. The exclusive subset, consisting of Snyder and

Table 2.2
Defining System Structure

Category	Source	Definition
1. actor taxonomy-based	Kaplan 1957: 11	actor classificatory variables specify the structural characteristics of actors that modify behavior. . . . nation state, alliance and international organization are examples of actors whose behavior will differ as a consequence of structural characteristics.
2. subsystem linkage-oriented	McClelland 1966: 22	leading characteristics in the performance of a complex system arise from the arrangement of its subsystems and of the relationships among these; behavior depends on structure.
3. relationship and stratification-based	Young 1968b: 30	characteristic relationships among actors in international systems over time . . . emphasize regularities in the interactions among actors. . . . also, stratification, or the ordering of actors in international systems in terms of their effective power.
a. exclusive	Snyder and Diesing 1977: 1989: 383	the number of major actors and the gross distribution of capabilities among them, along with the nature of military technology.
	Waltz 1979: 100–101	anarchy as an ordering principle and the distribution of capabilities among functionally undifferentiated units.
	Gilpin 1981: 29	dispersion of capabilities among system members, with bipolarity and multipolarity (or balance of power) as examples.
	Brecher and Ben Yehuda 1985: 17	how actors stand in relation to each other . . . the basic variables are the number of actors and distribution of power among them.
	Frankel 1988: 3	the characteristic relations between actors across time—rather than the 'process'—the more ephemeral forms and modes of interaction.
	Grieco 1988: 487	oligopolistic distribution of capabilities that conditions interaction.
	Holsti 1988: 24	distribution of capabilities.

Table 2.2 continued

Category	Source	Definition
b. inclusive	Ray 1980: 37	the way in which relationships—meaning *comparisons* between and among states or other entities and those based on *links* and *bonds* between them—are arranged. . . . states or other social entities are arranged either vertically or horizontally by both kinds of structural variables.
	Vincent 1983: 1	it is defined broadly to include agreements between states that presently have or have had an impact upon the behavior of states.
	Doran 1991: 2	at a minimum, structure involves the number of actors within the central or great power system, their relative power, their systemic roles, the extent of polarization (ideological as well as structural), the nature and extent of alliance association, and the nature of the norms and codes of governing behavior constituting the prevailing international regime.

Diesing (1989), Waltz (1979), Gilpin (1981), Brecher and Ben Yehuda (1985), Frankel (1988), Grieco (1988), and Holsti (1988), emphasizes the distribution of capabilities as the basic idea behind structure. The other subset, including Ray (1980), Vincent (1983), and Doran (1991), introduces more inclusive versions of structure, which entail links between actors and allow dynamic representations. It would be fair to say that, largely as the result of the influence of Waltz's exegesis of structural realism, the more limited idea of structure has prevailed over the last two decades in the field of international relations.

Waltz (1979, 1986), in thought-provoking assessments of system-level theory, international structure, and political realism, offers a very restricted meaning. The structure of a system, the basic conditioning factor in Waltz's vision of world politics, is represented by anarchy and a small number of prominent actors.[12] On the basis of this two-dimensional interpretation, Waltz (1979: 161–63) concludes that in "all of modern history [i.e., 1648 to the time of writing] the structure of international politics has changed but once"(163). The only known shift in structure occurred at the end of World War II, from multipolarity to bipolarity. The system remained one of anarchy, but the number of great powers decreased to just two.

States in a world of anarchy are presumed to be most interested in achieving and sustaining security, which in practice means trying to prevent others from improving relative capabilities. Thus Grieco (1988: 498, 487; see also 1990, 1993a, 1993b, 1993c) refers to the "positional" (487), as opposed to atomistic, character of international politics, with structure corresponding to the oligopolistic distribution of capabilities that conditions interaction. The term *positional* commonly is used to describe interpretations of structure like that of Waltz (1979), with anarchy inducing a competition for security among states. What emerges is a combination of positional analysis with the postulates of realism. States are expected to act out of self-interest and to attempt to maximize relative capabilities (effectively equated with security) within constraints imposed by a given structure. Anarchy plays an immanent role in conditioning behavior. According to Waltz (1988), in "developing a theory of international politics, neorealism retains the main tenets of *realpolitik*, but means and ends are viewed differently as are causes and effects" (40). Thus classical realism is merged with system-level theory, resulting in what has become known as structural realism or neorealism.

Opposite to neorealism would be a theory with a vision of structure that is qualitatively more inclusive. This would mean incorporation of systemwide characteristics that are enduring, presumably significant, but not strictly capability based. The analysis of international regimes is an obvious example to cite, in which norms and rules are the system's conditioning factors.[13] This goes well beyond capabilities and into more subjective dimensions of global politics. The behavior of states and other actors is explained in terms of the operation of a system of rights and rules. Thus regime analysis might be regarded as a rival system-oriented area of research with applications to both security and political economy. It even could be viewed as an uneasy compromise between realist and liberal thinking that includes ideas from each but fully endorses neither.

This exposition will not venture into *qualitatively* more inclusive notions of structure. Instead, it takes neorealism as the point of departure and offers a more encompassing treatment of structure that continues to be capability based. Thus the definition that follows is intended to facilitate progressive change in structural realism that preserves its basic character: *Structure consists of primary, secondary, tertiary, and higher-order elements of the international system that are (a) expressed in terms of the distribution of capabilities and (b) potentially able to affect the foreign policy decisions and outcomes achieved by states under rational leadership.*[14]

System structure consists of four categories of *elements*: primary, secondary, tertiary, and higher order, as just noted. These categories are mutually exclusive and exhaustive, with the presence or absence of *complex calculations* and *coalitions* deciding on membership.[15] Each set of elements is based in some way on the distribution of capabilities among states and will be explained in turn.

Primary elements require neither complex calculations nor coalitions. These components, collectively speaking, are closest to structural realism's sense of the distribution of capabilities. For example, the number of great powers is a primary element because it entails a simple counting of a subset of highly prominent states and is not based in any way on interstate coalitions.

Secondary elements require complex calculations but do not include coalitions. An example would be the concentration of capabilities in the system. The degree to which capabilities are dispersed evenly or held by a small number of states is open to calculation in any number of ways (Taagepera and Ray 1977). All such indicators constitute a departure from the initial variant of structural realism, which puts forward only one element, the number of great powers, at the primary level.

Tertiary elements include coalitions but not complex calculations. An example is the number of interstate alliances in the system. These coalitions are included in virtually all expositions on power politics but lack an explicit role in structural realism. Tertiary elements, which focus on linkages between and among states, are for that reason regarded as even further removed than secondary elements from the initial development of structural realism.

Finally, higher-order elements include both complex calculations and coalitions. An example of this type of element is the amount of polarization in the system. The idea is to measure how tightly connected members of each alliance are to each other, along with the degree of separation among respective alliances. The calculations required to identify polarization are complex (Wallace 1973; Bueno de Mesquita 1978), and, like other higher-order elements, polarization is at a maximum distance from the distribution of capabilities, conceptualized as the number of great powers, in Waltz's original exposition on structural realism.

Viewed in the context of the project of developing structural realism as a whole, the preceding delineation of structure offers at least two advantages.

First, the focus on the distribution of capabilities among states implicitly recognizes the consensus among social scientists that structure should encompass only relatively enduring aspects of a system. Rationality appears explicitly: unless an indicator of the distribution of capabilities can be linked to behavior that results from actors' real or hypothetical calculations about the international system, it does not qualify as an element of structure. While this restriction may seem excessively rigid and arbitrary, it is essential to strike a balance between the need for elaboration on the one hand and clear boundaries on the other. The preceding definition of structure is very encompassing in comparison to the treatment of this concept by Waltz, so an excessive amount of breadth becomes the principal danger to further efforts toward concept formation. In other words, if structure includes everything, it ultimately means nothing.

Second, the definition remains within the realist tradition but offers a more comprehensive approach toward the delineation of structure, which in turn creates the potential for a wider range of propositions about international processes. Several orders of salience are posited for indicators, from primary to higher order, based on the absence or presence of calculations and coalitions. This continuum recognizes the wider range of capability-based elements that could influence behavior, either directly or indirectly. The ordering from primary to higher order reflects the degree of distance that each type of element is deemed to represent in relation to Waltz's (1979) initial variant of structural realism.

These elements, all of which are based in some way on the distribution of capabilities, combine to form the structure of the international system from a *realist* point of view. It should be pointed out once again that, while structure could be enumerated in terms of other relatively enduring characteristics (with norms as one example that already has attracted attention in the context of an approach focusing on international society [Bull 1977; Kegley and Raymond 1990, 1991; Kacowicz 1998]), this would form the basis for a separate theory. So, too, would neotraditional realist concerns like the distribution of ideologies within the system. Of more direct concern at this point is how structure enters into the realist perspective on the world, which will be discussed in the next section. This discussion entails a precise identification of axioms for realism and structural realism that transcends chapter 1's overview of the realist tradition in international theory.

3. An Overview of Realism and Structural Realism

3.1 The Axiomatic Basis of Realism

Among the many critics of realism, Vasquez (1983) deserves credit for meticulous and thoughtful efforts to identify the degree of internal coherence and range of explanation for realist theory or "power politics." The maze of contradictions encountered in realist expositions and generally weak results from testing associated hypotheses came as a surprise at the time. From a later vantage point, however, the discoveries of Vasquez (1983) make sense and do not lead to obviously negative conclusions when placed in a frame of reference that is different from the most recent and equally authoritative study by Vasquez (1998). The typology of worldviews, ontologies, paradigms, and theories identified by Rosenau (1997: 31) helps to clarify the full implications of the seemingly dismal performance of realism as evaluated by Vasquez over the course of two decades. This typology will be expanded and explored in greater detail during the analysis in chapter 3 of scientific progress in the field of international relations, but for now it is useful in the more limited sense of helping to identify at least some degree of order in apparent chaos as related to realism.

Within any given worldview, such as realism, it is natural and even expected to find a range of ontologies, which in turn can encompass multiple paradigms and, ultimately, theories that may lack logical consistency with each other. To be more precise, a worldview is an overarching concept that invariably can be summed up in very few words or even just one, as in *realism, liberalism,* or Rosenau's (1988, 1990, 1995) neologism *fragmegration,* which refers to simultaneously unfolding processes of fragmentation and integration in the international system. Rosenau (1997) introduces a further series of concepts that move beyond the worldview to progressively higher levels of specificity about the subject of study, in this case international relations:

"[O]ntologies involve our most basic understanding of the nature of global politics, whereas paradigms specify the parameters or boundary conditions within
which political activities occur, and theories specify how the relationships
among individual or collective actors vary within any given set of parameters"
(30). The realist worldview, for example, might be represented in the following
way: it includes firm unit boundaries, states as the main units, and the primacy of security issues within its ontology (31).[16] In the realist paradigms (note
especially the plural here), the parameters (or boundary conditions) refer to the
existence of actors seeking relative gains in confrontational anarchic structures.
Finally, the key variables in realist theories are more diverse: threat, interests,
power, alliances, and security, each of which can be measured in various ways,
play central roles in respective realist theories (Vasquez 1997, 1998; Gibler
1999a; Legro and Moravcsik 1998).

    While the preceding typology from Rosenau is not the only way to establish
a hierarchy among the concepts ranging upward from theory to worldview, it
is sufficient to bring out the need to match the form of testing pursued with the
degree of generality entailed by respective constructs. A worldview, for example, is a concept that conveys an overall meaning, inclines toward the normative end of the intellectual spectrum for that reason, and, at least by intuition,
is not assessed effectively by gathering data and testing hypotheses. A more
effective way to evaluate realism's underlying ontology might be to identify discrete, internally consistent classes of theory within the parameters set by its paradigms and to appraise respective and overall performance of hypotheses.

    Realism's intricate set of theories, which is virtually certain to appear inco-
herent regardless of how parameters are set, may be traced to both its age and
its sustained popularity. Over the course of centuries and in the hands of many
exponents, the realist worldview stimulated a diverse collection of theories,
some of which have only superficial similarities to the others. An overview of the
assumptions entailed by respective modes of realist theorizing—as opposed to a
futile search for a single, unified theory—is the most promising path toward
improving structural realism or any other variant that might be selected for further development. In this way, neorealism can be placed in the context of one of
the realist paradigms for continuing work. Thus identification of a subset of logically consistent axioms is essential to eventual creation of an elaborated structural realism as a product of one of the paradigms *within* the realist worldview.[17]

    Four relatively recent and rigorous attempts to enumerate the axioms of
realism are sufficient to establish the credibility of the preceding argument
about diverse theories coexisting within a given worldview. Despite access to
the same classic texts and relatively similar objectives, Keohane (1989: 38–39),
Holsti (1995: 36–37), Kegley (1995: 5), and Schweller and Priess (1997: 6)
present lists that include three, five, ten, and four assumptions, respectively, for
realism.[18] The axioms from Keohane (1989), which are most restricted in number, will be reviewed first and used as a basis for comparison with the others.
As will become apparent, it is easy to identify dimensions related to beliefs

about actors and the level of analysis that is most important to understanding international relations.

From two standard sources, including one classic and one modern, Keohane (1989: 38–39) derives three fundamental assumptions of realism.[19] The assumptions focus on the units of the system, political processes, and interests, respectively, and may be summarized as follows:

1. The most important actors in world politics are territorially organized entities (city-states and modern states).[20]
2. State behavior is rational.[21]
3. States seek security and calculate their interests in terms of relative standing within the international system.[22]

Within the typology created by Rosenau (1997), this set of axioms might be summed up as a *contingent* realist worldview.[23] The emphases on rationality and security suggest a neutral view of human nature, even if nothing explicit appears on that subject in any given exposition. Free will and the ability to learn and improve upon previous choices are consistent with this line of reasoning and do not entail a liberal point of view.[24] The pursuit of security occurs in order to permit the satisfaction of other goals, which might include prosperity or even loftier things. Thus contingent realism is distinguished by the vision of decision makers as rational actors with a range of goals, seeking security as a foundation for any and all other activities.

Consider, by contrast, the following assumptions enumerated by Kegley (1995):[25]

1. A reading of history teaches that people are by nature sinful and wicked.
2. Of all people's evil ways, no sins are more prevalent, inexorable, or dangerous than are their instinctive lust for power and their desire to dominate others.
3. The possibility of eradicating the instinct for power is a utopian aspiration. (5)[26]

These assumptions combine to create the image of what might be called a *deterministic* realist worldview, a polar opposite from contingent realism as identified a moment ago. The darker side of human nature is stressed; power rather than security becomes the priority of the state in a world beset by evil: "There is no escape from the evil of power, regardless of what one does. Whenever we act with reference to our fellow men, we must sin, and we must still sin when we refuse to act; for the refusal to be involved in the evil of action carries with it the breach of the obligation to do one's duty." The preceding quotation, from Morgenthau's (1946: 201) classic exposition *Scientific Man and Power Politics*, sums up the deterministic end of the realist continuum.

Closer to Keohane's (1989) listing, but still at some distance, are the assumptions attributed to realism by Holsti (1995) and Schweller and Priess (1997). From Keohane's list, Holsti includes the first and second assumptions, while Schweller and Priess incorporate only the first, and in each instance the language is somewhat different. The latter two lists also include references to anarchy, suggesting another dimension: *system-level* as opposed to *unit-level* realism. The final two lists look like hybrids along the contingent/deterministic continuum; Holsti includes war and peace as the central questions of international relations, while Schweller and Priess incorporate power as a basic factor and international relations as conflict. Thus the list from the former is closer than the latter to the contingent end of the spectrum because power does not appear directly in Holsti's summary.

Some of the differences just summarized rise to the level of paradigmatic and possibly even ontological within Rosenau's (1997: 31) hierarchy of concepts. Key variables are not the same across the four summaries of realism, with the difference between seeking power and seeking security as sufficient to distinguish classes of theories. (To distinguish the goals of power and security seeking from each other in practice, it is essential to measure the latter in a way that focuses on more than just relative gains—otherwise, deterministic and contingent realism would appear to collapse into each other.) Variation also exists at the paradigmatic level: two of the lists refer to anarchy, while the other two do not grant it an explicit conditioning role. In terms of ontologies, the main units and boundaries appear consistent, and the basic issues are related to interstate rivalry, although the lists vary in how explicitly this final point is recognized. While dimensions of determinism and contingency, and unit and system levels, are identified, all four of the lists still appear to fit within a worldview that revolves around coping with the problems encountered by states in competition with each other.

Although the preceding survey of realist assumptions hardly can claim to be authoritative, that is not its purpose. Instead, the review shows that consulting just four sources is enough to reveal multiple theories and even paradigms within realism as a worldview. Thus, as expected, it is important to identify the assumptions to be retained in further theorizing in order to avoid the irony embedded in the title of Vasquez's compelling study *The Power of Power Politics* (1983; see also 1998 and Freyberg-Inan 2001), which suggests the apparent weakness of realism in everything *except* for its continuing ability to maintain allegiance as a worldview.[27] To move beyond the maze of contradictions and inconsistencies uncovered by Vasquez, it is essential to work within an identified class of theories: that is, some kind of paradigmatic grouping. In sum, a truly powerful variant of realism must begin with logical consistency in order to realize its potential.

Best (or even almost exclusively) known through structural realism (Waltz 1979, 1986), the more recent system-level theorizing may be expected to show greater internal consistency for two reasons: (a) its relative newness, which offers less time for subvariants to emerge, and (b) its creator's commitment to economy of explanation, which inherently limits the potential for self-contradiction.

3.2 The Axiomatic Basis of Structural Realism

State centrism, rational choice, and pursuit of security are the assumptions within structural realism that pertain to unit-level behavior. The preceding list (identified, as previously noted, by Keohane 1989) can be combined with three axioms about system structure to form the basis of structural realism (Waltz 1979: 91, 94, 100–1):

> 4. Anarchy is the ordering principle of international structure.[28]
> 5. States, the units of the international system, are undifferentiated by function.[29]
> 6. Structure is defined by the distribution of capabilities among states.[30]

The six axioms collectively represent system-level, contingent realist theorizing. The behavior of states is conditioned by the structure of the international system, which parallels something more familiar: "International politics is structurally similar to a market economy insofar as the self-help principle is allowed to operate in the latter" (Waltz 1979: 91). States are not inherently good or bad but must adapt to the distribution of capabilities in the anarchical international system.

Structural realism is a system-level theory based on principles borrowed from traditional realism and microeconomic theory (Ripley 1990: 22). Maximization of utility is represented by pursuit of security, operationalized in terms of positional standing, by each state as a self-interested, unitary actor. As in the standard metaphor of a free market populated by rational actors, *structure* "refers only to the spontaneously formed unintended conditions of action generated by the coactivity of separable firms" (Dessler 1989: 449). In the ideal version of a free enterprise system, devoid of collusion or regulation, producers and consumers strive for agreement on pricing based on the law of supply and demand. At some point an equilibrium emerges. The resulting structure, commonly known as the market, then has a life of its own. It conditions further interactions and is the selection mechanism for actors; only those who adapt to the market can be expected to survive for any length of time.

Units in the international "market," understood to be sovereign states, are differentiated by capability endowments and engage in interactions that reflect ongoing rivalry. Causal linkages are straightforward. Units arise and spontaneously form a structure, such as that of the system of states. The organizing principle is one of competition among independent actors. Members of the international system exist in a system of self-help, so the dispersion of capabilities will matter the most and determine the structure: "State behavior varies more with differences of power than with differences in ideology, in internal structure of property relations, or in governmental form" (Waltz 1986: 329). Given the lack of transnational authority, positional ordering among states is the crucial variable to monitor.

All of this can be summed up at a more general level. The assumption of anarchy—which holds true regardless of the specific membership of the international system at any given time—might be restated as follows: the only guarantee of survival for an individual unit in a closed system is assertion of sovereignty in whatever way becomes necessary. Thus it is assumed that either neutral or positive human nature can and will produce an anarchical result in such a system; it is not necessary to infer the existence of evil—as in the case of deterministic realism—to explain what happens under these conditions. The preceding inferences, to be more exact, effectively link Waltz's (1959) "first image" (i.e., the individual) to neorealism as a theory from the "third image" (i.e., the international system): each state will be concerned with its position in the hierarchy, and the capabilities possessed by other individual system members and coalitions (whether presumed to be hostile or friendly) will be monitored. Self-interest and insecurity have the effect of sustaining competition under conditions of anarchy. This will be true even in a system of generally weak states, as in the case of sub-Saharan Africa, where even concerns about implosion that might result from efforts toward external conquest are not sufficient to restrain competition at the interstate level (Saideman 2001: 154-99). It almost goes without saying that *changes* in the distribution of capabilities also make up an important part of the external setting; in the most extreme instance, a state might enter or exit the system, thereby altering the balance in a qualitative manner.

One of the positive traits of structural realism is its economy of explanation, a by-product of which is freedom from logical inconsistency between axioms. It falls clearly within the paradigm of system-level, contingent realism as these terms have been used so far. To place structural realism more explicitly in this context, consider the comparison of neorealism with realism as carried out by Schweller and Priess (1997). Their focus is on a wide range of dimensions: disciplinary setting, goals attributed to actors, presumed causal variables, interpretation of capability, substantive interest, and vision of the system. Traditional realism is associated with history, philosophy, and other disciplines from the humanities. Actors are assumed to seek power. Interests and power are the presumed causal variables. Capability is seen in terms of an interstate relationship, the substantive focus is on foreign policy, and the system (as a conditioning factor) includes interaction processes. Structural realism, by contrast, is seen as a product of microeconomic theory. Actors are assumed to pursue security, and the causal variables are anarchy and the distribution of capabilities. Capability itself is regarded as a structural attribute, the substantive focus is on international politics rather than foreign policy, and the system affects actors through its structure (Schweller and Priess 1997: 7).

(Neo)traditional realism and structural realism are orthogonal when viewed in terms of the preceding dimensions as articulated by Schweller and Priess

(1997). They are equated, respectively, with the deterministic actor-level, and contingent system-level, variants of realism. This comparison reinforces the point that neorealism already is perceived, at least implicitly, within a sector of the realist worldview, which provides the basis for its elaboration. The desire for greater understanding of international conflict, crisis, and war provides the immediate motivation for refinement of structural realism, so each of these concepts must be defined before that goal can be pursued further.

4. International Conflict, Crisis, and War

4.1 Defining International Conflict

Given the concern with breadth as well as depth, the goal of concept formation should be to include the widest possible range of conflicts within the international field of vision. To begin at the most general level, *political* conflict consists of interactions with the following properties (Gurr 1980):

1. Two or more parties are involved.
2. They engage in mutually opposing actions.
3. They use coercive behaviors "designed to destroy, injure, thwart or otherwise control" their opponent(s).[31]
4. These contentious interactions are overt; hence their occurrence can easily be detected and agreed upon by independent observers.[32]

Political conflict therefore is described as an explicit process involving groups that may be taken to approximate individuals. For such reasons, Gurr's definition may be regarded as a point of culmination for the events data movement that had commenced in the 1950s and had emphasized the study of interactions, usually between states, that could be observed, quantified, and probed for regularities (see East, Salmore, and Hermann 1978).

Gurr's encompassing definition serves as a natural lead-in to the problem of defining *international* conflict in an equally rigorous way (2). In an authoritative treatment of the subject, Haas (1970a: 8–10) identifies three kinds of international conflict: diplomatic (e.g., formal methods such as lodging protests), non-institutionalized (e.g., bilateral sanctions, imposed by one state on another), and military (e.g., declaring war). The exact boundaries between these categories are far less important than the general principle they establish, namely, that even when *international* is understood to mean *interstate* conflict, the range of behavior available for study is vast. Consider also the definition from Mitchell (1981), which refers to "[a] range of incompatible goals," "[a] range of psychological conditions experienced by the parties involved," and "[a] set of behaviours used to achieve the disputed goals" (17).[33] Once again, the range of actors, issues, and events that might be included is immense.

Comprehensiveness is reaffirmed as the key criterion by this admittedly brief discussion of prior concept formation as related to conflict in general and international strife in particular. From a vantage point three decades after Haas (1970a), it seems very unlikely that a longer review would produce a different verdict. The definition from James (1988), which will be used throughout the remainder of this study, is intended to encompass the wide range of phenomena that reasonably could be regarded as international conflicts. Thus an international conflict is defined as "any interaction delimited in time and space, involving two or more international entities (whether states or transnational actors) which possess non-identical preference orderings over one or more sets of alternative choices" (5).[34] From the standpoint of systemism, as introduced earlier, the definition refers explicitly to micro-micro interactions but does not foreclose the possibility of theorizing based on macro-macro or hybrid linkages. The preceding description of the processes of international conflict offers at least three further and specific advantages, each of which is related in some way to comprehensiveness.

First, actors may be sovereign states or may be transnational in character. As the intensity of conflict increases, the state-centric assumption within the realist worldview is regarded as likely to be approximated more closely. At one extreme, consider the negotiations over limited free trade between Canada and the United States in the 1980s (Doran and Drischler 1996; Lusztig 1996; Cameron and Tomlin 2000). The process involved many nonstate actors as well as governments and closely matched Keohane and Nye's (1989: 249) description of complex interdependence: multiple channels of contact among societies, no hierarchy of issues, and the absence of military force. At the other end of the spectrum, conflict that escalates to a very high level tends to restrict the range of involved actors. The threat and application of sustained military force are powers still virtually monopolized by states; even the various and sundry actions of terrorist, paramilitary, secessionist, fundamentalist, and other military forces operating across borders do not rival the resource mobilization that occurs during interstate strife. Thus structural realism, with its state-centric basis, is expected to explain conflict more effectively at that level. Events such as interstate wars and militarized interstate disputes (Small and Singer 1982; Gochman and Maoz 1984; Jones, Bremer, and Singer 1996), to cite two obvious examples, should be accounted for more effectively by some variant of realism rather than interdependence-based theories.

Second, the definition recognizes that international conflict is not a fully determined, zero-sum game. Incompatibility may be perceived with regard to some goals, but other interests continue to be mutual. For example, disputes are common within the Arab world, but the general disposition to unite against Israel endures, in theory if not always in practice. The possibility of mutual gain from conflict resolution serves as a constant reminder against determinism. To use Rapoport's terminology, international conflict is more of a "game" than a "fight" (Rapoport 1960, quoted in Deutsch 1988: 139–40, 143). It is characterized by strategic interaction among actors. An international conflict, for example, will arise over one or more issues where preferences differ and the techniques applied by actors range from pacific to violent (Brecher and Wilkenfeld 1997: 50).

Third, and finally, the definition of conflict is relatively free from ambiguity. Other treatments, possibly including the perceptions of actors and thereby entailing highly judgmental terms, could prove difficult to operationalize. Since the definition does not incorporate notions of blame, it is well suited to deal with the many instances in which responsibility for starting a conflict is less than obvious.

4.2 Defining International Crisis

Within the realm of international conflict, it is desirable to identify a focused, but still wide, range of events upon which an initial reassessment of structural realism, within the context of systemism, can be based. To begin with an obvious criterion, a conflict should be intense enough to challenge the existing structure of at least one international subsystem. Otherwise, it will be without basic implications for the international system even when the latter is considered only in terms of one or more subsystems. Since structure is defined as a multitier concept, that does not limit the investigation to the few historical instances of conflict that have created the possibility of (or resulted in) global transformation. Change in structure, as defined more specifically in chapter 5's overview of an elaborated structural realism, may refer to one or more of a multifaceted set of indicators. The following definition of an international crisis is used to identify an important class of events by the International Crisis Behavior (ICB) Project and is related directly to the definitions of system and structure already developed:

> An *international crisis* is a situation characterized by two [individually] necessary and [collectively] sufficient conditions: (1) distortion in the type and an increase in the intensity of *disruptive interactions* between two or more adversaries, with an accompanying high probability of *military hostilities*, or, during a war, an *adverse change* in the military balance; and (2) a *challenge* to the existing *structure* of an international system—global, dominant or subsystem—posed by the higher-than-normal conflictual interactions. (Brecher and Wilkenfeld et al. 1988: 3; see also Brecher and Wilkenfeld 1989, 1997, 2000)[35]

The 412 cases meeting this definition from 1918 to 1994 are listed and summarized in Brecher and Wilkenfeld (1997, 2000). A brief review of previous efforts toward definition of an international crisis will be sufficient to establish the advantages offered by ICB's treatment.

Efforts to define crisis as a process began with the events data analysis of the 1960s and 1970s.[36] McClelland (1968) referred to a "change of state in the flow of political actions" (160), with an "unusual volume and intensity of events" (161; see also McClelland 1961, 1972). Azar (1972) developed the idea of interaction beyond the threshold of a "normal relations range" (184). Snyder and Diesing (1977) refer to "a sequence of interactions between the government of two or more sovereign states in severe conflict, short of actual war, but involving the perception of a dangerously high probability of war" (6). Young (1968b: 15) and Hermann (1972: 10) combined interaction with structure; each identified an international crisis as a situation in which changing processes could produce effects on system structure. Definitions such as those just listed are not without value, but they are incomplete when considered from the standpoint of systemism. They focus on process exclusively and leave out components of a working international system, although Young and Hermann come closest by making note of structure. By comparison, the ICB definition is more complete; it refers either implicitly or explicitly to all of the components of an international system.

At this point the priority is to introduce the nature of international crisis as a process, with an emphasis on the role played by states. Brecher (1989: 209; 1993, 1999; see also Brecher and Wilkenfeld 1997) describes four interrelated domains of an international crisis: onset, escalation, de-escalation, and impact. In this process, unit-system linkage consists of a cycle. External change results in stress for the decisional elite of a state, which attempts to cope with onset and, later, escalation. Through information gathering and consultation, the elite identifies and evaluates alternatives. Depending on the complexity and protractedness of the situation, one or more choices emerge from that process. The resulting actions, which can range from verbal to violent, will produce war or some other form of resolution, leading in either instance to eventual termination of the crisis. Crises will have some kind of impact on the international system, possibly altering one or more aspects of existing structure (Brecher and James 1986).

Crisis participants have mixed motives that can reflect the characteristics of any number of game-theoretic scenarios, including "Chicken," "Stag Hunt," and others. Interactions are power oriented, and concern for security is brought out directly by the possibility of military engagement. Priorities vary with actors and circumstances; the balance between motives can change over the course of one or more crises (Hebron and James 1997). It also should be noted that a crude differentiation between "high" and "low" politics is not entailed by the above-noted definition of an international crisis. These events can encompass economic and other issues either directly or below the surface. For example, the crisis leading up to the assault on Pearl Harbor in December 1941 originated, at least in part, with intensifying resource constraints faced by the Japanese over the course of several years (Brecher and Wilkenfeld 1997: 405).

With regard to the role of the state in crisis, rationality is assumed to guide the process of choice. Rational choice does *not* imply a caricature consisting of a complete search for information and review of every imaginable alternative. At some point the costs entailed by further efforts to secure data are inferred to outweigh the benefits (Riker and Ordeshook 1973: 21–22). This trade-off becomes more severe under crisis conditions, when there is intense pressure to make decisions about important issues. A so-called "satisficing" response, in fact, becomes optimal once resources devoted to finding a better choice can be deployed more profitably elsewhere. For example, detailed assessment of the merits of alternative strategies becomes pernicious if it creates undue limitations on the time and energy available for executing the plan that is selected. In sum, the role of the state in an international crisis corresponds to that anticipated by structural realism in the general sense: a rational actor in pursuit of security that is engaged in strategic interaction under conditions of anarchy and time constraints.[37]

Unit-system linkage is achieved explicitly through ICB's definition of a *foreign policy crisis,* which derives from three interrelated perceptions held by a state's highest-level decision makers that are generated by a hostile act, disruptive event, or environmental change (Brecher and Wilkenfeld 1997: 3; 1989, 2000; Brecher and Wilkenfeld et al. 1988; Wilkenfeld and Brecher et al. 1988):

1. a *threat to one or more basic values;* along with
2. an awareness of *finite time for response* to the value threat; and
3. a *heightened probability of involvement in military hostilities.*

The literature on crisis decision making and attendant efforts toward definition is vast and will not be covered here. It should be noted, however, that the conditions within the ICB Project's definition of a foreign policy crisis are consistent with over a generation of improvements in theorizing and empirical research.[38] The 895 foreign policy crises meeting the ICB definition are listed in Brecher and Wilkenfeld (1997, 2000).

With both the definitions of an international crisis and a foreign policy crisis in place, the basic advantages of this concept formation in the context of eventual testing of an elaborated structural realism can be summarized. First, the definitions are well integrated with each other. The adversaries in an international crisis account for one or more foreign policy crises.[39] Second, from the standpoint of systemism, ICB's definitions create the potential to examine a full set of linkages, including macro-macro and micro-micro along with the hybrids, or macro-micro and micro-macro. Thus the preceding definitions of crisis are both internally consistent with each other and relevant to testing priorities.

While these are laudable achievements, perhaps a more general question about crises in world politics needs to be answered before going any further. Given the demise of the Soviet Union and events in Eastern Europe over the last decade, what is the continuing relevance of studying international crises? Does the apparent resolution of the superpower conflict mean that analysis of crises holds only historical interest? After all, the term *crisis* itself would seem like a good candidate for the seemingly dated collection of Cold War–associated concepts cited earlier from Holsti (1996).

Several points argue against the conclusion that crisis is an artifact of either the Cold War or some earlier era and therefore less relevant to the present and future: the probable inability of even a Russian-U.S. condominium (if one emerged) to put an end to crises, the nature of politics in the developing world, the process of change itself, the likelihood that crises will not be restricted to a few increasingly irrelevant places, and the evidence available about the likelihood of violence when crises do occur. Each of these five points is developed in turn.

First, the two leading military powers are incapable of preventing (or at least controlling) all of the events that might cause them to experience further crises, mutual or otherwise. This is true especially of the former Soviet Union, which is beset by nationalist strife from within and without. Even if the bilateral rivalry has been dampened, third parties still may cause the United States and the reconstituted Russian state to engage in direct confrontation. States such as Libya, China, and Israel remain capable of generating intense international conflict, and the unfolding situation in the former Yugoslavia already has raised tensions between the United States and Russia to levels not seen since the Cold War. It is very unlikely that future disputes involving these and other actors will elicit an identity of interests between the two leading powers, especially as the trauma of the final Russian Revolution of the twentieth century recedes. As a result of actions by client (or other) states, the United States and Russia still could be involved as adversaries in a major crisis. Furthermore, as Ray (1995: 346) points out, the former USSR, China, and India have about half of the world's population, and the future of democracy—and, presumably, a relatively stable foreign policy—is at best uncertain for these states.

Second, it would be extremely optimistic to assume that changes in Europe, whether at the national or regional level, will counteract the legacy of a generation of superpower conflict in the developing world. Crises occurred frequently there in spite of U.S.-Soviet cooperation on security matters throughout the Cold War. Although each superpower usually acted with restraint toward its rival's vital interests, the United States and USSR also proved unwilling to "forego perceived opportunities to advance their own interests at the other's expense *unless and until the threat of a dangerous confrontation appear[ed] to be imminent*" (George 1988a: 591; see also George 1988: 584 and 1988b, 1988c). The superpowers competed under the shadow of nuclear war, with factional rivalry in Angola, the struggle between Ethiopia and Somalia over the Ogaden, and various conflicts in the Middle East—to cite a few prominent examples—resulting in numerous international crises. The potential for more crises is considerable, especially if lessons from past protracted conflicts are a guide to the future (Brecher and Wilkenfeld 1997: 820–34).

Third, the international system still could be prone to crises because of the process of change itself. Consider the unsettled situation in central Europe, a traditional site of great-power rivalry. As it becomes more entrenched, the reunification of Germany could produce greater insecurity among various states in Europe, including Britain, France, and especially Russia. It is possible and even likely that the leading powers and other states will disagree intensely on some of the issues related to the future of Europe, possibly producing a new series of crises.[40] With so many more independent governments functioning in Eastern Europe, it is not at all clear that the leading powers will find management of global or regional security any easier.[41]

Fourth, in the course of arguing that major war appears to be on the way to being obsolete, Mueller (1988: 252) implicitly challenges the idea that crisis will continue to be of general relevance.[42] He observes that, since 1945, war has occurred "almost entirely within the *fourth* [i.e., the most impoverished] world." This would appear to suggest that intense international conflict and crisis will be restricted to zones of extreme poverty, with deprivation as the fundamental cause of continuing violence. Thus, although crisis might persist, research on it could appear to have a very restricted geographic mandate.

Events in the last decade, however, suggest that such an argument is incorrect. The Gulf War unfolded between Iraq and a U.S.-led coalition, with the main prize being the impressive energy resources of Kuwait. Thus the war involved technologically advanced states, took place in the "Third" rather than the "Fourth" World, and counteracted the notion of "immunity" from physical coercion for small states (Watson 1992: 300). Although this is only one case, it does suggest that military conflict among advanced states remains a viable subject for study, especially given the flare-ups that continue in the tense diplomacy between Iraq and the United States. The still relatively new situation in Europe, with the virtually simultaneous creation or transformation of many states, also argues in favor of skepticism about the impending irrelevance of realist practice and resulting crises. Tensions among the former Soviet Republics, if anything, reinforce this view. The prospects for a stable peace in post-Yugoslavia, the Transcaucasus, or the Trans-Dneister region of Moldova would appear limited in years to come (Brecher 1993: 545–46). Central Asia, in particular, is a power vacuum with immense potential for further crises in the aftermath of the Afghan War. The events of "9/11" bear out that assertion.

Fifth, and finally, research suggests that the most likely crises are those with a relatively high potential for violence, which in turn tends to produce more of the same. Consider the following examples from various world regions: Morocco/Polisario, Ethiopia/Somalia, Chad/Libya, Rwanda/Burundi (Africa); India/Pakistan, Afghanistan/Pakistan, North Korea/South Korea, China/Taiwan, India/Sri Lanka, Russia/China (Asia); Arab/Israel, Greece/Turkey, Iran/Iraq, Iraq/Kuwait (Middle East); and Italy/Croatia, Serbia/Croatia, Serbia/Bosnia-Hercegovina, Russia/Ukraine (Europe).[43] These pairings, many of which produced numerous conflicts in the twentieth century, generally conform to the series of characteristics identified by Brecher (1993) for violent crises: "geographic contiguity between the adversaries; a military-security-type issue in dispute, notably over territory, or several issues combined; the unfolding of the conflict within a subsystem; a structure of fragmented decisional authority, i.e., polycentrism, whether accompanied by power bipolarity or unipolarity; considerable heterogeneity; and authoritarian regimes" (547–48; see also Brecher 1994). The unfortunate tendency of the dyads "at risk" for crises to be violence prone as well creates an important by-product. Crises that do occur can be expected to lean toward violence, which in turn creates potential for spillover, more crises and protracted conflict. In sum, the simmering conflicts in the international system today are exactly the kind that are most worrisome with regard to escalation potential.

All things considered, international crisis emerges as a continuing high priority for research. Although international politics among the states at the top of the system appears relatively peaceful, trends do not constitute laws (Popper 1974). Relations among the United States, Russia, and the European states might continue to improve; it also is conceivable that they will deteriorate. The developing world, of course, is likely to experience further strife regardless of what happens in Europe. Moreover, through contagion or diffusion effects, these conflicts might undermine stability among the great powers, however defined. All of this takes place with the rising power of China in the background—a development that is very likely to result in some uncomfortable days ahead for world leaders.[44] In sum, the study of crises in world politics seems certain to remain an important subject in the era of rapid change and complexity.

4.3 Defining International War

It is easy to grasp the concept of war intuitively but far more challenging to give it a rigorous definition. Visions of war emerge from across the social sciences and even beyond. Wright's (1942: 9–13) classic exposition acknowledged legal, sociological, philosophical, and psychological ways of looking at war. Lider (1977: 6–29) offers an authoritative list of disciplinary approaches that encompasses and transcends those identified by Wright: biological, psychological and sociopsychological, anthropological, ecological, geopolitical, legal, moral, military-technical, sociological, political, politico-economic, and multidimensional. With so many fields contributing to the study of war, it therefore is to be expected that a variety of definitions have been proposed. This brief review, of necessity, will search for convergence among them.

Wright (1942) defined war as "the *legal condition* which *equally* permits two or more *hostile groups* to carry on a *conflict* by *armed* force" (8). This definition, which Wright characterized as suitable for contemporary conflict because it is narrower than conceptions that would apply to earlier eras, also is taken to be "a species of a wider genus" (Wright 1942: 12). This description recognizes implicitly that war exists as a subset of conflict and that in the modern world it refers to states as the basic entities involved. Malinowski ([1941] 1968), writing from an anthropological point of view, defined war as "an armed contest between two independent political units, by means of organized military force, in the pursuit of a tribal or national politics" (247). This definition, which also appeared long before the behavioral revolution, resembles that of Wright because of its recognition of war as a type of intergroup conflict.

Even closer to the notion of war as a subset of conflict is Malinowski's observation that "aggression is a by-product of cooperation" (252). Thus conflict (C') is regarded as the complement of cooperation (C), and war (W) is a subset of C' (see also James 1988; Kugler 1993a: 483).

While a great many other definitions appeared during the twentieth-century study of war, it is beyond the scope of this exposition to cover even a few of them. Instead, the classic definitions from Wright and Malinowski are sufficient to establish that a sense of war as a separate *class* of events existed long ago. Rather than pursuing more examples from many decades past, it is useful to turn to the summary of such efforts presented by Most and Starr (1989):[45]

1. at least two parties, one of which is a state
2. conflictual goals
3. parties that are aware of their conflicting goals
4. parties that are willing to attain a goal that they recognize conflicts with the wishes of the other(s)
5. situations in which at least one party is willing to use overt military force to attain its goal
6. situations in which at least one party is able to resist another's use of overt military force to the extent that it avoids "immediate" defeat, suffers a minimal number of casualties, and/or inflicts minimal casualties on the other(s)
7. situations in which no party that is willing to use overt military force can attain its goal with only a single use of force or with a series of such acts that are highly dispersed over time (73)

Most and Starr (1989) bring these components together as follows: "[W]ar is a particular type of outcome of the *interaction* of at least dyadic sets of specified varieties of actors in which at least one actor is willing and able to use some specified amount of military force for some specified period of time against some other, resisting actor and in which some specified minimal number of fatalities (greater than zero) occur" (73). This summary, as will become apparent, reflects convergence in the field toward a standard definition for international war.

Movement toward a fully *operational* definition took place within the context of the Correlates of War (COW) Project, the most sustained among the data-based, collective efforts to explore international conflict. Singer and Small (1972: 18–19) used an inductive process to identify a valid and reliable list of interstate wars. Wars from a merged list, derived from classic studies such as Wright (1942), had to survive further tests in order to achieve inclusion. The criteria included (a) political status of participants, measured in terms of diplomatic recognition, and (b) minimal thresholds for battle-related casualties or troops in combat. At the end of this process, an interstate war had to include two or more member states of the international system and produce a minimum of one thousand battle-related casualties among the participating states (Singer and Small 1972: 37, 39). It would not be an exaggeration to say that the preceding definition is the most recognized and accepted definition offered so far for any kind of international conflict.[46] At the very least, the COW definition has been the standard for empirical research on interstate warfare over the last three decades (Geller and Singer 1998). This will become apparent during the review of findings in chapter 4.

While finding great favor among scientifically inclined students of international conflict, the COW Project's definition is not without its faults. Critiques of the definition have tended to start with refinements and move on to more extreme ideas about its replacement. Levy (1983: 52–63), for example, provides a valuable discussion of how criteria such as the one thousand battle death threshold for inclusion might be applied to potential cases (a) over time and (b) in general versus those involving great powers. More recent critics have attacked the validity of the COW definition, either implicitly or explicitly, along a number of fronts. Guilmartin (1988: 153) asks whether European conceptions of war are appropriate for analysis of conflicts involving the Ottomans and, by implication, other cultures. Even more skeptical is the assessment offered by Holsti (1996: 14), who observes that most post–World War II conflict has occurred *within* states. (This point derives from the more general one raised in chapter 1, in which Holsti and others questioned the continuing relevance of theorizing based on realism and state centrism in particular.) Thus, with at least implicit reference to the COW definition of war, Holsti (1996) asks the following question: "Are we to understand the Somalias, Rwandas, Myanmars, and Azerbaijans of the world in classical European terms?" (14). Marshall's (1999) critique of mainstream concept formation about war goes a step further, seeing the need to focus more on "social identity" groups rather than states as abstractions (26). Thus it might be asked whether the COW definition of war continues to have empirical relevance, even if it might be seen as suitable concept formation about interactions between and among states.

Despite the problems identified in the preceding discussion, evidence exists that the COW definition can continue to provide the foundation for empirical research about interstate war. As Kugler (1993b) observes, "[M]uch has been learned about the characteristics and effects of war" (965). Wallensteen and Sollenberg (1996: 353, 356–57; see also Gleditsch et al. 2001 on armed conflict) confirm that most armed conflicts in the 1990s have concerned internal issues but also note the existence of "at least one interstate armed conflict each year [from 1989 to 1995], with the exception of 1993 and 1994. Thus interstate conflict is not extinct" (353). Furthermore, the sheer number of conflicts of one sort or another may not correlate with the overall danger posed to global and regional systems as a whole. From that point of view, short but intense conflicts such as the Gulf War of 1991 or the Afghan War of 2001 can prove most important of all if the parties involved have both the capacity and possible inclination to use weapons of mass destruction.

Perhaps the most promising recent development is one that builds on the COW definition by distinguishing among different types and thereby identifying continuity and change in the evolution of war over several centuries. Levy, Walker, and Edwards (2001) identify wars between (a) great powers, (b) great powers and other states, (c) other states alone, and (d) states and nonmembers of the international system (which had been labeled by Singer and Small [1972] as extrasystemic or imperial or colonial wars). This taxonomy is used to identify trends that would not be obvious from the fully aggregated data on war. For example, the frequency of great-power war has been declining for most of the previous five hundred years, yet the severity and proportion of great powers participating has gone up. Levy, Walker, and Edwards (2001) hypothesize that the higher number of great-power participants in great-power wars may reflect the increasing interdependence within the modern great-power security system. If anything, that would tend to contradict the idea that interstate war is in the process of being swept away by globalization; ironically, what if the risks of escalation to full-scale global strife actually are increasing with time?

Considerations such as those raised by Wallensteen and Sollenberg (1996), along with Levy, Walker, and Edwards (2001), suggest that it is too soon to write off the COW definition. As will become apparent from the review of research in chapter 4, the COW definition has enabled multiple generations of scholars to compile an impressive array of findings about the causes of war. Adoption of the COW definition thus completes this subsection on concept formation as related to war.

5. Conclusions

Systemism has been introduced as an alternative that is superior to either individualism or holism with regard to theorizing about international relations. Basic concepts that are fundamental to later creation of an elaborated structural realism, the international system and its structure, have been defined. An overview of realism and structural realism helps to place in context efforts to develop a theory in the tradition of system-level, contingent realism. Finally, international conflict, crisis, and war, which would be the substantive concerns for an elaborated structural realism at the initial stages of its development, have been defined. This completes the derivation of basic concepts that started in chapter 1 and sets the stage for chapter 3, which will assess the meaning of scientific progress in the field of international relations.

CHAPTER THREE

International Relations and Scientific Progress

I haven't seen much progress.
> —Kenneth N. Waltz, quoted in Halliday and Rosenberg, "Interview with Ken Waltz"

1. Objectives and Plan of Work

This chapter will develop a framework for evaluation of scientific progress in international relations. It builds on concept formation from the preceding chapters and sets the stage for an overview and assessment of structural realism in part 2. The task of developing the overarching concept that will guide evaluation of progress, the *scientific research enterprise,* is carried out in four additional sections. Each is summarized at this point.

First, the meaning of scientific progress in international relations is explored. Work begins with identification of useful concepts from the philosophy of social science. A continuum of aggregation for concepts is described, with *worldview* and *hypothesis* as the polar points representing generality and specificity, in that order. An intermediate zone along the continuum, which encompasses paradigmlike creations, is identified as optimal for evaluation of scientific progress within international relations. Illustrations at each point of aggregation are taken from realism, for which the nuances among various ways of thinking are most familiar and easily placed in context. Three types of comparison—pragmatic, revolutionary, and evolutionary—are designated for (a) worldviews and ontologies and (b) the external and (c) internal performance of paradigmatic entities, respectively. While this discussion entails some degree of abstraction, an ongoing effort is made to maintain a connection with the concerns of international relations as a field of study. In other words, substantive illustrations are used to establish the relevance of analysis from philosophy of science to progress in international relations as a discipline.

Second, each of the preceding types of comparison is developed at greater length. Pragmatic comparison is summarized as a naturally occurring historical process that unfolds primarily beyond the boundaries of the research community. Desirable traits for a paradigmlike entity are identified through a review of competing and complementary efforts toward concept formation. The resulting criteria form the basis for development and later application of the scientific research enterprise as the focal point for carrying out revolutionary comparison as noted above. Priorities for effective theorizing within paradigmatic boundaries are enumerated and provide the foundation for evolutionary comparison. Familiar terminology is involved, but the analysis extends the existing concepts. For example, explanatory power is identified as a concept that contains multiple dimensions, among which trade-offs exist.

Third, as a point of culmination for the preceding analysis, the concept of a scientific research enterprise is introduced for application to the field of international relations. This paradigmlike entity is presented through an analysis of costs and benefits associated with alternative versions of theorizing within its boundaries. Concepts such as economy of exposition, along with descriptive, explanatory, and predictive power, are used to give meaning to assessment of costs and benefits. The analysis relies upon a diagrammatic exposition to bring out potential trajectories of development within a scientific research enterprise.

Fourth, and finally, the accomplishments of this chapter are reviewed and placed in the context of the study as a whole. The conclusion ends by introducing the task to be carried out in part 2 of the book: presentation and evaluation of structural realism as a scientific research enterprise.

2. The Meaning of Scientific Progress in International Relations

Where is the appropriate place to begin the process of reassessment and reconstruction of theory about international relations? A myriad of concepts relate to the development of theory in some way or another, so this is not an easy question to address. The answer offered here can be summed up in the concept of a scientific research enterprise: *Within a given worldview and ontology, a scientific research enterprise consists of (a) a set of assumptions with parametric status known as the hard core; (b) rules that prohibit certain kinds of theorizing, labeled as the negative heuristic; and (c) a positive heuristic, meaning a series of theories for which the solved and unsolved empirical problems (along with anomalies), which focus on the description, explanation, and prediction of actions and events, continue to accumulate.*[1] The as yet unfamiliar terminology that appears in the preceding summary statement is introduced as this chapter moves forward. The scientific research enterprise is intended to be synthetic in the best sense that is possible. It builds on previous concept formation and strives for a higher degree of integration than that exhibited by previous frameworks for evaluation of research progress. The discussion that follows will begin at a relatively high level of abstraction and move increasingly toward a more applied form of analysis that bears upon international relations.

While international relations as a discipline can be traced back much further, the review that follows will concentrate on the era after World War II. As it turns out, however, this period of about a half-century is sufficient to reveal diverse viewpoints across the key dimensions. Disagreement is sustained over (a) basic issues related to theory construction in general and (b) realism in particular. For such reasons the discouraging words from Waltz in the epigraph to this chapter begin to make sense.

With regard to theory construction, debates ebb and flow over scope, including dichotomies such as middle range versus grand theory[2] and system versus unit,[3] as related to prospects for the growth of knowledge. Methods of both creation and evaluation also evoke a wide range of views on progress; deductive versus inductive theorizing and quantitative versus qualitative testing continue to stimulate intense debate over the best ways to move international relations forward as a discipline.[4] Comparative reviews and chronologies, which sometimes include efforts toward integration of approaches, occur periodically but either do not seem to create any sustained consensus on the meaning of progress in the field or are too recent to be assessed in such terms.[5]

One approach, realism, obtains by far the most attention in the era since World War II. Many scholars have advocated realism as the best hope for progress and, even when critical of the approach, suggest its revision rather than abandonment.[6] Others, with the numbers growing especially in the last decade, reject realism either completely or overwhelmingly and call for development of theories that are different in kind rather than merely in degree.[7]

These arguments have had the effect of raising more general concerns about the pursuit of knowledge within international relations as a discipline. Lapid (1989: 237–38) articulates the idea of a new era of reflection in terms of a "third debate" linked to the "confluence of diverse anti-positivistic philosophical and sociological trends" (237). This new debate "is typically expected to facilitate trailblazing ideas about the nature and progression of knowledge in the international relations field" (238–89). The key themes in the debate, according to Lapid (1989), are preoccupation with meta-scientific units ("paradigmatism"), a focus on underlying premises and assumptions ("perspectivism"), and drift toward methodological pluralism ("relativism") (239).[8] A little over a decade later, it is clear that Lapid's assessment of the field's direction should be regarded as prescient. The English School, world society, postmodernism, feminism, classical realism, neotraditional realism, structural realism, neoliberalism, liberalism, world systems theory, and neo-Gramscian Marxism all compete across the dimensions identified by Lapid (see also Wendt 1999: 32). Debate continues but without closure, so perhaps the reaction should be somewhere between "celebration and despair," as so aptly put by Ferguson and Mansbach (1991: 376) soon after the appearance of Lapid's exposition.

Given the sheer volume of debate and resulting uncertainty about knowledge claims in the discipline of international relations, it seems wise to begin with fundamental issues in developing a vision of progress. Ideas about the means of theorizing and how disciplines move forward are the natural domain of the philosophy of science. The discussion therefore shifts in that direction, with an eye to identifying a useful set of concepts for evaluation of progress.

Although many thoughts have been expressed about how to aggregate ideas and research, all available concepts within the philosophy of social science fall somewhere along a continuum from the general to the specific.[9] The exposition that follows will seek to develop the most salient concepts, including polar points. This process begins with reference to Rosenau (1997), in which four

Table 3.1
Realism Along the Continuum of Aggregation:
From Worldview to Hypothesis

Concept	Degree of Aggregation	Summary of Meaning	Illustrations from Realism
worldview	most general	understood by *gestalt*	international relations as power politics
ontology	general	identification of what is to be observed: main units, unit boundaries, main issues	assumption of firm boundaries, states as the main units, and war versus peace as the main issue
paradigms	intermediate	designation of parameters	actors seeking relative gains in confrontational anarchic structures
			actors seeking a mixture of relative and absolute gains in confrontational anarchic structures
theories	specific	designation of key variables	number of great powers
			concentration of capabilities
			number of alliances
			polarization of alliances
hypotheses	most specific	'if-then' statements	if two states experience a transition in relative capability, then war between them becomes more likely

major points—worldview, ontology, paradigm, and theory—have received some attention already. The current treatment will build on that concept formation in two ways. It will expand on the description of the preceding points and will cover one other as well, to facilitate use of the continuum in a wider range of comparison with respect to scientific progress.

Table 3.1 provides an illustration of how concepts ranging from worldview to hypothesis can be situated at respective degrees of aggregation. The table's continuum of aggregation summarizes each concept's meaning and includes illustrations taken from realism. The immediate advantage of the continuum, applied in this way, is that it provides an organized and coherent means for moving from the most encompassing ideas to precise manifestations: in other words, it enforces a higher degree of clarity on theorizing in order to facilitate comparison and cumulation. A more specific benefit is provided with respect to the eventual creation of an elaborated structural realism, which would become exceptional among theories because of "conscious reflection on its philosophical bases or premises" (Biersteker 1989: 265). Each of the concepts summarized in the table will be explained in turn; the discussion naturally begins by contrasting opposite ends of the continuum.

Polar points of specificity and generality are identified with the concepts of the individual hypothesis and worldview, respectively. The former is the most specific, theory-laden statement that can be made, while the latter is the most general among potential concepts.

A hypothesis is a contingent statement about the connection of one entity to another, such as "If x, then y with a greater likelihood." A prominent example from international relations appears in table 3.1: "If two states experience a transition in relative capability [x], then war between them [y] becomes more likely."[10] As with all hypotheses, this example includes terminology that is embedded at higher degrees of aggregation (Quine 1953). Thus terms like *relative capability* and *war* are understood within a prior and more abstract context, which in this instance would refer to the relatively familiar language of power transition theory within the field of international relations (Organski 1958; Organski and Kugler 1980; Kugler and Organski 1989; Kugler and Lemke 1996; Tammen et al. 2000).

At the other extreme, a worldview is a holistic concept that expresses a belief system or way of understanding the world, as opposed to a presentation that is based self-consciously on some combination of logic and evidence. Thus the realist worldview is summed up in table 3.1 as power politics, which leaves a lot of room for variation (and even contradiction) as it is manifested at increasingly specific points along the continuum. The Hobbesian view of human nature, as articulated by Morgenthau (1946) and others designated in the preceding chapter as deterministic realists, fits within the worldview. So does contingent realism, with its emphasis on free will and learning within the boundaries imposed by anarchy and security seeking. Thus it is obvious immediately that worldview, understood in such terms, is not the place to look for analytical consistency. Rather, as noted in the table, understanding is holistic in nature.

Treated as polar points, worldviews and hypotheses also differ in terms of normative versus positive emphasis. This is a product of the ways in which general and specific concepts, at the extremes, are comprehended.[11] A worldview is understood by *gestalt* rather than through an explanation based on some mixture of formal logic and evidence from observation. Thus the concept represents something fundamentally normative in character; a worldview shapes interpretation of reality from a perspective that is not subject to any prior rational reconstruction. A worldview, moreover, may even remain implicit and unnamed; a formal exegesis is not necessary to confirm its presence because self-identification occurs naturally through adoption of arguments that can be traced back to a fundamental system of beliefs. At the other extreme, a hypothesis, while always ultimately connected to one or more worldviews (and unintelligible to, or even ruled out by, others), is a positive statement in the sense of specifying a connection between things that have some empirical basis. Tentative support for, or refutation of, a hypothesis may have important normative implications, but that is a matter beyond the domain of the contingent statement itself.[12]

Neither a worldview nor a hypothesis, given their respective properties, is the appropriate point of aggregation at which to pursue assessment of scientific progress in a discipline such as international relations. The problems with analysis that might be conducted at each polar point are considered in turn. This discussion moves on to establish a taxonomy of comparison at respective intermediate degrees of aggregation, which include ontologies, paradigmlike creations, and theories.

A series of increasingly basic questions asking "Why is this argument correct?" eventually produces an infinite regress because no further answer based strictly on some combination of logic and empirical evidence is available. This identifies the point of generality at which the worldview rests. The worldview underlying the current project can be used to show how this process works. It can be summed up as *scientific systemism,* a belief that social life can be understood as a system that reflects the choices of individuals under constraints, which in turn can be understood through application of the scientific method.[13]

Scientific systemism makes it possible to interpret international relations in a certain way; as noted in chapter 1, political interactions are believed to produce patterns that can be detected by systematic research. Ultimately, concepts such as "political interactions," "patterns," and "systematic research" can be reduced to their most primitive levels and derived from the belief system labeled scientific systemism. Thus this worldview can encompass a wide range of research that shares its commitment to the principles of science, understood most fundamentally as logical consistency in theory and pursuit of reproducible evidence, along with systemism.

Any set of concepts combined to produce an ontology, a paradigm, a theory, or a hypothesis can be recast in more encompassing terms to represent a worldview. Incommensurability with other worldviews is not assured but becomes highly probable when ideas are put forward with this degree of generality. The example of social constructivism in relation to scientific systemism is useful in highlighting this point. The worldview of social constructivism represents, as closely as anything that might be imagined, the antithesis of scientific systemism. It emphasizes the social construction of reality and rejects the pursuit of knowledge through a direct application of the scientific method (Wendt 1992, 1999; Onuf 1995; Adler 1997).[14]

Although sometimes difficult to identify in terms that are accessible to a wide audience, the alternative method entailed by social constructivism appears to be described most effectively as historical hermeneutics (Habermas 1975). Conventional scientific thinking, which holds to the possibility of objective knowledge based on reproducible evidence, is regarded as inadequate for understanding of international relations and social life in general. Instead, social constructivism's emphasis is on the role played by participants in consciously interpreting the world and thereby setting boundaries for behavior.[15] Thus constructivism rejects materialism and individualism in favor of idealism and holism (Wendt 1999: 23–31, 376).

Taken together, scientific systemism and social constructivism do not appear to offer common grounds for comparison precisely because each entails incommensurable criteria for *evaluation*.[16] While other worldviews could share some grounds for assessment (perhaps more likely to be identified on a pairwise than on a collective basis), the obstacles at this degree of generality are inferred to be formidable across the board.

Consider the basic issue of what is taken to be true. If truth is regarded as a social construction or convention, then every social group may be said to have its own set of truths. Truth becomes "coextensive with consensus: agreement makes truth, rather than truth inviting agreement" (Bunge 1996: 97). To the extent that it accurately represents social constructivism as a worldview, this set of beliefs represents the antithesis of scientific systemism. While ideas can travel across worldviews and exert potentially progressive influence (as in the case of constructivism's reminder about the importance of ideas in shaping reality[17]), competition initiated by design and based on a priori performance criteria should be granted a lower priority than in the past at the degree of aggregation represented by worldview.

One potentially troubling point that emerges from the preceding discussion is that, while conflicts at the degree of aggregation represented by worldview are most fundamental, this line of reasoning could be construed as saying "Ignore them." The later discussion of comparison at more specific degrees of aggregation will return to this issue and include an explanation of why inter-worldview debates are best left to resolution primarily through naturally occurring processes in society as a whole.

What about focusing debate on the individual hypothesis, which represents the opposite extreme from a worldview? This option, alas, is too self-limiting; even widely divergent philosophies of science are skeptical about the existence of would-be crucial experiments (Kuhn 1962; Feyerabend 1970; Lakatos 1970). In principle it is difficult to imagine how the apparent failure of any hypothesis, or even a few in combination, could generate wide enough *implications* to justify a fundamental shift in perspective. This point is reinforced in reference to the earlier discussion of terminology in a hypothesis; in every instance it will be proposed within some larger context that provides a vocabulary for expression. While that property does not entail incommensurability in interpreting results, it further reduces the likelihood that any one proposition can "thread the needle" in competition at a higher degree of aggregation.

Consider, for example, how realists have reacted to historical evidence that suggests an absence of power balancing in some cases. The worldview is preserved, but a search for other manifestations in behavior gets underway. Vasquez (1998: 372–73) sees a proliferation of "realisms," including both offensive and defensive, that suggest degeneration in the face of evidence. However, from a realist standpoint, the problem might appear somewhat different. Perhaps there is nothing wrong with an expanding range of tactics to be attributed to actors in a realist world, as long as the conditions within which each will apply are specified. For instance, threat (Walt 1997) may be balanced under some circumstances and interests (Schweller 1997) under others. Or, as will be suggested in chapter 5, threat and interests can serve as components in building a more complete model of the state as an actor.

Proliferating ideas about state behavior can coexist in realist theories and paradigms, but not without a sense of where competition and complementarity, respectively, exist. Vasquez (1997: 91) is accurate in noting contradictory propositions within realism, but that points to the latent existence of multiple paradigms and theories that need to be properly identified and separated from each other. It becomes clear why, in both this instance and others that might be raised fully outside of realism, the failure of one or more hypotheses does not necessarily mean the "beginning of the end" for a paradigm, ontology, or worldview. It may instead be, as Winston Churchill put it, "the end of the beginning." As research accumulates within a high level of aggregation, such as an ontology, competing and complementary theories and paradigms can be expected to accumulate. Thus it becomes crucial to avoid the chaos identified by Vasquez (1997: 905), where realism allows itself to find support from balancing of power, balancing of threat, bandwagoning, and other forms of behavior without any designation of circumstances under which each in turn is expected to operate.

For the reasons that come out in the preceding example, it is unlikely that scientific progress could be evaluated in a compelling way within the narrow context of either articulating or testing a single hypothesis. Instead, it is likely that the performance of individual hypotheses can be assessed more effectively in a wider frame of reference.

Intermediate concepts, whether referring to paradigms or related constructs that might be identified along the continuum, would appear from the outset to be better suited than either hypotheses or worldviews to the task of assessing scientific progress. The challenge is to designate, among this still very wide range of options, concepts that offer varying blends of the general and the specific in the appraisal of international relations. Each concept then can be used to evaluate the performance of international relations and perhaps other disciplines from a series of progressively more (or less) general vantage points along the continuum. The extent to which judgments are consistent at varying degrees of aggregation, of course, will be a matter of great interest.

Philosophers of science and specialists in international relations have developed concepts and arguments that are useful in assessing scientific progress, but in the end, synthesis remains elusive. As will become apparent from the overview that follows, the story of defining scientific progress within the field of international relations is one of trade-offs. While not contradictory, the essential components do create conflicting priorities at the margins.

Among the trade-offs to be considered at various stages of the analysis, degree of generality, as already noted, is prior to all others. To identify the proper range along the continuum from worldview to hypothesis for making one sort of comparison or another, it is essential to think about a balance between the need for (a) some degree of stability in an overall framework within which research occurs (Ball 1976: 171) and (b) the desire to remain open to potentially transforming changes in outlook (Rosenau 1997).

What, then, is the most promising option from within the intermediate range along the continuum? The answer to this question, as it turns out, will depend on the task at hand. The salient points identified so far are ontology, paradigm, and theory. Used by Rosenau (1997) to identify the components of alternative worldviews about international relations, these concepts are helpful in reaching a decision about how and where to pursue a synthesis among existing ideas. While in principle an infinite number of other intermediate points could be identified, this limited set of concepts is both necessary and sufficient to bring out differences in kind rather than mere degree. The five-point continuum's ability to meet the preceding needs will be demonstrated more effectively after the remaining three points have been introduced.

Ontology focuses on the nature of existence and, as such, remains too general and normatively focused to serve as a promising avenue for evaluation by a community of scholars. The problem of incommensurability as related to concept formation, which initially became associated with interparadigmatic debate as defined by Kuhn (1962), seems germane to this point along the continuum and, of course, to those that might reside even closer to worldview. The crucial condition to fulfill is clarity—an ontology must be specified in a way that is intelligible and consistent, or research based upon it cannot build toward a higher purpose.

Terms such as *paradigm, paradigmlike creation,* and *paradigmatic entity* will be defined here differently from Kuhn's (1962) *research paradigm.* The former refer to concepts found within a zone along the continuum that is greater in specificity, while the latter is more consistent with the idea of ontology or even worldview, depending upon the exposition in which the term is found. The treatment offered later in this section also reflects a desire to establish consistent usage for *paradigm* as a concept; through its placement within an identifiable zone along the continuum of aggregation, self-defeating proliferation of meanings can be averted for this prominent theoretical term (Masterman 1970).

Intended originally for application only to the natural sciences, Kuhn's (1962) research paradigm is the most heavily debated conception of progress across an even wider range of disciplines over the last several decades. The basic idea is that paradigms entail different and incommensurable frames of reference for interpretation of evidence. Differences extend to units of observation, boundaries between them, and issues to be resolved. Thus critical experiments between research paradigms are not feasible because each is founded upon a different ontology. Instead, research takes the form of "normal science" within a paradigm, and it is "precisely the abandonment of critical discourse that marks the transition to a science" (Kuhn 1977: 273). Attempts are made to solve "puzzles" of limited scope, and unless they persist and increase significantly in number, anomalous results do not bring the paradigm into question. Ultimately, the frame of reference is sociological (or even societal): no *exclusively* logical criterion can dictate allegiance to one research paradigm versus another (Kuhn 1970: 260–61).

One example within international relations of a paradigm, understood in the general terms conveyed by Kuhn, is the behavioral research on linkage politics that spanned the 1960s and 1970s.[18] The characteristics of a paradigm are clear to see in the major compilation from Wilkenfeld (1973). The frame of reference for this area of research began with a commitment to behavioral science and quantitative methods; all of the findings relied upon correlation, regression, factor analysis, or related techniques. As Wilkenfeld (1973) points out, the purpose of studying linkage politics was to gain a more complete understanding of events by "taking account of a large number of variables that have a bearing on the ultimate behavior of a nation, whether this behavior be manifested in the domestic or international spheres" (1). While state centric, linkage politics also was somewhat removed from realism because of its emphasis on the potential impact of domestic systems on interstate relations. The Kuhnian "puzzles" focused on identifying various forms of linkage between foreign and domestic conflict, which presumably depend on the types of state, behavior, temporal relationship, and conflict situation and context (Wilkenfeld 1973: 4). A decade or so later, research priorities moved elsewhere because of a persistent "anomaly" that pertained to the paradigm as a whole: aside from action-reaction processes, coefficients from quantitative research remained modest in spite of creative and comprehensive efforts to study conflict linkage (Wilkenfeld et al. 1980). Thus both theorizing and methods moved away from aggregate data analysis of linkage politics—a paradigm shift in the terms introduced by Kuhn.

Variation in ontology creates the potential for disagreement about the meaning and even the content of what is observed. Although debates ultimately might be resolved within some expanding domain of common language, the process of comparison would appear to be inefficient from the outset.[19] Resolution of differences about ontology, as with worldview, would seem better left to the natural processes to be described at a later point.

Another point along the continuum is the paradigmlike creation, which emphasizes variation at the *parametric* level. As will become apparent, this type of aggregation emerges as optimal for comparison of rival approaches because a focus on parameters creates the most useful balance between generality and specificity. To illustrate this point it is helpful to consider, in turn, the boundaries for interparadigmatic consensus and potential disagreement.

Agreement on units, boundaries between them, and issues within interactions is a precondition for identifying a set of paradigms within an ontology (Rosenau 1997). In the language of international relations, this refers to units within a system and the substantive questions to be answered through assessment of their interactions. As noted in table 3.1, an ontology identifies what is to be observed, which includes the main units, along with unit boundaries and the main issues. Thus, to be considered within the same ontology, paradigms have to agree on a designation of units and a maximum feasible agenda of issues.[20]

A parameter can be understood as a determining factor or characteristic. (This is the language favored by Rosenau [1997].) Setting parametric boundaries means identifying ranges for the determining factors or characteristics. (By convention these ranges are referred to as epistemic conditions, within which generalizations are expected to hold.) For example, in domestic politics, theorizing about a form of behavior such as voting might begin with the requirement that the political system not be undergoing a revolution. Other epistemic conditions also might be enumerated: complex, multivariate theorizing about voter choice would be relevant, for instance, only with a secret ballot. Thus paradigmatic boundaries do not have to be expressed in a highly technical form; instead, epistemic conditions can be specified as a series of dichotomies that distinguish when generalizations are anticipated to be valid.

Consider the differences that appear in table 3.1 with respect to realist paradigms. A "hard line" version of realism might hold that actors seek only relative gains, while a "soft line" alternative allows for pursuit of both absolute and relative gains, although with greater emphasis on the latter. (A similar comparison might be made between "offensive" and "defensive" realism and other salient pairs of variants [Legro and Moravcsik 1998, 1999].) In either instance, of course, states are the actors, existing within confrontational anarchic structures.

The more mathematical sense of the term *parameter,* which refers to a constant within a function that determines its specific form, is useful in establishing paradigmatic aggregation rigorously as the crucial breakpoint along the continuum from generality to specificity.

Parametric values express the range of application for some set of functional relationships. Connections might be monotonic in one context, nonmonotonic in another, and nonexistent once a threshold value of some kind is reached. The sustained and prominent debate between neorealism and neoliberal institutionalism can be used to illustrate the forms such differences can take.[21] For each contending outlook the principal units of the system are states, with different parametric values for the input of other actors such as intergovernmental organizations, multinational corporations, and individuals. Thus the "neoneo" debate occurs within a common ontology.

For each paradigm, the "mapping" of unit behavior in terms of scope and impact looks different. In neorealism the anticipated breadth and depth of impact for units other than states are more highly restricted than in neoliberal institutionalism. Parametrically speaking, neorealism would assign a value approximating zero to the expected impact of nonstate actors in security issues and somewhat more than that for other areas, assuming for the moment that such boundaries between substantive concerns are meaningful (Lipson 1984). In other words, the functional form for translation of actor behavior into outcomes would be monotonic for states (i.e., more actions by states ———➤ more change in outcomes within all issue areas) and nearly nonexistent and attenuated for nonstate actors in security and other issue areas, respectively (i.e., more actions by nonstate actors ———➤ negligible change for security issues and marginal change in outcomes for nonsecurity issues). In contrast to neorealism, neoliberal institutionalism would assign higher parametric values (understood as inequalities: i.e., direct versus marginal impact) for nonstate actors in each instance, with a greater magnitude, as expected, for issues other than security.

Debates phrased in this manner take place at a maximum feasible point of aggregation, which is efficient from the standpoint of scientific progress. Observation of units and interactions does not pose a problem, as it would at the degree represented by ontology. Yet major differences exist about *why* things happen as they do and can be expressed in the language of parameters, as in a moment ago. While this might look like parsimony in a new guise, the point at issue here is more fundamental. It concerns the identification of a degree of generality for debate within which major issues can be addressed but short of unproductive exchanges in which normative arguments intervene and move the discussion toward irreconcilable differences.

Interparadigmatic debate, to sum up the preceding discussion, is the most efficient forum within which to pursue resolution of general differences.[22] (It should be acknowledged, of course, that efficiency is not an intrinsic value but rather is defined in the canons of science.) A common set of observation statements, due to shared assumptions, facilitates dialogue (Barbour 1974: 96). The search for limits in the application of paradigms is expected to be mutually intelligible among respective adherents. Arguments can be anticipated to converge on assumptions about the role of parameters within an agreed-upon ontology and worldview.

Efficient comparison of paradigmatic creations requires that each be represented by the best available theory within its boundaries. This leads naturally to the question of what is meant by a theory and how such entities should be compared to each other in a paradigmatic context.

Theories within a paradigm share a belief in common parametric settings but differ in terms of the presumed network of effects observed in the empirical world. A theory designates a hypothetico-deductive system that produces an interrelated set of propositions (Bunge 1996: 114).[23] As noted in table 3.1, the designation of key variables is what distinguishes one theory from another. Thus various realist theories might include different combinations of variables, with two among many possibilities listed in the table. Both the number of great powers and concentration of capabilities among actors will factor into an example of theory building to be developed momentarily.

Theories are highly suited to direct competition with each other (Bunge

1996: 118). Each will consist of a set of assumptions from which are derived a logically consistent class of hypotheses that pertain to the empirical world. As assumptions are combined to produce hypotheses that may be either wholly or partially inconsistent with each other, competing theories emerge. This variation is not only possible but certain because no set of axioms will be sufficient to provide the basis for an exhaustive set of propositions (Gödel [1931] 1988; see also Stein 1999: 224, n. 80). Introduction of further assumptions accounts for the divergence between theories and ultimately defines the boundary between intraparadigmatic competition and the shift to a new paradigm. A theory remains within a given paradigm as long as its system of variables does not entail assumptions that contradict those granted parametric status.

Perhaps the chaos detected by Vasquez (1997, 1998) can be placed in the preceding context and viewed in another way. A wide range of concepts has developed with some loose connection to realism. As Vasquez (1997: 905) points out, if the items on the menu of choices for confirming realism are allowed to coexist, then falsification criteria are certain to remain out of reach. For example, under what conditions should balancing against power, threat, interests, or anything else, for that matter, be expected? When is balancing of any kind likely to fail? These and other questions must be answered, or realism would seem destined for the same fate as astrology.

Consider the example of theories A and B, each of which accepts that variables V_1 and V_2 define a system of relationships and that parameters P_1 through P_6 fall within the range of values associated with neorealism.[24] Theories A, B, and potentially others can be compared to each other within the consensus on parameters. Causal relations will vary among the theories, and comparison becomes meaningful in more specific terms.

Suppose that theories A and B are stated as they appear in figures 3.1a and b, with arrows and signs representing presumed cause and effect and substantive impact (i.e., positive or negative, from one variable to the other). The theories agree that V_1 affects V_2 but differ on the anticipated direction of impact. This disagreement can occur without a paradigmatic shift because theories A and B may have added assumptions that create different expectations, but without contradicting any of the beliefs about the six parameters noted a moment ago. Now consider theory C in figure 3.1c: it is consistent with theory A on the issue of how V_1 and V_2 are connected, and it adds V_3 as a cause of V_2. Assume for the moment that the addition of V_3 to the system is consistent with the parameters as described earlier, so that theory C also remains within the paradigm.

Theory D, from figure 3.1d, looks like theory C but adds in V_4, which, as it turns out, entails assumptions that are incompatible with the parameter values that provide the basis for theories A through C. Thus theory D represents a paradigmatic shift because it contradicts at least one of the axioms from P_1 through P_6.

This story corresponds approximately to the origins of the debate over international stability and polarity (Waltz 1964; Deutsch and Singer 1964), with some "twists" thrown in to show the diverse potential for development of

Figure 3.1
Theories Within and Outside of Paradigmatic Boundaries

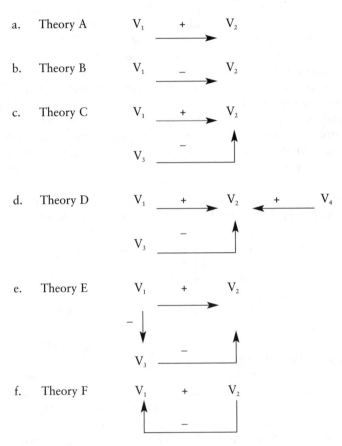

a. Theory A

b. Theory B

c. Theory C

d. Theory D

e. Theory E

f. Theory F

even very simple-looking theories, both inside and outside of paradigmatic boundaries. Let V_1 equal polarity, either bipolar or multipolar; V_2, stability, meaning stable or unstable; V_3, concentration of capabilities in the system, from low to high; and V_4, the number of international organizations in the system, from low to high. Theories A and B represent the rival arguments over polarity's impact on the stability of the system. Since P_1 through P_6 are taken as the parameters set by the axioms of structural realism, theories A and B can coexist within its boundaries. Theory C, which introduces the concentration of capabilities as a variable and retains theory A's version of how V_1 is related to V_2, also remains within the parametric boundaries of structural realism.[25]

However, theory D, which incorporates through V_4 the basic sense of transnational relations (Keohane and Nye 1972), reaches the parametric degree of difference with theories A through C. It contradicts the state-centric axiom of structural realism (i.e., P_1) by including a causal effect from the number of international organizations. Thus a paradigmatic difference emerges between theories that include V_4 and those that remain consistent with P_1 through P_6.

One obvious objection to the preceding differentiation of theory and paradigm should be addressed: Is addition of a single discordant variable to a system that is common to a set of theories sufficient to identify paradigmatic difference? In practice, however, this concern rarely will arise because paradigmatic difference, when it occurs, is anticipated to entail a process that does not end with adding just one variable. As will become apparent, interparadigmatic discrepancies in the field of international relations tend to be defined sharply at the level of parameters, and the shift in a system of variables from one to another is likely to produce a wide range of differences.

Theories, as identified here within a paradigm, can vary in important ways. Even in a system with only a few variables, a vast range of specific and potentially important differences can produce many theories. Consider just the possibilities that are restricted to abstract relations within the network of variables depicted by figure 3.1: (a) exogenous versus endogenous roles, (b) direct versus indirect effects, (c) direction of anticipated substantive impact, and (d) unidirectional versus bidirectional effects.[26]

First, theories can disagree about endogeneity; theory C treats V_3 as exogenous. Consider, however, theory E as an alternative. Figure 3.1e includes a plausible effect of V_1 on V_3, namely, that a bipolar system might contribute to further concentration of capabilities in general. (The negative sign in the figure follows from the way in which the categories of these variables have been ordered.) This might occur as a result of returns from economy of scale; the two preeminent powers would be expected to accumulate even more capabilities relative to others, which in turn would increase concentration.[27]

Second, the network of effects may include both indirect and direct types or just the latter, as in theory E versus A, B, C, and D. In theory E, V_1 is hypothesized to affect V_2 both directly and through V_3.

Third, the direction of anticipated substantive impact may be positive or negative, as in the case of how V_1's effect on V_2 is seen by theories A and B, respectively. Depending on whether each parametric setting is (or is not) preserved, the different signs for $V_1 \longrightarrow V_2$ have the potential to create theories inside (outside) of the paradigm.

Fourth, and finally, cause and effect can be unidirectional or bidirectional. Theory F, depicted by figure 3.1f, introduces bidirectional cause and effect. Multipolarity leads to war, which in turn (for the sake of argument) contributes to bipolarity. Bidirectional causation would not appear to entail a paradigmatic shift because the parametric settings of structural realism, P_1 through P_6, do not rule it out. Thus some variants of structural realism might permit only unidirectional effects, from structure to process, at the system level, while others might include bidirectional (or, perhaps, feedback) effects. The former of the two options appears to be the choice of Waltz (1979) in putting forward the initial version of structural realism.[28]

Efforts to resolve differences between and among theories within a paradigm naturally converge on empirically oriented issues related to research design and interpretation of evidence. Aggregate data versus comparative case studies, preferred data sources, specification of monotonic versus nonmonotonic relationships, lags and leads between variables, and a host of other interrelated issues become meaningful only within a consensus about parameters. Although evidence still can be interpreted in different ways, the ability to assess competing hypotheses in a common context exists in principle and can be improved through incremental efforts.

This process corresponds to normal science as defined by Kuhn (1962, 1970, 1977). It is not, however, the only research activity that is anticipated or hoped for in pursuit of scientific progress. Instead, some ongoing attention to interparadigmatic differences also is needed in order to maintain a balance between the need for cumulative knowledge and skepticism about its foundations. The basic questions for international relations, as indeed for all disciplines, focus on the proper amount and timing of comparison writ large versus pursuit of cumulative knowledge that does not (or, at least, is not intended to) challenge beliefs about parameters.

Analysis of options for comparison, from worldview thorough hypothesis, produces some basic conclusions. Worldviews and ontologies are not well suited to comparison initiated by design within a research community defined in the terms conveyed by Kuhn (1962); instead, these very general entities should compete primarily in a natural way outside of such boundaries. Paradigms can be compared more effectively because differences arise in parametric terms, which are mutually intelligible to those involved in debate. Theories can compete directly within the context of a paradigm. Hypotheses form within theories and combine to enable comparison at that degree of aggregation.

Three kinds of comparison, *pragmatic, revolutionary,* and *evolutionary,* result from the preceding discussion of the degrees of aggregation suitable for assessment of scientific progress:

1. *Pragmatic comparison* refers to the assessment, through natural processes within society as a whole, of performance between or among ontologies in respective worldviews.
2. *Revolutionary comparison* refers to the assessment, carried out by design within the research community, of performance between or among paradigms in an ontology.
3. *Evolutionary comparison* refers to the assessment, carried out by design within the research community, of performance between or among theories in a paradigm as manifested through testing of alternative hypotheses.

Each of the five salient points along the continuum of aggregation, from world-view to hypothesis, plays a role in assessing progress. In all instances the concepts are matched with objectives and those who might act toward achieving them.

Comparison at the ontological degree of aggregation, as will become apparent, does not lend itself to the listing of specific criteria to be applied by field specialists. Thus it will be put forward in a global sense that is consistent with the significant normative element inherent in ontology as a concept. For the latter two types of comparison, however, performance indicators must be devised for application by the research community. These standards are introduced in the latter two parts of the chapter's next section.

Discussion of comparison so far has remained preoperational, although several of the major themes related to that process have been touched on already. The next section explores each type of comparison in greater detail, with appropriate examples from international relations.

3. Comparison at Respective Degrees of Aggregation

3.1 Pragmatic Comparison of Ontologies

Debate over what is to be observed, along with the main units, unit boundaries, and main issues, inherently will contain a relatively high element of value-laden judgment. The decision to place the world in one frame of reference or another may have the effect of biasing analysis toward or away from the status quo.

Consider, for example, structural realism in the (ongoing) absence of a model of agency and, in particular, without a more developed exposition on state behavior. The resulting analysis of international relations is open rather easily to criticism that it exhibits a conservative bias.[29] This point comes through most directly in the previously noted debate over stability and polarity; the quest for the most "stable" international system indirectly reinforces the normative value of the underlying social order. From the standpoint of ontology, attention in a realist-oriented analysis of structure is directed toward observation of great powers and away from alternatives such as that of Galtung (1964), who perceived a world composed of "core" and "peripheral" states, with the latter being exploited by the former. The main issue in Galtung's ontology, to cite the most important difference in relation to the debate over stability and polarity, is the intended distribution of *wealth,* with an underlying concern for greater egalitarianism. Thus the agenda widens from great-power rivalry to include income distributions both within and across national boundaries, human rights, and other considerations. In sum, ontology entails, at least indirectly, a greater normative element than more specific degrees of aggregation, and this must be recognized in efforts to decide on what is best.

How should ontologies be compared to each other? The key insight is that a natural process of selection, by a community wider than the scholarly one (once again, understood in the terms set forth by Kuhn's [1962] classic exposition), is the most promising way to decide between relatively holistic, normatively oriented concepts at such a high degree of aggregation. This argument is based on a triangulation of ideas and information borrowed from the following diverse areas of knowledge: the sociology of anticipated behavior in declining organizations, the Condorcet jury theorem from the theory of public choice (which refers to the application of economic principles to nonmarket decision making), and empirical research about both the limitations of experts and the growing competence of ordinary citizens (Hirschman 1970; Mueller 1979, 1989; Chan and Bobrow 1981; Rosenau 1990, 1997). One set of ideas focuses on how scholars can be expected to confront the problem of incommensurability in ways that produce distortion, while the others suggest that some judgments may be made most effectively through gradual processes that unfold beyond a given community of experts. Thus the argument, as it develops, is pragmatic: the life cycle of an ontology and overarching worldview is believed to begin with its demonstrated utility to scholars (defined in discipline-specific terms) and to end when society no longer sees the value of products based on that way of interpreting the world. In sum, sustained irrelevance in pragmatic terms renders the ontology obsolete; hence the use of that adjective to describe comparison at this degree of aggregation.

For present purposes the community of scholars in international relations will be treated as an "invisible college" with the potential, at certain times, to exhibit the range of behavior attributed by Hirschman (1970; see also Rafferty 2001) to members of declining organizations.[30] The meaning of organizational decline is taken to be intellectual; more precisely, when the reigning ontology faces what are perceived to be severe and possibly irreversible problems, exit and voice move to the forefront as options.

Reactions anticipated among membership to the decline of an organization provide the starting point in the series of steps leading to pragmatic comparison. The framework of exit, voice, and loyalty, developed by Hirschman (1970) to explain choices made under such conditions, is useful in coming to grips with the rise and decline of ontologies. In brief, two options exist for members of an organization who confront the problem of how to deal with its decline. Exit is one possibility, and voice—that is, speaking in an effort to change the organization—is the other. Resort to each of these options can be expected to vary with circumstances (Hirschman 1970: 77–78):

> [E]ven with a given estimate of one's influence, the likelihood of voice increases with the degree of loyalty. In addition, the two factors are far from independent. A member with a considerable attachment to a product or organization will often search for ways to make himself influential, especially when the organization moves in what he believes is the wrong direction; conversely, a member who wields (or thinks he wields) considerable power in an organization and is therefore convinced that he can get it "back on track" is likely to develop a strong affection for the organization in which he is powerful.

This line of reasoning suggests some patterns that may be exhibited by organizations facing either real or perceived decline. Efforts to deal with problems, rather than abandonment, are likely to emerge from those who are either most powerful within or most committed to the organization. These characteristics are likely to be mutually reinforcing (Hirschman 1970: 77).

What, then, should be anticipated from members of an organization faced with decline as described in this instance? Within the frame of reference created by Hirschman, the expectation is that responses to a sense of crisis about ontology will entail distortions that transcend those found in scholarly debates under ordinary circumstances. Two processes, which create opposing biases for different subsets of members, will be at work. The first problem is that the exit option—referring here to a shift away from an embattled ontology—looks easier (all other things being equal) to new and recent entrants into a field, so the exercise of voice will tend to be underrepresented among such scholars. The second source of bias concerns those heavily invested in an ontology; for them, exit is perceived as costly and may cause bias toward voice and persistence in the face of overwhelming and even irreversible evidence.[31] The resulting problem, in Hirschman's language, is that loyalty is too narrow and shallow in the former group and too wide and deep in the latter to facilitate scientifically based, collective decision making at the degree of aggregation represented by ontology or worldview. An ontology in apparent decline will not receive a representative sample of opinion from critics who advocate revisions versus one or more qualitatively different alternatives. For this reason in particular, competition initiated by *design* is best carried out at the degrees of aggregation represented by theory and paradigm.

One recent example of a debate over ontology should be enough to establish the preceding point. Basic questions are posed in the debate: Is the world of international relations populated by rational entities? Or is rational choice, embodied in formal modeling, just a "red herring" in the study of international security? Walt (1999a, 1999b) makes a frontal assault on rational choice at the level of ontology—his answers to the preceding queries are "no" and "yes," respectively. The world according to Walt is *not* made up of leaders who can be modeled according to the mathematical means favored by formal theorists. Instead, he argues that the findings based on formal models in areas such as deterrence theory are either unoriginal or off base altogether. Walt also asserts that formal modeling is in the process of taking over major journals devoted to security studies—to the likely detriment of the field as a whole.

Walt's polemic, along with the responses to it that appeared in a recent symposium from International Security (Walt 1999a, 1999b; Bueno de Mesquita, Lalman, and Morrow 1999; Martin 1999; Niou and Ordeshook 1999; Powell 1999; Zagare 1999), are summed up well by Martin (1999: 82): "While presenting these challenges as a plea for diversity and tolerance, Walt adopts an approach that is likely to generate just the opposite: conflict, defensiveness, and countercharges." Even the titles of respective entries into the debate are enough to make this point—for example, "Return of the Luddites" (Niou and Ordeshook 1999). In an overall sense, the exchange is crushed under its own weight, imposed by a focus on ontology that produces deadlock rather than synthesis in the hands of the experts.

While the community of specialists is not expected to be at its best in assessing ontologies, why would those without such training be preferred to make fundamental decisions? To begin, knowledge claims that result from an ontology (and its underlying worldview) are social products. Something useful must be transmitted to the general public, or an ontology and its worldview will be undermined in the long term. Practical value presumably would involve some combination of interpreting the world of international relations in an accessible way and with relevance to public policy. At this point normative considerations come to the fore: to remain viable, an ontology must contribute to the well-being of society defined in terms of its ability to grasp the nature of continuity and change manifested in contemporary events.

Given the above-noted problems concerning bias within research communities, the public at large may be the better judge of respective ontologies because it is the *consumer*, not the producer, of the ideas being created. A wider range of opinion may even be essential to distinguishing a "scientific revolution" from a mere "ideological revolution," with the latter representing nothing more than an "intellectual fashion" (Popper 1981: 106). Relevant here is the idea of "groupthink," where a relatively small and like-minded collectivity reaches unwarranted conclusions as a result of efforts to prevent criticism and preserve cohesion (Janis 1972). At certain periods of its existence a research community might exhibit some of these symptoms, first identified among elite groups making foreign policy under crisis conditions. The field of international relations, for example, may end up experiencing such a process with respect to the democratic peace: in particular, exponents of quantitative research may have some tendency to see a "perfect" correlation as a Rosetta Stone rather than just another research finding.

Preference for nonspecialists as arbiters of ontology, an idea that runs counter to intuition, finds further support through reference to the Condorcet jury theorem. The theorem, which requires only a few assumptions, generates a result with applications well beyond voting, its original intended domain. Assume that each individual in a group making a binary choice is more than 50 percent likely to select the option that is better for his or her group's common interest. The theorem is straightforward in its implications: the larger the group composed of such individuals, the more likely it is that the "correct" choice will be made in a majority vote (Mueller 1979, 1989). If it can be assumed that individuals are more likely than not (on average) to accept the more useful social products from competing ontologies, then this "jury" may even be preferred to one composed of professional specialists.[32] Thus the very size of the general public becomes an asset to its decision making as long as members are even marginally above the threshold of chance in understanding what is better for them.

This argument about how to assess ontologies continues with the introduction of evidence, admittedly preliminary in character, about the rising competence of ordinary individuals and limitations of experts. Rosenau (1990: 275–310) provides an array of evidence that active participation by a wider range of people in politics is underway on a global basis. A resulting "skill revolution" may produce a higher level of competence on average and greater ability to engage in informed filtering of information. A related point concerns the uniformity of information. The Cable News Network (CNN) is available around the globe and might even be described as the principal common source of information for mass publics at the turn of the millennium. The general public becomes a meaningful concept because of the significant and increasing level of common knowledge that is disseminated by CNN and other global networks of communication, most notably, the World Wide Web. So pervasive is the audience for this network that public officials and other commentators are apt to use the same humorous description of its importance: "Nothing is real until it's on CNN."

Apparent trends toward common and improving knowledge among mass publics is consistent with the idea that the Condorcet jury theorem is becoming more relevant with time as a basis for selection of ontologies. The theorem's key assumption about the mean level of understanding of collective interest among members of a group would seem more credible now than ever before. While bias could prolong the life of an ontology, no reason exists a priori to expect a tendency toward intellectual conservatism in mass publics. Extension of the voting franchise in stages, as seen in British history, could be cited as an example of the process by which narrow self-interest is overcome gradually by a combination of superior argument and more enlightened self-interest. Instead, risk propensity with regard to ontology should follow an approximately normal distribution in any large population. Only an appeal to "false consciousness" or conspiracy theories (Bunge 1998) can produce the opposite conclusion, namely, that knowledge claims are self-perpetuating due to the control they exercise over society.[33]

Expert opinion, by contrast, may be less useful than presumed in making some kinds of decisions. The present context, in which a specific point is made about selecting ontologies, is not the only one in which a case can be presented for either eschewing or at least supplementing expert opinion. Fascinating examples are available of equal or superior forecasting by nonexperts in areas that range from handicapping of horse races to anticipation of international crises (Chan and Bobrow 1981). In each instance the explanation is that expert advantages are minimized because, in spite of efforts to the contrary, theory as a guide to action remains either rudimentary or virtually nonexistent for some kinds of subject matter. In some instances, such as security markets, reliable forecasting would bring the process itself to an end almost as a matter of course. The degree of uncertainty inherent in international relations suggests that, at or above the degree of aggregation represented by ontology, the general public may be a viable and even superior choice for purposes of adjudication.[34] This speculation, of course, is linked to the earlier point about bias in reactions from the expert community: the two ideas combine to shift the balance in favor of natural processes of selection through the general public.

Perhaps the best way to continue this phase of the discussion is with a dramatic historical instance of how such natural processes can work: astronomy versus astrology in describing and (especially) explaining and predicting events. (The separate aspects related to entertainment or other dimensions of value that might favor astrology and explain its persistence in a residual role will not be covered here.) Over the long term the demonstrated superiority of astronomy along these salient dimensions of knowledge rendered debates about respective ontologies (and underlying worldviews) superfluous. For example, it became pointless for astronomers to confront astrologers about the nature of celestial bodies, which might be thought of crudely as the units of observation, because one ontology simply won out over the other as a matter of *pragmatism within society as a whole.* The utility of astronomy in navigation alone is sufficient to settle the issue.[35]

While such graphic differences are much less likely to occur within a social science like international relations, the principle remains the same. An argument based on efficacy comes into play as a by-product of beliefs about the likely destination of debates about ontology among specialists: some degree of breakdown in communication due to incommensurability is virtually inevitable and should be prevented by directing arguments elsewhere. It is pseudoscientific to advocate a discourse that would occur without at least the potential for introduction of reproducible evidence.

All of the preceding discussion about why decisions at the degree of ontology should be made through natural processes among society as a whole is acknowledged as speculative. No attempt will be made to produce systematic arguments or evidence that support this process in either normative or empirical terms.[36] Instead, the purpose is to identify and give initial credibility to an assumption that will be embedded within scientific systemism as a worldview, namely, that decisions about ontology are made most effectively through the means just described. The process of adjudication at this high, normatively influenced degree of aggregation should take place in a natural way among the general public.

Scientific systemism recognizes the appropriate degrees of aggregation at which to strive for progress through, respectively, intentional comparison conducted by the research community and natural evaluation by society as a whole. Intellectual resources should be allocated to create the greatest likelihood of further learning about international relations. Variation therefore arises in degree of aggregation (from general to specific), mechanism (intentional or natural) and scope (specialists or society as a whole) with respect to evaluation.

Although it might seem to lead in such a direction, the preceding analysis does not weaken the case for a scientific understanding of international relations. It instead establishes within the worldview and ontology an understanding of the time-honored point that normative conclusions cannot be derived from strictly existential statements. Put simply, the "ought" cannot follow directly from the "is." The research project, however, is itself infused by norms, which in the present context are those that underlie scientific systemism. A bridge of some kind, including normative principles, is needed to transform empirical knowledge into understanding and judgment. In sum, the idea of pragmatic comparison represents the normative application of scientific systemism.

3.2 Revolutionary Comparison of Paradigms

Constructive criticism is less frequent than destructive criticism, however, not only because it is harder, but also because it calls for fairness and friendliness, qualities that get lost when the race for power replaces the quest for truth.
—Mario Bunge, *Finding Philosophy in Social Science*

While defining conditions for a paradigmlike creation already are established, more work is needed to identify a concept that is useful in application. The status of international relations as a discipline continues to stimulate fundamental disagreement, but systematic efforts to measure progress have been few.[37] Thus the process of deriving a paradigmatic entity for applied analysis of international relations begins most effectively through a review of concept formation within the philosophy of science at a general level.

Two prominent concepts from the philosophy of science, research programs and research traditions, approximate the paradigmatic degree of generality (Lakatos 1970; Laudan 1977). References to these concepts appear to exhaust the limited range of explicit allegiances found at this degree of aggregation within international relations as a field. Instead, scholarly self-identification tends to be expressed in the paradigmatic terms described by Kuhn: that is, at the degree of *ontology* as that word is understood in the present exposition. As expected from the discussion in the preceding section, this invariably proceeds along a series of divisive dimensions such as quantitative versus nonquantitative methods, rational choice in opposition to political psychology, and realism versus liberalism (Lamborn 1997; Harvey 1998; Brecher 1999).

Debate needs to be recast at the paradigmatic degree of aggregation, as described in table 3.1. A paradigm in this context represents an intermediate degree of aggregation that focuses on designation of parameters. As noted in the table, room exists within the realist worldview and ontology for parametric variation. Actors might seek either relative gains or some mixture of absolute and relative gains in confrontational anarchic structures. Other examples of how parameters can be designated in varying ways also could be provided, but one is enough to establish the basic commensurability inherent in paradigmatic competition. The values assigned to parameters can vary in either qualitative or quantitative terms (e.g., pursuit of relative gains alone vs. a mixture of absolute and relative gains), but the vocabulary is held in common.

Explicit support for work within a paradigmlike creation as just described, which measures progress in international relations, is the exception rather than the rule. Elman and Elman (2002a) observe that, while Lakatos's framework is referenced quite heavily, "the great majority of citations appear in boilerplate footnotes." Discussion seems restricted to the two concepts already noted: that is, research programs and traditions, with more attention to the former than the latter.[38] As will become apparent, the latter two concepts can be synthesized to facilitate assessment of scientific progress within international relations. Each of these concepts is consistent with scientific systemism, so the principle of cumulation argues in favor of building on what already exists rather than beginning anew. Thus research programs and traditions will be summarized and compared as a means toward the end of developing a paradigmlike creation that brings together their best points and also achieves operational relevance for international relations.

Introduced by Lakatos (1970), sophisticated methodological falsificationism is a framework that emphasizes cumulative progress through systematic replacement of theories within a substantive domain of research.[39] It is the foundation for the concept of a scientific research program, which is cast at the paradigmatic degree of aggregation and represents a counterpoint to Kuhn's idea of a paradigm. A brief introduction to falsificationism will place the idea of such a program in context.

Lakatos's outlook on the advancement of knowledge follows in the Popperian tradition of attempting to falsify theories, with the objective being replacement of whatever exists with a superior version. Rather than merely accumulating observations, the priority in Popper's frame of reference is to move forward by discarding theories. Once a theory is found to be inconsistent with evidence, it is time for something new (Popper 1969: 215; see also [1935] 1959).[40] Conjectures and refutations thus form a sequence leading progressively to higher levels of truth or, perhaps put better, lower levels of falsehood.

With a focus on the practical questions that researchers in any field must face, Lakatos moved beyond Popper's vision of conjectures and refutations. For example, if a theory is considered to be refuted, what is to be put in its place? Some frame of reference is necessary to place observations in context, so more than just a negative decision needs to happen at the time a theory is repudiated. Something must replace the old theory as an arbiter of experiences. A similar practical question arises about the threshold for change: Is a refutation of *any* kind sufficient to justify abandoning a theory, even one that has succeeded in many other instances? This question becomes even more pressing in a social science like international relations, where it is reasonable to expect a margin for error for even the best theories.

For Lakatos, these considerations moved the question of falsification to a higher degree along the continuum of specificity to generality. Attention shifts from hypothesis to theory. Thus a scientific research program is defined as a *series* of theories that reflect accumulated learning and challenges from new experiences. Each iteration consists of a set of assumptions and derived propositions, with a deeper set of convictions about ontology and methods of inquiry present at all stages. The goal of research is to engage in "sophisticated" testing of the research program; evaluation transcends the potentially misleading results of a single experiment or particular set of observations. Falsification criteria therefore move up one degree of aggregation, from hypothesis to theory, as a product of what might be viewed as risk aversion about the research process.

These ideas resonate in a field like international relations, where what are regarded as data in relation to past events can change significantly on relatively short notice. For example, much more is known now than before the demise of the communist regime about high-level decision making in the USSR (Gaddis 1997). Still further changes in interpretation of past diplomacy can be expected as more material on Soviet foreign policy decision making becomes available. This example is just one of many that could be cited as giving reason for a cautious verdict about any theory on the basis of one or a small number of seemingly refuted hypotheses.

Although every theory makes predictions (at least implicitly) and therefore can be assessed on an individual basis in terms of accuracy, Lakatos argues that it is more useful to focus on the progress represented by a program of research as a whole. This constitutes the most fundamental difference from Popper (Nickles 1987: 195), for whom a theory stands alone against the evidence that confronts one or more of its hypotheses. More specifically, according to Lakatos (1970), a theory is *falsified* "if and only if another theory T' has been proposed with the following characteristics: (1) T' has excess empirical content over T: that is, it predicts *novel* facts, that is, facts improbable in the light of, or even forbidden by, T; (2) T' explains the previous success of T, that is, all of the unrefuted content of T is included (within the limits of observational error) in the content of T'; and (3) some of the excess content of T' is corroborated" (116). The replacement of one theory by another within a scientific research program is based on explanatory power. This vision of progress is consistent with the deductive-nomological approach toward scientific explanation, which, as noted in chapter 1, bases knowledge on general laws (Hempel 1965: 337, 345). The goal of theorizing is to identify more encompassing laws—an assertion that, for any student of international relations in the last century or so, must arouse a mixture of admiration with curiosity and even skepticism. To pose the most general question, what does "content" potentially mean in a field that pertains to human experience rather than, say, observations from laboratory or field experiments? This query and others related to it will be explored at a later point.

According to Lakatos, with respect to the process of replacement of theories, the preferred option, T', can come from within or outside of a given research program. If the latter is the case, the program itself is considered to be refuted. Of course, at a later point, a still better theory could emerge from within, thus restoring the program to viability. This potential sequence of events reveals one of the principal insights credited to the framework developed by Lakatos. Unlike earlier treatments that emphasized discarding theories, Lakatos's version of falsificationism is able to counter charges of premature termination (Ball 1976: 171). Even after experiencing more than one setback, a research program can be rehabilitated. Progress in Lakatos's frame of reference is "compatible with all theories having false empirical consequences"; hence the toleration of anomalies, which later may be explained by a superior version of the theory at hand (Smart 1972: 270). Within Lakatos's frame of reference, scholars "should not be too impatient, nor require instant gratification" (Elman and Elman 2002b). In more prosaic terms, this recognizes that not all good ideas come at once; coping with an anomaly may be a matter of time to think through its implications more than anything else.[41]

With respect to international relations, realists might point to the end of the Soviet Union as one such example. Perhaps it is just a matter of time before one of the variants of realism provides a compelling explanation for the most recent revolution in Russia and its aftermath. (One possibility is Wohlforth's [1995] power-oriented argument that Gorbachev pursued perestroika because the economic burden of the ongoing arms race had weakened the Soviet economy to a point at which further efforts at balancing could not achieve the desired results.) It seems unlikely that the full effects of the sweeping changes in Eastern Europe can be comprehended fully from any vantage point just yet; put differently, is a decade long enough to obtain an accurate reading of events? Sometimes the answer definitely is "no"; consider, for example, how the Treaty of Versailles would have looked in the late 1920s as opposed to a decade later. The more general point to be made is that the framework developed by Lakatos entails important judgments about the meaning and time frame for assessment of anomalies but does not offer guidance on such matters. These unanswered questions therefore should not be overlooked in any potential application of sophisticated methodological falsificationism.

Three more concepts—the *hard core, negative heuristic,* and *positive heuristic*—must be developed to identify Lakatos's scientific research program with the paradigmatic degree of aggregation. These concepts combine to describe and explain the relationship of any given theory (T) to a potential successor (T').

The term *hard core* refers to the axiomatic basis of the program. During its lifetime, these assumptions are not questioned. Only if the program as a whole is refuted by the emergence of a superior alternative (i.e., a program that still looks better after a reasonable passage of time) is the hard core discarded. For example, advocates of structural realism might identify the parameters P_1 through P_6 as the hard core of a research program understood in Lakatos's terms. State centrism, pursuit of security, and other axioms with parametric status would continue as the foundation until a better program emerged and retained its edge for long enough to cast aside doubt. This observation, of course, returns to the earlier point raised about the treatment of anomalies: What might "long enough" mean in practice with respect to an irreversible demonstration of superiority for one program over another? For either a research program or alternative paradigmatic entity, this matter and others of a practical nature must be confronted at the stage of application.

For a research program the negative heuristic consists of a set of methodological principles that protect the hard core from experimental refutation and rule out qualitatively different kinds of theorizing (Lakatos 1970; Koertge 1971: 161). The basic concepts in the hard core are assumed to remain valid even when specific propositions appear to be refuted by testing. Instead, the failure of a hypothesis is assumed to be a product of one or more of the series of connections between it and the foundation of the program. A faulty research design, inferior data, one or more invalid interpretations, or other factors—not an inadequacy within the hard core itself—are inferred to be the reasons why a proposition might have been refuted. To maintain falsifiability, at least in principle, the program also must rule out fundamentally different classes of explanation. Straightforward assessment of what is sufficiently distant would seem to depend on parametric designation. In other words, the research program presumably would prohibit development of theories that contradicted any of the axioms in the hard core.

Consider realism, writ large, as a research program. What exactly does it prohibit? It is precisely at this point, where the negative heuristic is addressed, that the full force of Vasquez's (1983, 1997, 1998) criticism becomes evident. So many realisms exist that merging them into a single research program is impossible. As an illustration, assume instead that Walt's (1990, 1997) balance of threat is articulated in such terms. The negative heuristic of that research program would prohibit balancing behavior that granted priority to any consideration over and above threat as perceived by an actor. A rigorous treatment then would require an operational rendering of threat in order to link the negative heuristic to the empirical side of the research program. Only at this level of specificity can realist research programs be designated without inviting inconsistency and confusion.

Hypotheses derived from the hard core and other assumptions create the positive heuristic for a research program, which takes the form of a surrounding belt of empirical findings that always are open for review.[42] It incorporates unrefuted hypotheses and anomalies that continue to challenge the program. Given that the empirical range of a viable program is presumed to be expanding, the presence of puzzling cases is natural and important in establishing priorities for further research. The process of coping with anomalies will involve experimentation with alternative theories, which entail assumptions beyond those present in the hard core. Several of the theories about international stability from figure 3.1 can serve as examples here. (The exception is theory D, which introduces a change at the parametric level and therefore would find a place in a research program separate from theories A-C and E-F.) These theories, all of which use the distribution of capabilities among states to explain the amount of international instability, build in varying assumptions about endogeneity and other matters that are not settled by the hard core of structural realism. The respective versions are in a position to compete with each other in accounting for stability and other aspects of the international system without challenging the hard core. In other words, these theories could form a series, based on expanding empirical content and corroboration relative to each other.

"Progressive" and "degenerative" research programs are distinguished by the nature of the theories they produce (Lakatos 1970). Progress is manifested in development of theories that continue to satisfy the requirements noted above with respect to empirical content, while hypotheses that focus on a single case and lack more general implications serve as a warning of the onset of decline. As already noted, progress can be restored via a breakthrough that brings together a set of anomalies within a more encompassing version of the theory that claims status as T' in relation to T. This possibility shows that Lakatos's idea of a scientific research program is flexible enough to avoid the determinism inherent in the original falsificationist regime for replacing theories. The advantages of the research program for application in the social sciences are summed up by Elman and Elman (2002b): the program "deserves to be taken seriously as a consequential and plausible candidate for how to describe and appraise the trajectory of theoretical developments. We like its emphasis on tolerance and tenacity, and on rewarding innovation."

One implication of the preceding analysis might be that long-established research programs should steer away from an overwhelming allocation of time and energy to apparently new and emerging anomalies. It may require time to detect the common and overarching traits of a series of puzzling events, and a fixation on any one seeming anomaly may produce degeneration as a result.

Consider the following landmark example from physics at the outset of the twentieth century (Einstein 1996): "Henri Poincaré had posited three outstanding problems to which current physics had no satisfactory explanations: the apparent absence of ether drift, Brownian motion, and the photoelectric effect. Within a period of fifteen weeks in 1905, Einstein submitted to the *Annalen der Physik*, from the Swiss Patent Office in Bern, papers that revolutionized—and, implicitly, interconnected—the way in which all three problems were perceived" (33). This case stands out in history because it is so decisive, compelling, and, unfortunately, unusual. Effective linkage of seemingly disparate problems—perhaps relabeled as anomalies within the five-year period of the preceding example—is too much to expect in the ongoing conduct of research over the short term. Partial successes over longer time lines are more likely to occur in international relations and other disciplines in which the human element is central. The study of beings who act on the basis of logic and reason—surely the "best case" scenario—still presents difficulties that transcend those of the natural sciences. Intentional action among subjects, in short, ensures that the human sciences will move forward with greater difficulty.

Realism, for example, may encounter stubborn anomalies in a given time interval, such as a decade, simply because this worldview has been able to last so long in one form or another. Thus it might appear to be degenerative within almost any arbitrary time frame—if the interval is kept short enough—perhaps even "too concerned with sustaining the paradigm and not concerned enough with providing new insight" (Freyberg-Inan 1999: 50). Some decades, however, may be more "friendly" than others for a sustained program of research, so anomalies could be regarded as opportunities for improvement (or revival), not just a threat to existence. For example, major cooperative agreements in the 1990s, in particular the North American Free Trade Agreement (NAFTA) and the European Union (EU), may trigger creative and progressive change in one or more variants of realism. No reason exists a priori to assume that realism cannot improve in response to a new set of challenges.

Although the idea of a scientific research program represents a step forward in the philosophy of science, it is clear that Lakatos did not offer a set of operational rules to permit ready identification of the major components (Kuhn 1970: 238). Identifying and setting boundaries for the hard core, along with negative and positive heuristics, becomes a matter of individual judgment, not the application of firm criteria (McMullin 1978: 245; Rosenberg 1986: 135-36). To move toward a clear demarcation, it is useful to think in terms of Buchdal's (1969) "metaphysical" and "phenomenal" levels of explanation (73). The abstract, logical relations of a research program, expressed in terms of its parameters, would constitute the hard core. The metaphysical (i.e., theoretical) axioms would be unfalsifiable in principle, while the *empirical meaning* of each might be open to interpretation in various contexts during the testing of hypotheses. The positive heuristic, by contrast, would encompass the phenomenal level, which consists of solved and unsolved empirical problems, along with anomalies. It is empirical in nature, with issues such as operationalization and measurement error creating room for interpretive differences over the program's level of progress and prospects for the future. Finally, the negative heuristic would present the program's rules, which prohibit challenges to the hard core and demand that explanations in the positive heuristic remain consistent with its parameter settings.

For structural realism, as one possible instance of a scientific research program, the parameters P_1 through P_6 from chapter 2 would serve as axioms and stand as the hard core. Terms such as *state centrism, rationality,* and others from the axioms would take on empirical meaning in deriving and testing propositions about cooperation and conflict. This process, in turn, would create the positive heuristic.[43] The negative heuristic would consist of a prohibition on rejecting the parametric settings created by P_1 through P_6, along with ruling out explanations that contradicted one or more of those axioms. Thus, at least by intuition, it seems feasible to enumerate the conditions of the negative heuristic and to set boundaries between the hard core and positive heuristic.

Although more specific than the classic exposition from Lakatos (1970), the preceding discussion about a particular discipline indirectly reveals the still-limited operational value of the research program as a concept. Smart (1972) observes that the scientific research program as presented by Lakatos is "not a very precise" notion, with the likelihood being that its creator intended the concept as more of a general guide to progress than something amenable to direct measurement (271). In the context of international relations, Snyder (2002) observes that Lakatos's scheme "leaves the practicing scientist without needed guidance" (see also Bennett 2001). This point can be made at an even more general level: the debate among Kuhn, Popper, and others who followed them reveals the elusiveness of falsifiability as a criterion when applied to the history of science, whether natural or social in content (Simon 1985: 291). As Kuhn (1970: 239, 240, 256; see also Blaug 1980 on the lack of certainty for deciding on acceptable scientific theories) asserted in comparing his influential concept of a paradigm to Lakatos's framework, scientists also must "*decide* whether a given programme at a given time" is progressive, thereby making the criteria for change social in nature.[44]

While Kuhn's observation seems on target, it also could be taken as a challenge: Is it possible to move beyond the general idea of a research program to a concept with greater precision that provides more objective criteria for assessment of progress? The answer given here is "yes"—it is possible to do better than the quasi-constructivism inherent in Kuhn's vision of scientific progress. As will become apparent, success can be achieved through application of the existing concept of a research program, but only in a limited domain. A more extreme departure is needed to achieve relevance when the focus is on international relations as a whole.

When the empirical domain is restricted sufficiently, a more objective and convincing assessment of how members of a series of theories relate to each other becomes possible even on the basis of the very limited instructions provided by Lakatos. This ability is demonstrated by the respective assessments of research programs that appear in table 3.2 on institutional theory (Keohane and Martin 2002), power transition theory (DiCicco and Levy 1999), liberalism (Moravcsik 2002), the democratic peace (Ray 2002), expected utility theory (Bueno de Mesquita 1988, 1993), neoclassical realism (Schweller 2002), and operational code analysis (Walker 2002).[45] All but one of these thorough applications appear in a recent collection that seeks to test the limits of Lakatos's framework in practice (Elman and Elman 2002c). The table (a) conveys examples of presumed innovations and recommendations for improvement for the respective programs and (b) notes the verdict reached by the scholars who carried out each study.

While it would be beyond the scope of the current exposition to cover these studies in detail, each is able to offer a range of insights that derive, at least to some extent, from application of the framework developed by Lakatos. Bueno de Mesquita (1988, 1993), for example, points to the shift from a static expected utility theory of outcomes (meaning whether a war occurs between a given pair of states) to one that includes interactions as clearly fulfilling the criteria for status as T' in terms of excess empirical content, prediction of novel facts, explanation of T's unrefuted content, and corroboration of at least some excess content. Ray (1999, 2002) is able to identify a hard core and both negative and

Table 3.2
Research Programs in International Relations

Program	Examples of Presumed Innovations	Recommendations	Verdict
Institutional[a] theory	information is treated as a variable that can be influenced by human action; multiple equilibria exist	integrate the distributional struggles along the Pareto frontier with efforts to move that frontier forward	progressive
power transition[b]	multiple hierarchy model; alliance transitions[c]	conceptual development and operationalization of states' (dis)satisfaction with the status quo; construction of an explanation for the timing of war that is fully consistent with the hard core; better specification of causal mechanism leading to war, including the role of bargaining between dominant state and challenger	tentatively progressive
liberalism[d]	distribution of preferences shapes state behavior; democratic peace; explanation of long-term change	investigate state-society relations and implications of interdependence[e]	progressive
democratic peace[f]	inter-democratic peace, alliance and trade; democracies winning wars	seek complementaries with realism	progressive
expected utility theory[g]	specification of necessary conditions of war; probability estimates for war; explanation of crisis interactions as well as outcomes	continiue to develop game-theoretic framework	progressive

Table 3.2 continued

Program	Presumed Innovations	Recommendations	Verdict
neoclassical realism[h]	impact of capabilities on foriegn policy is indirect and complex; unit level variables mediate connections	investigating changes in perceptions of power to explain apparently anomalous behavior	progressive
operational code analysis[i]	beliefs have autonomous effects on strategic interaction	resolve inconsistencies between personality and cognitive versions of foriegn policy	tentatively progressive

[a] Keohane and Martin (2002).

[b] DiCicco and Levy (1999, 2002).

[c] This may represent an "interprogram shift" (DiCicco and Levy 2002).

[d] Moravcsik (2002) indentifies ideational, commercial and republican theories competing within the program.

[e] These recommendations are inferred from the discussion of the current directions of liberal theorizing.

[f] Ray(1999, 2002).

[g] Bueno de Mesquita (1988, 1993).

[h] Schweller (2002).

[i] Walker (2002).

positive heuristics for the research program on democracy and peace, while DiCicco and Levy (1999, 2002) enumerate these same concepts for the power transition, elegantly averting confusion with power cycles, long cycles, and related approaches. In each of the preceding instances the concept of a research program is able to provide a sense of how much has been accomplished, along with salient priorities, in a given domain of research.

Several properties stand out when the table is viewed as a whole. First, of the seven programs, five are judged to be progressive and two tentatively progressive. (These verdicts are provided explicitly by respective authors or inferred as a "bottom line" on the basis of what has been written.) Second, each of the programs seems to have innovations to offer; in other words, the positive heuristic shows at least some recent record of accomplishment. Liberalism and neoclassical realism, for example, are very different from each other, yet each is able to identify innovations that relate to the unit level. Liberalism shows how the distribution of preferences can shape state behavior, while neoclassical realism demonstrates that the impact of capabilities on foreign policy is indirect and complex (Keohane and Martin 2002; Schweller 2002). Third, the recommendations generally are expressed in language consistent with realism: states, power, conflict, and even complementarities with realism are prominent concepts among the summaries of ideas about further progress. Fourth, and finally, the table arranges the programs in approximate order from most holistic to most individualistic, and there is no obvious pattern in terms of relative success. While the programs are generally regarded as progressive, it is easy to conclude that they might be doing even better if recast in the terms suggested by systemism.

Table 3.2 at once reveals both the strength and the weakness of Lakatos as a guide to evaluation of research. The terminology enables scholars to enumerate areas of learning and to identify what has been accomplished. However, the general tendency toward concluding in favor of progress is not entirely a result of selection effects—that is, a focus on only relatively successful programs. Instead, the basic problem identified earlier—a lack of specificity—contributes to the tendency to see all of the programs as progressive. Rather than seeing this as bias on the part of those carrying out the evaluations, we should recognize it as an inherent property of the methodology of scientific research programs in application.

While the preceding examples are somewhat encouraging to advocates of systematic evaluation of progress, the success cannot be replicated for international relations as a whole. The basic problems related to application of the research program as a concept concern measurement of content and rigidities in the rules for replacement of one theory with another. Even the very positive treatment of Lakatos's concept formation in DiCicco and Levy (1999: 689, 700) draws attention to vagueness about how empirical findings are to be aggregated in reaching a judgment about whether to label a research program as progressive or degenerative. An exegesis of the research tradition (Laudan 1977), the main alternative to the research program at the paradigmatic degree of aggregation, will highlight the main areas of difficulty and offer ideas for improvement.

While generally consistent with Lakatos's sophisticated methodological falsificationism as a philosophy of science, Laudan's (1977) research tradition also introduces modifications that are useful in answering Kuhn (1970) and a host of other critics who have commented on the idea of a research program from the perspective of either the history or the philosophy of science.[46] The point of departure for the concept of a research tradition is that "rationality and progressiveness of a theory are most closely linked—not with its confirmation or falsification—but rather with its *problem solving effectiveness*" (5). An empirical problem corresponds to "anything about the natural world which strikes us as odd, or otherwise in need of an explanation" (15). Thus, in Laudan's frame of reference, a theory is repudiated when a more effective alternative has emerged, measured in terms of the number and importance of empirical problems solved versus the number and importance of anomalies and conceptual problems generated. "Experience," according to Laudan, "teaches us that it sometimes takes a number of intra-theoretic adjustments before a problem can be convincingly solved" (39–40). Theories rise and fall within a given research tradition, defined as *"a set of general assumptions about the entities and processes in a domain of study, and about the appropriate methods to be used for investigating the problems and constructing the theories in that domain"* (81). With agreement about units of observation, boundaries between them, and issues, conflict at the level of ontology is foreclosed, and debate focuses on the progressiveness of a sequence of theories in the research tradition.

Laudan and Lakatos are complementary along some lines. Laudan's conception of a research tradition appears to combine Lakatos's hard core, negative heuristic, and positive heuristic; it incorporates general assumptions and methods of empirical inquiry and theorizing. Each framework also refers to a *series* of theories within some overarching field of study, recognizing the usually incremental nature of scientific progress. Furthermore, both Laudan and Lakatos emphasize the need to evaluate theories in a comparative context. Performance, in other words, is meaningful only in light of available alternatives (Laudan 1977: 71).

Laudan (1977), however, also introduces some valuable amendments to the doctrine conveyed by Lakatos. Laudan points out that, on the basis of compelling examples from intellectual history, "the succession of specific theories within a maxi-theory involves the *elimination* as well as the addition of assumptions, and there are rarely successor theories which entail their predecessors" (77). Thus, within a research tradition, some previously solved problems may re-emerge as anomalies, clearly at odds with Lakatos's notion that a later version of a theory always incorporates the confirmed content of those coming earlier.

Laudan (1977) also observes that "the attempt to specify content measures for scientific theories is extremely problematic if not literally impossible" (77; see also Watkins 1978: 367). This conclusion follows from a review of important cases in the history of science, as opposed to abstract reasoning about research progress in some ideal form. As a result, Laudan asserts that solved problems, as opposed to potential range of application, should be most important in selecting one theory over another. In particular, this modification diminishes the force behind Kuhn's (1970) assertion that "no exclusively logical criteria" can entirely dictate the choice among theories (288). Identification of empirical problems is an exercise that can be carried out through a survey of research completed and in progress; this would seem more feasible than a specification of overall content, for which no a priori measurement exists. The former approach is inductive within some overarching frame of reference and entails identifying boundaries for problems relative to each other, while the latter is not facilitated by any obvious point of departure.

From the standpoint of international relations, this improvement brings both good and bad news. The positive side is that attention is directed away from inherently futile debates about content in an overall sense; the example from chapter 5, a dialogue on realism conducted in the underspecified language of Lakatos, will establish that point decisively (Vasquez 1997; Christensen and Snyder 1997; Elman and Elman 1997; Schweller 1997; Walt 1997; Waltz 1997). The idea of empirical content for international relations is so elusive that a focus on problem solving emerges almost by default as the preferred alternative. But this is where the news is not so good; to borrow a phrase from Winston Churchill about democracy versus other forms of government, it becomes apparent that "measurement of solved and unsolved empirical problems, along with anomalies, is the worst way to assess progress—except, of course, for all of the others." A later discussion will show that the operational side of the research tradition is not well developed at the level of international relations as a discipline, but it does have potential. While the obstacles to assessment in these terms are not prohibitive (which they do appear to be with respect to empirical content), the work is challenging.

Another advantage of Laudan's reformulation is that it contains some needed flexibility in the quest for progress. Multiple paths in a series of theories from T to later versions are not only permitted but even expected. Consider, by contrast, the rigidity of the decision rule from Lakatos: later theories in a research program must retain all past explanations. Theories then must fit together like a series of Russian dolls: each is situated entirely inside the next, with some room to spare. However, no evidence exists that the most rapid path toward knowledge will look just like this. What if alternate routes, which permit re-emergence of anomalies if overall progress is achieved, prove faster? This possibility cannot be ruled out, and thus a flexible approach, which allows for the exercise of either rule of replacement, is appropriate.

When viewed through the lens of international relations as a discipline, uneven development emerges as more likely to be a norm than an aberration. Since empirical problems must pertain in some way to real events, and history provides these data in a continuous stream, it is virtually certain that at least some anomalies will be resurrected even when solutions are accumulating elsewhere (see Blaug 1980: 38).

Ironically, the argument from Laudan about how to replace theories parallels the one offered by Lakatos about Popper's version of falsificationism. Within Popper's scheme of analysis the process of replacement seems too quick and easy, while for Lakatos it appears unlikely to occur at all.[47] In particular, problems solved near the outset of a sequence of theories in a research program are granted a privileged position and, by fiat, become more important than those encountered later. No increase in quantity for the latter, under the criterion adopted by Lakatos, ever could be enough to balance off the loss of even one among the former. The potential to produce results opposite to those intended by Lakatos and Popper argues in favor of a more flexible approach in each instance. Progress could be held back just as easily by either form of extremism in decision rules for replacement of theories. In sum, the regime advocated by Lakatos might be regarded as a Weberian (Weber 1949) "ideal type" of progress rather than a practical guide to action. It might have some utility for a limiting case such as pure mathematics, where neither existing nor potential knowledge can be altered in quantity by real events, but international relations obviously stands in counterpoint as an inexact science that poses a qualitatively different set of challenges.

Combination of the most useful elements of the frameworks developed by

Lakatos and Laudan provides the foundation for assessment of revolutionary progress within international relations: that is, at the paradigmatic degree of aggregation. This pathway parallels the one recommended by Moravcsik (2002) at the conclusion of a sustained effort to use Lakatos's framework in a reassessment of liberalism: "[T]he central challenge facing IR today is not selecting the correct philosophy of science most likely to help us to develop a universal theory of IR, but selecting frameworks that permit us to engage in *rigorous theory synthesis*" (see also Vasquez 2002). The properties that a paradigmlike entity should possess are enumerated at this point. From the perspective of utility for revolutionary comparison, these characteristics must find a place in the development of the concept of a scientific research enterprise, which serves as the point of culmination for this chapter.

Commitment to falsificationism, as opposed to mere accumulation of evidence, is fundamental. A hard core must be specified in metaphysical terms. It will consist of a set of assumptions that receive parametric status and allow for a range of empirical referents. The hard core is exempted from evaluation on the basis of results obtained through testing of individual hypotheses. This is because the negative heuristic directs that such instances be dealt with through reassessment of case selection, data analysis, or other possible components of the process that could account for one or more disappointing research results. Realists, for example, might quarrel over measurement of national capabilities while continuing to agree that security depends directly on that variable. Thus hypothesis testing could result in failure but produce the tentative conclusion that capabilities had not been measured accurately. If refutations persist in spite of various measurement regimes, then attention naturally shifts to improved theorizing. As ever, questions such as "How soon should that happen?" lack answers.

Operational rules about replacement of theories are crucial and require further development at this point. The key assumption to be introduced is that *content for a theory is expected to be proportional to the number and significance of solved empirical problems.* This assumption is trivial at one level and more subtle at another. Obviously, every time an empirical problem is solved, that adds to the confirmed content of a theory. This might be labeled a simple "bottom-up" estimation of overall content. The "top-down" side of things is more problematic: What would it mean to say, for instance, that one theory is blessed with more content than another and should receive priority for further development? Measurement problems quickly become intimidating, if not overwhelming, unless the domain is restricted from the outset.[48] Research on some category of behavior, such as war or trade, might be more amenable to measurement of content—and even then, immense conceptual difficulties can arise as rates of change accelerate—but international relations as a whole presents a fundamentally different challenge.

For example, a theory may be put forward to account for major wars and then may be extended to a wider range of conflicts. This process appears to have occurred with some success in the case of power transition theory

(Organski 1958; Organski and Kugler 1980; Kugler and Lemke 1996; DiCicco and Levy 1999; Tammen et al. 2000). The comparison of the initial variant of power transition theory to those that followed, however, is feasible in relative rather than absolute terms. While later versions account for more kinds of war and even other varieties of conflict, it is impossible to say what that means in relation to some kind of outer limit.

Even development of categories for measurement of content seems awkward from the beginning. Suppose that cooperation and conflict are put forward as basic types of behavior in international relations. Would it be desirable to count individual instances of action in each category and then check whether a theory can explain them? This seems impractical, especially with regard to specification of overall content. How would all potential acts of cooperation or conflict be identified? While more sophisticated ideas could be developed on this point, the basic problem already is established. Any "bottom line," "100 percent level," or "denominator in a fraction" for content can be achieved only with arbitrariness for an encompassing field like international relations.

By contrast, a focus on the combination of empirical problems that are solved and still outstanding—to the extent that such things can be appraised in a valid and reliable way—may have potential as a meaningful *indicator* of content. This presumed correspondence shifts the problem of measurement from empirical content, for which a baseline of performance is elusive, to empirical problems, which can be identified and enumerated on the basis of experience. The assumption that the number of problems will correlate positively with content, the unobserved variable, becomes more credible as the would-be domain of a theory increases in scope. In fact, an even weaker assumption is sufficient to justify designation of problem solving as the indicator of content: unless content is correlated *inversely* with identification and resolution of empirical problems, this effective synthesis of ideas from Lakatos and Laudan is viable as a guide to decision making about progress. All other things being equal, a wider range of solved and unsolved empirical problems, along with anomalies, seems unlikely to point toward narrower content. After all, what reason exists to expect an *easier* task when it comes to identifying and resolving empirical problems in a theory that is more limited in content? Probability alone suggests that, if anything, the opposite is likely to be true. Although not directly measurable, a higher level of content should make it easier to locate empirical problems.

There are two rules for replacement of a theory within a paradigmatic entity: (a) consistent with Laudan, the challenger must solve more empirical problems than the reigning theory; and (b) in keeping with Lakatos's concerns about expanding content, the combination of problems addressed by the later version—entailing those solved, those unsolved, and anomalies—must be greater than that of the earlier one. These rules allow for the desired flexibility with respect to roles played by solved problems and anomalies from one theory to the next; progress is measured on the basis of aggregate performance rather than the status of any individual empirical problem.

Revolutionary assessment at the paradigmatic degree of aggregation depends on (a) the direction of movement exhibited by a series of theories and (b) how that pattern looks in relation to one or more proposed alternatives. Assume, for purposes of illustration, that P is the current paradigmatic choice and Q is proposed as a challenger. Let the respective theories within each paradigm be denoted by P_0, P_1, P_2, . . . and Q_0, Q_1, Q_2, ... Four logical possibilities can be identified for the relationship of the two paradigms to each other; these scenarios are created by combinations of internal performance by P with its problem-solving effectiveness in relation to Q. Only scenarios in which Q is progressive are relevant to the analysis, which produces the limit of four to be discussed. If Q is degenerative, it presents no challenge to P regardless of the latter's performance. The more substantive points of comparison are covered here, while a technical exposition appears in appendix A-1.

When P is both progressive and better than Q in problem solving, it continues as the paradigm of choice. This rule follows intuition, provides a degree of stability for research, and reflects the assumption that it is worthwhile to stay with a paradigm such as P until its full value is realized. The second scenario, when P is progressive but Q already is superior in terms of problem-solving ability, is more complicated but has an authentic feel to it. Efforts by the rival paradigms to establish sustained superiority over each other—with advocates of P tending to see Q's advantage as temporary—are both expected and worthwhile. When P is degenerating but still ahead of Q in problem solving—the third scenario—the choice of one over the other will depend on whether advocates of the reigning paradigm can restore progressiveness. (This may even result in a synthesis—see Pouncy 1988.) If not, Q is certain to supplant P within a discipline-specific time frame. Fourth, and finally, when P is degenerating and Q already is ahead in problem solving, this is the exemplar of falsification.

This discussion of alternative scenarios is helpful in bringing out the nuances that may exist in real cases of comparison. Exploring the properties of theories will contribute to understanding of evolutionary change, which in turn clarifies how revolutionary comparison is expected to work in practice.

3.3 Evolutionary Comparison of Theories

Direct falsificationist arguments, which originate with Popper ([1935] 1959, 1969), represent one extreme with regard to decision rules, where theories are discarded as soon as evidence of any kind arises against them. For several reasons it is argued that the best path to progress entails a more gradual outlook on the overthrow of theories, even allowing for the fact that inertial effects may cause some schools of thought to stay around too long. Arguments in favor of departing somewhat from the strictly falsificationist perspective are at least threefold and range from the philosophical to the practical.

First, from a philosophical standpoint, it appears prudent to be skeptical about (to use the terms introduced by Popper's falsificationism) both conjectures and refutations. The significance of an apparent anomaly, for example, is usually not self-evident (Rosenau 1995: 114). As a matter of basic disposition, it seems prudent to give theories a "fighting chance" (Ball 1976: 171).[49]

Second, and more specifically, falsifying evidence must be viewed in context. Theory and observation can be difficult to separate in practice, whether the reference is to a "hard" scientist using a microscope or a "soft" scientist accessing a data set. The act of the former shows faith in optics, while the latter is indirectly affirming theories used to define the variables within the compilation at hand. The interpretation must allow for the interplay between theory and hypotheses on the one hand and a body of evidence on the other (Glymour 1983: 110).[50] Tentative support for a hypothesis is *hypoprobable* (to use the term from Cioffi-Revilla and Starr 1995; see also Cioffi-Revilla 1998), meaning that the overall probability of confirmation is less than the likelihood of any one of the components that must be combined to make it happen. A true hypothesis may appear to fail testing because of faulty logic, measurement error, flaws in research design, random error, and even other reasons as yet unanticipated. The likelihood that a valid proposition will obtain support is calculated as the *product* of the complement for each preceding possibility (e.g., 1 minus the probability of measurement error), so it is prudent to regard failure of a hypothesis as *part* of a greater and challenging process of evaluation.

Third, and finally, practical benefits may accrue from persistence. Efforts to test a theory with high face validity but weak performance in prior evaluation may produce helpful knowledge about alternative variables that are more fundamental in importance. Applied research, or normal science, can have valuable by-products; examples range from technological advances to policy advice (Couvalis 1997: 109). While this line of reasoning should not be taken as encouragement to stay with a theory long past its time, it does make the point that such entities have multiple uses, some of which disappear more quickly than others.

Research on arms races from the Correlates of War (COW) Project over the last two decades provides a useful illustration of the three preceding points about falsificationism in action.[51] In this instance, a theory designated here as t_0 links arms races to the outbreak of war. The initial version put forward by Wallace (1979a) is dyadic or micro-micro in specification; interstate war (w) is expected to correlate with the presence of an arms race (a) between a pair of states, or, in the language of systemism, a ———➤ w is the implicit causal linkage (i.e., lower-case characters representing a micro-micro connection between an arms race and war). Wallace claimed that the COW data on militarized disputes between major powers supported the theory, which produced skepticism and a series of further tests in response. Critics pointed to interdependence between and among dyads in the years leading up to World Wars I and II, which had the effect of shifting attention to a macro-macro version of the theory, T_1, where A ———➤ W. This version of the theory did not fare as well when tested; no connection at all, rather than a mixture of results, sums up the findings. Debates in this area of research continue over the proper definition and measurement of an arms race, and Geller and Singer (1998: 81) report that the issue appears far from settled after two decades of intensive effort. This continuing research represents an area of "normal science" in Kuhn's (1970) terms, albeit rather unsatisfying in the absence of an overarching agreement on theory after so much focused effort.

Even this short and simple illustration of theorizing in a relatively restricted domain is sufficient to bring out the three preceding general points about philosophy, context, and practical value with respect to departing from a strict regime of falsificationism. First, the research on arms races and war is permeated with skepticism about both theory and data, which has produced a lively and constructive debate over a series of theories (Geller and Singer 1998). Second, refutation of t_0 by the failure of T_1 to find support from COW data is just one possible conclusion when the findings are placed in the context of earlier remarks (see Duhem 1977) about seemingly failed propositions; another reasonable reaction is to explore issues related to research design and measurement before passing judgment. Reactions have varied and debate continues over the meaning and impact of arms races. Third, and finally, while embattled, the theory of arms races and war continues to stimulate inquiry intended to improve understanding of the causes of war. The burgeoning study of enduring rivalries, for example, is rooted in efforts to go beyond arms races in understanding how relationships evolve into war versus other outcomes (Goertz and Diehl 1992, 1993; Diehl and Goertz 2000).

All of this serves as an excellent bridge to the operational issues about scientific progress through replacement of theories. On the basis of the earlier discussion of paradigmatic development, theories can be identified in sequence through a common hard core and negative heuristic and a presumably expanding positive heuristic. Evolutionary comparison of theories requires that criteria be developed for each of these components. The goal of the discussion that follows is to reach an understanding of what it means to say that one theory is better than another, bearing in mind the points made a few moments ago about the need to be cautious in reaching such judgments.

Neither the philosophy of science in general nor international relations in particular can boast of a definitive set of criteria for evaluation of theory.[52] This is as expected because the balance between general rules and discipline-specific priorities will vary. Furthermore, while some principles accord with common sense, they may always prove difficult to use for assessment in practice. Who would *not* want a theory that was precise and distinct from others (Kuhn 1977: 291; Bunge 1996: 103–4; Legro and Moravcsik 1998: 5), was coherent with other theories and background knowledge (Barbour 1974: 92; Kuhn 1977: 291; Bunge 1996: 103–4), brought order and meaning to reality (McClelland 1966: 15; Puchala 1991: 59–60; Thompson 1994: 22), raised new questions and was increasingly comprehensive (Jeffrey 1971: 40; Puchala 1991: 59–60; Berger and Zelditch 1993: 5–6; Thompson 1994: 22), and accumulated empirical support (Barbour 1974: 92; Kuhn 1977: 289; Berger and Zelditch 1993:

5–6; Bunge 1996: 103–4)? Some of these obviously desirable traits are more amenable to measurement than others. The exposition that follows will introduce basic principles for theory while blending in concerns from international relations in particular, at each stage bearing in mind the eventual need for application.

Within a paradigm, the hard core is established in the initial version of a theory, T_0 (or t_0 if it consists strictly of micro-micro connections). (Later versions appear as T_1, T_2, and so on.) Two principles, *logical consistency* and *efficiency*, apply directly to the creation and use of the hard core. Each will be presented in a way that includes the potential for operational rendering.

Logical consistency, the first and perhaps more obvious of the two principles, is applied when the hard core is created at the outset of a series of theories. Since all assumptions that receive parametric status are treated as unfalsifiable for purposes of applied research, it is essential that each be logically consistent with the others. The need for consistency is well established in prior expositions both within and beyond international relations (Legro and Moravcsik 1998: 6; Bunge 1996: 103–4).

Efficiency, the second principle, is applied as theories develop in sequence and relates to how the assumptions of the hard core are working out in practice. Efficiency is maintained when all of the axioms are playing significant roles in development of the positive heuristic. If an assumption is granted parametric status, it must not be relaxed at any time, and that rules out any number of hypotheses. Thus the decision to include an assumption in the hard core reflects the belief that the overall impact on theorizing will be favorable in spite of the reduced flexibility involved.

Assessment of the negative heuristic will take place indirectly through development of the positive heuristic. If anomalies can be identified without ambiguity, then the negative heuristic, which rules out theories that violate the hard core, is said to be functioning well. Thus *precision,* noted a while ago among the traits that would be desirable for any theory, comes to the fore with respect to the negative heuristic.

Theories serve four basic purposes: description, explanation, prediction, and control of the subject matter. The relative importance of each goal and the trade-offs between and among improvements in achieving them will vary with the field of study.[53] Consider, by way of introduction, meteorology as an example of a field in which relative priorities seem fairly obvious. Yet even here trade-offs occur, and the emphasis on one objective versus another can be expected to change. Prediction is a preeminent priority because improvement in this area contributes directly to preservation of life and property. Even small increments in warning time can help to reduce substantially the human costs inflicted by several kinds of dangerous weather (e.g., cyclones). Description and explanation of weather can be expected to contribute to forecasting, but these are lower priorities in and of themselves. Control, an even more ambitious goal than prediction, becomes more important to pursue as feasibility increases. The ability to prevent disasters such as hurricanes or floods would be even more coveted than warning of them. Thus priorities across the purposes ranging from description to control can be expected to change. If knowledge increased to a point at which control over certain meteorological dangers seemed within reach, then efforts could be expected to shift in that direction.

International relations, by comparison, is a more difficult field to assess in these terms. The initial decision about priorities is whether all of the objectives listed above can be compared in commensurable ways within the paradigmatic degree of aggregation. The earlier discussion of ontologies and worldviews makes it clear that one of the goals, control over what happens, is inappropriate for intra- or even interparadigmatic dialogue. Discussion of control in mutually intelligible terms would imply the ability to agree on the terms of a debate on normative grounds. Unlike the other goals just noted, control implies some action that would be taken to change the world in a particular way.[54] By contrast, description, explanation, and prediction are worthy goals even in the absence of certainty regarding what might be done with such knowledge about international relations (Bunge 1996: 2; Brecher 1999: 217).[55] (For example, neoliberals and dependency theorists might celebrate their ability to reach agreement that free trade increases economic inequality within states but might derive very different policy implications from that point onward.) The balance between and among description, explanation, and prediction as priorities and how each is related to the axioms of a theory are important questions in search of answers.

Appendix A-2 conveys a diagrammatic exposition of how description, explanation, and prediction are expected to vary as a function of the number of axioms included in a theory. In each instance the functional form is monotonically increasing, but the curves vary in shape and expected upper limit for performance. For present purposes it is sufficient to identify description, explanation, and prediction as the tasks that theories of international relations must perform and to show how the ability to carry out each depends on making assumptions. This makes it possible to return more effectively to the question of how to designate solved and unsolved empirical problems, along with anomalies.

What constitutes either a solved or an unsolved empirical problem? How does something come to be called an anomaly? The answers to these questions are established in a specific manner by neither Laudan (1977, 1981), who developed the preceding series of terms, nor anyone else. Two decades after putting forward the idea of a research tradition, Laudan (1996) himself acknowledges that the technical problems of application remain "enormous" (82). In particular, it is not clear how problems are to be counted (Kukla 1997). Thus measurement difficulties, which stood in the way of implementing the idea of empirical content within a research program, also must be addressed for the concepts of empirical problem and anomaly as created in reference to a research tradition.[56]

Fortunately, an important difference helps to separate the two cases with respect to prospects for application. For empirical content the basic difficulty is its open-ended nature. The concept requires some idea of what a theory would need to achieve in order to reach an ultimate limitation on performance. In other words, how much content exists in relative terms is a function of how much ultimately *might* exist, and the latter seems almost beyond comprehension with respect to measurement. An empirical problem (solved or unsolved) or anomaly, by contrast, represents a different and more limited set of challenges with respect to operational use. Neither concept is defined in *relation* to an upper boundary. Thus the task at hand is to identify these concepts in a way that will permit consistent judgments to be made about their status at any given stage of theorizing within a paradigmatic entity.

We can meet these concerns by returning to the nature of a theory of international relations along the continuum of aggregation. A theory consists of a system of variables. Agreement exists about the nature of units of observation and boundaries between them. One further assumption is needed to move ahead with defining an empirical problem, namely, that every observation can be classified as either a behavior or an event (Cioffi-Revilla 1998). Behavior is described in terms of an action within a specified domain. Events combine actions into a collective entity with greater meaning. For example, the army of one state might cross the border of another, which in turn would produce resistance from the army of the latter. Invasion is one action and resistance is another. These actions might be combined and referred to as a "battle" or "war."

Theories of international relations seek to describe, explain, and predict actions and events. The following definitions result from this set of objectives:

1. A *solved empirical problem* is a set of actions or events that have been described, explained, or predicted (or retrodicted, when referring to thep ast) by a theory.

2. An *unsolved empirical problem* is a set of actions or events that have yet to be described, explained, or predicted (or retrodicted, when referring to the past) by a theory.

3. An *anomaly* is a set of actions or events that a theory can describe, explain, or predict (or retrodict, when referring to the past) only in violation of one or more of the axioms from its hard core.

The first two of the preceding definitions are complementary. Description, explanation, *or* prediction of an event or action counts as a solved empirical problem. For example, a set of events might be described and explained but not predicted; this would count as two solved problems and one unsolved. If the unsolved problem posed a threat to the hard core, however, it would be relabeled as an anomaly. The issue of designating boundaries for sets of actions and events, which would affect the number of items placed in each major category, is expected to take care of itself in the context of an individual discipline. Comparison of theories within a paradigm permits resolution of such differences because of the preexisting agreement on units of observation and boundaries between them.

Theories seek to describe, explain, and predict, so the natural tendency is to add assumptions in order to achieve more in each area. From a scientific point of view, however, assumptions are costly, and additions to an existing set should occur judiciously. Consider these words of warning from Shanker (1988):

> Axioms are constantly being invented or revised in order to . . . address problems which would defy the reach—i.e. the intelligibility—of the preexisting axioms. The evolution of a . . . field typically consists, therefore, in the gradual development of such system-families. But the further this process advances the greater become the pressures for rationalization if the subject is to remain manageable: Like the unplanned development of a medieval city these systems soon become too cumbersome for efficient communication, and interest shifts accordingly to refashioning the axiom set without diminishing the scope of the system (by introducing alternative— possibly more abstract—axioms). (197–98)

What makes this admonition especially interesting is that it is aimed at *mathematics,* presumably the most rigorous of all disciplines, not international relations or any of the other social sciences.[57] The quotation also offers implied support to the earlier criticism of strict incrementalism. Successful theory building is likely to include setbacks, albeit temporary ones, that may look like the initial stages of degeneration. Experimentation with overlapping versions of a theory in search of a successor is likely to be the norm rather than the exception. Thus the path from T_i to T_{i+1}, where the latter of the two theories demonstrates superiority over the former, easily can take place after an interval of, as Shanker puts it, "rationalization" and "refashioning." If such things can happen to the demigods of mathematics, should there be any shame in the experience for the mere mortals of international relations?

All of this points toward the need to strike a balance between the complexity of a theory in relation to what it creates in terms of description, explanation, and prediction. While the importance of economy of explanation is well established, a firm sense of what this idea means in practice still is lacking. A better term might be *economy of exposition,* since explanation is only one of the three objectives designated for a theory of international relations. All other things being equal, simplicity, manifested in a smaller number of assumptions, is more attractive (Barbour 1974: 92; Lave and March 1975: 61; Kuhn 1977: 291; Glymour 1983: 331). Yet it is unlikely in practice that economy of exposition will be amenable to measurement along any single dimension. What if a theory is parsimonious but turns out either to be wrong or capable of explaining very little (Haggard 1991: 417)? The complications raised by this question alone are sufficient to justify the kind of assessment suggested by Maoz (1990):

"Parsimony is a ratio between the number of premises a logical system contains and the number of inferences that can be deduced from them. The more inferences that can be drawn from a small number of premises, the more parsimonious the system" (14). Similarly, Lave and March (1975) call for a "relatively large number of interesting predictions per assumption" (64). However, "prolific" rather than "parsimonious" would seem like a better way of describing this criterion, which then might stand as one dimension of economy of exposition. Thus a theory might become more or less prolific as assumptions are added, since this term is understood as a ratio rather than an absolute number.[58]

Theories, to sum up the preceding series of points about comparison and progress, should be approached from an evolutionary perspective with regard to deciding upon falsification. Logical consistency and efficiency are the properties desired for the hard core, with precision as the priority for the negative heuristic. Description, explanation, and prediction are the goals pursued in the positive heuristic. The positive heuristic consists of solved and unsolved empirical problems, along with anomalies, expressed in terms of the description, explanation, and prediction of actions and events. Finally, expansion of the positive heuristic must be pursued with some attention to economy of exposition, a term that refers to the number of axioms and how prolific they are in generating hypotheses.

3.4 Summing up the Continuum of Aggregation

Scientific systemism, as envisioned in this book, puts forward the preceding apparatus, centered on the continuum of aggregation, as its vision of scholarship. Progress in international relations can be assessed in multiple ways at any stage of development. This brief subsection will address two issues that are prior to an exposition on the scientific research enterprise, which puts the principles developed in the earlier sections of this chapter into practice. One issue is whether the five-point continuum of aggregation is both necessary and sufficient for assessment of scientific progress. The other concerns the logical connections involving respective types of comparison.

Perhaps either a smaller or larger number would be better than the five points, ranging from hypothesis to worldview, that have been designated along the continuum of aggregation. This is a difficult question to answer for at least two reasons. First, discipline-specific considerations are likely to enter into any compelling reply. This response leads into the second reason: before application, it is hard to know where either more nuances might be recognized or redundancies eliminated along the continuum. For these reasons the analysis that follows should be regarded as tentative and speculative rather than authoritative. At this stage it seems fair to say that evolutionary and revolutionary comparisons balance off concerns about replacement of theories and paradigms. Practical matters of application will arise because of the conflicting priorities that exist between "making the mistakes as quickly as possible" (to use the colorful and commonly repeated way of conveying Popperian thinking) and prematurely terminating a potentially worthwhile line of research in the face of ultimately surmountable obstacles. Thus the points represented by theory and paradigm along the continuum would appear to play essential roles in assessing progress; one generates incremental comparison within a consensus about parameters, while the other brings fundamental, axiomatic differences into sharp relief. Whether a greater amount could be learned by looking at performance at more nuanced points between theory and paradigm is a question that may answer itself after the entire framework is seen in application.

Pragmatic comparison of ontologies serves as a necessary bridge between the discipline of international relations and concerns in the world beyond academe. Policy makers, for example, can benefit from knowledge produced by international relations, but it is essential for scholars to produce an "orderly"—perhaps *intelligible* would be a better word—presentation of the variety of data they have to offer (George 1993: xxiv). As noted earlier, with the general public improving in its ability to judge ideas and information, and the bias among experts in assessing ontologies being expected to continue (i.e., in the latter sense, an anticipated tendency toward Kantian phenomenalism), pragmatic comparison begins to emerge as common sense. A discipline such as international relations must produce, at least as a by-product, concepts and information that help to inform public discourse. After all, how otherwise could the allocation of capital and labor to such a frequently arcane subject ultimately be justified?[59]

Logical relations between pragmatic, evolutionary, and revolutionary comparison also should be explored in at least a preliminary way. Does fulfillment of any one kind of progress imply the existence of either of the other two? Two possible kinds of connection exist: "up" or "down" between pragmatic and revolutionary comparison, and evolutionary and revolutionary comparison, respectively. The third possible type of linkage, between pragmatic and evolutionary comparison, is ruled out a priori. Replacement of one theory by another should be of interest to academic specialists alone; only at the stage of revolutionary change, where parameters are shifted, could effects be anticipated to reverberate at the degree of ontology and therefore affect the general public or the policy-making community in some way. The same inhibition operates in the other direction as well. If a major change in public thinking about international relations did take place, it would be reasonable to expect that impact would be transmitted downward to the paradigmatic level rather than directly into a shift from one theory to another.

Revolutionary change supersedes evolutionary change. If a series of theories in one paradigm $(P_0, P_1, \ldots)$ is replaced by another $(Q_0, Q_1, \ldots)$, then the conclusion is that Q_j is regarded as superior to P_i in an irreversible way, where these theories are the best versions available in each series. This judgment could be reached as versions of the former paradigm, for example, P_i, P_{i+1}, and P_{i+2}, respectively, show an inability to match Q_j and therefore produce a judgment that paradigm P is degenerative. Since this process could occur without any evolutionary progress in Q over the same time interval, revolutionary change does not imply the existence of ongoing evolutionary change.

Evolutionary change can produce revolutionary change when the shift within a new paradigm, from Q_j to Q_{j+1}, is decisive in its implications for the future of the established paradigm, P. If P_i is the best version of P and the above-noted shift in versions of Q establishes superiority, then a revolutionary change may occur. As noted earlier in the chapter, however, this decision becomes more difficult if P still is progressive; its research community can be expected to increase efforts to find $P_{i+1} > Q_j$. If P is degenerative, then the shift in paradigms follows from the evolutionary change in Q.

More difficult to specify are the linkages involving pragmatic and revolutionary change. Given the large-scale nature of pragmatic change, it is expected to be rare and therefore difficult to anticipate on the basis of cumulative developments involving theories or paradigms. Thus the transmission of effects from revolutionary to pragmatic change also should be uncommon. At least some instances of the more common event of revolutionary change will not produce pragmatic change. Instead, it is more likely that a series of revolutionary changes will be required to produce pragmatic change. The inherently normative and subjective elements that enter into ontology virtually guarantee that transmission of effects from revolutionary to pragmatic change will take a cumulative and conditional form.

Effects from pragmatic to revolutionary change are not expected. The reason is that such developments, when in evidence, are expected to be simultaneous rather than unidirectional. A major overhaul in public beliefs about ontology is anticipated to be a process informed by the social by-products of sequential revolutionary change in the research community. The language of public debate can be expected to shift and the processes of revolutionary and pragmatic change to become symbiotic.

4. The Scientific Research Enterprise

Analysis of a series of issues, ranging from the general meaning of progress to specific criteria for comparison of theories, culminates in definition of a paradigmatic entity that is most useful for the field of international relations: the scientific research enterprise. The components in the definition offered at the outset of this chapter, which include the hard core, negative heuristic, and positive heuristic, have been introduced in previous sections. The hard core is assumed to be logically consistent and efficient and is protected by a precise negative heuristic, as described previously. For a theory in sequence within a scientific research enterprise, empirical content is assumed to correlate with the solved and unsolved empirical problems, along with anomalies, that it includes. For present purposes let it be assumed (admittedly, a herculean assumption) that it is possible to aggregate the solved and unsolved empirical problems (plus anomalies) across the categories of description, explanation, and prediction. A diagrammatic exposition, which conveys an analysis of benefits and costs, then can be used to assess scientific progress. The cost-benefit analysis that follows is intended to show how changes in empirical content might be related to the expansion of the axiomatic basis of theories.

Figure 3.2 presents a cost-benefit analysis of research progress for ideal types of scientific research enterprise. The contents of the figure will be first explained in generic terms and later applied, in a preliminary way, to structural realism in chapter 5. Rather than focusing on a given scientific research enterprise, the figure will be used to bring out the range of possibilities that exists for the trade-off between axioms and marginal empirical content. The horizontal axis corresponds to the hard core plus auxiliary assumptions: that is, the overall number of axioms. The value for the number of axioms (A) ranges from zero (where nothing is assumed and content is nonexistent) to infinity (a point never to be reached). For the sake of argument it is assumed that each additional axiom represents an approximately equal increment in cost in terms of economy of exposition; the fact that some assumptions are likely to prove more prolific than others in practice, a point introduced in the previous section, is not incorporated here. (Although no genuine quantification is involved, the degree of truth and generality of the axioms—obviously the most important consideration—is assumed to be independent of their number.) *The positive heuristic refers to the range of empirical problems addressed and solved, along with anomalies; its expansion is assumed to correlate with empirical content.* Thus the vertical axis in the figure corresponds to marginal empirical content (C). It is important to distinguish content from *marginal* content. Empirical content increases as long as any further marginal gains are made. Allowing a role for economy of exposition shifts the focus to marginal empirical content, as depicted by the figure. Thus the cost-benefit analysis focuses on how marginal empirical content changes as a function of the number of assumptions.

Starting at (0, 0), the curve for marginal empirical content traces out an inverted "u." The curve returns to the horizontal axis where, at (A_0, C_0), no further empirical content can be obtained.[60] The height it would reach, along with the slope of ascent and descent, can be anticipated to vary in practice.

How many axioms are worthwhile? The answer depends on the price of A on one hand and the value or price of C on the other. While maximizing C looks like the obvious decision rule, other criteria enter into the picture and make (A_0, C_0), where the number of axioms is at the maximum, an unlikely choice.

For ease of exposition, assume the value of knowledge to be constant within some time frame. Several alternatives are given by the marginal cost of axioms to users. Two basic cases can be identified: constant versus increasing marginal costs. In the first instance, each axiom is as costly as the one before. This would be represented by a horizontal line at some level above the axis in the figure. The outer limit of achievement is reached when this line intersects with the curve, meaning that marginal costs and benefits are equal. The second possibility, in which each axiom is more costly than the one before, would produce a curve that slopes upward. Once again, intersection with the curve for marginal benefits determines the optimal point. Each of the basic possibilities

Figure 3.2

Axioms and Marginal Empirical Content for Ideal Types of Scientific
Research Enterprise

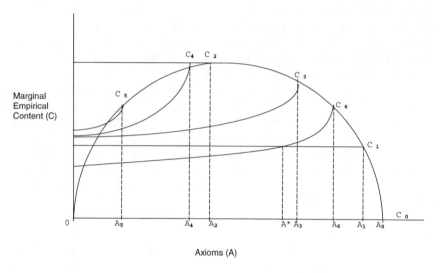

Axioms (A)

creates an ideal type of scientific research enterprise and is considered in turn.

Constant marginal costs create a range of possibilities, three of which, (A_0, C_0), (A_1, C_1), and (A_2, C_2), are salient for purposes of comparison. It is assumed that complexity always is costly, so its level will exceed the horizontal axis. This rules out the choice of C_0, which corresponds to Veblen's (1912: 363–400) knowledge for its own sake, or as practiced by members of the "leisure class," idle curiosity. Only when axioms are cost-free will the result be C_0. A more normal expectation would be C_1, where marginal costs are greater than zero and the better of the two intersection points is the one with more empirical content. Note that C_1 is much further along the curve for marginal empirical content than C_2. The latter would be selected only if marginal costs reached a much higher constant value, as depicted by the horizontal line that intersects (A_2, C_2). Anything above that level would make the entire research enterprise nonscientific by definition because marginal costs exceed marginal benefits from the outset. The assumption of constant marginal costs at such a high level also rules out all points to the left of C_2 because in all instances the curve for marginal empirical content is exceeded.

Increasing marginal costs also allows for more than one outcome. The most obvious possibilities would be in the neighborhood of C_3 or C_4, which differ from each other in a qualitative way. The costs per axiom rise gradually in one instance, so $C_3 > C_2$, while the sharper increase in marginal costs in the other results in $C_2 > C_4$.[61] In other words, depending on the steepness of ascent for the cost curve, it could produce an outcome better or worse than the relatively high constant costs, yet neither reaches the intersection point for comparatively lower constant costs, so $C_1 > C_3 > C_2 > C_4$.

A more unusual scenario would be that represented by (A_5, C_5), where the marginal cost curve rises so rapidly that it barely intersects with the marginal benefits curve at all. Curves that rise more rapidly and start out high enough to miss the marginal benefits curve, of course, represent theorizing that is not scientifically viable from the outset.

One more scenario is needed to complete the assessment of ideal types. When marginal cost curves do not cross each other and one is always less than the other for all values of A, superiority is clear and sustained; for example, this holds true for the curves leading to (A_4, C_4) and (A_1, C_1), respectively. The second possibility is that the marginal cost curves cross each other, meaning that regions exist in which one could be chosen over the other and vice versa. This final scenario is represented by the curve leading to (A_6, C_6) in relation to the previously unchallenged (A_1, C_1). Note that, until the point A^* along the axis where the curves cross, the path leading to (A_6, C_6) looks better. The crucial question becomes the desired range of application for a theory. Are further increments of knowledge, as generated by a given theory, worth the effort? The answer depends on the theory's achievements and prospects in relation to alternatives. Thus it would be possible to seek protection for a research enterprise, such as the one leading to (A_6, C_6) in the figure, by restricting the domain of its applicability.

Three basic dimensions emerge from discussion of ideal types of scientific research enterprise in the figure: (a) viable versus nonviable, (b) increasing versus constant marginal costs, and (c) intersecting versus nonintersecting cost curves. Some expectations exist about the curves that will be encountered in practice. First, curves that are nonviable should be rare because the research community can be expected to find more promising avenues from the outset. Second, increasing rather than constant marginal costs should be the norm. Third, and finally, intersecting curves create the greatest potential for destructive debate between advocates of one research enterprise versus another; comparison at or around A^* coincides with a time of crisis and incipient degeneration for an enterprise that had demonstrated sustained superiority.

Many more curves could be imagined, but those in the figure are sufficient to bring out the basic properties under the range of assumed conditions. First, the point ultimately reached by a curve with respect to marginal empirical content could be better or worse with either constant or increasing marginal costs from axioms. At the same time, intuition favors the choice of a research enterprise with constant marginal costs. Second, only curves that intersect the curve for marginal empirical content are viable. Those that either start off too high or rise too sharply to produce an intersection with the curve for marginal content are irrelevant from the outset. Finally, a curve may cross with another or remain beneath it until the intersection point with marginal empirical content is reached. In other words, while one curve may be unambiguously preferred to another at all points along the horizontal axis, it also is possible that they will cross over, resulting in zones of superiority for each.

Structural realist theories will be compared to each other in terms of curves for marginal empirical content in chapter 5. At that point it will be argued that the trajectory resembles the favorable scenario leading to (A_1, C_1) in figure 3.2, as opposed to rivals that appear destined to fall by the wayside as a result of rapidly rising costs relative to marginal benefits.

5. Conclusions

This chapter started off with an assessment of the meaning of scientific progress in general terms, with the intention of developing a framework that could be applied to the field of international relations. The process involved deciding on the proper scope and mechanism for evaluation of worldviews, ontologies, paradigmatic entities, theories, and hypotheses.

Pragmatic, revolutionary, and evolutionary comparisons emerged as the appropriate approaches toward ontologies (and, implicitly, worldviews), paradigms, and theories, respectively. Pragmatic comparison is regarded as appropriately carried out as a natural process occurring beyond the boundaries of a community of research specialists. Revolutionary and evolutionary comparisons are expected to be carried out by intention within that community.

Theories, which are the crucial unit of analysis for assessing progress within a paradigmatic entity, are based on a hard core of axioms and develop a positive heuristic within the rules instituted by a negative heuristic. The hard core is made up of axioms that are granted paradigmatic status; it is judged in terms of logical consistency and efficiency. The negative heuristic forbids revision of the hard core and rules out theorizing inconsistent with that foundation. Precision is the principal characteristic needed by the negative heuristic. Finally, the positive heuristic is composed of solved and unsolved empirical problems (and anomalies), measured in terms of the description, explanation, and prediction of actions and events.

All of this work set the stage for definition of a scientific research enterprise, a paradigmatic entity that is intended to produce effective assessment of progress. Analysis of costs and benefits for respective ideal types of scientific research enterprise provides the basis for application to research carried out in a specific discipline.

Completion of the preceding set of tasks creates the framework needed for a more substantive evaluation of structural realism. Part 2 will provide that assessment. Chapter 4 describes the foundation and evolution of structural realism, while chapter 5 begins evaluation of it as a scientific research enterprise.

Part 2

Structural Realism as a Scientific Research Enterprise

[Student, reading aloud from a book] "*Understanding Poetry*, by Dr. J. Evans Pritchard, Ph.D. To fully understand poetry we must first be fluent with its meter, rhyme and figures of speech, then ask two questions: (1) how artfully has the objective of the poem been rendered? and (2) how important is that objective? Question one rates the poem's perfection, question two rates its importance, and once these questions have been answered, determining the poem's greatness becomes a relatively simple matter. If the poem's score for perfection is plotted on the horizontal of a graph, and its importance is plotted on the vertical, then calculating the total area of the poem yields the measure of its greatness."

—from *Dead Poets Society*, © Touchstone Pictures, 1989.

CHAPTER FOUR

The Foundation and Evolution of Structural Realism

1. Objectives and Plan of Work

This chapter conveys the foundation and evolution of structural realism as a scientific research enterprise. It builds on the concept formation related to scientific progress from the preceding chapter, which focused on the need to move toward a framework with greater potential for application to a social science such as international relations. The review of structural realism as described above will take place in five stages.

First, the hard core and negative heuristic are identified on the basis of Waltz (1979), the initial exposition of structural realism. The hard core requires one significant adjustment that is based on a source other than Waltz's initial study. This permits designation of a series of theories within structural realism as a scientific research enterprise.

Second, the theories that follow in sequence from T_0, which is based on Waltz's initial exposition, are presented. This is the first stage of identifying the positive heuristic, within which the surrounding belt of auxiliary hypotheses plays a central role. The discussion focuses on description of empirical problems by theories that have been built on the foundation of structural realism (i.e., T_0). This process of description, in turn, provides the basis for a review of propositions with the potential to be integrated with a more advanced version of structural realism.

Further identification of the positive heuristic takes place in the third section. The focus is on explanation and prediction of solved and unsolved empirical problems, along with anomalies. The survey includes hypotheses that use capability-based indicators (each of which corresponds to a potential element of structure as identified in chapter 2's typology) to account for conflict, crisis, and war. While these propositions generally are ad hoc in the manner communicated by Lakatos (1971), their potential for integration into a more encompassing version of structural realism makes it worthwhile to conduct such a review.

Fourth, the portrayal of the positive heuristic for structural realism is completed through a more intensive look at war as an empirical problem. This exercise complements the previous stage of review by focusing on the central substantive concern for the research enterprise, as opposed to performance of capability-based indicators in accounting for a wider range of events. In terms familiar to social scientists, attention shifts from a set of independent variables to a dependent variable.

Fifth, and finally, tentative conclusions are offered about the evolution of structural realism. This discussion sets the stage for the following chapter, which evaluates the performance of structural realism as a scientific research enterprise and derives priorities for an elaborated structural realism.

Before we move ahead on the objectives just noted, it is important to distinguish what will take place in this chapter from preliminary reassessment of structural realism as a scientific research enterprise in chapter 5. Several aspects of review and evaluation are carried out more appropriately after elaboration of structural realism. Thus chapters 4 and 5 will not draw upon the diagrammatic exposition for description, explanation, and prediction of empirical problems that appeared in appendix A-2. These chapters also will not address (except very briefly) the issue of trajectory, in terms of marginal costs and benefits conveyed by figure 3.2, for structural realism as a scientific research enterprise. The aspects just noted, along with the general issues of pragmatic, revolutionary, and evolutionary comparison, are addressed in a preliminary way by chapter 5. Since the preceding tasks can be carried out much more effectively once an elaborated structural realism is presented in some form, the priority in part 2 will be to describe and evaluate structural realism as it exists now, in order to set an agenda for a new version of the theory.

Some caution and even humility are in order before moving forward with the proposed agenda. It always is possible to propose a measurement scheme of some kind, as in the absurd "area-based" assessment of poetry noted in the epigraph to part 2. The teacher, in that instance, wisely had his students destroy their copies of *Understanding Poetry*. This permitted them to appreciate poetry for itself, rather than forcing it into a procrustean bed of pseudoscience based on calculation of greatness. In a sense, the goal of part 2 of this book is to avoid the same fate as *Understanding Poetry*. While an attempt to measure scientific progress in international relations makes more sense than trying to quantify the greatness of poetry, at least on the basis of intuition, it is all too easy to miss the mark and end up in much the same place as J. Evans Pritchard, the author of the work just mentioned. As will become apparent, the abstractions that pervade the philosophy of science require considerable adjustment in order to achieve some connection with the evolution of a real discipline in the social sciences, such as international relations. For such reasons it becomes prudent not to laugh too soon or hard at the fictive author and book noted a moment ago.

2. The Hard Core and Negative Heuristic of Structural Realism

2.1 The Hard Core

Table 4.1 lists the assumptions granted parametric status by structural realism that make up the hard core.[1] This exposition, it should be noted, is derived implicitly from Waltz (1979), the original presentation of structural realism.

Waltz's exegesis is not written in the language developed either in the previous chapter or elsewhere in the philosophy of science, so the contents of the table represent an effort to translate structural realism into the context of the hard core as that concept is understood here. The six parameters are regarded as beyond any challenge based on empirical testing alone, and they provide the foundation for structural realism as a scientific research enterprise. In metaphysical terms, the parameters might even be referred to as the "constitution" of structural realism. Given the decision rule from chapter 3, which stipulated that violation of even one assumption is sufficient to remove a theory from the paradigm in question, the metaphor seems apt: that is, the axiomatic basis of structural realism is constructed in the very limited way associated with a constitution.

Table 4.1
The Hard Core of Structural Realism: Identifying Axioms with Parametric Status

Parameter	Meaning
P_1	The most important actors in world politics are territorially organized entities (city-states and modern states).
P_2	State behavior is rational.
P_3	States seek security and calculate their interests in terms of relative standing within the international system.
P_4	Anarchy is the ordering principle of international relations.
P_5	States, the units of the international system, are undifferentiated by function.
P_6	Structure is defined by the distribution of capabilities among states.

One point of contention about the axioms involves the creator of structural realism directly, which in turn raises the question of how the "original" version of a theory within a research enterprise should be identified. Is it best to stay only with the text itself or to "correct" any error that could have been found at the time of writing? The two possible answers to this question have the potential to create somewhat different versions of the hard core. The controversy is over including P_2, which asserts that state behavior is rational. This difference of opinion must be resolved immediately and will entail a brief discussion of how Waltz (1979, 1986, 1997) and Keohane (1986b; see also Guzzini 1998 and Kahler 1998) disagree about the assumption of rationality in particular.

While rational choice appears as one of the axioms with parametric status in table 4.1, it would meet with disapproval from Waltz (1979, 1986, 1997), who continues to argue that structural realism does not entail this assumption. In particular, Waltz (1986) asserts that political leaders cannot make the "nicely calculated" decisions implied by rationality (330). Instead, the structure of the system is regarded by Waltz (1979, 1997) as an evolutionary mechanism, with states who follow (or defy) its imperatives having a better (or worse) chance of survival. This holistic argument, however, creates inconsistencies in the theory: "The realm of reason within neorealism remains ambiguous. Under tight structural constraints of international competition and selection, the rationality of agents seems superfluous. Waltz fails to demonstrate that structures have such consistent and predictable effects, however" (Kahler 1998: 925). In the language of systemism, the *macro-micro connection* that is needed to explain why some states survive and prosper while others do not is missing from the theory.

By contrast, Keohane's (1986b) intuition that structural realism implies rational choice by states seems much more on target. The easy way to make that point is to take rationality temporarily out of play. If rational choice is *not* the norm, then how does the states system continue to avert hegemony? Only by assuming an economic model, with survival as the goal and behavior that approximates calculation of costs and benefits toward that end as the norm, can the presumed effects of market (i.e., anarchical) constraints be understood (Guzzini 1998: 129). Logically, if only a few system members are making policy in a prudent way, the balance of power will fail to operate and one of two possibilities seems likely: (a) world empire under an exceptional great power that also happens to be rational or (b) replacement of the collectively irrational states system with one based on another kind of unit that acts out of self-interest. Thus, paradoxically, two versions of the hard core become possible: in a somewhat humorous way, they might be described as "the one Waltz wants and the one Waltz needs."

Systemism's basic principles intervene decisively to favor inclusion of the rationality axiom in the hard core. Macro-micro connections, for example, cannot be explored otherwise. In addition, commitment to doctrine would seem less important than practical considerations that have been paramount during all prior stages of the analysis.[2] The point, then, is not to identify the "real" Waltz in some exploration of the academic record. Instead, the hard core for structural realism needs to be constructed as it might have been at the time of the theory's creation in order to achieve the potential for consistency as theories develop.[3]

Table 4.1's axioms are theoretical; specific actors, events, times, and places are not entailed. States are expected to pursue positional standing in Europe, Asia, or elsewhere, before and after the invention of nuclear weapons, and independent of who is governing them. Anarchy is anticipated to pose the same problems for modern states as it did for Athens and Sparta in antiquity. Variation from one structurally analogous situation to the next must be explained by factors other than state centrism, rational choice, and the other components of the hard core.

2.2 The Negative Heuristic

Structural realism, as noted already, is a theory put forward in a frame of reference other than the one developed by Lakatos and his fellow travelers. Thus it is not possible to read out an explicit presentation of the negative heuristic from Waltz (1979). The alternative is to engage in rational reconstruction, as in the case of the hard core a moment ago. What, then, reasonably could be identified as methodological principles that (a) protect the hard core from experimental refutation and (b) rule out qualitatively different kinds of theorizing?

Structural realism is an empirical theory and therefore should seek protection for its hard core at the level of measurement. Capability is at the center of this process. Security seeking by states in terms of relative capabilities implies that such things can be observed and measured. If behavior among states either individually or in the aggregate seems to contradict expectations derived from structural realism, then measurement of capabilities and security become priorities for making revisions. In other words, the concrete manifestations are opened up for review while the hard core, stated in the abstract, remains intact. Substantive arguments over the millennia have not brought closure on the subject of what power means, so the suggestion that capabilities might be measured in ever-improving ways does not plunge structural realism into a debate over either a settled or a trivial matter.

Although capability is the natural focus of contention over findings that appear to contradict structural realism, the negative heuristic also calls for skepticism about research design-related issues in general. The example of arms races and war from the previous chapter reinforces this point. A conservative reading of results, whether friendly to structural realism or not, would be the norm derived from long-standing scientific practice. This point becomes even more important to consider as the number and complexity of steps in the research process continue, on average, to increase. As the "distance" between a theory and testing of its propositions becomes greater, the need for caution in drawing implications from results—especially at the more general level of evolutionary progress versus stagnation—comes to the fore.

Another basic question about the negative heuristic concerns what kinds of theorizing are ruled out altogether. This matter is crucial to scientific status because a theory cannot be falsified otherwise. Two limits on theorizing can be identified. One pertains to the status granted to a particular level (i.e., micro or macro) in the network of effects, and the other focuses on the nature of actors.

Structural realism rules out any explanation that is purely reductionist in nature. Waltz's (1979: 20–30) scathing indictment of the theory of imperialism, which refutes the notion that the economic superstructure of units can be used to account for imperialistic behavior, is the best illustration of that point. In the language of systemism, the contention is that no theory consisting of micro-macro linkages alone (i.e., x ———► Y) ever can be sufficient. Furthermore, structural realism also argues for theory construction that begins with macro-macro connections and strives for economy of explanation, so actor- or micro-oriented complications generally are regarded as more appropriate for models of foreign policy.

Another implicit methodological rule in structural realism prohibits behavior that will be designated as *strategic altruism*. If a state takes action that reduces its relative standing without a reasonable expectation of a later and greater improvement as a result, this other-regarding behavior—if such examples accumulate—creates the basis for eventual falsification of structural realism. Strategic altruism, if encountered, can be accounted for only by a theory that contradicts a parametric setting of the structural realist hard core. This is a crucial point because the research enterprise must be open to replacement by a potentially superior rival. *Tactical altruism,* by contrast, poses no threat to structural realism. If one or more states engage in actions that strengthen others at their expense, but they do so with the belief (even if mistaken) that it will result in eventual overall improvement of relative standing, that is nothing more than yet another manifestation of power politics.

Germany's participation in the Maastricht Treaty provides an example of tactical altruism in action. Given its preeminent position on the European continent, why would Germany agree to an economic and monetary union that reduced its autonomy in relation to the other states involved? On the surface, this behavior looks altruistic, with the Germans giving up potential and even likely relative gains under the alternative scenario of no such treaty. The need to balance capabilities at different levels, however, can account for Germany's participation in the Maastricht Treaty. While without question the leading state on the continent, Germany also needed to accept some restrictions on its influence in Europe in order for the European Community to balance in monetary affairs against Japan (Grieco 1995: 38). Thus German conduct in this case can be classified as a likely instance of tactical rather than strategic altruism.

Since states must be concerned with politics at multiple levels, ranging from global to intrastate, trade-offs are virtually certain to occur. Thus apparent anomalies-in-the-making may reflect instead the common and ongoing practice of tactical altruism among states that are seeking security through the best means available.

Structural realism's hard core and negative heuristic create its foundation. The parametric settings focus on both unit and system, so the potential for a full range of linkages, from micro-micro through macro-macro, already exists. Structural realism's negative heuristic designates capability and security as concepts that are subject to revision (as needed) at the level of measurement in order to protect its parametric settings. In other words, the failure of a hypothesis produces questions about the empirical meaning of capability, security, and other concepts within a particular analysis rather than the hard core of axioms itself. The negative heuristic also emphasizes the need for skepticism about empirical findings, especially those resulting from complex research designs that operate at some distance from the theory that presumably is being tested. With regard to qualitatively different kinds of theorizing, the negative heuristic rules out reductionism as a point of departure and prohibits strategic altruism. Thus the hard core and negative heuristic combine to form the basis for the positive heuristic of structural realism as a research enterprise devoted to international relations as a whole.

3. The Positive Heuristic of Structural Realism: Theories in Sequence

Identification of the positive heuristic for structural realism is a three-stage process. The first step, to be carried out at this point, focuses on description of empirical problems by the initial variant of structural realism and theories that build on its foundation: that is, T_0, T_1, T_2, ... The other stages, which cover explanation and prediction, are carried out more effectively through separate but interrelated reviews of (a) empirical testing that focuses on capability-based variables in connection to conflict, crisis, and war; and (b) war in particular as an empirical problem. These phases of the review take place in the following two sections of this chapter. When the first of those two stages is introduced, the role of each in representing the positive heuristic will be explained.

Structural realism's vision of international relations enables it to describe empirical problems that can be derived from its parametric settings (i.e., axioms P_1–P_6). An empirical problem takes the form of a *question* about an action or event, the value of which is expected to become clear on the basis of subsequent research findings. Thus the empirical problems described by structural realist theories will focus on the actions of states, the main units of the system, and the events that involve them. An action can be classified as one of two basic types, cooperation (C) or conflict (C'). By its very nature, structural realism focuses more on conflict, but it does not exclude the possibility of interstate cooperation. Given the presence of parameters P_3 and P_4 in particular (i.e., with anarchy and competition as governing principles), cooperation between and among states is anticipated to be tactical: that is, the ultimate concern always is for enhancement or at least preservation of security.

As noted, systemism identifies four kinds of connections that a theory might put forward: micro-micro, micro-macro, macro-micro, and macro-macro. This typology is useful in providing a basis for discussion of what structural realism can offer with regard to problem solving through description, explanation, or prediction. From the outset, it should be noted that description of empirical problems is theoretical. This component of the positive heuristic focuses on *articulation* of empirical problems, not the actions and events that already have occurred in world politics. Explanation and prediction are qualitatively different in that each of these constituents of the positive heuristic naturally pertains to the specific contents of the historical record. Thus further discussion of how empirical problems are to be described will focus on classes of actions and events in the abstract.

Since cooperation and conflict stand as the basic action categories, description of empirical problems will consist of questions about these actions or aggregations of them. It is the ability to ask a question about some manifestation of C or C' that counts toward descriptive achievement for a theory. Explanation and prediction, by contrast, require formally stated hypotheses.

With structural realism from Waltz (1979) designated as T_0, the initial variant of the theory, descriptive ability begins with the problem of interstate war as a manifestation of conflict. The problem of the causes of war is identified at the macro level by T_0's inclusion of anarchy (P_4) and pursuit of relative standing (P_3) among states, the principal units of the system (P_1). Relative standing, by definition, exists in finite quantity, and thus the ongoing potential for war (and, indeed, other forms of conflict) is created. Note that in describing the causes of war as an empirical problem, the onus is on a theory to show that it possesses a subset of concepts with the potential to appear, when combined in a formal sense, in an explanation. Thus, as put forward by Waltz, war as an event emerges as the basic empirical problem articulated by structural realism.

Cooperation also entails a main macro-level problem: power balancing—or, perhaps more accurately, capability balancing. States form balancing coalitions because of the concerns for security (P_3) associated with a given profile of capabilities in the system (P_6) under conditions of anarchy (P_4). As in the case of conflict, T_0 is able to articulate a basic problem of cooperation at the system level.

Each of the problems just described in the language developed in the current exposition corresponds to one of the basic claims made by Waltz (1979) for his theory of international politics, namely, that structural realism can address the recurrence of war and capability balancing in the system.[4] These are events rather than actions, and, as Waltz (1979: 122) acknowledges, the latter are another story. Thus initiation, for example, is a problem separate from whether a war occurs. Moreover, if an event such as war is assessed as a process, any number of other empirical problems of definite interest from a structural realist perspective can be identified. What about, for example, the questions of who joins in, and who exits, from a war? These and other action-related empirical problems become part of a research agenda beyond T_0, the initial variant of structural realism.

Efforts to advance the descriptive component of the positive heuristic as it developed after T_0 can be divided into two subsets. One consists of attempts to build upon T_0 through creation of full-fledged theories that are consistent with its hard core and negative heuristic. A theory can qualify for this status whether or not it is put forward exclusively as an extension of T_0; the important criterion is that it reasonably can be represented in that way. The other subset consists of what Zinnes (1980a, 1980b) and Nicholson (1989: 18, 218) describe as ad hoc hypothesis testing. Empirical problems in these instances are explained and (or) predicted on the basis of capability-oriented factors that appear consistent with the parametric settings of structural realism yet lack any explicit connection to the theory. These studies, as noted earlier, are reviewed in the following two sections of this chapter.

Perhaps the most amazing aspect of Waltz's (1979) structural realism is the *distribution* of time and effort in reaction to it: "[T]here have been attempts to apply Waltz's theory, attempts to debunk it, and some sympathetically critical attempts to defend it. But so far there has been surprisingly little sustained attempt to develop it" (Buzan, Jones, and Little 1993: 6). In over two decades, only a pair of subsequent studies would seem to approximate full-fledged, self-conscious efforts to build directly on the foundation created by Waltz. Each of these efforts, by Gilpin (1981) (i.e, T_1) and Buzan, Jones, and Little (1993) (i.e, T_2), will be summarized in the context of its continuity with, and points of departure from, the original exegesis in Waltz (1979). In other words, although T_1 and T_2 are not actual lineal descendants of T_0, they can be constructed effectively as extensions of T_0 within the hard core and negative heuristic of structural realism. At the conclusion of this review, the natural questions about why these and not other expositions are included as theories will be answered.

Gilpin's (1981) study on war and change in world politics stands on its own as a major work, with great influence on the application of hegemonic stability theory to international political economy in particular. This study, however, also can be read as an important extension of structural realism as a scientific research enterprise. It is at once consistent with the hard core of structural realism and also a step beyond the relatively static treatment of world politics implied by that theory. Thus Gilpin's theory is designated as T_1.

Gilpin identifies the problem of political change as a serious concern for system-level realist theory. On the one hand, Gilpin (1981) starts out by endorsing the basics of structural realism: "[T]he fundamental nature of international relations has not changed over the millennia. International relations continue to be a recurring struggle for wealth and power among independent actors in a state of anarchy" (7). On the other hand, Waltz's inherently static vision of the international system is developed further through Gilpin's specification of the process of political change (12). A system begins in a state of equilibrium and is disturbed by differential growth in capabilities among states. This produces a redistribution of capabilities in the system, which in turn leads to disequilibrium. The process is completed through resolution of the systemic crisis. Change at the level of the system is rare because it entails change in the "international distribution of power [i.e., capabilities], the hierarchy of prestige, and the rules and rights embodied in the system" (42). Thus incremental change in capabilities ultimately can alter the structure of the system itself, although so infrequently that the idea of the latter as a relatively enduring characteristic is preserved in T_1.

Gilpin's ability to address system-level change adds an important empirical problem to those that can be addressed by structural realism. As a theory, T_1 adds the assumption that incremental change in capability can produce a new structure at the system level. In the language of systemism, this qualifies as a micro-macro connection, of which none appeared in T_0. Thus, in the context of describing empirical problems, T_1 is an improvement over T_0: (a) it describes an additional and significant empirical problem; and (b) it introduces a qualitatively different kind of linkage, micro-macro, into what had been a strictly macro-macro theory.

While Gilpin's vision of international political change is somewhat removed from Waltz's version of structural realism—it introduces unit-level and governance-related factors into the treatment of system-level change and produces implications that war will occur over hegemonic status rather than for balancing purposes alone (Gilpin 1988)—this theory remains within the structural realist research enterprise. The reason is that the distribution of capabilities effects change in such nonrealist characteristics as prestige, rights, and rules. The extent to which any of the latter even exist is a reflection of control exercised by the system's great powers, so the structural realist vision of anarchy and competition among states remains intact.

Buzan, Jones, and Little (1993) are even more explicit than Gilpin in building on structural realism as articulated by Waltz, which they prefer to label as "neorealism" (6). Thus the theory put forward by Buzan, Jones, and Little is designated as T_2. It moves much further away than Gilpin from the original formulation, however, and can be regarded as paradigmatically different than T_0 if read literally. Its points of continuity and difference with the initial variant of structural realism will be addressed in turn.

Buzan, Jones, and Little (1993) claim to follow in the realist tradition, with an emphasis on the primacy of politics and "acceptance of Waltz's basic definitional framework for international structure" (11). Three key differences from Waltz are noted: (a) a more comprehensive definition of structure is deployed; (b) structure is not regarded as the only systemic-level factor in operation; and (c) the analogy with microeconomics is discarded. The nature and implications of each of these developments will be explored in turn.

Buzan, Jones, and Little (1993) view capability and therefore structure as multidimensional: "The end result of disaggregating and de-restricting the distribution of capabilities is a fairly limited set of possible distributional structures based on four types of attribute: military capability, economic capability, political cohesion, and ideology" (64). This proposed disaggregation reflects a desire to address a wider range of issues through a context-dependent measurement of the distribution of capabilities. The shift to four kinds of capability, according to Buzan, Jones, and Little, does not challenge the "simplicity of deep structure" (59); anarchy continues as the foundation of the international system. Instead, the change is consistent with the idea that capabilities can vary in importance from one situation to another (Keohane and Nye 1977, 1987, 1989).

Another shift from the initial variant of structural realism concerns introduction of interaction capacity to complement structure as a system-level factor. *Interaction capacity* refers to the quality of technological and societal capabilities across the international system (Buzan, Jones, and Little 1993: 79). This factor defines a range within which structural realism is relevant. If interaction capacity is too low, no international system exists; should it instead become too high, that could turn into a society of states as envisioned by Grotius (Guzzini 1998: 22; see also Bull and Watson 1984; Watson 1992; Kacowicz 1998). Within the boundaries just noted, the distribution of interaction capacity could affect the pace of events and even their outcomes; for example, greater complexity might be harmful if it accelerates escalation of conflict. Thus interaction capacity creates the potential to address an additional set of empirical problems.

Buzan, Jones, and Little (1993: 234) also move away from structural realism's microeconomic analogy. The door therefore is open to diverging internal structures among states. The reason is that external pressures, when interacting with the individual circumstances of states, can produce different yet equally viable strategies and tactics. Consider the assessment offered by Rogowski (1999): "The classical realist position, according to which domestic institutions quickly and automatically evolve toward a single 'best adapted' form, finds little support in the research to date. Countries differ greatly in their institutional forms—extent and effectiveness of franchise, methods of election, decision rules—and there is good evidence that these differences profoundly affect the style and relative success of their foreign policy" (135). Whether recognition of this preceding argument constitutes a rejection of structural realism's fifth parameter—that states are undifferentiated by function—is a matter of emphasis.

Buzan, Jones, and Little (1993: 241) assert that anarchy can produce states with different structures, and they obviously are correct. Even under the intense pressure of Cold War competition, states survived by relying upon widely diverging economic and political systems. Thus it is possible to distinguish *input* as a process from *output* in functional terms. States as different as Canada and Cameroon sustain mandatory taxation and provide public goods that show remarkable uniformity of type; in particular, the very small number of states without a military security establishment of some sort should be noted. Convergence of function is visible almost everywhere, while the *means* toward such ends vary greatly.

Furthermore, the greater success of one state versus another in providing the standard public goods, most notably military security, should be equated with a difference in degree rather than in kind. With assorted factor endowments among states, it is reasonable to expect variation in both means pursued and ends achieved. This point is reinforced by the ongoing character of a basic component of structural realism, namely, the distribution of capabilities, which never features strict equality.

This discussion of the same goals being pursued through various means is ironic on the surface because it can be derived in a straightforward way from P_2, the parameter asserting rational choice. Comparative advantage in human and material factors of production implies variation in internal structure. States can be expected to use different means toward the end of security seeking as a result of what they have to offer both in terms of self-help and as possible coalition partners.[5] Thus the claim that Buzan, Jones, and Little make about introducing functional differentiation can be interpreted in one of two ways. If it is taken literally, the result is initiation of a research enterprise that departs from structural realism. However, a focus on different means rather than ends preserves continuity; states are expected to react to structural imperatives by deploying resources efficiently, which creates internal differentiation as a by-product.

Perhaps a deeper point of irony emerges when the call for functional differentiation is linked to Buzan, Jones, and Little's recommendation that capabilities be disaggregated into four categories. The latter idea shows recognition that power will be exerted in context through application of appropriate means. States will vary in capabilities and can be expected to resort to mixtures of approaches and substitution in efforts to maintain or enhance security. Thus the acknowledgment of variable degrees of relevance for capabilities across situations also suggests an awareness of diversity in means pursued at the intrastate level. The rationality axiom demands nothing less.

With the respective efforts of Gilpin (1981) and Buzan, Jones, and Little (1993) described as the successor theories to Waltz (1979), it becomes feasible to answer the questions noted at the outset of this phase of the review: (a) Why designate these two entities as theories? and (b) Why exclude others? Since T_1 and T_2 have been compared to T_0, and the idea of a series of theories is central to the concept of a research enterprise, it also is appropriate to ask another question: (c) How do T_1 and T_2 look relative to each other?

For an answer to the question of what should appear in the sequence T_0, T_1, ... for structural realism, it is useful to return to figure 3.1, which showed six theories in the context of a discussion about the role of parameters in setting boundaries for membership in a paradigm. Recall that theories A and B linked stability to polarity and had opposite signs for the anticipated connection but resided, according to the parameter-based criteria, within the same paradigm. Although each theory looks on the surface like an individual hypothesis, that is misleading. The discussion of these theories connected each of them to common parametric settings for an identified paradigm—a point not conveyed in the diagrammatic exposition. Thus both of the theories have a foundation in the hard core and negative heuristic for a research enterprise.[6]

Within the world of international relations, however, formation of a context in the manner of a moment ago is *not* the norm. As Waltz (1997: 913) points out, individual propositions or sets of them, of which there is no shortage, do not stand as theories. Although these entities can *develop* into theories, creation of the deeper foundation of an axiomatic basis and methodological rules is found only in exceptional instances. While the existence of one or more propositions can be regarded as necessary for an entity to claim status as a theory, it does not constitute a *sufficient* condition. This argument can be linked to the way in which concepts are arranged along the continuum of aggregation from hypothesis to worldview. The continuum possesses the basic property of a scale, which in this context means that each more general point encompasses those more specific than itself. Thus one or more freestanding statements of the nature "If x, then y" count as hypotheses rather than theories because they are not grounded in the principles of an overarching paradigmatic entity, which in turn "flies the flag" of a designated ontology, and so on.

When the expositions of Gilpin (1981) and Buzan, Jones, and Little (1993) are placed in the context of the analysis just concluded, status as theories in a sequence following Waltz (1979) becomes much more obvious. T_1 and T_2 are consistent with the hard core of T_0, and each of these theories builds on that foundation. As for T_2's place in sequence after T_1, more than mere chronological order is involved in that designation. Buzan, Jones, and Little do not contradict Gilpin on the subject of political change; instead, they introduce a series of innovations that make it feasible to explore Gilpin's micro-macro linkage more effectively. The expanded definition of structure, which recognizes the need to match capabilities with context, certainly enhances that potential. So too does Buzan, Jones, and Little's analysis of internal differences between states with regard to the means that might be used to obtain security. Interaction capacity as described by Buzan, Jones, and Little serves as a refinement of Waltz's general sense of epistemic conditions—a question that Gilpin did not pursue. Thus all of the developments put forward in T_2 either build on T_1 in an indirect way or open new vistas. This establishes the place of T_2 after T_1 in the sequence starting with T_0.

One component of the positive heuristic, a series of theories based on the hard core of structural realism, has been identified. The others will be specified in the following two sections.

4. The Positive Heuristic of Structural Realism: Elements of Structure

Review of the positive heuristic so far is consistent with the general frame of reference established by Lakatos (1970, 1971), in which a series of theories is identified. The key difference, introduced via the concept of a scientific research enterprise, is a focus on empirical problems rather than content. At this point the ideal vision of a positive heuristic conveyed by Lakatos and its application to international relations as a discipline diverge in important ways. The points of difference emerge because of two features associated with the framework derived from Lakatos when applied to a specific field of study: (a) extremely high standards for programmatic coherence and (b) a lack of operational instructions. The difference between Lakatos's sense of a positive heuristic and what it is reasonable to expect from a review of structural realism (or, for that matter, any other paradigmatic entity in international relations) will be explained at this point.

Lakatos (1970, 1971) presents a vision of the positive heuristic that is intended for general application, but its use in explicating research from a particular discipline requires considerable adjustment to circumstance. Lakatos (1971) sees the positive heuristic as defining problems, constructing auxiliary propositions—even foreseeing anomalies and turning them "victoriously" into examples—and all according to a preconceived plan (99). This vision, to put it mildly, is intimidating and impractical when treated as a literal account of how science should take place. As described by Lakatos, the scientists working within the positive heuristic look like an advancing army that uses superb strategy and tactics to win one victory after another. To social scientists, alas, this sounds more like fantasy than reality. The academic "armies" of international relations, for example, fall victim to surprises, find fault with their generals, and seem to spend a significant amount of time in retreat as well as advance.

Use of the preceding metaphor, of course, proves nothing, but it does set the stage for showing where adjustments need to be made if the positive heuristic is to play a useful role in application to research in practice, whether for international relations or elsewhere. This point refers to compromises beyond the substitution of empirical problems for content, a change that already is in place. Some further accommodations are needed before the framework can be used to complete an overview of research in relation to structural realism.

To begin, the degree of integration between empirical research in the positive heuristic and the foundation of a research enterprise, expressed in terms of a hard core and negative heuristic, often borders on invisible in practice. This disjunction already is recognized by Lakatos (1971) at a general level, and the point certainly finds particular application to capability-oriented research in international relations. As noted in chapter 3, Lakatos (1971) posits the existence of three kinds of ad hoc hypotheses; since the concern here is not with content measures, only the third type, ad hoc$_3$, is relevant.[7] The reference is to propositions that do not form an "integral part" of the positive heuristic. It seems implied that an effort to review such hypotheses, with an eye to potential integration with the positive heuristic, would not be misplaced. This idea is not put forward by Lakatos, but it seems like a natural derivation from his analysis.

With regard to empirical research on capability-based indicators and international relations, the above-noted course of action becomes essential. An enormous amount of research connects potential elements of structure—that is, indicators based on the distribution of capabilities among states—to various forms of cooperation and conflict (Brecher 1993; Vasquez 1993, 1998; Geller and Singer 1998; Leng 1999). As will become apparent from the continuing process of review, very little of the theorizing or testing reveals more than a tenuous association with the hard core and negative heuristic of structural realism. Connections can be established, but that is a quest for an elaborated structural realism rather than the current review, which focuses on the existing positive heuristic.

From the preceding analysis emerges the first adjustment that is made in further identification of the positive heuristic: To create maximum potential for expansion of structural realism's problem-solving capacity, it makes sense to address capability-based research in general rather than the restricted subset of instances with an established connection to the hard core as described in table 4.1.

Another area of adjustment concerns how much to include in the forthcoming stages of review. A compromise between comprehensiveness and feasibility becomes necessary. While creation of maximum potential for problem solving is an admirable goal, it is beyond the scope of a single study to address the full range of hypotheses and evidence that connect the distribution of capabilities to international cooperation and conflict. A process of sampling therefore becomes necessary, which explains the presence and character of each respective phase of the review.

First, connections involving elements of structure with conflict, crisis, and war will be enumerated. The elements in the survey are organized according to the typology presented in chapter 2: primary, secondary, tertiary, and higher order. Conflict, crisis, and war, the full set and two important subsets of C' identified in chapter 2, provide a wide variety of actions and events for the review. Thus hypothesis generation and testing map a domain composed of elements of structure onto a range of empirical problems that fall within the intended purview of structural realism as a scientific research enterprise.

Second, a specific subset of empirical problems—those related to the causes of war—will be singled out for a closer look. This is a natural complement to the preceding exercise because sampling takes place on what social scientists would describe as the dependent variable. Thus one stage of review focuses on what a set of independent variables can say with respect to a range of dependent variables, while the other features an attempt at a more precise description of what is known about a particular dependent variable. Given the agenda of structural realism, the natural starting point for the latter account is the causes of war.

Taken together, the impending surveys of structural elements and knowledge about the causes of war should be sufficient to produce a tentative sense of "what is out there." Two further adjustments, one of which already exists implicitly, will make it feasible to move forward with the two-stage review. One is that conflict, in the encompassing sense for the first stage and manifested by war in particular at the second stage, is the focal point for the survey. It simply would be overwhelming to include cooperation as well—the range of substantive issues is daunting from the outset (Axelrod 1984; Martin 1993, 2000; Lusztig 1996). The other compromise concerns the evidence considered. Findings based on quantitative analysis are more conducive to the kind of aggregation and synthesis at issue here. In particular, the rules for tentative acceptance or rejection of a hypothesis tend to be more explicit and agreed upon among research participants. Furthermore, aggregate data analysis of conflict, crisis, and war converges over the decades toward the use of data from the International Crisis Behavior (ICB), Correlates of War (COW), and Militarized Interstate Dispute (MID) Projects, which further increases the comparability of results. To include case studies as well would make both stages of the review unmanageable.

Neither of these adjustments should bias the review and later assessment toward a favorable treatment of structural realism. It is more appropriate to begin with analysis of what capability-based variables can say about conflict rather than cooperation because this constitutes the "home field" for structural realism.[8] Failure to perform well in accounting for conflict, therefore, would constitute a greater setback because this behavior is more central to the self-appointed mandate of structural realist theorizing. The focus on data analysis rather than case studies also tends to raise the bar for capability-based explanations. No matter how rigorously they are conducted, the results of case studies are more prone to reinterpretation that favors a given proposition. The summary statistics and measures of association generated by aggregate data studies, by contrast, must be assessed with caution but ultimately are more difficult to defy when they continue to refute one or more propositions.

Attention shifts, at this point, to theory and evidence about elements of structure as related to conflict processes. Primary, secondary, tertiary, and higher-order elements are considered in turn. In each category, respective elements are identified, along with associated research findings on war and other manifestations of conflict. No attempt is made to provide a rigorous ordering of elements within each level.[9] Instead, elements appear in an order that approximates relative familiarity.

Table 4.2 provides an overview of the specific findings that derive from the review that follows. As will become apparent, the pattern is one of single factors being used to explain "more complex and dynamic processes" (Leng 1999: 138). The characteristics of findings summarized by the table will be discussed collectively at the end of the review.

4.1 Primary Elements of Structure

Primary elements of structure are based on the distribution of capabilities but entail neither complex calculations nor coalitions.[10] Five elements—great-power status, first and second place in the hierarchy, the number of great powers, and overall size of the system—have attracted attention so far with respect to formation of hypotheses and empirical testing. The logic and findings related to each element are summarized in turn.

Great-power status is a basic element of structure. (Although this element and the two that follow might appear to be actor attributes, each nonetheless is a visible product of the distribution of capabilities in the system and therefore qualifies as a primary element.) Bremer (1980: 58) cites several reasons why such states might be more prone to war. A state may have gained from war; hence its high level of capabilities and positive disposition toward further

Table 4.2

Capability-Based Elements and International Conflict, Crisis, and War: Characteristics of Findings

Type of Element	Elements Included in Review	Characteristics of Findings
primary	great-power status	great powers are more likely to be involved in war, militarized interstate disputes and crises
	first-place state in hierarchy	most likely to be involved in wars
	second-place state in hierarchy	most likely to initiate war
	number of great powers	mixed results for unipolarity and war; multipolarity is linked to war in the twentieth century; polycentrism is most prone to crisis-generated turmoil
	overall size of system	a larger system is more prone to interstate disputes
secondary	concentration among great powers	moderate degree of concentration is associated with war; low level of concentration for either great powers or leading state is linked to crisis-generated instability
	rank-ordering	higher ranking states are more likely to initiate and participate in wars
	position along capability cycle	crisis and war involvement increase for great powers in proximity to critical points
	dyadic transition	likelihood of war increases at transition in capabilities
	dyadic transition coupled with concentration	likelihood of war increases with transition and systemic deconcentration
tertiary	extent of alliance commitments	alliances correlate with war in twentieth century, opposite for nineteenth century, most relevant to great powers
	size of alliances	larger alliances are more war-prone
	alliance status in dyads	war is more likely when one state is allied to a major power and the other is not
higher-order	alliance polarization	war is more likely at high and low levels of polarization; militarized interstate disputes build up under high polarization
	balance of overall capabilities in a dyad	parity is associated with war
	distribution of capabilities within alliances	even distribution linked to dispute buildup

military activity. Other concerns of the most powerful states might include regulation of the system or protecting a reputation for assertiveness, either of which could lead to additional involvement in war. Thus great-power status might be linked to either initiation or participation in international conflict.

Small and Singer (1970, 1982) use COW data (from 1816 to 1980 by the second set of tests) to show that major power involvement in war is greater than that of minor powers.[11] This finding is reinforced, with some nuances, by Geller's (1988: 367, 371) analysis of all states that fought in two or more wars from 1816 to 1965. Geller discovers that major powers are more likely to fight severe wars and less likely to fight moderate wars than are minor powers, while both are equally likely to fight small wars.

Three studies focus on capability status in relation to conflicts other than war. Eberwein's (1982) replication of Bremer's (1980) study offers reinforcement through linkage of great power status to more frequent use of military force. Gochman and Maoz (1984: 611) find that major powers are more active in militarized interstate disputes. Brecher (1993: 76) reports a similar connection: 37 percent of foreign policy crises from 1918 to 1988 involve great powers (or superpowers), which is a far higher proportion than would be expected by chance.

Some studies focus on the specific positions held by individual states in the hierarchy of capabilities. The first- and second-place states are singled out for attention because of the special qualities that might be expected from contenders for leadership. Various theories, from hegemonic stability to power transition, have ascribed certain characteristics to these special states (Gilpin 1987; Organski and Kugler 1980).

Köhler (1975) uses COW data to assess whether the highest-ranking state in the system varies in war involvement in comparison to the times at which it lacks that designation. The study of fifteen leading states reveals a significantly lower amount of participation in war once this special status is gone. Bremer (1980) provides further evidence for this finding and adds an important detail: the highest-ranking state had the greatest frequency of involvement in war, but the second-place power most often *initiated* wars. This difference is consistent with Organski and Kugler's (1980) power transition theory, arguing that, through challenges, a second-place state will seek to improve its position relative to the leader.

Perhaps the most important aspect of structure, if the sheer volume of debate provides an indicator, is the number of poles in the international system. This concept has been the subject of long-standing controversy; the debate over polarity and stability combines "elements of what are called polarity and polarization" (Hart 1985: 33). In more specific terms, Goldmann (1974) notes that "a clear distinction is not always made between the international power structure ('polarity') on the one hand and the structure of international interaction ('polarization') on the other" (103).[12] The frequently cited concepts of pole, polarity, and polarization need to be clarified: What does each putative element mean, and where might it belong in the typology of structure? Poles and polarity will be covered at this point, with polarization being addressed later as a higher-order element of structure.

Some degree of consensus seems to have emerged about the first of these concepts over the last two decades. Bueno de Mesquita (1979) identifies the "number of poles, blocs, or clusters of nations in the system" (114) as one of the two principal aspects of polarity to consider in the context of the causes of war. Østergaard (1983), describing the world of the 1980s as one of "multipolarity," reveals a similar perspective: "The key states are the USA, the Soviet Union, Japan and two groups of states, the EEC and the Third World" (249). Although these designations would appear to mix states and groups of states together, that is a step beyond prior treatments of polarity. Bueno de Mesquita, for instance, separates the number of poles—or blocs of states—from the characteristics of the bonds linking states, most commonly assessed in terms of interstate alliances. This distinction removes at least one source of confusion from the debate, since characteristics of the alliance infrastructure then can be dealt with separately as higher-order elements of structure.

Linked most commonly to the subset of great powers in world politics, polar status is identified on the basis of observed or potential behavior, measured in terms of relatively high capabilities (Levy 1983: 16; Domke 1989: 161; Stoll 1989: 136). For example, a state that exerts influence on politics in multiple regions also will tend to be polar, in the sense that its policies attract the support of some states and repel others. More explicit designations appear in studies by Levy (1984) and Wayman (1985: 118–19). "Whereas size refers to the number of Great Powers," Levy argues, "polarity is best defined in terms of the distribution of military capabilities among the Great Powers" (345). In a like manner, Wayman identifies two dimensions, describing power polarity in terms of the number of prominent power centers, with *cluster polarity* referring essentially to the tightness and discreteness of coalitions. Although the terminology is somewhat different—size versus power polarity—it is clear that, in each instance, the number of major powers is equated with the number of poles.

Given that the number of poles is a distinct element of structure, what is its presumed linkage with systemic propensity toward conflict? Two basic points of comparison have culminated in efforts toward testing. One concerns the potential desirability of a unipolar world juxtaposed with others. The other concerns systems with two or more poles in comparison to each other. Each comparison will be explored in turn.

One idea, borrowed from Kindleberger's (1959, 1973, 1977) analysis of economic system management, is that a unipolar world would be more stable and less prone to destructive conflict. The leading state could be expected to maintain order (Organski 1958). The existence of one or more challengers, by contrast, is expected to provide the basis for instability across the board (Organski and Kugler 1980; Gilpin 1981).

Sustained debate over how the number of poles might be connected to conflict started with advocates of bipolar systems versus those with more centers of capability. The classic argument over the issue took shape almost forty years ago, with bipolarity confronting multipolarity as basic options (Waltz 1964; Deutsch and Singer 1964). Disagreement over the most stable system persists (James and Brecher 1988; Brecher and James 1989; Dougherty and Pfaltzgraff 1990, 1996; Kegley and Raymond 1992; Kim and Bueno de Mesquita 1995; James 1995; Brecher and Wilkenfeld 1997).

Some arguments in favor of the relative stability of a bipolar system can be traced directly to Waltz (1964: 882–87; see also 1967), the most persistent advocate of bipolarity, while others that will be acknowledged have more recent origins.[13] Each argument in favor of a system with two poles will be presented in turn, with appropriate extensions.

First, with only two leading powers, the system has no peripheries and should be simpler to manage (Waltz 1964; Morgenthau and Thompson 1985: 391; Gaddis 1986, 1987). The most obvious advantage is the absence of coalitional dynamics among great powers. Although the two leading states naturally could be expected to vie for influence around the globe, each also would have a relatively clear understanding of its situation. Conflicts over spheres of influence would be easier to manage and even resolve; all other things being equal, it is less difficult to obtain agreement from two parties than a larger number.

Second, all changes are deemed relevant by the two major actors as part of their competition, so developments are monitored closely (Waltz 1964). Failure to keep up with the rival power is one way in which bipolarity could become unstable, so it is important that the leaders remain attentive (Gilpin 1981: 235, 237). Since coalitions are ruled out in attempting to restore equality—by definition, other states are too weak individually to tip the balance—only efforts from within each actor have the potential to preserve the equilibrium.[14] A shift in the bilateral balance of capabilities involving the two principal states therefore could occur because of asymmetric levels of military spending, unequal support for client states, or other differences in policy.[15] Given the presumed concern for relative capabilities, neither duopolist is expected to allow its rival to achieve an overwhelming position. Should the adversary engage in escalated military expenditures or aggressive deployment, it can anticipate a response in kind (Richardson 1960). Of course, this property does not rule out short-term, reversible increases in resource allocations toward domestic needs in order to reduce internal political pressures.

Third, and closely related to the previous point, preponderant power should encourage the two leading states to act as system managers (Waltz 1964; George 1988b: 644). Although eager to improve its relative position, each great power also would be aware of how much there was to lose. Being evenly matched, the leading states would have to weigh marginal gains against potentially much greater losses from a conflict that could escalate beyond control. Adventurism by proxies would be likely to be restrained, at least to some degree, because that sort of behavior ultimately could endanger the very status of the leading powers. Aggressive actions would be expected under conditions of anarchy, but only if gains could be made without seriously endangering the vested interest of superior status.

Midlarsky (1988: 49–52), in a discussion of the dynamics of resource distribution, provides a fourth argument in favor of bipolarity. If capabilities are distributed randomly, with an equal likelihood that over time any state will receive a given item, it is possible to estimate the number of states that will receive any particular level of endowment. In a bipolar system, the expectation is that equality will result. However, that property holds for multipolarity only if the overall amount of resources is large.[16] Thus bipolarity can be expected to produce an equal and presumably stable distribution of capabilities under a wider range of conditions than multipolarity.

Fifth, and finally, recurrent crises are expected to provide a substitute for war, with disagreements being handled in an incremental fashion. With preponderant power and close monitoring, the crises that do arise are anticipated to focus on secondary matters. The potential for escalation is minimal, with the principal value of such confrontations being cathartic in nature. Rather than storing grievances, which could explode into world war, tensions are dissipated through third-party conflict in a series of contained environments. While this argument might appear cynical, it is motivated by a realist-oriented belief that some degree of conflict is inevitable.

Other scholars suggest that a system with more than two poles would be preferable.[17] In a salient counterpoint to Waltz, Deutsch and Singer (1964: 390–406) noted a basic advantage for multipolarity, namely, that a larger set of vital actors allows for a greater number of interaction opportunities. This property would make confrontation less likely because each system member would direct a smaller share of its attention to any other specific actor. In particular, the potential for highly destructive conflict would be lower. Sporadic conflicts involving different subsets of the international polity, all other things being equal, would be less likely to produce an overall buildup of hostility in the system. Thus the probability of an all-encompassing war also would be reduced.

Given the lower level of dyadic confrontation between pairs of states, a further effect of the proliferation of central actors would be the dampening of arms races (Deutsch and Singer 1964; Copper 1975: 415). By contrast, in a world of two competing superpowers "each action by one will be viewed as a strategic gambit by the other" (Rosecrance 1966: 314–27). The resulting danger of misperception thus would be very high, along with the likelihood of an arms race.

According to a formal analysis of balance of power politics, a world with two leading powers poses special problems (Niou, Ordeshook, and Rose 1989: 78). Any established advantage in relative capabilities should lead to a war of conquest. With only two significant powers, only strict equality will ensure stability. By contrast, consider a world with three major powers, each of which controls less than 50 percent of total capabilities. If two align against a third, the latter always can attempt to split the coalition by offering one of its members a better deal. Such manipulations might continue indefinitely, meaning that coalitions actually could assist in the prevention of war.

Finally, multipolarity "lessens the total nature of war" (Copper 1975: 415). With more than two actors, a main axis of conflict is less likely to develop. Cross-cutting cleavages could help to prevent division of the major powers into two exclusive coalitions. If and when warfare occurs, it is less likely to be all-inclusive.[18] In comparisons of bipolarity to multipolarity, plausible arguments emerge on each side.[19] Either configuration could be regarded as superior without contradicting structural realism as it currently is constituted. Rosecrance's (1966) suggestion of "bimultipolarity" (322) as a preferred system reveals the nature of the impasse that results from this situation. In this mixed option, bipolarity at the global level is complemented by important powers that "act as mediators and buffers for conflicts between the bipolar powers" in at least some regions (322). This attempt at compromise, however, reveals the deeper nature of the problem within the debate over poles and conflict: the motives behind state behavior, including both great and ordinary powers, are by no means obvious. Given the assumption of self-interest that is at least implicit on both sides of the debate, why would local powers have an incentive to seek compromise between the two leading states? Would the existence of important, albeit regional, centers of capability not complicate the world and therefore diminish one of the crucial advantages associated with bipolarity? In fact, there is no reason to decide that, under conditions of anarchy and self-interest among states, bimultipolarity necessarily would be any more stable than the basic alternatives. Further assumptions are required to reach such a conclusion. In particular, systematic weighting of the various factors would be required to reach any compelling judgment.

Consider some interesting speculation on the conditions under which bipolarity or multipolarity might be preferred: "The relative simplicity of forces and relationships in a single-tier, two-power situation is the optimum condition of equilibrium, or stability, when both powers are rational and conservative. Complexity, and unpredictability of political and military responses, may be the only deterrent to offensive thrusts by an expansionist power which is ruthless but rationally calculates its risks and probabilities of meaningful gains" (Liska 1962: 276). Once again, in order to anticipate the level of conflict resulting from a given state of polarity, the reactions of *units* in the system must be accounted for in some way.

Bueno de Mesquita (1980b) points out the need for unit-system linkage in a more specific and explicit manner, focusing on the role of risk propensity in the argument over two versus multiple centers of capability. He asserts that multipolarity is preferred if actors are assumed to be risk averse because a more complex environment discourages the initiation of war or other forms of intense conflict. By contrast, the argument against multipolarity as a more stable system entails the assumption that leaders are not averse to risk. Thus Bueno de Mesquita concludes that neither bipolarity nor multipolarity should be superior if preferences for risk taking are assumed to be distributed normally among the population of states. This assessment reinforces the point that assertions about relative stability ultimately depend on building in macro-micro and micro-micro connections, among others.

Arguments over tripolarity, a three-actor variant of multipolarity, also illustrate the difficulty associated with finding determinate differences. With three principal actors, each of which possesses no more than 50 percent of the system's resources, Niou, Ordeshook, and Rose (1989) predict that "no nation will be eliminated" (95). When any two line up against the third, the latter always can offer a better deal to one of its rivals, escaping termination through transfer of resources. Gilpin (1981), by contrast, considers tripolarity to be the most unstable system of all: "[T]he emergence of a powerful China, Japan or united Europe would undoubtedly prove to be a destabilizing factor in contemporary [bipolar] world politics" (91). This expectation implies either a war between a firm coalition of two actors against a third or a series of intense conflicts that involve shifting alliances. The basis of disagreement over tripolarity is clear: in one exposition, potential countercoalitions are considered likely to preserve the viability of actors; in the other, these complications are presumed to increased the likelihood of war. The crucial difference of opinion is over potential for escalation inherent in the sequence of conflicts among the great powers. Of course, either line of reasoning about tripolarity (and, indirectly, multipolarity in general) would be consistent with structural realism in its current form. So are some obvious contemporary and historical instances. China, the United States, and European Union (a tripolar set, for the sake of argument) seem to coexist without war, at least so far, while France, Britain, and Spain (allowing for France's possibly marginal polar status due to persistent civil strife [Mattingly 1959]) proved incapable of avoiding that outcome in the late sixteenth century.

When summing up the debate over poles and stability, it is clear that arguments on both sides rest on hidden assumptions. Why, for example, would presumably self-interested great powers or superpowers want to bear the burden of acting as system managers? Multipolarity might allow for sharing of obligations among a few more states, making it less costly on an individual basis to maintain order. Of course, it is not clear that dispersing responsibility would be a good idea either. Consider another standard item in the debate, referring to the lower level of global confrontation expected in a multipolar world: Why should it be assumed that a proliferation of bilateral arms races would not occur? If that is acknowledged as a possible and even likely result, why would these many rivalries be more desirable—meaning less likely to produce a conflict spiral—than a simple, bilateral competition? Of course, it is just as easy to claim on behalf of multipolarity that the many dyadic contacts would tend toward cooperation. In the absence of further assumptions about actor responses to the system, however, that is not a compelling response.

All of this points toward one inescapable conclusion: it is possible to construct a reasonable argument in favor of bipolarity, multipolarity, or even a hybrid system.

To generate specific, falsifiable assertions about the number of capability centers and system-level instability in terms of either war or other indicators, additional premises are required. Perhaps Kegley and Raymond (1992) have put things best: "[T]he inferences generated by both formal and informal deductive modeling must be tempered by the insights generated by inductive empirical analysis" (574). Thus it is useful at this point to turn to the evidence about capability centers and instability.

Only a few studies focus on unipolarity, in all likelihood because it is regarded as such an exceptional state of affairs. The results, at any rate, are mixed. Thompson (1986) uses both COW and other data on war that span the years from 1494 to 1983; he finds unipolarity and quasi-unipolarity to be less war prone than either bipolarity or multipolarity. Mansfield (1988), with a similar time frame (1495 to 1980) but a somewhat different data set and indicators, reports that the frequency of war per annum is higher during unipolarity. Finally, Spiezio's (1990) tracking of the capabilities of Great Britain, the system leader from 1815 to 1939, produces a noteworthy inverse correlation with the frequency of war. This finding would seem to favor unipolarity in terms of hegemonic leadership. Given the rare and temporary nature of unipolarity in the modern states system, it probably is much more significant to understand the relative qualities of configurations with two or more centers of capability.

Several studies use aggregate data on international war to assess how the number of poles might be connected to international conflict. Haas (1970b) examines patterns of stratification and instability from the eighteenth century onward for twenty-one geographic subsystems. He defines stratification as the degree of concentration of capabilities within a subsystem, effectively isolating a set of major powers, and conceives of instability in terms of "rates of incidence of warfare" (99–100). The results are not directly comparable to those of the other studies that will be reviewed—the data cover a longer time span than the standard compilation from the COW Project—but they do possess a certain degree of similarity. Haas (1970b; see also Roskin and Berry 1990: 504, 505) summarizes his discoveries in the following manner: "The choice between bipolar versus multipolar arrangements now seems clear. If a state or group of states is willing to accept long wars that are won by aggressor states, bipolarity provides an escape from the more warprone character of historical multipolar subsystems. Multipolarity entails more violence, more countries at war and more casualties; bipolarity brings fewer but longer wars" (121). Such mixed results, as will become apparent, are by no means unusual for bivariate testing of propositions based on elements of structure.

Singer and colleagues (Singer, Bremer, and Stuckey 1972; Singer 1979: 165–69, 173) use COW data for the period from 1820 to 1965 to conduct bivariate testing that links the number of poles to the pervasiveness of war. They measure the concentration of capabilities among major powers, with a lower level viewed as corresponding to a greater degree of multipolarity. With regard to the dependent variable, warlikeness, Singer and colleagues measure the average annual amount of war underway in the system at half-decade intervals. In the nineteenth century, bipolarity shows a positive linkage to the pervasiveness of war, with the reverse being true in the twentieth century.

With a different treatment of the dependent variable, Cannizzo (1978: 951–53, 957) replicates the study by Singer, Bremer, and Stuckey. Adopting a state-level orientation, she measures the average annual nation-months of interstate war in which a given major power was involved. Like others, Cannizzo finds an intercentury breakpoint within the period from 1816 to 1965. In the nineteenth century, the summary statistics—considered for each state in turn—did not approach the level attained for the system. The concentration of capabilities in the system, taken to be an approximate measurement of its extent of bipolarity, predicted war involvement for the individual state much less accurately than it had for the collectivity of major powers. In the twentieth century, a major power's involvement in war tended to follow periods of parity and rapid change toward parity, although the model could explain 50 percent of the variance in warlikeness for only one state, China.

On the basis of data from the COW Project for the period from 1824 to 1938, Ostrom and Aldrich (1978) found the probability of war to be "moderately large" in a bipolar system, minimal with three poles, greater with four and five actors, and drastically lower with six powers. A more sophisticated, regression-type analysis of the same data supported a combination of "Balancer [i.e., N = 3] and Deutsch-Singer hypotheses [i.e., multiple points of contact]" (762–63). This pattern, meaning that the probability of war is lower with either three or more than five great powers, is consistent with the initial set of results. Unfortunately, the results of the study as a whole are inconsistent. While three centers of power permit balancing in favor of the power on the defensive, so do five if approximate equality is assumed. A third power can join an existing coalition that favors the status quo, thereby standing in the way of the revisionists. Yet the results point toward the warlike nature of a system with five powers. Furthermore, on the basis of the data analysis, six or more great powers must be regarded as sufficient to disperse attention and lessen the impact of confrontation, while five are not. To explain these results, it is necessary to develop a more complex model of the impact of centers of capability on the probability of war or conflict in general. Otherwise, only ad hoc explanations can cope with the twists and turns in the above-noted results.

While investigating the impact of the number of poles on several indicators of war among greater powers from 1495 to 1975, Levy (1984) identifies two complicating factors. Levy relies on three indicators of systemic war proneness: "The *frequency* of war is the number of wars in a given period. *Magnitude* refers to the total nation-years of war among participating Powers and reflects its spatial-temporal scope. The *severity* of war reflects its human destructiveness and is measured by the number of battle fatalities" (349). No connection emerges for war and the number of poles in a system, ranging from four to eight. Since the size of the Great Power system has changed very little, it cannot explain significant variations in stability (350–52). Effective arguments about the number of poles therefore must rely on *discontinuities*. In other words, since the absolute number of major powers always is small, expectations should be formulated in terms of breakpoints: for example, in the classic debate over stability and polarity, the difference between two and three or more such entities is regarded as crucial. Another complication to bear in mind is the multidimensional nature of war as just one example among conflict processes. Had differences emerged between magnitude and severity, for example, they might be a product of the differential impact of the number of poles—or, for that matter, any other element of structure—on various aspects of interstate warfare.

Wayman (1984, 1985: 126, 131) uses COW Project data from 1815 through 1965 to examine the impact of the number of poles on the magnitude (i.e., nation-months) and frequency of interstate wars fought by major powers. A measure of capability concentration based on the share of major power capabilities held by the two greatest powers identifies a system as "power bipolar" when that exceeds 50 percent of the total. Although Wayman finds the multipolar years to be "slightly less war prone," 75 percent of the wars within those years were of high magnitude, with the percentage being practically reversed for the wars during bipolarity (1985: 131).

Bueno de Mesquita and Lalman (1988) compare systemic and dyadic explanations of international conflict, with the number of capability centers occupying a prominent role in several formulations. The most comprehensive model, which includes other structural variables as well as the number of poles, reduces the probability of error in predicting war by only 10.7 percent.[20] Bueno de Mesquita and Lalman therefore conclude that "structural dimensions, contrary to arguments in the literature and to conventional wisdom, show no sign of significantly altering the likelihood of international warfare" (13). This stands as one of the most prominent apparent refutations for use of variables related to system structure in the explanation of international conflict.

Hopf (1991: 478, 486; see also Midlarsky 1993 and Hopf 1993) focuses on the European system and compares multipolarity (1495–1521) to bipolarity (1521–1559). The frequency, intensity, and duration indicators reveal a small difference in favor of bipolarity as a less warlike system than multipolarity.

One set of studies, from the International Crisis Behavior (ICB) Project, relates the number of poles in the system to conflict other than war. Brecher, Wilkenfeld, and James (1989) compare multipolar (1929–1939), bipolar (1945–1962), and polycentric (1963–1985) systems along several dimensions of international crisis. (*Polycentrism* refers to a system with two centers of military power and a greater number of independent centers of decision making.)

Bivariate testing, which includes indicators such as the annual number of crises, intensity of violence, and number of involved actors in a crisis, generally favors bipolarity. The latter system exhibits relatively high turmoil on only two of the eleven indicators. Furthermore, for the "potentially preeminent indicator—subsequent tension level—it is far and away the most stable system" (51). Multivariate testing also favors bipolarity.[21] An index of instability, based on behavioral variables (consisting of the nature of the triggering event, management techniques and intensity of violence), identifies polycentrism as the most unstable system. Bipolarity ranks as more stable than multipolarity, although the difference is not dramatic.

Brecher and Wilkenfeld (1997: 746–59) test several propositions about the number of poles and several crisis-based indicators. Polycentrism is most unstable for four indicators (frequency, violence in trigger, severity of violence, and major power effectiveness), bipolarity for one (stress experienced by decision makers), and multipolarity for one (lack of major power activity); bipolarity and multipolarity are tied for one (legacy in terms of subsequent crises). The basic pattern in the data supports the idea of polycentrism as most unstable, most notably for indicators related to both the frequency and intensity of crises.

Taken together, the evidence about the number of poles is complex and should be interpreted with caution. The most visible pattern for both crisis and war favors bipolarity in the twentieth century, although the results appear quite sensitive to measurement. Several studies produce evidence that a system with two central powers will be less prone to damage from warfare (especially in the twentieth century), while no study offers uniform support to multipolarity. The research, however, raises more questions than it answers.

Although it receives less attention than the subset of major powers, the number of states in the system is an equally basic aspect of structure.[22] As in the case of the number of poles, the size of the system is the subject of disagreement with regard to implications for the level of conflict. Deutsch and Singer (1964) suggested that a greater number of states in the system would create more interaction opportunities. This property, in turn, is expected to lower the amount of confrontation. If dyadic and higher-order combinations of states were counted, the potential points of contact would expand at much more than a linear rate. Thus even the addition of a few actors could have a major impact on the level of tension in the system. Similarly, Thompson, Rasler, and Li (1980) identify the stabilizing role of "multiple actors and issue areas" as a basic component of the "pluralistic process" in world politics (59). Thus, for somewhat overlapping reasons, these studies suggest that a larger international system would tend to experience less warfare.

Others, however, argue that additional actors are likely to create problems. According to Waltz (1967), "[E]xtreme equality is associated with instability" (228), whether referring to an economy or a polity. A large number of relatively weak actors therefore are expected to lack leadership, most notably in conflict management. If new actors tend to have revisionist objectives, the proliferation of states will be associated with greater conflict (Buzan 1981: 165; Gilpin 1981: 225).

While greater interaction opportunities certainly could lower the level of dyadic confrontation, what about the potential lack of conflict management in a world of many actors, including some revisionist states? It is not obvious which set of forces should be expected to have greater impact.

Hypothetical examples can be used to demonstrate that expanding the system's size may have a more complicated impact than expected by either side in the preceding argument. Consider a system with specific numbers of major and minor powers. A dyad in this system, using the terminology of Most and Starr (1987), is "balanced" (235) if it consists of two approximately equal states and unbalanced otherwise. The number of unbalanced dyads in the system then is regarded as an indicator of potential for war. (While debatable, that assumption ultimately does not affect the line of argument; it would apply just as well if instead balanced dyads were linked to war potential.) Most and Starr used a system with three major powers to illustrate some unexpected effects: "Simple expansion of system size—in addition to changes in the number of major powers—has a dramatic effect on the numbers of imbalanced and balanced dyads. *Tri*polar systems with 3, 5, 10 and 15 nations would have 0, 6, 21 and 36 imbalanced dyads respectively." Thus, in terms of dyadic interactions, it is not obvious that a larger system should be less war prone. Opportunities for aggression could increase with a greater number of states, depending on the distribution of capabilities. For example, a further proliferation of weak states might simply create new and inviting targets for more established powers. If, by contrast, *parity* is inherently more dangerous, then an increasing number of balanced dyads, within a larger system, will be the source of worry.

One data-based study explores the connection of interstate conflict to the size of the international system. Gochman and Maoz (1984: 593) focus on militarized interstate disputes (MIDs) from 1816 to 1976 and find the post–World War II era to be the most prone to disputes, with the increase over time attributed at least in part to expansion of the international polity. This suggests the potential relevance of assessing the effects of the system's size after normalizing for the number of states or possibly dyads. For example, if two systems are of sizes N and 2N, and the latter has more conflicts, that would lead to the inference that a larger system is more conflict prone. However, when the number of dyads is controlled for, the margin of difference in terms of frequency of conflict becomes crucial in making that judgment.

4.2 Secondary Elements of Structure

Secondary elements are based on complex calculations about the distribution of capabilities but do not make reference to interstate coalitions. The discussion in this section includes several elements: concentration of capabilities among the great powers and in the leading state (respectively), rank ordering, position along a cycle, and dyadic transition, and dyadic transition coupled with concentration. In each instance, possible connections with international conflict, crisis, and war are reviewed, along with results from testing.

Concentration, also known as *stratification,* refers to the degree of inequality exhibited by the distribution of capabilities among system members. While extreme points in the distribution would seem obvious (ranging from exact equality to all of the capabilities being in the hands of one actor), many intermediate possibilities exist and may be calculated in any number of ways. Fortunately, authoritative work is available for reference on the meaning of concentration. Ray and Singer (1973) and Taagepera and Ray (1977) provide thorough discussions of the theoretical and practical issues entailed in creating an overall assessment of stratification. The process leading to adoption of the Concentration of Capabilities (CON) Index included extensive comparison with other methods of calculation. The expression derived by Ray and Singer (1973) and evaluated by Taagepera and Ray (1977) yields scores ranging from 0 to 1, which represent minimum and maximum concentration, respectively, regardless of the size of the system. (The index can be used to calculate concentration either within the system as a whole or a subset such as the great powers. The latter is the norm in subsequent research.) CON is "conceptually satisfying" because it can be interpreted as a "normalized standard deviation" (Taagepera and Ray 1977: 373, 378). The index also is less prone than other measurement options to respond only to the proportion of capabilities held by the largest state. On the basis of CON's positive qualities, the meaning of the concentration of capabilities is established in a rigorous manner.

With regard to the impact of the concentration of capabilities on the system's propensity for international conflict, contradictory opinions can be traced to philosophical origins. A highly stratified system might be more prone to dictatorial behavior by those in favored positions, especially if one state ever managed to achieve hegemonic status. The need for leadership and collective responsibility, however, suggests that dispersion of capabilities will create problems. A classic example in the latter sense is provided by the Tragedy of the Commons, which carries a disturbing message about equal power and effective action (Bartlett 1980: 615; Hardin 1977). With capabilities widely distributed, the public good—in the classic example of the tragedy, land under collective administration—suffers because of uniform pursuit of self-interest. All farmers desire access to the commons, but unrestricted grazing by cattle will deplete this scarce resource. Since the farmers are approximate equals, leadership for a movement to conserve the resource is unlikely to emerge. The result is destruction of the commons through unrestrained exploitation.

Specific issues in politics at the international level are available to be cited by the respective sides in the debate over concentration of capabilities. A system with either a monopoly or an oligopoly of capabilities would present certain risks. Unrestrained behavior by a hegemonic power or bitter rivalry among members of an inner circle could be very destructive. By contrast, the danger of collective irresponsibility suggests the utility of a highly stratified system.

For example, regional arms races involving relatively equal states would be less subject to regulation and control by greater powers. In sum, alternative hypotheses are viable: either a high or low level of concentration in capabilities could be associated with conflict, crisis, and war.

Concentration of capabilities also may be linked to such events in a more complex way: "[T]he 'coefficient' governing the relationship between capability concentration and international conflict is not constant, but is itself determined by the proportion of the capability in the system held by satisfied powers" (Stoll and Champion 1985: 77). (The more general question of whether, from a realist point of view, any state is ever truly satisfied is not addressed here.) With a low proportion of the capabilities held by satisfied powers, war becomes more likely when the concentration factor is high because a disparity tends to favor revisionist states. When a moderate percentage of power is held by satisfied states, less war is expected; of course, a high proportion of capabilities among such states will be more stable if capabilities also are concentrated.

With a focus on the period from 1820 to 1965, Singer and colleagues (Singer, Bremer, and Stuckey 1972; Singer, Bremer, and Stuckey 1979: 173) use CON and COW data to assess the impact of concentration of capabilities on magnitude (i.e., nation-months) of major power war. The linkage proved to be significant for the period as a whole, but an intercentury difference is notable. In the nineteenth century, greater concentration of capabilities is associated with the amount of war in progress, while the reverse is true for the twentieth century. Thus one century supports the idea that parity is associated with peace, while the next one favors preponderance.

Cannizzo's (1978) replication study, which focuses on the magnitude of war for individual great powers ($N = 14$ per century) from 1816 to 1965, produces the same pattern. The results, however, are much stronger for the twentieth than the nineteenth century. Another replication study focuses on the occurrence of war rather than its magnitude. Bueno de Mesquita (1981a) finds that the presence or absence of war over five-year intervals from 1820 to 1965 is unrelated to the concentration of capabilities.[23]

One study puts forward a nonmonotonic relationship between concentration and war. Mansfield (1992: 10, 12) focuses on wars involving at least one major power over five-year intervals from 1825 to 1965. The data analysis reveals an inverted u-shaped relationship; over CON's range of 0 to 1, a value of 0.27, or a moderate degree of concentration among those observed in history, is associated with a maximum frequency of war.

Stoll and Champion (1985) test the connection between capabilities held by satiated versus revisionist powers at a given level of concentration and the amount of war in the system. Expert-generated data are used to measure the respective satisfaction levels. The model developed by Stoll and Champion is supported by COW Project data from 1820 to 1965, without the usual intercentury difference, although it underestimated the magnitude of World War I significantly. As expected, when capabilities are concentrated, war becomes more likely as the proportion held by revisionist states increases. It also is interesting to link these findings about satiated and revisionist powers to earlier results concerning first- and second-place states. While the leading state is most active, possibly including intervention intended to stabilize the system, the second-place power issues the most challenges. This pattern is consistent with what Stoll and Champion find in terms of an interaction effect between concentration and revisionism among those holding most of the capabilities.

Concentration is assessed in an especially interesting way by Rasler and Thompson (1994: 60–61), namely, as an indicator of the propensity toward war when changing in a particular way at regional and global levels, respectively. The specific connection involves the narrowing of the gap between global concentration and regional concentration as a danger signal for war. If the regional concentration is increasing, in relative terms, that will be expected to correlate with the rise of a challenger and a greater likelihood of war. Data analysis on great powers interactions from 1490 to 1990 offers strong support for this hypothesis with respect to the frequency of war (Rasler and Thompson (1994: 67).

One study uses concentration to account for variation in crisis-generated instability. James (1993a: 17, 20) relies on the ICB Project's Severity Index, weighted by duration, to assess the instability created by each international crisis. Measured at five-year intervals from 1925 to 1980, concentration is linked inversely to crisis-generated instability at the global level and for all but one region (i.e., the Western Hemisphere). The same pattern exists for instability when linked to concentration of capabilities in the leading state, only this time Europe is the exceptional region.

Another secondary element to consider is rank ordering. This is a variation on the primary elements defined in terms of the highly visible first- and second-place states. With a focus on the *full* rank ordering, complex calculations are involved. On the basis of the argument already presented from Bremer (1980), it is expected that higher-ranking states will be more prone to involvement in conflict, crisis, and war. Once again this logic finds support: Bremer (1980: 69) compares the capability rankings and war experiences of states over the years from 1820 to 1964 and finds that higher-ranking states are more likely than lower-ranking states to initiate and participate in wars. Of course, it would be interesting to see how this connection holds up for other dependent variables; most notably, lower-ranking states might emerge as more likely *targets* of war initiation.

Doran (1985: 297) draws attention to the potential effects of changes in the share of capabilities held by individual states, most notably the great powers. As a great power's relative capabilities rise and decline, its behavior toward the international system is expected to change: structure and stability take on meaning in the context of the long-term continuous evolution of systems accompanying changes in the various state cycles of power and systemic role."

Especially important are critical points along the cycle, when, for example, an actor shifts from decline to improvement in *relative* capabilities. At such points, the probability of involvement in warfare is expected to increase (Doran 1989a: 90). When a number of leading powers pass simultaneously through points of transition, the likelihood of major war becomes greater (Doran 1991). This logic could be extended to cover involvement in other forms of conflict, such as militarized interstate disputes and international or foreign policy crises.

Doran (1985: 307; see also Doran 1989b, 1991), in an effort to test the connection between cycles of capability and the outbreak of major war, charts the shares held by the great powers over the period from 1875 to 1914. He finds nine critical points during that era, including four in the last five years. In statistical terms, the structural change prior to World War I was "unusually severe," with the period before World War II also being above average in that regard. These findings obtain further credibility from the data analysis of Doran and Parsons (1980), which links both initiation and participation in war to a great power's proximity to critical points along its cycle. Hebron and James (1997) find additional support for capability cycles in an investigation of foreign policy crises for great powers from 1918 to 1985. The analysis, based on ICB Project data, produces mixed but generally favorable results for a series of hypotheses about the timing of crises in relation to critical points.

Another major sector of research on secondary elements of structure is concerned with transitions between states. In other words, what are the potential implications for conflict when states exchange positions in the ranking of capabilities? The answer to this question for some is the "power transition," which argues that peace is most endangered when one state is in the process of moving past another (Organski 1958; Organski and Kugler 1980; Kugler and Lemke 1996; Tammen et al. 2000). The scholarship in this area is expansive and tends to confirm the impact of capability transition, so only a few recent studies will be summarized at this point.

Geller (1992b) focuses on serious disputes from the COW data set over the interval from 1816 to 1976. The probability of a contender dyad going to war increases significantly when relative capabilities shift for that pair of states. Over an even longer period, from 1490 to 1990, Rasler and Thompson (1994: 45) find that great-power dyads in which one member is equal and overtaking have a higher relative likelihood to produce war than pairings in which no overtaking occurs. Kim and Morrow (1992: 908, 914–16, 917) focus on war from 1816 to 1975 over twenty-year intervals, which in turn produces 115 dyad-periods for the great powers. They find that risk-acceptant and dissatisfied rising states are more willing to use force to challenge the status quo, risk-averse declining states are more likely to fight to forestall change, and relatively equal capabilities make both sides willing to go to war.

Among the studies that link secondary elements to war, Geller (1992a) stands out for its integration of capability-based indicators expressed at the systemic and dyadic levels. Geller hypothesizes that dyadic transitions among contender states are more likely to be linked to war when the system is diffuse rather than concentrated in capabilities. For eighty-five such dyads, change in concentration alone is not linked to war, but deconcentration and dyadic capability shifts, when they occur together, show a strong connection to war.

Considered collectively, research on the concentration of capabilities and the positions of states within a given hierarchy tends to link a diffuse and relatively even distribution to the occurrence of war, most notably in the twentieth century. This result is consistent with the earlier conclusions reached about multipolarity. More subtle points, however, must be considered as well. The linkage of concentration to international conflict may be nonmonotonic (see Vasquez 1998: 297 on further complications related to Mansfield's [1992] results) and also appears to be mediated by the identities of those who hold the capabilities. Interesting associations between secondary elements and conflict, crisis, and war pertain to cycles and transitions, which serves as a reminder that micro-micro and micro-macro connections are likely to play an important role in an elaborated version of structural realism. Finally, one study explores the interaction between two elements, concentration and transition, and finds a compelling connection to war. The need to look at "compounds," rather than elements alone, also develops as a theme in further theorizing based on structural realism.

4.3 Tertiary Elements of Structure

Tertiary elements are based on interstate coalitions but not complex calculations. Three such elements are covered in this phase of the review: extent of commitments, size of alliances, and asymmetric alliance status in dyads. Propositions and testing based on these elements are considered in turn.

Most general among the issues to consider is how the magnitude or extent of alliance commitments might be linked to the occurrence of conflict, crisis, and war. In a highly influential study written from a nonrealist perspective, Singer and Small (1966) hypothesize that a greater number of alliance commitments in the international system will result in more warfare. Pursuing a line of argument that parallels Adam Smith's "invisible hand" within a market, they assert that "anything which restrains or inhibits free or vigorous pursuit of the separate national interests will limit the efficacy of the stabilizing mechanism. And among those arrangements seen as most likely to so inhibit that pursuit are formal alliances" (249). When flexibility is reduced, in other words, states are more likely to engage in destructive forms of conflict.

Alliances also have been advocated as a potential means of stabilizing the system. Traditional realist notions of balance of power suggest that aggressive behavior by one state can be restrained by a combination of others. If x is menaced by w, a stronger state, it is rational for x to seek assistance. Thus x may form an alliance with y, or perhaps y and z, to discourage an attack by w on any of those concerned.

Schroeder's (1986) analysis of European diplomacy in the central subsystem after the Napoleonic era is consistent with interpretation of alliances as stabilizing mechanisms. The treaty system of 1815 and the network of small powers on the continent combined to make political life relatively stable; the Concert of Europe operated flexibly, and its members shared an interest in preserving the autonomy of small states. Rather than removing interaction opportunities, the Concert nurtured cooperative linkages among the powers.[24] This assessment of how alliances might function, however, is consistent with the postulates of structural realism only under specific circumstances. A network of defensive alliances would entrench the status quo in the system. If risk aversion is assumed for those engaged in defense pacts, then the orientation toward preserving instead of gaining status becomes understandable. By contrast, the logic of Singer and Small depends less on assumptions about risk propensity; alliances might just as easily be intended for offensive as well as defensive purposes.

Efforts to test the connection of alliances to international conflict have focused primarily on the frequency and intensity of interstate warfare. Singer and Small (1966) use six measurements of the pervasiveness of alliances (with the most basic being the percentage of overall dyads exhausted by alliance commitments) to represent the independent variable. Using COW data through 1945, they chart the magnitude and severity (nation-months and battle deaths, respectively) of wars that began within three different periods—one, three, and five years—following measurement of the alliance configuration. From the complex tables of statistics, Singer and Small (1966) produce the following summary:[25] "[W]hen alliance aggregation or bipolarity [i.e., pervasiveness of major power defensive pacts] in the nineteenth century increases, the amount of war experienced by the system goes down, and vice versa. And in the twentieth century, the greater the alliance aggregation . . . in the system, the more war it experiences" (283). The same results obtain on an individual basis.[26] Thus the twentieth century is consistent with the arguments concerning flexibility, while the nineteenth reflects the vision of alliances as mechanisms that restore the balance of power.

Two more specific points also should be made concerning the research design and results from Singer and Small. First, the use of three different time lags showed recognition of how little is known about the impact of alliance aggregation on variables such as the outbreak and intensity of war. In other words, the transmission of effects from structure to process is another aspect of the realist vision that requires further specification. A second point concerns the intercentury difference that emerged, paralleling the results obtained for some analyses that focused on the number of poles. Structural realism ultimately must be able to account for diversity across time periods, so the need to incorporate variables beyond those in the basic Waltzian or positional treatment of structure is reinforced.

Some studies confirm the findings of Singer and Small, although with variations. Ostrom and Hoole (1978) conduct a similar, COW-based investigation of alliance aggregation and war. For each year from 1816 to 1965, they calculate the ratio of defense dyads and dyads of interstate war, respectively, to the size of the system. Using statistical procedures that differ from those of Singer and Small, they find no connection between the two ratios. However, Ostrom and Hoole also compare the percentage of states in the system involved in alliances with five measurements of war magnitude. The results from this phase of testing parallel those of Singer and Small.

Using COW data, Thompson, Rasler, and Li (1980: 63, 77) investigate the linkage between interaction opportunities and war from 1816 to 1965.[27] A statistical analysis of the data, with a three-year time lag, partially confirms the results from Singer and Small. Reducing interaction opportunities predicts to war for 1919–1939 and the reverse (albeit weakly) for 1816–1914. However, for 1946–1965 the expected linkage does not hold. Once again, the intercentury difference—this time coupled with variation in the twentieth century—cannot be explained on the basis of a single bivariate treatment.

With a focus on the great powers from 1495 to 1975, Levy (1981) probes the connection between war and international military alliances. He uses a wide range of measurements for the former: frequency, duration, number of great powers involved, and several others. For the latter, Levy focuses on the number of alliances and how many powers formed alliances. From rank-order correlations he finds that alliance formation is associated with relatively low levels of war, measured in various ways. However, he also computes "the proportion of alliances followed by war within five years and the proportion of wars preceded by alliances within five years" as more specific tests of the general hypothesis (596–97). "With the exception of the nineteenth century," Levy finds that "defensive and neutrality alliances when they have occurred, have been excellent predictors of wars involving (or between) the Great Powers, appearing thus to have nearly constituted sufficient conditions for war in some periods" (612). (The results, of course, may not have causal implications, as pointed out by Vasquez [1987]; instead, the near-constant conjunction of alliances and war may correlate with deeper, more determining conditions for such events.) As in the cases of Singer and Small, and Thompson, Rasler, and Li, the use of a time lag plays a determining role in the generation of results. While it is understandable that a delay of some kind is certain to occur in transmission of effects, the choice of periods such as one or five years must be made on the basis of criteria with general application.

Oren (1990: 216–17, 226–27) looks at the size of membership in alliances for a possible connection to war. Alliances with at least one major power and wars from 1816 to 1980 make up the data set. The analysis produces a noteworthy connection between alliance size and war proneness, even when controlling for alliance duration.[28] It also is interesting to note that the frequently encountered intercentury difference is absent, suggesting that the discrepancy may depend more on the overall amount of war rather than the function of alliances or other variables.

Siverson and Sullivan (1984: 5–6, 10–12) examine alliances and war in a context different from that of the preceding studies. They focus on the initial dyad in each war, to observe more directly the process of onset, and also develop a "baseline population" to permit more meaningful comparison. Among the wars from 1815 to 1965 identified by the COW Project, fifty-nine of the one hundred initial participants did not belong to an alliance. This result is inconsistent with the usual logic regarding interaction opportunities and war. However, Siverson and Sullivan also discover an interaction effect involving alliances and capability status: "[M]ajor powers with alliances are more likely to be an initial war participant than major powers without allies," and "minor powers with an alliance were less likely to be an initial war participant than minor powers without an alliance" (12). This difference suggests that the argument about pervasiveness of coalitions formulated by Deutsch and Singer may be more relevant to major powers because alliances reduce flexibility for such actors. By contrast, alliances may enhance security for minor powers, which tend to be less autonomous in the first place. A related study confirms the importance of alliances for anticipating the war behavior of major powers from 1815 to 1945. In the post–World War II environment, however, border effects outweighed those of alliances (Siverson and Starr 1989).

Siverson and Tennefoss (1984) focus on dyads from 1816 to 1965 and probe whether alliance commitments impact upon the likelihood of war. Militarized interstate disputes are most likely to result in war for asymmetric dyads: that is, dyads in which one state is allied to a major power and the other is not.

From the review of research on the extent of alliance commitments, two basic conclusions emerge. One is that a relatively consistent difference exists between the nineteenth and twentieth centuries. Alliances appear to correlate with stability in the former and the reverse in the latter. In the twentieth century, perhaps, alliances are more likely to represent explicit commitments toward the defense of endangered client states, while in the nineteenth century alliance formation reflected the stereotypical game of "musical chairs" associated with a highly flexible system. Some of the especially unsuccessful alliances of the last century—such as those involving France and small powers in Eastern Europe during the 1930s—tend to suggest this hypothesized difference. The importance of developing a model of state behavior is reinforced by this line of reasoning. Depending on the objectives of its participants, the impact of an alliance on the likelihood of conflict, crisis, and war could vary dramatically.

Another basic conclusion is that the effects of alliances can be evaluated accurately only within a more comprehensive linkage of elements of structure to conflict. Levy (1981) suggests that intercentury and other differences and patterns related to alliances and war probably reflect underlying environmental factors rather than the direct impact of coalitions. In other words, alliances should be interpreted as elements of structure that interact with others in order to produce effects. This idea is implicit in the two points made by Vasquez

(1987) in his summation of research on alliances and war: "First, alliances do not prevent war or promote peace; instead, they are associated with war, although they are probably not a cause of war. Second, the major consequence of alliances is to expand the war once it has started; in this way, alliances are important in accounting for the magnitude and severity of war" (119). In sum, additional capability-based elements must be used to complement alliances in order to explain the frequency and intensity of war and other forms of international conflict.

Renewed attempts to link elements of structure to conflict processes should devote more attention to the reasons behind alliance formation. Depending on the objectives of its members, an alliance may encourage either restraint or aggression.

4.4 Higher-Order Elements of Structure

Higher-order elements of structure entail both complex calculations and interstate coalitions. The following elements are covered in this phase of the review: polarization (including tightness and discreteness), balance of overall capabilities in a dyad, and distribution of capabilities within alliances. Propositions and testing based on these elements are considered in turn.

Among the specific properties of alliance configurations, the most prominent are the closeness of attachments within coalitions and the amount of distance (i.e., relative dearth of common attachments) between them. These characteristics combine to represent polarization, or the system's degree of rigidity. "Polarization," according to Goldmann (1974), "is a process characterized by an increase in positive interaction between certain members of the system and a decrease in positive interaction between them and other members of the system" (107). In equally general terms, Jackson (1977) urges scholars to "reserve the concept of polarization for description of patterns of interaction, i.e., the structure(s) of conflict in the system" (92). This formulation became more explicit with Bueno de Mesquita's (1979: 126) dimensions of discreteness and tightness, referring to the distance separating clusters of states and their degree of cohesion around the respective poles in the system. Similarly, Rapkin and Thompson (1980) refer to the "extent to which a system's actors form two separate systems or blocs with inter-bloc and intra-bloc interaction being characterized, predominately and respectively, by conflict and cooperation" (378). Later descriptions of polarization or "bipolarization" also reveal the general agreement concerning the nature of its two dimensions (Brecher and Ben Yehuda 1985: 24; Brown 1988: 27).

More agreement than diversity exists with regard to the presumed impact of each of these structural attributes. Greater tightness and discreteness are expected to result almost uniformly in a higher amount of disruption in the system. With an overriding axis of conflict, prospects for compromise are minimal. The gulf between such coalitions cannot be bridged easily; issues become more encompassing, thereby increasing the difficulty of trade-offs based on varying intensity of preference. Disputes accumulate more quickly than they can be resolved (Midlarsky 1988: 30–32). Aggregation of capabilities by members of rival alliances also enhances the perception of threat, especially when each coalition increasingly acts as a unit (Vasquez 1987: 128).

For an illustration of how the process of polarization can lead to war, the standard historical reference is the sequence of events culminating in August 1914. In the years leading up to the general European crisis, Austria-Hungary and Germany confronted France and Russia, with Britain increasingly identified as sympathetic to the latter of the two alliances. As July 1914 progressed, the two armed camps within Europe drew further away from each other, while simultaneously showing greater cohesiveness. Communication increasingly consisted of hostile statements toward the rival coalition, along with reassuring comments to allies (Holsti 1972). The opportunity to prevent disaster slipped away, and World War I ensued.

Investigations of the impact of polarization have focused on interstate conflicts, disputes, and wars. Wallace (1973) uses COW Project data to assess the impact of polarization on the magnitude (nation-months) and severity (battle deaths) of war from 1815 to 1964. His Polarization Index, based on smallest space analysis, encompasses tightness and discreteness. Wallace (1973, 1979b) observes that "where the system is highly polarized, the great majority of nations will be clustered in as few as two tightly knit groups at a considerable distance from one another. On the other hand, where polarization is low, the nations will form many loose clusters distributed in random fashion throughout the [geopolitical] space" (97). When testing a simple linear model, he found no significant connection between the Index and either dependent variable. A curvilinear fit, by contrast, performed extremely well. The explained variance ranged from 0.58 to 0.77, suggesting that war becomes more likely at both very low and high levels of polarization (105). In theoretical terms, however, it is not obvious why such results would be expected. Furthermore, the presumably high level of polarization during the Cold War did not produce all-out war, which creates at least one highly salient anomaly for Wallace's model.

For the years from 1816 to 1965, Bueno de Mesquita (1978: 126, 131, 136) uses COW data to assess the occurrence of interstate war in general and among major powers in particular. Using statistical procedures, he measured tightness and discreteness (along with the change in each) on the basis of alliance commitments. Highly similar states ended up in the same cluster, at various distances from those in other groups. In Bueno de Mesquita's formulation, closer proximity among the states in a cluster represents tightness, while discreteness corresponds to the relative distance from other groupings. Thus the exposition parallels Wallace (1973), but with different measurement techniques. A variation on one of the above-noted structural factors had by far the most significant connection to the occurrence of war in the twentieth century. Increasing systemic tightness correlated very positively with war, and the duration of war in the twentieth century could be predicted best by the change in tightness.

Gochman (1980: 93, 114) probes the connection of polarization to interstate conflicts, described as events in which "one or more major powers explicitly threatened or actually employed military force against other members of the interstate system" (93). Excluding World Wars I and II (a potentially problematic exclusion), he focuses on the experiences of the major powers in the period from 1820 to 1970. As in so many other data-based studies, an intercentury difference emerges. In the nineteenth century, the degree of polarization into two camps predicted to involvement in conflict, especially for the United Kingdom, Germany, and Italy. In the twentieth century, the effects are mixed. For the United States, the USSR, the United Kingdom, and France, participation is greater as the system becomes more polarized, while the linkage is reversed for China, Japan, and Austria-Hungary and nonexistent for Germany and Italy. The diversity of results within and across each century serves as a reminder that linkages of conflict experiences for individual states with elements of structure can be expected to vary. States seem to react differently to the same degree of polarization in the environment, so it is reasonable to anticipate that regional and other variations also may emerge. This reinforces the point that an important role exists for specification of macro-micro linkages within a more encompassing version of structural realism.

Wayman (1985: 122, 133) hypothesizes that "cluster bipolarity"—analogous to high levels of tightness and discreteness in the system—will be associated with subsequent interstate warfare (122). This proposition follows from the fact that "two important conflict-reducing agents—namely, intermediary relationships and cross-cutting cleavages—exist in a cluster multipolar setting but are eliminated in a cluster bipolar one" (122). Using the magnitude and frequency of war as dependent variables, he finds support for the hypothesis in the twentieth century, although the reverse obtains for the nineteenth.[29] Wayman (1984: 72–73) also probes the connection using first differences in cluster polarization and finds a negative correlation between the level of change in polarization and the magnitude of war in the current century. This is consistent with Bueno de Mesquita's discovery that increasing tightness is associated with the subsequent amount of war underway. Taken together, Wayman's findings are consistent with prior differences identified between the centuries, although once again it is difficult to locate a theoretical rationale for this outcome.

Midlarsky (1988: 32, 39) links the beginning and ending of interstate disputes to polarization in the system. He discovers that, under conditions of relatively high polarization, there is a tendency toward buildup in the number of disputes in progress. In other words, existing disputes are not resolved as quickly as new ones begin. In the period before 1914, according to Midlarsky, the accumulation of disputes contributed to the likelihood of systemic war.

Some degree of consistency exists among the studies that focus on aspects of polarization. The findings by Bueno de Mesquita about increasing systemic tightness, by Wallace regarding very high levels of polarization, by Wayman concerning cluster bipolarity in the twentieth century, and by Midlarsky about the accumulation of disputes point in one direction. When the pattern of interstate coalitions becomes more precise—meaning that the configuration of alliances tightens or already is highly visible—the danger of war increases. As for Wallace's finding that very low polarization also increases the risk of war, and the similar linkage uncovered by Wayman for the previous century, these patterns may be related to the earlier findings about the effects of alliance pervasiveness. Given the flexible system of bargaining within nineteenth-century Europe, more alliances may have meant additional stabilizing factors in operation, with extremely "loose" alliances being less helpful than more obvious connections.

Another higher-order element to consider is the balance of capabilities in a dyad when the potential contributions of alliance partners are factored into the equation. This element raises once again the basic issue of preponderance versus parity. For the period from 1816 to 1975, Kim (1989: 269) finds a 32 percent higher probability of war when opposing coalitions are approximately equal rather than unequal in capabilities and all other variables are held constant. A follow-up study of great powers in the same period produces a similar result, with major power dyads that possess relatively equal overall capabilities being more than two times as likely to go to war as those with unequal capabilities (Kim 1991).

One further characteristic of alliances, the distribution of capabilities within them, may have important effects on international conflict. Midlarsky (1988: 163, 167) observes that, in political systems, coalitions with a relatively even distribution of capabilities among members are more prone to entropy, or internal disintegration. Within an alliance, for example, a significant gap in capabilities between the great and small partners would be preferred, in order to facilitate leadership and coherence in policy. Of course, this property is desirable if and only if it is assumed that durable coalitions promote systemic stability. Put differently, it is better for an alliance to have minimal entropy if volatile alignments contribute to misperception and increase the danger of war. The buildup of disputes between the Triple Entente and Triple Alliance, each of which consisted of great powers, in the years before World War I would appear to confirm this line of reasoning. It is clear that, as in so many previous instances, assumptions beyond the usual boundaries of structural realism are required to complete the argument.

When the propositions and findings for higher-order elements are summed up, there is a parallel with what appeared at the other three levels. Both theorizing and evidence seem to call for integration into an overall framework, but so far that is lacking.

This is an appropriate point at which to revisit table 4.2, which summarized the characteristics of findings about conflict, crisis, and war across the types of element within international structure. Six surface traits and one deeper analytical point can be derived from the review and summary table. Each is considered in turn.

When the findings are viewed collectively, six characteristics stand out. First, the results based on aggregate data are overwhelmingly bivariate. Second, the elements of structure do receive support from the data in a substantial number of instances, although the connections generally are limited in both strength and scope across all four types. The third trait concerns a general lack of exploration with respect to the effects that might result from interactions between elements. Fourth, with a few exceptions, testing takes a linear functional form. Fifth, the vast majority of data analysis focuses on interstate war. These various limitations of the positive heuristic suggest priorities for elaboration of structural realism in terms of both formulation of hypotheses and selection of evidence. Sixth, and finally, it should be noted that the vast majority of the data analysis has been carried out by nonrealists. This is not to suggest that there is bias against variants of realism in the results, only that the opposite seems rather unlikely, thus increasing the power of the test in an overall sense.

One deeper analytical point also comes out of the review and summary table: the positive heuristic as described in terms of research findings is linked to the other apparatus of structural realism in at best an implicit way. A more direct connection to the hard core is needed to sort out contradictory propositions and create an inventory that is consistent within and across the types of element. The story in relation to the negative heuristic is more encouraging. While the table consists of capability-based variables as a matter of deliberate selection, it also seems free from either strategic altruism or other obvious violations of theorizing within structural realist parameters.

5. The Positive Heuristic of Structural Realism: War as an Empirical Problem

Review of the positive heuristic so far includes a series of theories and overview of how elements of structure have been used to explain conflict, crisis, and war. This final component of the "mapping out" of the positive heuristic will be more focused. It is concerned with war as an empirical problem. The causes of war is a subject of vast scope, as recent comprehensive efforts to address these matters will attest (Vasquez 1993, 2000b; Harvey and Mor 1997; Geller and Singer 1998; Wolfson 1998; Midlarsky 2000). The current overview, by contrast, is more modest in its agenda. A series of tables will be created to summarize what is known about the connection of *capability-based indicators* to basic dimensions of the causes of war. The goal is to obtain an overall sense of what elements of structure, which are integrated so far only in a typology, might be able to say about war as an empirical problem.

Tables 4.3 through 4.8 provide an overview of research findings for actions and events. Tables 4.3 through 4.6 focus on *actions*, while tables 4.7 and 4.8 pertain to *events*. Within the first set of tables, 4.3 and 4.4 include findings related to the frequency of war with respect to initiation and participation by states, respectively. Tables 4.5 and 4.6 cover research results related to the intensity of war, once again for initiation and participation in that order. Tables 4.7 and 4.8 convey findings about the frequency and intensity, respectively, of war as an event. The six tables, taken together, provide a mapping of research results on war for (a) events and actions, in the latter sense including both initiation and participation; and (b) frequency and intensity, the two basic dimensions of any action or event.

Each table takes the same form. Independent variables, in all instances capability-based elements of structure (or, in a few instances, combinations of them), are listed from primary through higher order. In some instances, multiple studies have used the same variable, so these appear together (e.g., the six tests pertaining to balance of capabilities in table 4.3). The unit of analysis, designated as (a) monad, (b) dyad, or (c) region and system, is noted. Functional form is identified as either monotonic or non-monotonic; the few examples of the latter are explained in some instances by notes to the respective tables. Hypotheses based on the independent variables are noted as supported or not supported in each instance. Finally, the source of the hypothesis and testing is listed.

Several points of explanation about the contents of the tables are in order before the analysis begins.[30] First, the tables focus only on bivariate results; no attempt is made to somehow synthesize and communicate the findings from multivariate analysis. Second, the hypotheses in some instances are stated in the reverse ordering of what the authors put forward so that all will take the positive form: for example, "The more of independent variable x, the more war is expected." In each instance the characteristic associated with war is noted; for example, in the case of capability status from table 4.4, that means designation as a great rather than ordinary power. Third, while not all of the studies use the COW definition of war, even those that do not are in at least a close approximation to that data set's meaning, which facilitates a general comparison of the kind conducted here. Fourth, and finally, a very simple designation is used for whether the independent variable showed a connection to some manifestation of war, namely, supported versus not supported. Since this is a mapping exercise, greater precision, which would entail much more difficulty in aggregating the results by introducing issues such as significance tests, relative size of N, and like matters, is not regarded as a virtue. Instead, the purpose of each table is to provide a sense of the central tendency in research findings for each aspect of the causes of war.

Table 4.3 reveals some patterns that will be common to each of the others that follows. Since war initiation is the question, the unit of analysis is always either the monad or dyad, with three and eighteen instances, respectively. All but two studies feature a monotonic connection of the independent variable to initiation of war. The relatively common time frame, from the post-Napoleonic era onward, reveals the predominance of COW data in this area of research. The various end-points correlate with the version of the COW data set available when each respective study occurred. It is interesting to note that seventeen of the tests support the proposition about war initiation. Variables such as the number of poles (in this instance referring to bipolarity versus multipolarity), challenger status, concentration, the balance of capabilities, advantage for the initiator relative to the target, parity/overtaking, concentration coupled with capability transition, supersatisfaction, dissatisfaction, asymmetry in alliance commitments, systemic tightness, and the number of alliances involving a state all show some connection to the initiation of war. Disagreement is notable with respect to the balance of capabilities in a dyad; while three studies find a connection, three others do not.

Table 4.4, which focuses on the frequency of war participation, conveys a similar set of results. In the twenty-two instances of testing, the frequency of each unit of analysis is monad (fourteen), dyad (six), "n-ad" (i.e., a number greater than two) (one), and region or system (one), respectively. This is expected once again because the focus here also is directly on the experiences of individual states. The functional form is monotonic in each case, and once again the time frame is consistent with use of various releases of data from the COW Project. The hypotheses are supported in twenty out of twenty-two instances. Once again, quite a few independent variables show at least a minimal connection to war, in this case referring to participation by states. These variables are great power status, hegemonic change, rank, balance of capabilities, parity, capability cycle, difference in global versus regional concentration of capabilities, alliance size, alliance commitments, balance of overall capabilities, alliance commitment coupled with status, and alliance polarization. For one variable, the amount of capability held by a state, the studies report contradictory findings.

Intensity of war provides a change of pace in tables 4.5 and 4.6. As noted by table 4.5, only one study looks at the intensity of war initiation. Its characteristics are much the same as those reported in the preceding tables. The one finding to report is that a state's position along its capability cycle shows a monotonic linkage with the intensity of its war initiation. Meanwhile, table 4.6 includes just two independent variables. Capability status and alliance commitments both reveal a monotonic connection to the intensity of war participation. In both tables the unit of analysis, as might be expected, is the monad.

Table 4.7, which covers the frequency of war as an event, features greater diversity in units of analysis. The frequencies are region/system (twenty-six), dyad (seven), dyad/N (one), and monad (two), respectively. Region and system predominate, as would be expected, because the focus here is on events rather than actions. Once again, the monotonic functional form accounts for almost all of the tests, in this instance, thirty-one out of thirty-six. The time frames, however, show a little variation: four of the tests include data from the fifteenth century onward. Results are mixed: twenty-two out of thirty-six tests support a connection between the independent variable and frequency of war. Variables for which at least some connections exist are the number of great powers (both in sheer number and in terms of bipolarity versus multipolarity), size of the

Table 4.3
War Initiation as an Empirical Problem: Frequency

Type of Element	Independent Variable	Unit of Analysis	Functional Form	Time Frame	Results	Source
primary	poles - more than two great powers in the system	dyad	monotonic	1815–1965	supported	Bueno de Mesquita and Lalman 1988
		dyad	monotonic	1816–1984	supported	Huth, Gelpi and Bennett 1993
	challenger status-second ranking state in terms of monadic capability	monad	non-monotonic	1820–1864	supported	Bremer 1980
secondary	concentration - degree of concentration of capabilities among system members	dyad	monotonic	1815–1965	supported	Bueno de Mesquita and Lalman 1988
	balance of capabilities - degree of equality in capabilities in a dyad	dyad	monotonic	1969–1973	supported	Garnham 1976
		dyad	monotonic	1816–1970	supported	Mihalka 1976
		dyad	monotonic	1815–1965	supported	Bueno de Mesquita and Lalman 1988
		dyad	monotonic	1815–1965	not supported	Bueno de Mesquita and Lalman 1989
		dyad	monotonic	1816–1976	not supported	Geller 1992b[a]
		dyad	monotonic	1816–1985	not supported	Gochman and Hoffman 1996
	capability balance - initiator versus target state	dyad	monotonic	1816–1974	supported	Bueno de Mesquita 1980b
	parity - capabilities of one state are overtaking another	dyad	monotonic	1816–1985	supported	Geller 1992b[a]
		dyad	monotonic	1490–1990	supported	Rasler and Thompson 1994[a]

Table 4.3 Continued

Type of Element	Independent Variable	Unit of Analysis	Functional Form	Time Frame	Results	Source
	capability transition/ concentration - capability transition under conditions of more diffuse distribution	dyad	interactive and monotonically increasing	1816–1985	supported	Geller 1992a[a]
	capability cycle - proximity to critical points along cycle for a state	monad	monotonic	1816–1975	supported	Doran and Parsons 1980[b]
	supersatisfaction - capabilities are above a state's current standing in system	dyad	monotonic	1816–1980	supported	Anderson and McKeown 1987
	dissatisfaction - capabilities are beneath a state's current standing in system	dyad	monotonic	1816–1980	supported	Anderson and state's McKeown 1987
tertiary	alliance commitments - great power ally with one side and not the other	dyad	monotonic	1816–1965	supported	Siverson and Tennefoss 1984
higher-order	tightness - degree of cohesion within an alliance	dyad	monotonic	1815–1965	supported	Buenode Mesquita and Lalman 1988 Scarborough 1988
	alliance commitments - number involving a state	monad	monotonic	1815–1965	not supported	Siverson and Sullivan 1984

Notes for Table 4.3

a. This hypothesis is tested with "contender dyads".
b. This hypothesis also appears in Doran (1989a).

Table 4.4
War Participation as an Empirical Problem: Frequency

Type of Element	Independent Variable	Unit of Analysis	Functional Form	Time Frame	Results	Source
primary	poles – more than two great powers in the system	monad	monotonic	1820–1970	not supported	Gochman 1980[a]
	capability status – status as a great power	monad	monotonic	1816–1980	supported	Small and Singer 1970, 1982[b]
		monad	monotonic -	1816–1965	supported	Geller 1988[c]
	rank – highest ranking state	monad	monotonic	1820–1964	supported	Bremer 1980
	hegemonic change – status as leading state versus other points in history	monad	monotonic	1816–1965	supported	Kohler 1975[d]
secondary	balance of capabilities – degree of equality in capabilities	dyad	monotonic	1950–1969	supported	Weede 1976[e]
		dyad	monotonic	1945–1974	supported	Mandel 1980
		dyad	monotonic	1816–1939	supported	Moul 1988[f]
		dyad	monotonic	1865–1965	supported	Bremer 1992
		dyad	monotonic	1816–1986	supported	Geller 1993
	capability level – amount of capability held by a state	monad	monotonic	1820–1970	not supported	Gochman 1980[g] 1996
		monad	monotonic	1816–1965	supported	Bremer 1980
	capability distribution – parity	monad	monotonic	1816–1965	supported	Cannizzo 1978[h]
	capability cycle – critical points along cycle of capabilities for a state	monad	monotonic	1816–1975	supported	Doran and Parsons 1980
	difference in concentration – narrowing for global minus regional	region or system	monotonic	1490–1990	supported	Rasler and Thompson 1994[g]
tertiary	alliance size – number of state in an alliance	n-ad	monotonic	1816–1980	supported	Oren 1990[i]

Table 4.4 Continued

Type of Element	Independent Variable	Unit of Analysis	Functional Form	Time Frame	Results	Source
	alliance commitments – number involving a state	monad	monotonic	1815–1945	supported	Singer and Small 1966
		monad	monotonic	1815–1965	supported	Siverson and Sullivan 1984[j]
		monad	monotonic	1815–1965	supported	Siverson and Starr 1989[k]
higher-order	balance of overall capabilities – degree of equality in capabilities including alliances	dyad	monotonic	1816–1975	supported	Kim, 1989, 1991[i,l], 1996
	alliance commitments - great power with alliance, minor power without alliance	monad	monotonic	1815–1965	supported	Siverson and Sullivan 1984
	alliance polarization – tightness and discreteness of alliances	monad	monotonic	1820–1870	supported	Gochman 1980[l,m]

Notes for Table 4.4

a. Gochman (1980: 112,114) finds that bipolarity is associated with war involvement in the nineteenth century and results are "mixed" for the twentieth century.

b. Small and Singer (1970) produce analogous results on the basis of data from 1816 to 1965.

c. Great powers are more likely to fight severe wars and less likely to fight moderate wars than are minor powers.

d. The hypothesis focuses on the war involvement of 15 leading states at different stages; when leadership status is lost, war-proneness diminishes.

e. The hypothesis is tested with data on contiguous Asian dyads.

f. The hypothesis is tested with data on European great powers.

g. The results refer to great powers.

h. The results obtain for the twentieth century and refer to great powers.

i. The unit of analysis in this study is the individual alliance involving at least one major power, which varies in size.

j. The hypothesis is tested with data on great powers.

k. The connection for alliance membership and war holds during the period from 1815 to 1945.

l. This study refers to initial war participants.

m. Polarization predicts to war participation in the nineteenth century, with mixed results for the twentieth century.

Table 4.5
War Participation as an Empirical Problem: Intensity

Type of Element	Independent Variable	Unit of Analysis	Functional Form	Time Frame	Results	Source
secondary	capability cycle – critical points along cycle of capabilities for a state	monad	monotonic	1816–1975	supported	Doran and Parsons 1980

Table 4.6
War Participation as an Empirical Problem: Intensity

Type of Element	Independent Variable	Unit of Analysis	Functional Form	Time Frame	Results	Source
primary	capability status–major powers	monad	non-monotonic	1816–1980	supported	Geller 1988[a]
tertiary	alliance commitments–number involving a state	monad	monotonic	1815–1965	supported	Singer and Small 1966[b]
		monad	monotonic	1648–1965	supported	Gibler 1996[c]

Notes for Table 4.6

a. Major powers are more likely than minor powers to fight severe wars (more than 15,000 battle deaths), less likely to fight moderate wars (between 1000 and 15,000 battle deaths), and equally likely to fight small wars (less than 1000 battle deaths).
b. The magnitude and severity of war, as defined by the COW Project, are assessed.
c. This hypothesis is tested for major powers. The dependent variable is the number of years in which a great power is involved in wars against other great powers.

Table 4.7
War Events an Empirical Problems: Frequency

Type of Element	Independent Variable	Unit of Analysis	Functional Form	Time Frame	Results	Source
primary	poles – number of great powers in the system	region or system	non-monotonic	1824–1938	supported	Ostram and Aldrich 1978[a]
		region or system	monotonic	1865–1965	not supported	Beer 1981
		region or system	monotonic	1495–1975	not supported	Levy 1984
		region or system	monotonic	1494–1983	supported	Thompson 1986[b]
		region or system	monotonic	1495–1980	not supported	Mansfield 1988[c]
		region or system	monotonic	1918–1994	supported	Brecher and Wilkenfield 1997[d]
	poles – two or more great powers in a system	region or system	monotonic	multi-century	supported	Haas 1970b
		region or system	monotonic	1815–1965	not supported	Wayman 1984[e]
		region or system	monotonic	1495–1559	supported	Hopf 1991[f]
		dyad	monotonic	1816–1965	not supported	Kim and Bueno de Mesquita 1995
	size – number of states in the system	region or system	monotonic	1816–1976	supported	Gochman and Maoz 1984
	leading state – highest ranking in terms of capability	monad	monotonic	1820–1964	supported	Bremer 1980
secondary	concentration – degree of concentration of capabilities among system members	region or system	monotonic	1820–1965	not supported	Singer, Bremer, and Stuckey 1972[g]
		region or system	monotonic	1820–1965	not supported	Bueno de Mesquita 1981b[f]
		region or system	monotonic	1820–1965	supported	Stoll and Champion 1985[h]
		region or system	non-monotonic	1825–1965	supported	Mansfield 1992[i]
	change in concentration – change in concentration of capabilities among system members	region or system	monotonic	1820–1965	not supported	Singer, Bremer, and Stuckey 1972[g]
		region or system	monotonic	1825–1965	supported	Mansfield 1992[i]
	movement in capabilities – rate of relative capabilities movement among system members	region or system	monotonic	1820–1965	not supported	Singer, Bremer, and Stuckey 1972[g]
		region or system	monotonic	1825–1965	supported	Mansfield 1992[i]

Table 4.7 continued

Type of Element	Independent Variable	Unit of Analysis	Functional Form	Time Frame	Results	Source
secondary	balance of capabilities – degree of equality in capabilities	dyad	monotonic	1816–1975	not supported	Kim 1989[j]
	parity – capabilities of one state are overtaking another	dyad	monotonic	1816–1975	supported	Kim 1989[j]
		dyad	monotonic	1816–1975	supported	Kim and Morrow 1992[k]
	capability cycle s – critical points along cycles of capabilites for states	region or system	monotonic	1816–1975; 1816–1985	supported	Doran 1985; 1989a[f], 1991[l]
	capability ranking – rank of state in terms of capability	monad	monotonic	1820–1964	supported	Bremer 1980
	growth – increase in capability	dyad	monotonic	1816–1975	not supported	Kim 1989[j]
tertiary	alliance pervasiveness – percentage of states with any alliance	region or system	monotonic	1820–1965	not supported	Singer and Small 1979
		region or system	monotonic	1816–1965	supported	Thompson, Raster and Li 1980[m]
	alliances – absent or present	region or system	monotonic	1495–1975	supported	Levy 1981[n]
higher-order	alliance polarization – tightness and discreteness of alliances	region or system	non-monotonic	1815–1964	supported	Wallace 1973[o]
		region or system	monotonic	1816–1965	supported	Bueno de Mesquita 1978[p]
		region or system	monotonic and non-monotonic	1815–1976	not supported	Moul 1993
	alliance capability margin – equality in capabilities between alliances	dyad	monotonic	1816–1975	supported	Kim 1989[j]
		dyad	monotonic	1816–1975	supported	Kim and Morrow 1992[k]

Table 4.7 continued

Type of Element	Independent Variable	Unit of Analysis	Functional Form	Time Frame	Results	Source
	hierarchical equilibrium – absence of two greatpowers with respective alliances	region or system	monotonic	1816–1964	supported	Midlarsky 1988
	alliance dyads/system size – number of alliance dyads controlling for system size	dyad/N	monotonic non-monotonic	1816–1965	not supported	Ostrom and Hoole 1978

Notes for Table 4.7

a. The probability of war is at a local minimum with three poles and at an absolute minimum with six.
b. The data analysis reveals unipolarity and quasi-unipolarity to be war-prone.
c. The data analysis shows that unipolarity is more war-prone.
d. The ICB Project variable 'severity of violence' is used to measure war, with polycentrism experiencing higher severity than bipolarity or multipolarity.
e. Multipolar years are somewhat less war-prone than bipolar years.
f. This hypothesis is tested for the great powers.
g. Concentration and increasing concentration are associated with more (less) war in the nineteenth (twentieth) century; movement is connected with war in the twentieth century. See also Singer, Bremer, and Stuckey (1979).
h. Concentration is linked to war when revisionist powers are stronger.
i. This hypothesis is tested for wars involving at least one great power within five-year intervals. The linkage is curvilinear, with frequency of war anticipated to reach a maximum at some intermediate level of concentration.
j. This hypothesis is tested for great power dyads within 20-year intervals.
k. This hypothesis is tested for great power dyads within 20-year intervals. Risk propensity also is factored into this research design.
l. Doran (1991) uses the longer time interval indicated.
m. The connection between alliances and war holds for 1919–1939, reverses for 1816–1914, and is absent for 1946–1965.
n. The nineteenth century is an exception to the overall pattern in which alliance engagements among major powers are followed by war.
o. War is very probable at low and high levels of polarization.
p. Increasing tightness predicts to war.

Table 4.8
War Events as an Emperical Problem: Intensity

Type of Element	Independent Variable	Unit of Analysis	Functional Form	Time Frame	Results	Source
primary	poles – number of great powers in the system	region or system	monotonic	1495–1975	not supported	Levy 1984[a,b]
		region or system	monotonic	multi-century	supported	Haas 1970b[b,c]
		region or system	monotonic	1495–1559	supported	Hopf 1991[a]
secondary	capability cycles – critical points along cycles of capabilities for states	region or system	monotonic	1816–1985	supported	Doran 1991
tertiary	alliance pervasiveness – percentage of states with any alliances	region or system	monotonic	1815–1945	supported	Singer and Small 1966[b]
higher order	cluster polarization – lower ratio of actual to potential poles, i.e., cluster bipolarity	region or system	monotonic	1815–1965	supported	Wayman 1984[a,d]
		region or system	monotonic	1650–1965	supported	Gibler 1999a[f]
	alliance polarization – tightness and discreteness of alliance	region or system	monotonic	1815–1965	supported	Bueno de Mesquita 1978[e]
		region or system	non-monotonic	1815–1964	supported	Wallace 1973[b]
		region or system	monotonic and non-monotonic	1815–1976	not supported	Moul 1993[b]

Notes for Table 4.8

a. This hypothesis is tested for the great powers.
b. Both the magnitude and severity of wars, as defined by the COW Project, are assessed.
c. Haas (1970b) reports that the connection is reversed for the duration of war.
d. This hypothesis is tested for magnitude only. "Cluster" polarity as defined by Wayman (1984) is analogous to polarization.
e. This hypothesis is tested for the duration of war.
f. The relationship reverses for the period from 1650 to 1799, where cluster multipolarity is linked to the magnitude of war.

system, leading status for a state, concentration, change in concentration, movement of capabilities, parity, capability cycles, capability ranking, alliance pervasiveness, presence of alliances, alliance polarization, alliance capability margin, and hierarchical equilibrium. Of course, some of these variables, such as the number of great powers, obtain mixed results from testing.

Finally, table 4.8 conveys results for the intensity of war. In all instances the unit of analysis is the region or system. Eight of the ten tests include a strictly monotonic functional form; seven rely on COW data. The same fraction also happens to hold for the number of independent variables that find support from testing.

Through the preceding mapping exercise, it is possible to detect some overall patterns in research on war that is based on aggregate data analysis. It is clear that a wide range of elements of structure have appeared in respective propositions and tests. These elements also represent all types; in the four tables with a minimum of four variables represented, at least one example appears from every one of the categories, that is, primary through higher order. The dyad is the predominant unit of analysis for actions and also is relatively visible for the frequency of war as an event. Consensus seems to exist on the maximum feasible range for data analysis (from the Napoleonic era onward) and the operational meaning of interstate war. These preceding points of agreement arise from the fact that the vast majority of systematic research on war adopts the data and measurements of the COW Project. Results from testing are mixed, but a sizable majority of elements show a connection to one or more of the basic aspects of the causes of war, which consist of initiation and participation, along with war in and of itself, with both the frequency and intensity of these actions and events being included in the analysis. As in the previous stage of identifying the positive heuristic, it is not obvious how the diverse elements and findings about war based on them would be integrated into a coherent whole.

6. Conclusions

This chapter has reviewed the hard core, negative heuristic, and positive heuristic of structural realism. The hard core consists of six parametric settings, with rationality being included, in spite of some controversy, as a result of the current project's commitment to systemism and the need to establish a coherent foundation for structural realism as a research enterprise. The negative heuristic excludes strategic altruism as a form of behavior and prohibits explanations for conflict, crisis, and war that otherwise violate the hard core.

Analysis of the positive heuristic requires some movement away from conventional expositions in the philosophy of science but becomes feasible with appropriate adjustments. Three components of the positive heuristic for structural realism are identified. One is a series of theories that shows an increase in the range of empirical problems. The initial variant of structural realism could address only macro-macro linkages, whereas the latter two versions either include or create the potential for all four logical possibilities. The second stage in identifying the positive heuristic consisted of a review of explanation and prediction (or, in practice, retrodiction) of conflict, crisis, and war by the full range of elements of structure. While many linkages have been put forward and more than a few confirmed with an overwhelming emphasis in the research on the causes of war, capability-based research stands largely in isolation from the hard core of structural realism. Third and finally, a review of findings about the causes of war as an empirical problem reinforces the preceding point about the disjunction between theorizing *writ large* and quantitative research findings. This is perhaps the most daunting challenge to be faced by any effort to produce an elaborated structural realism.

This review sets the stage for evaluation of structural realism, as it exists so far, in the following chapter. Each basic component of structural realism as a scientific research enterprise, including the hard core, negative heuristic, and positive heuristic, has been described. The goal of the analysis conducted in that chapter will be to derive priorities for a more advanced version of structural realism.

CHAPTER FIVE
An Assessment of Structural Realism

1. Overview and Objectives

This chapter will provide a preliminary assessment of structural realism as a scientific research enterprise. Both the hard core and positive heuristic will be appraised. The evaluation should be regarded as tentative, however, because it represents the first of a two-stage process. Although several aspects of the framework developed in chapter 3 will be applied to structural realism as conveyed by chapter 4, others come into play more naturally as part of a future research agenda: that is, after an elaborated structural realism appears in full as a theory and experiences testing. Thus, as noted near the outset of the previous chapter, analysis of structural realism at this stage will include neither (a) a diagrammatic exposition of description, explanation, and prediction nor (b) appraisal of marginal costs and benefits from greater complexity in theorizing. Two more specific aspects of evaluation covered by chapter 3—assessment of the hard core with regard to efficiency and the negative heuristic in terms of precision—also will form part of the future research agenda.[1] The present chapter, however, will carry out the following five tasks.

First, the hard core will be assessed in terms of logical consistency. The six parametric settings for structural realism are evaluated for congruity on a pairwise basis. As will become apparent, a potential difficulty with one of the pairings arises as concern at the empirical level as well.

Second, the positive heuristic is appraised initially in terms of the exposition from Waltz (1979), which is identified as T_0, a purely positional theory of international politics. The theory put forward by Waltz is found wanting along several dimensions, some of which are addressed, at least in part, by the subsequent efforts of Gilpin (1981) and Buzan, Jones, and Little (1993), previously designated as T_1 and T_2.

Assessment of the positive heuristic continues in the third section with a focus on the research findings summarized in the preceding chapter. A few basic and representative patterns in aggregate research are identified and then assessed in terms of potential for generalization. If these results are to be considered credible as solutions for empirical problems, that is the natural point to probe. This section also includes a brief review of measurement issues with the potential to affect tentative research findings, most notably as related to alliances.

Fourth, priorities are identified for an elaborated structural realism, or T_3. These ideas are described in some detail, most notably the need for a model of state behavior and more inclusive vision of international structure. The discussion culminates in a schematic presentation of T_3, designated as elaborated structural realism. T_3 is *not* presented at this point as a full-fledged theory. Instead, a diagrammatic exposition is used to guide the discussion of what such a theory should aim to include. The schematic version, however, will be evaluated in a preliminary way within the context of the model of scientific progress presented in figure 3.2.

Fifth, and finally, the accomplishments of the preceding sections are reiterated and the agenda of part 3 is introduced.

2. The Hard Core:
Are the Parametric Settings Consistent with Each Other?

Two criteria are applied in assessment of the hard core for structural realism as a scientific research enterprise. As identified in chapter 3, the benchmarks are logical consistency and efficiency. The first of these two criteria can be addressed without reference to the positive heuristic, so logical consistency provides the natural starting point for discussion. As noted a moment ago, the second criterion, efficiency, can be evaluated more thoroughly after an elaborated structural realism is presented in full (see James 2002a).

With six axioms, fifteen possible pairs exist. Table 5.1 summarizes the ways in which the axioms with parametric status are related to each other. Among the combinations listed, nine are regarded as related and six as independent of each other. Pairs deemed independent are those in which neither axiom implies the other. For example, state centrism (P_1) and anarchy (P_4) are regarded as autonomous from one another. State centrism does not imply anarchy; the Grotian perspective on international society, for example, points toward the possibility of a fundamentally different alternative with respect to an ordering principle (Bull 1977; Kacowicz 1998). Neither does anarchy denote state centrism; it is possible to envision a system that lacks both hierarchy and a single type of unit. The long-enduring medieval world is the obvious example that comes to mind.

Rational choice (P_2) and anarchy (P_4) make up another unrelated pair. Rational choice among states could produce hierarchy rather than anarchy as an ordering principle; other assumptions are needed to predict which of these structures is more likely to prevail. (For example, is this a unit-determined system?) Similarly, anarchy does not guarantee rational choice by states. Some states conceivably could be eliminated because of a failure to pursue their interests while the system of anarchy continued unabated.

One example of a related pair of axioms would be state centrism (P_1) and rational choice (P_2). If state centrism is the norm, then rational choice is implied; otherwise, selection would be expected to "weed out" the state as a political unit. (The question of whether irrational units might be capable of exerting influence during their temporary existence is assumed to be a minor one.) Rational choice, however, does not guarantee a state-centric world; another type of unit could prevail in spite of the best efforts of states across the board.

Table 5.1
Logical Consistency for the Hard Core of Structural Realsim: Independent and Related Axioms

Axioms	P₁ State Centrism	P₂ Rational Choice	P₃ Security Seeking	P₄ Anarchy	P₅ Status Undifferentiated by Function	P₆ Structure as Capability Distribution
P₂	related, preeminence of states implies rationality					
P₃	independent	related and potentially problematic				
P₄	independent	independent	related, anarchy encourages competitive security-seeking			
P₅	independent	related, rationality encourages sameness of functions	related, competitive security-seeking encourages sameness of functions	related, anarchy encourages sameness of functions		
P₆	related, state-centrism provides basis for capability distribution as structure	independent	related, competitive security-seeking produces structure	related, anarchy produces structure based on distribution of unit capabilities	independent	

While it is beyond the scope of this exposition to account in detail for each of the cells from the table, the main properties are worth pointing out:

1. Every parameter is related to at least one other.
2. Each parameter is independent of at least one other.
3. No pair exists for which $P_i \longrightarrow P_j, P_j \longrightarrow P_i$, where $i \neq j$.
4. One pair is related in a potentially problematic way.

The first three properties, taken together, are favorable or at least neutral to structural realism. The research enterprise grants parametric status to axioms that are independent in some cases and potentially related in others. Most important is the third property, which means that no axiom constitutes both a necessary and sufficient condition for one of the others. Thus none of the parametric settings is redundant. The fourth and final prominent feature of the table, which refers to the possibly problematic connection involving rational choice (P_2) and pursuit of security (P_3) through relative standing in the international system, merits further discussion.

Rationality implies self-interest. But who is the "self" in this case? This question is not answered at length by either Waltz (1979) or subsequent structural realist expositions, but the implication is something like Bueno de Mesquita's (1981b) "gatekeeper" (i.e., decision maker with the final opportunity to prevent war) or Putnam's (1988) "Chief of Government" (COG), who represents the state at each tier in a two-level (or, perhaps more accurately, multilevel) game (see also Tsebelis 1990; Buzan 1991; David 1991; Ayoob 1995). Yet the gatekeeper or COG in Waltz's vision of international politics seems afflicted with partial blindness. While leaders are taken to be rational, they seek security only at the international level. This combination of axioms creates potential inconsistency in pursuit of anything beyond macro-macro connections. In particular, what should a COG do about internal threats? If the leader's goal is to represent the state adequately, some rate of substitution must be designated for security inside versus outside of national borders (Simon and Starr 2000). Otherwise, it could be deemed rational for a leader to allow the state to collapse as a result of one type of pressure but not the other.

This discussion leads naturally into the more encompassing subject of comparative politics. If both internal and external security are of fundamental interest to a national leader, then factors such as the type of government at a general level and other more specific elements would enter into calculating the trade-off.[2] Put differently, it is reasonable to expect that the balance of concerns between internal and external security will vary on a cross-national basis and perhaps also for a given state over time.

While it would be getting too far ahead of things at this stage to explore either the meaning of internal security or its potential trade-off with external security, the basic point is clear. Without further development of the apparatus surrounding the rationality axiom—meaning specification of a state-level utility function that remains consistent with structural realism's other basic postulates—the hard core cannot pass the test of logical consistency. Thus a model of state behavior becomes a high priority for an elaborated structural realism as a result of the need for congruity between and among its parametric settings, not to mention other reasons that will become clear.

3. The Positive Heuristic: Starting with Waltz, or T_0

For many students of international politics, the positional version of structure conveyed by Waltz (1979) and reiterated in later expositions (1986, 1997) is regarded as problematic, although reassessments emerge from several vantage points.[3] Despite the diverse range of opinion, several basic criticisms can be identified. One problem is that structural realism seems deterministic, leaving virtually no room for human agency. Another is that the perspective is static and cannot account for many recent and contemporary changes in the international system. A third problem is the inherent lack of detail in the explanations and predictions (or retrodictions) that structural realism out of Waltz can produce directly. The fourth and final difficulty pertains to the general relevance of capabilities as resources. Further discussion of these problem areas will suggest potential paths toward improvement of structural realism.

Structural realism links processes at the level of the international system, such as the pervasiveness of warfare, directly to positional standing. For this reason it attracts criticism, not surprisingly, for apparent determinism (Holsti 1991a: 5; Howe 1991: 327, 328). More specifically, many theorists are skeptical about the ability of structure alone to determine state behavior (Bueno de Mesquita and Lalman 1988: 3; Wendt 1999: 17–18). With a specific focus on Waltz's expositions, Achen (1989) characterizes structural realism as a "puzzling sort of social theorizing in which human volition is largely absent" (3), and various other critiques emphasize an "alleged disregard for history as a process that is continually undergoing redefinition, in which individuals contribute to the molding of each successive era" (Dougherty and Pfaltzgraff 1990: 126; see also 1996, 2001). (For example, crises—one of the main focal points envisioned for hypothesis generation and testing for an elaborated structural realism—would be envisioned by the initial variant of structural realism in strictly macro-level terms.) Although Waltz (1979, 1997) always is careful to assert that he developed structural realism as a theory of international politics rather than foreign policy, the resulting holism seems increasingly self-limiting. In the language of systemism, the theory appears restricted, at the instruction of its creator, to macro-macro connections.

Critics seem to agree that, in particular, structural realism lacks a convincing treatment of unit-level response to structural imperatives or, in the language of systemism, macro-micro and micro-macro linkages. On the basis of historical experience, change and stability "can be generated at any level (from micro to macro) in the world polity" (Brown 1991: 217–18). Consider the rather fatalistic implications of anarchy combined with states seeking maximization of security through relative positional standing. It is true by definition that some states will have a military advantage over others at any given time, so rational choice, if taken in a superficial way, seemingly would predict a virtually uninterrupted series of conquests. Thus, it would appear, warfare should be underway constantly (Howe 1991: 328). Nothing in the hard core of structural realism contradicts this argument because restraining factors are not incorporated among the axioms with parametric status. Yet, in reality, states with favorable positions do not always exploit them, and war is not always in progress, although it could be observed that great-power warfare occurred almost constantly in sixteenth- and seventeenth-century Europe. Thus the meaning of rational choice among states seeking security under conditions of anarchy needs to be developed further, in order to preserve consistency at the empirical level and counteract structural realism's tendency toward holism.[4] This point reinforces the need, noted toward the end of the discussion of the hard core, for a model of state behavior (i.e., foreign policy [Walker 1987]) within a more advanced version of structural realism.

Inability to account for change is a second shortcoming attributed to structural realism (Buzan and Jones 1981: 2; Katzenstein 1989: 21; Wesson 1990: 7–8; Mastanduno and Kapstein 1999: 9; Wendt 1999). The axioms listed in table 4.1 do not refer to means of change; to borrow Kaplan's (1957) terminology, transformation rules for the international system are not specified. For example, how and why, according to structural realism, would a multipolar system shift into hegemonic war, bipolarity, or some other configuration? It is not clear whether such a conversion would be expected to occur by design or through the normal pursuit by individual states of enhanced relative capabilities. In either instance, the method of transformation does not follow logically from the axioms that have been granted parametric status by structural realism.

Given that Waltz's (1979) interpretation identifies (at its time of writing) only one transition in structure over the course of several centuries—from multipolarity to bipolarity at the end of World War II—questions about an inability to address the issue of change seem justified (Levy 1983: 4). If the structure of the system is to help explain processes, which are multifaceted and in some instances defined in ways that encompass rapid change, it should include components that can address variation. How otherwise can a virtually immutable structure account for changes in world politics aside from rare, dramatic, global transformations? Qualitative change in the number of great powers, which for Waltz (1979) means either (a) a shift from two to three or more or (b) back the other way, is uncommon; to explain anything that varies more rapidly, such as the frequency or intensity of international conflict, it becomes necessary to look toward a wider range of capability-based indicators that remain consistent with the hard core of structural realism.

This line of reasoning is relevant especially to any comparative analysis of regions. Contrast, for example, evolution of the roles played by the United

States, the acknowledged leading world power for many decades, in Latin America and Southeast Asia. In Latin America, sustained political and military activity by the United States suggests hegemonic regulation. Southeast Asia reveals more variation, with the salient impression being a decline in the U.S. level of engagement since the end of the Vietnam War. This difference across regions cannot be explained in terms of a change in the number of great powers in the global system, but it might be accounted for by one or more elements of an inclusive treatment of structure. Other capability-based indicators might be able to explain the preceding differences between regions while maintaining consistency with the hard core of structural realism, rather than simply leaving the field of explanation to rival theories.

Structural realism also is attacked from many quarters because its predictions lack specificity. The theory is "hard pressed to explain single-handedly the myriad forms of state behavior and regional outcomes, let alone their evolution and change" (Solingen 1998: 5). Power balancing, for instance, is predicted for a world of anarchy, but not which coalitions will form as a result (Garst 1989: 19). A system of two principal powers may be seen as more (or less) conflict prone than one in which capabilities are distributed with greater equality, but the timing and scope of warfare or other manifestations of instability cannot be anticipated without further information. As a rule, only aggregate tendencies can be estimated. Even if multipolarity (or bipolarity) could be linked to the outbreak of war, what would the connection imply for the many other conflicts in which states might engage? What about specific expectations regarding regional or national patterns of warfare? Furthermore, can war be reduced to a one-dimensional concept? What if the frequency of war could be linked positively with bipolarity, but that connection disappeared or reversed with the introduction of some measure of intensity? Clearly, structural realism as applied by Waltz (1979) is not equipped to deal directly with such precise queries. The more specific the process at issue, the less structural realism at version T_0 is able to say about any patterns that might become visible.

Consider as an example the period of rapid decolonization in the decade following World War II, which added many new states to those already in the system. It is clear that interaction opportunities, both bilateral and multilateral, increased dramatically as a function of the global polity's membership. Three possibilities regarding conflict proneness of the system therefore would arise: increased, decreased, or no change. (The speed and pervasiveness of decolonization as a process in and of itself, of course, would represent a separate challenge for a new variant of structural realism—in other words, "How and why did it all happen so fast"?) Waltz's structural realism does not generate a prediction about the effects of expanded membership; all three interpretations are feasible. Under conditions of anarchy, a greater number of interaction opportunities could lead self-interested states to engage in fewer sustained bilateral conflicts, resulting in a lower level of strife in the system. It also is possible that the complexity created by the emergence of new actors could pose new difficulties for external relations, perhaps leading to more intense multilateral conflicts as compared to those experienced before by individual dyads. Finally, each of these effects—along with others—might come into play, with the net result being little or no change.

Efforts to derive hypotheses from the parametric settings also bring out the highly general nature of the positive heuristic in the sense of Lakatos (1970). Take Grieco's (1988) propositions that (a) states behave as "unitary-rational agents," sensitive to the costs imposed by the system on members who act otherwise, and (b) "international institutions affect the prospects for cooperation only marginally" (188). The first of these propositions can be derived from the assumption of state centrism. If states remain the principal actors in world politics, that is because they have maintained rational choice as units. Depending on the state and its circumstances, that could mean a number of things, thus allowing for the observed variation in foreign policies. Security could be pursued through internal or external means (or both in some combination), which in practice would be primarily defense spending and alliances (or informal coalitions), respectively. The second hypothesis is derived by Grieco from the assumption of anarchy. If anarchy is dominant, then international institutions, by implication, are not very important. Force, latent or manifest, explains the resolution of conflict.

Furthermore, when Grieco (1988: 499) turns to development of a more specific proposition regarding the viability of interstate cooperation, he argues that positional considerations may inhibit the making of deals. And what if the partner will derive a greater benefit from the trade, thus producing a *loss* in bilateral status for the actor? Grieco (1988) concludes that such trades are not acceptable in a system of anarchy, for which *relative* capability is the prime consideration. No determinate answer to the question of when to cooperate can be obtained without further assumptions than those adopted explicitly by Grieco due to a wide range of complicating factors: "[C]oncerns for relative gains within a bilateral relationship can be muted by the relative gains such a relationship affords vis-à-vis third parties" (Kirshner 1999: 82; see also James 1988). Virtually all interstate trades entail a loss in bilateral standing for one party, yet some cooperation takes place anyway. To remain viable, structural realism must be able to account for this sort of variation in state behavior—the need for "secure microfoundations" could not be greater (Lake and Powell 1999: 25).

Even allowing for the primary intended role of system-level theory, which is to provide a *context* for the explanation of individual events, it is necessary to go beyond what can be derived from its initial variant, that is, T_0 as put forward by Waltz. The prevailing conception of international structure "is not unlike the corresponding views of Newtonian mechanics" (Ruggie 1989: 27). Factors intervene and further postulates are needed to account for the resulting patterns. For example, how is cooperation to be explained in a world of *unchanging* anarchy (Mansbach and Vasquez 1981: 11)? Similarly, what about the declining frequency of war? In sum, the positive heuristic viewed through the lens of T_0 resembles an underdetermined system of equations: with more unknowns than expressions, multiple solutions remain viable.

Keohane (1989: 62; see also Buzan, Jones, and Little 1993) raises a fourth problem for structural realism—the general relevance of capabilities viewed as resources. This line of argument is well established among scholars of international political economy and focuses on the limits on capabilities possessed by states in an increasingly complex, interdependent world. The particular issue in relation to structural realism or any other state-centric vision of world politics is the relevance of military capabilities. Is interstate rivalry the only issue, with resolution of differences depending on relative ability to threaten or exert military force? Or is it more appropriate instead to separate at least some issues from each other, with relevant resources varying by circumstance (Vasquez 1986)? These questions pose a basic challenge to the initial variant of structural realism, which grants priority to military security and the capabilities of states in its analysis of world politics.

Structural realism at T_0, to sum things up, is problematic in terms of the positive heuristic. *It is deterministic, static, capable of yielding only a few very general explanations and predictions, and based on at least one strongly challenged assumption.* Escalating challenges to the research enterprise demand that these difficulties be addressed.

It is fair to say that both T_1 and T_2 deal with some of the preceding aspects directly. Gilpin's theory makes it possible for structural realism to address the problem of political change, which in turn reduces the degree of determinism. Buzan and colleagues experiment with the disaggregation of capabilities into four categories tailored to circumstance. Overall, however, more work is needed. The developments by T_2 in particular move structural realism forward, but the range for explanation and prediction remains quite limited. Thus structural realism should be elaborated in a way that responds further to each of the main strands of criticism from the preceding review.

4. The Positive Heuristic: A Review of Research Findings

Chapter 4 reviewed a myriad of findings about conflict, crisis, and especially war in relation to primary, secondary, tertiary, and higher-order elements of structure. No attempt will be made in this section to assemble these diverse elements into a coherent whole—that is a mission designated for a fully elaborated structural realism (James 2002a). At present the priority is to continue evaluation of structural realism's positive heuristic as manifested through the variety of what Lakatos (1970) labels ad hoc$_3$ hypotheses. Many of these propositions fit into middle-range theories of one sort or another, but the purpose here is not to establish or assess those linkages either. Instead, the first of two subsections will (a) offer a few generalizations on the basis of the findings; and (b) present a critique that connects the lack of integration among the various frames of reference that generated the hypotheses to the latter's collective inability to demonstrate cumulation. A second, brief subsection will explore the potential role of measurement in influencing the findings presented. Examples related to alliances will be used to show how the results presented in tables 4.3 through 4.8 are more of a starting point than a conclusion for assessment of the positive heuristic.

4.1 Another Look at Findings Based on Elements of Structure

While many nuances might be brought out in the findings described in the last chapter, a few prominent and general patterns from that review, when subjected to scrutiny, will be sufficient to establish the point that the ability to generalize on the basis of the results is burdened by fundamental problems. The patterns just noted are as follows: in the twentieth century, multipolarity and a less concentrated distribution of capabilities are linked to the occurrence of war. Alliance formation and tightening of existing commitments also are associated with systemic war proneness. On the basis of these results, a bipolar system with a concentrated distribution of capabilities and a few loose alliances may be described as the preferred structure. Larger questions about why these results occur must await the development of a more integrated treatment of elements of structure in relation to conflict: that is, an elaborated structural realism.

Other interesting generalizations also could be culled from the wide range of findings reviewed in chapter 4 and used to illustrate the points made in this section, but those above are sufficient for present purposes. For several reasons the preceding generalizations should be regarded with caution, both individually and collectively, as cumulative knowledge about the impact of structure on international conflict, crisis, and war. One problem is that auxiliary assumptions vary across investigations, which creates the potential for inconsistency between and among them. Another is inadequate range among the studies as a whole in assessment of international conflict. A further difficulty is the relative lack of understanding about sufficient conditions for conflict. Finally, complications from potential intervening variables and multivariate effects must be addressed. Each of these difficulties will be considered in turn.

Assumptions vary, sometimes dramatically, from one capability-based study to the next. Aside from the six axioms of structural realism, which seem to enjoy at least implicit endorsement, inconsistency characterizes theorizing that links elements of structure to conflict, crisis, and war. In fact, differing expectations invariably can be traced to contradictory premises. Consider, for example, the opposing conclusions reached by Gilpin (1981) and Niou, Ordeshook, and Rose (1989) concerning tripolarity. Different assumptions about constraints on coalitional dynamics explain this contradiction quite readily. Gilpin expects tripolarity to be very war prone, with a coalition of two powers attacking a third as the obvious and persistent scenario. However, as Niou and colleagues point out, any coalition of two actors is inherently unstable because the excluded power—faced with possible destruction—can offer one of the aggressors a deal that is better than whatever already is in place. This line of reasoning implicitly assumes that agreements can be overturned in pursuit of greater gain. Similarly, for Gilpin, the anticipation of war is produced by the opposite assumption: once a coalition forms, it will tend to be firm. Expected value calculations might make the members of an alliance reluctant to forfeit their benefits in order to gamble on a better payoff. Depending on what else is assumed, either set of expectations regarding tripolarity can be reconciled with structural realism.[5]

Examples of assumptions built into a specific study that produce either direct or implicit inconsistencies with others that focus on the same subject matter are not difficult to find. A few instances should be sufficient to demonstrate this point. To begin, the time between cause and presumed effect can vary significantly from one instance to the next, sometimes including more than one lag in the same research design. While exploratory analysis reasonably can include multiple measurement options, some connection to an underlying model of transmission of effects also is desirable. For example, why would some effects be anticipated to appear over the course of years, as opposed to months or decades or even as yet unmentioned intervals?

With regard to risk propensity, no consensus exists in empirical studies (or, for that matter, in theory) on where or when to assume neutrality, acceptance, or aversion. Leaving aside the roles played by individual leaders, is it reasonable to suppose that one outlook or the other will predominate on a cross-national basis? Furthermore, what is the operational basis for risk propensity and, in particular, aversion to risk?

Collective action also plays different roles within the research summarized in chapter 4. Advocates of bipolarity obviously would argue that, with more than two centers of capability, it becomes difficult to formulate and implement a scheme of management for power politics. Elsewhere, bipolarization is identified as menacing, but its presence would seem to imply the existence of a more coherent system of alignment. Collective action, in other words, should be facilitated by the straightforward pattern of alliances represented by bipolarization. Given the different expectations commonly expressed for bipolarity and bipolarization, it is obvious that the role of collective action should be made clear and consistent.

Given the assessment of conflict in the overwhelming majority of previous systematic studies, another reason suggests caution about would-be generalizations for the findings enumerated in chapter 4. International strife invariably has been equated with warfare, most notably as expressed in terms of the measurement options conveyed by the COW Project. While some capability-oriented studies have focused on militarized disputes or crises, much more is known, at least in terms of sheer data analysis, about war than any other form of international conflict. Furthermore, many interpretations are based upon the collective experiences of the great-power subset, as opposed to states in general. It is not obvious that inferences based on that evidence also should apply without qualification to other actors and forms of conflict.

Aside from the question of measuring conflict, the results from testing collectively have more to say about the necessary, as opposed to sufficient, conditions for war (James 1988). To cite a specific example, changes toward tightness in alliance configurations and more diffuse distribution of capabilities do not serve as causes of interstate warfare. It instead is appropriate to view these developments as reducing external constraints on choice by the leadership of a given state in favor of war over peace. Suppose, for example, that more clearly defined coalitions and greater uncertainty about relative capabilities (in the latter sense, a trend toward parity) take hold in an international system. A higher *likelihood* of both confrontation and misjudgment about the likely outcome of a struggle might be the result, tending to encourage the outbreak of violent conflict.

Intervening variables and multivariate effects provide a further reason to be wary of reading too much into the patterns that seem to have been gleaned from aggregate testing. Intervening variables may have a profound effect on presumably straightforward linkages involving international conflict, most notably war, and individual aspects of structure. The role played by pervasiveness of alliances in the system, to cite an example from the findings, is likely to depend on the intentions behind their formation. Similarly, whether those holding extensive capabilities are satisfied with the system (a nonstructural variable) is anticipated to have a mediating effect on the linkage of capability concentration and war.

Multivariate effects are as yet poorly understood because an integrated treatment of elements of structure in relation to conflict—incorporating a full range of independent, intervening, and dependent variables—is yet to be specified and tested. Consider, for example, interaction of the number of poles with concentration or polarization. Potential effects from combinations such as these rarely are considered and could have important implications for either seemingly established or repudiated bivariate linkages. While well-constructed and often quite elaborate, research designs have tended to focus on the most prominent elements of structure on an individual basis. Even more unknown are the combined effects of capability and cluster polarity, concentration of capabilities and the pervasiveness and characteristics of alliances, and so on. None of the existing frameworks of analysis pertaining to structure offers a full set of expectations across these elements. Problems such as inconsistency among propositions (Burgess and Moore 1972: 361) and the inability to account for change (Buzan and Jones 1981: 2; Katzenstein 1989: 292; Keohane 1989: 36) might be addressed through a more integrated sense of structure.

Another closely related area that is not well understood, but is certainly crucial to a full treatment of the issues, is *intrastructural* effects. In other words, what impact can various elements of structure be expected to have on each other? Such effects would seem important to model in an effort to understand fully the impact of structure on process. An example of this unusual kind of theorizing is provided jointly by Aron (1966: 136) and Gilpin (1981: 88, 89; 1988: 596–97), although the latter takes things one step further. Both Aron and Gilpin assert that bipolarity will produce bipolarization, using those terms as they have been explained previously in chapter 4. Thus an intrastructural effect is posited from a primary to a higher-order element. Gilpin extends this causal chain into processes, with the next link being a greater propensity toward war.

To sum things up, several obstacles stand in the way of generalization on the basis of the results obtained from testing ad hoc hypotheses about elements of structure and international conflict. Auxiliary assumptions are seen to vary, and the investigations tend to focus almost exclusively on war. In addition, the research findings bear much more on facilitating (as opposed to necessary or sufficient) conditions for conflict-related actions and events and are subject to revision when potential intervening factors and multivariate effects are taken into consideration. The results bring to mind the flawed dichotomy noted by Brecher (1999) with regard to quantitative versus qualitative analysis. Findings based on aggregate data analysis seem to dwell in relative isolation from "grand theory" within international relations—to the detriment of both.

One question to raise at this point concerns the relevance of empirical findings to realist theories other than structural realism. The implications of the results from testing for structural realism will be explored in the next main section, but what about other variants that have been noted? This question ends up being self-defeating because of the nature of the theories at issue. Neotraditional realist theories, which collectively form the salient alternative to structural realism, are not ready for elaboration in response to research findings. A lack of falsifiability, resulting in virtual incoherence, will become apparent from a brief review of neotraditional theorizing.

Neotraditional realism, also referred to as neoclassical realism (Legro and Moravcsik 1998, 1999), represents one reaction to the perceived excesses of Waltz's (1979, 1986) structural theory. Other than this rejection of holism, adherents of neotraditional realism probably have little fully in common, but they do seem committed to opening up the unit level for consideration along several fronts. New and reconstituted directions include traditional realist notions of power balancing (articulated in terms of concerns about relative gains [Grieco 1988]), but also other ideas about the focal point of interstate competition. Prominent examples include balance of threat (Walt 1997) and balance of interests (Schweller 1997). Thus neotraditional realism might, on the surface, appear to be on a more dynamic and promising path than structural realism.

All, however, is not as it might appear with neotraditional realism. In brilliant and authoritative reviews, Vasquez (1997, 1998) shows that the diverse set of ideas about balancing create a basic problem, namely, a lack of falsifiability for the realist paradigm as a whole. Vasquez (1997, 1998) concludes that realism is unscientific because virtually all observed behavior of states, including "bandwagoning" *with* superior power, seem consistent with one or more variants of the theory. Examples of this problem continue to accumulate; consider the following seemingly positive assessment of realist explanations for some major events in the last decade: "After the Cold War, U.S. security and economic strategy have diverged. Security strategy has been more consistent with the predictions of balance-of-threat theory, while economic strategy has followed more closely the expectations of balance-of-power theory" (Mastanduno 1999: 168). In sum, if power, threat, or interests being balanced all are acceptable as evidence in favor of realism, then, one might ask, "How can it lose?"

Systemism can help to put the preceding difficulty into a wider context that facilitates an improved approach. Pursuit of a full set of linkages, beyond the recently near-standard micro-micro specification, would have the potential to push neotraditional realism in the direction of falsifiability.

Consider, for example, Walt's (1997: 933) treatment of balance of threat. While Walt claims that states will balance against the most serious threats as opposed to the mere aggregation of power, he sees the latter as being relevant to threat assessment. This might be restated, clarified, and linked to other variants of realism through use of language provided by systemism: anarchy produces a concern among states for balancing against threat, understood in terms of the distribution of power and interests—that is, a macro-micro connection.

Ironically, this formulation *already exists in the form of expected utility theory* (Bueno de Mesquita 1980a, 1981b; James 1988; Bueno de Mesquita and Lalman 1992). Furthermore, unlike Walt's treatment, expected utility is explicit about functional form, which from the standpoint of systemism puts it another step ahead of balance-of-threat theory. While it would be beyond the scope of this chapter to delve into expected utility in much greater detail, a brief description of the components from its basic equation related to war should make the preceding point. In words rather than symbols, for ease of exposition:

> Expected Utility of War (for state i versus potential enemy j) = (utility or value of winning for i) x (i's probability of winning) + (utility or value of losing for i) x (i's probability of losing)

The formulas in use today in applied work on expected utility theory go far beyond the preceding simple presentation. (Examples of applied research on expected utility are legion and appear regularly in virtually all of the major journals in international relations; this work is not cited by Walt 1997.) However, even the rudimentary expression from above is sufficient to show that neotraditional realism could be strengthened by consulting expected utility theory, which works with the same concepts but offers an explicit functional form to bring them together. To be more exact, the value of winning, or utility, is assessed in terms of the *interests* at issue between states i and j. The probabilities of winning and losing are based on relative *power* between i and j. The overall expression for expected utility might even be conceived of, in

Walt's terminology, as the degree of *threat* posed by i to j (or, by reversing roles for i and j in the expression, the threat from j to i). Note that in this form, the concepts that currently find favor among neotraditional realists—interests, power, and threat—come together in a coherent functional form that even can be linked to the system level. In other words, efforts to maximize expected utility would derive from system imperatives created by anarchy: that is, a macro-micro linkage.

While expected utility is not the only potential source for enhanced rigor and system-level connections, neotraditional realism would do well to review its need to improve falsifiability within the preceding context. Only a coherent and falsifiable variant then would be ready to go through the process of elaboration that is envisioned for structural realism.

4.2 Measurement Issues and Further Research

This brief subsection is intended to show that measurement issues make the interpretation of any compilation of findings a matter for great caution. The discussion is a by-product of the point made in chapter 3 about the multifaceted possible explanations for failure of a hypothesis (Duhem 1977). Recall that the list included faulty logic, measurement error, flaws in research design, random error, and even reasons as yet unanticipated. While any of these problems deserve detailed consideration, only one will be considered within the constraints imposed by this discussion. Measurement error will be explored in the context of some recent and interesting assessments of how alliances should be assessed as part of the practice of world politics.

Studies by Gibler (1996, 1997, 1999a, 1999b; see also Gibler and Vasquez 1998) and Leeds, Long, and Mitchell (2000) suggest that the findings reported for alliances in tables 4.3 through 4.8 may need reconsideration: in particular, "white noise" may be masking stronger and more significant connections.

Gibler (1996: 89) produces an authoritative review of alliance documents from 1815 onward and reaches the conclusion that those focusing on the resolution of territorial disagreements are fundamentally different from others. He labels such agreements territorial settlement treaties (TSTs). Gibler (1996: 86) produces evidence that suggests that previous studies have erred in combining TSTs with alliances writ large. Specifically, TSTs do not focus on third parties in the conventional way expected for an alliance; they specify neither a potential threat nor a potential target. An analysis of MIDs and TSTs from 1815 to 1988 confirms this suspicion: dispute involvement for rivals reduces dramatically and is less intense (if it occurs) after a TST has been signed. Thus it is difficult to justify representing TSTs as alliances in the way that this term is understood in realist practice.

Another seemingly subtle point of measurement, explored by Leeds, Long, and Mitchell (2000: 691, 692), concerns the obligations listed in alliances: more concretely, when is an ally obligated to offer support, and what form should it take? Reexamination of treaties produces the conclusion that a wide range of requirements exist for allies: defense, offense, neutrality, nonaggression, and consultation. Controlling for these kinds of obligation, Leeds and colleagues (2000: 695) find that 74.5 percent of allies meet their commitments in time of war—a relatively high level compared to previous findings. The analysis implies that it is crucial to establish that alliances are *relevant* before trying to link them to war (Leeds, Long, and Mitchell 2000: 698).

Given the findings from Gibler and Leeds, Long, and Mitchell, the results for alliance-based hypotheses reported in tables 4.3 through 4.8 should be regarded as an *understatement* of connections that may exist in a fully specified model. Alliances, in various ways, have been connected to war, but the recent studies suggest that measurement error may have attenuated the findings. While further research would be needed to confirm this point, at the very least it shows that the development of the positive heuristic is an ongoing process in which measurement matters. Thus the potential for realist explanations of war, in which alliances play a key role, may yet to be realized in full.

5. Toward Elaborated Structural Realism

Problems have been identified in both the hard core and positive heuristic of structural realism. In particular, the relationship of rational choice to security seeking among states needs to be clarified. The range of empirical problems addressed by the series of theories currently linked to structural realism remains rather limited. In addition, research findings based on systematic data appear to lack integration and therefore cannot be linked effectively to any version of structural realism that is available at present.

For such reasons, two priorities arise for elaboration of structural realism: that is, creation of a T_3 in the existing sequence of theories. One is development of a model of state behavior, which should help to address both the difficulty noted with respect to the hard core and the range and coherence of propositions about conflict processes. The other priority is a more inclusive treatment of structure. The rationale for each priority will be developed at some length because these changes, if instituted, constitute major steps beyond structural realism as it currently exists. This discussion will be followed by an overview of a proposed T_3: that is, elaborated structural realism.

5.1 Identifying Priorities

System-level or macrotheory naturally rests on the assumption of micro-level foundations (Elster 1983: 23; Nicholson 1989: 218). Thus, in elaborating structural realism, there is need for an explicit model of state behavior. Various scholars have called for an explicit treatment, realist or otherwise, of the role of the state in world politics (Mastanduno, Lake, and Ikenberry 1989: 471; Keating 1990: 34), which structural realism has depicted in a very general way as maximization of security through enhanced positional standing.

Perhaps the best way to counteract the ethereal, even fatalistic character of system-level realism as constituted in Waltz (1979) is to specify how units are expected to cope with their environment, as expressed in figure 2.2's portrayal of the international system. Structural realism assumes that states function as rational actors, with utility being maximized in terms of relative positional standing. But what does that mean in terms of even aggregate patterns of behavior? How, for example, is a leader to assess security while contemplating escalation of a conflict with one or more states? Are the capabilities of all actors regarded as equally menacing? Is the relevant balance global or regional? Furthermore, under what conditions can fundamental change be expected to occur? Other questions could be posed, but these few are sufficient to demonstrate that structural realism requires a more explicit unit-system linkage to move beyond holism and determinism. As opposed to operating on assumption, the need is for a focus on connections that transcend the macro-macro level, which in turn require a model of state behavior (Booth 1987: 42).

With regard to addressing the elusive issue of change, progress requires that restrictions on the defining conditions of structure be relaxed. As opposed to the dichotomy involving two versus three or more centers of power at the global level, the distribution of capabilities should be interpreted in more inclusive terms. This can be accomplished without violating the requirement that structure consist only of relatively enduring attributes of the system. The previously developed typology of primary, secondary, tertiary, and higher-order elements begins to address the issue.[6] It is a step beyond the "disaggregating and de-restricting" of the distribution of capabilities introduced by Buzan, Jones, and Little (1993: 64) in T_2, wherein military capability, economic capability, political cohesion, and ideology are introduced as providing the basis for parallel structures. The difference is that the typology ranging from primary to higher-order elements refers to the makeup of indicators in terms of calculations and coalitions (as opposed to empirical measurements), which moves past structural realism's usual focus on polarity alone as the motive force in international relations.

One example of a dynamic component that already shows some ability to account for conflict processes is the capability (or power) cycle. According to Doran (1985), structure should be viewed as *dynamic* in a positional sense because change can occur without reference to a shift in the *number* of great powers. Variation in the structure of the international system is taken to depend on two factors: one concerns the balance of capabilities among leading states, while the other "emphasizes the upward and downward mobility of states within the international system"—that is, their capability cycles (297). Thus structure may be altered by the rise and fall of individual states in an existing configuration described by a primary element, such as bipolarity or multipolarity in terms of the number of poles. Since structure can change without the number of prominent actors being altered, the concept becomes more elaborate than before through incorporation of the relative standing of individual states. Changes in relative position, which can have important effects on subsequent interactions, still tend to unfold over relatively long periods of time (Doran 1991). Thus the addition of a dynamic component would not violate the enduring character that structure, to remain a meaningful concept, must uphold. It remains stable in comparison to changes in process.

Elaboration of structural realism will need to enhance its potential for explanation and prediction. Referring to Waltz's approach as "ultra-exclusive," Jones (1981: 14–16) introduces "capability" and "relational" structures. These components have the potential to explain more of world politics without repudiating the system-level character of structural realism. Enduring aspects of the system other than the number of great powers can be identified. Coalitions, which might explain developments that a purely positional analysis could not, qualify as relational structures.[7] Elaborated structural realism therefore should include the characteristics of alliances as tertiary and higher-order elements of structure. Institutions that are not based on military security, however, are excluded and regarded as more appropriate for rival paradigms.

Consider the example of an economic market: cooperative arrangements between business and government, along with regulations of commerce by the latter, are pervasive in advanced, industrial states. The fundamentally market-oriented nature of economic activity under these regimes remains intact, with departure from the "hidden hand" analogous to introduction of a more elaborate structure. With respect to international relations, arrangements that focus on the security dilemma (Herz 1950, 1951; Jervis 1979) could be regarded as efforts to reduce uncertainty in an otherwise unregulated "market of power." By implication, a more encompassing notion of structure becomes viable because a greater number of developments have the potential to be explained or predicted.

For an inclusive approach toward structure, the crucial departure from the positional model is incorporation of intentionally produced items, such as coalitions.[8] In the domain of international politics, alliances are products of interstate interactions, which in turn provide a context for subsequent conveyance among actors. By contrast, in the positional model, "entities that are intentionally produced, such as alliances, cannot be part of structure" (Dessler 1989: 462). When such media do not exist, the positional outlook is valid: "Waltz's causal claims (anarchy accounts for war, bipolarity for stability, and so on) can thus be considered special limited cases of the transformational [i.e., more inclusive] theory, much as Newton's laws are a special case of relativity theory" (465). In the overwhelming majority of historical instances, however, intentionally produced entities of some kind do exist. The actions of states depend on two media: resources, or "the physical attributes that comprise 'capability'," and rules, or "the media through which they communicate with one another and coordinate their actions" (Dessler 1989: 454). Resources and rules affect interaction among units, which gradually—and, on rare occasions, rapidly—change the nature of the system itself. This belies the atomistic picture of world politics provided by existing variants of structural realism.

One objection to inclusion of alliance commitments in a theory such as elaborated structural realism is that these arrangements may require national forces to be placed under integrated command, thereby violating sovereignty. The example of France's role in the Gulf War (among many other possible choices), however, should be sufficient to counteract that argument. France allowed the United States (which had the single greatest commitment of personnel and equipment) to assume control of its forces, but only in the interest of *tactical effectiveness*. At no time did that policy include permission to use those resources in a manner contrary to the perceived national interest of France. Alliances and coalitions per se, in short, can be undone if the advantages of coordination are outweighed by divergence in policies. The problems associated with UN peacekeeping certainly come to mind as an example here.

Some treatments of structure, to begin with alliances and the relative capability endowments of states as examples, already seem to incorporate relational elements (Liska 1962: 161–68; Singer and Small 1979: 227; Ray 1980: 37, 39–40; Goldmann 1981: 123). These modifications of structure, which both incorporate and transcend positional standing, implicitly seek to explain a wider range of events. With an explicit focus on the problems of narrowness and lack of specificity in predictions, Dessler (1989: 444–49) advocates a more inclusive demarcation of structure. A "transformational" model, as opposed to the positional version advocated by Waltz, would have greater potential for grounding discussion of a wide range of events. A positional interpretation of structure, as Dessler observed, is one that focuses on the arrangement, position, organization, or situation of units. The transformational model is an elaboration of the levels of structure and action that have been described in positional terms (Dessler 1989: 451–54, 459–62).

With respect to structure, *rules* are brought in to complement *resources*, which already are incorporated in the positional perspective. State behavior depends on both of these media of action, not just the distribution of capabilities. In a "scientific realist" interpretation of the world, the assumption of rational self-interest is the manifestation of rules (Dessler 1989; see also Ellis 1985; Gutting 1985). A model of state behavior would specify how the rational state is expected to interpret its position in the world. Adaptive behavior would consist of choice from a set of feasible policy options, leading to the maximization of security as assessed by the actor.

From a transformational point of view, structure therefore incorporates more than just anarchy and the distribution of capabilities. It also includes "the media through which rational action is effected" (Dessler 1989: 459). Dessler's vision of structure is transformational in the sense that resources and rules are reproduced or transformed through action. Of course, it is assumed that the impact of rule-oriented elements of structure would be subject to assessment through observation, which parallels the treatment of existing capability-based aspects. Depending on the nature of interactions, structure evolves or remains effectively constant. World War II, to cite a dramatic example, shattered the multipolar environment of the interwar years and generated new rules and power endowments. After 1945, two superpowers presided over opposing coalitions of states and engaged in a global rivalry that persisted for decades.

The most potentially encompassing treatment is proposed by Morrow (1988), who claims that structure "resides in those elements of the international system that resolve conflicts in preferences" (79). Three obvious examples would be "the capabilities of states, durable alliance systems, and international regimes" (85). The attributes of the system condition and maintain interactions; the outcome and impact of a given conflict are determined by features of the system that do not reside within a specific actor and also clearly are not processes. A system is transformed when a "critical mass of actors need that change to achieve their preferred policies" (94). The circle of cause and effect is closed by the impact of behavior on the system itself: that is, through a micro-macro connection.

Without elaboration, only a few predictions are likely to result from a framework such as structural realism as put forward by Waltz (1979). Moreover, these assertions are unlikely to be specific, concerning instead the balance of power and its general connection to intermittent war.[9] While transformation of the global system after World War II from multipolarity to bipolarity had great importance, it cannot explain everything. What can be said on that basis about evolving patterns of great-power or superpower rivalry? How can regional variations in conflict be accounted for if structure so seldom is altered? A more inclusive notion of structure, bringing in positional dynamics and intentionally produced components, would have greater potential to answer such questions.

While arguing on behalf of economy of explanation, Olson (1982) brings out this point in a different but equally valuable way. The persuasiveness of a theory "depends not only on how many facts are explained, but also on how diverse are the kinds of facts explained" (13). A theory that illuminates the behavior of the great powers toward each other under varying circumstances and over a long period would be valuable, but not so much as one that also could account for other patterns of interaction. The events of 1648, no matter how important at the time, obviously cannot account for changes in the frequency and intensity of conflict in recent years. Even the dramatic change that took place in 1945 is very unlikely to explain, for example, the transformation of the Soviet sphere of influence that, several decades later, took place in just a few short years. Limitations on structural realism are notable especially with regard to the direction of further developments: that is, prediction of actions and events in conflict processes.

Another reason to favor an inclusive treatment of structure is that more diverse evidence will tend to discourage biased selection. Including in a definition of structure the configuration of alliances, for example, almost certainly allows a wider range of assertions about processes to be deduced. To test such hypotheses it would be necessary to bring in evidence beyond the positional standing and war involvement of the great powers; the situation of actors in general and regional configurations are obvious possibilities. In sum, a narrow and potentially self-serving focus on one region or time period becomes more difficult to justify with an inclusive definition of structure.

One objection to the inclusive approach is that it might encourage the "pernicious practice of summoning new systems into being in response to every salient change within a system" (Waltz 1986: 329). *Structure* has been extended to refer to bonds and links, but many other things also are encountered in the vast scholarship on international relations, which creates the danger of rendering the concept useless (Singer 1989: 4). Among the meanings Singer identifies are observed and proposed regularities in "the behavior of social entities," hypothetical and real "statistical associations among many sets of variables," conditions of any kind that "change slowly," and even regularities "for which no other word comes to mind." A concept that means everything ultimately explains nothing. To prevent that from happening to the centerpiece of an elaborated version of structural realism, the warnings from Waltz and Singer imply that criteria for inclusion must be very clear and consistent.

Among the various problems that could result from overextended concept formation, the most salient is that structure may become confused with process. Vincent (1983), to cite an extreme example, regards structure as "something that helps stabilize the international system and makes it more predictable" (1).[10] In other words, its existence is to be inferred from the degree of stability exhibited by the system. This approach makes it rather difficult to estimate the impact of structure on the level of disruption observed, except for after the fact and in a tautological way. A restricted demarcation can guard against such problems but is found wanting for other reasons. Where, then, is the right place to draw the line?

Structure, as defined earlier in a general way, should be relatively enduring and should have significant implications for behavior by rational units. Waltz (1986) objects to the latter criterion, but the argument against including other system-level characteristics appears to be inconsistent. "Asking whether something is important," he asserts, "cannot tell us whether it should be included or excluded" (328). Yet Waltz, as noted earlier, also argues that the distribution of capabilities among states should be recognized—with variables based on the dispersion of other characteristics being left out—because state behavior varies more with changes in relative standing than with differences in other things. This appears to pose a contradiction regarding selection criteria for the composition of structure. At the very least, it is obvious that a more precise demarcation of structure is needed.

One approach to this problem, to be manifested in elaborated structural realism, is to adopt a capability-based rule of inclusion. Some examples should help to explain the nature of this criterion. Alliances could be included because the formation of blocs affects the distribution of capabilities by potentially altering the balance at the global or subsystemic levels. In other words, the pervasiveness of alliances should be regarded as a capability-oriented, distributional attribute of the international system.[11] The concentration of capabilities *within* an alliance also could have important implications for the behavior of its members. For example, a coalition with a prominent leading state may tend toward higher cohesion and a lower likelihood of involvement in conflicts with those outside its domain. By contrast, an alliance composed of relatively equal states could be more prone to internal rivalry and even warfare. Inconsistent behavior by the alliance as a whole then might lead to conflicts with other system members.[12]

Also appropriate for inclusion in a capability-based model would be the *dynamics* of dispersion. New actors change the distribution of capabilities by definition. Thus variation in the number of states in the system as a whole and in regional subsystems should be considered as potential causal factors. Shifts in the concentration of capabilities among existing states also would be worthy of attention. Extensions such as these move the agenda of capability-based research beyond the boundaries of the great powers, with implications for the conflict-related behavior of states in general, most notably the neglected interactions among those in the peripheries.

With regard to the great powers specifically, the rise and decline of relative capabilities also would qualify as structural change. While the *number* of great powers might not change over the course of a few decades, the share of capabilities held by each actor will evolve and, in all likelihood, affect processes. It is apparent that such variation could be appraised in a number of ways, with some efforts already in evidence (Ray and Singer 1973; Taagepera and Ray 1977). The examples that follow are not exhaustive but appear for clarification because examination of individual units is especially distant from standard treatments of structural realism. The standing of the leading state, for instance, may have implications for the likelihood of stabilization through what has been labeled "hegemonic" leadership (Gilpin 1981). Along similar lines, the probability of conflict building up, potentially leading to systemic war, could be affected by the shifting balance between the first- and second-place powers (Organski and Kugler 1980). It also is possible to derive insights from the evolution of the relative standing of *each* great power; for example, over the last two centuries involvement in war can be linked to points of transition (Doran and Parsons 1980). When relative capability reaches a maximum or minimum, or the rate of ascent or descent is transformed (e.g., the state continues to make gains but at a progressively slower pace), a great power is more likely to become involved in war. In addition, when several states are near points of transition, conflict and even war on a grand scale is more likely than otherwise. A longitudinal perspective on structure therefore would appear capable of generating some interesting propositions about patterns of conflict, crisis, and war among the great powers.

Of course, when components of structure are at issue, change should be measured in years, not a mere matter of days or weeks. The notion of an enduring aspect of the system may be arbitrary, but it does imply that structure is not subject to truly short-term fluctuations. Change is regarded as evolutionary and cumulative, as opposed to sporadic and sudden.

All of the preceding concerns, which focus on excluded but potentially important causal factors, derive from the restricted nature of structural realism. As interpreted by Waltz (1979), it cannot address the effects of coalitions, capability-based dynamics, and many other things. The potential range of capability-oriented theory is not exhausted by estimating the effects of the size of the system and number of principal powers, so it is essential to seek a more comprehensive vision. Structural realism is an appropriate candidate for that type of theory building, bearing in mind that it is important for the elements of an inclusive approach to remain logically consistent with each other.

5.2 Toward Elaborated Structural Realism, or T_3

Elaborated structural realism is a theory that follows in the realist tradition, yet takes more than a few steps beyond preceding system-level variants. Figure 5.1 is a schematic presentation of elaborated structural realism's vision of world politics. This diagrammatic exposition contains no specific hypotheses; instead, it is intended as an overview of how structures, actors, and processes are expected to relate to each other in a functioning international system. In that sense the schematic presentation can be linked closely to figure 2.2, which conveyed Brecher and Ben Yehuda's (1985) international system. The components of an international system—actors, structure, process, issue, context, and environment—are represented at various points in figure 5.1. Each will be discussed in greater detail.

Elements from the four levels of structure will be organized into a *periodic table* when elaborated structural realism is articulated in full (James 2002a). These elements, as noted in chapter 1, combine to form the structure of the international system from a realist point of view. The typology consists of the following elements of structure, each of which appears with defining characteristics and a familiar example: (a) primary—neither complex calculations nor coalitions are entailed (e.g., number of great powers); (b) secondary—complex calculations, but not coalitions, are entailed (e.g., concentration of capabilities among system members); (c) tertiary—coalitions, but not complex calculations, are entailed (e.g., number of alliances in the system); and (d) higher order—both complex calculations and coalitions are entailed (e.g., the tightness of alliances in the system). The above-noted periodic table would be intended to convey order and meaning among the wide range of elements it conceivably can include.

As described in figure 5.1, a full set of potential intrastructural effects would need to be considered. These appear at the left side of system structure in the figure and are virtually unexplored in previous capability-based research on conflict, crisis, and war.[13] To make the possible connections easier to see, those for the primary elements appear closest to the edge, followed by the ones corresponding to secondary elements, and so on. Intrastructural effects based on primary elements will be used as an example to illustrate what is involved here. Primary elements might have effects on each other; hence the arrow that originates with and points back into the primary level. One or more of these elements also could affect those at other levels, which explains the additional three arrows tracing out from the primary level.

Elements of system structure are anticipated to produce direct and indirect effects on processes. Direct effects are from elements to *macro processes*, which refer to events in the aggregate. Thus cooperation or conflict in various forms might be accounted for in either global or regional terms. An example of this type of linkage from Waltz's (1979) structural realism would be from the number of poles to system stability, with bipolarity expected to be less war prone than other configurations. In the language of elaborated structural realism, this would be a direct effect from the number of poles as a primary element to the macro process of the frequency of war.

Elements of structure also are anticipated to affect *micro processes*, which entail actions and events below the regional level of aggregation. These include dyadic, monadic, and intrastate processes. As figure 5.1 reveals, these linkages are mediated by *state behavior*. Cooperation and conflict manifested as micro processes are subject to influence by elements of structure, but pursuit of security by states, which is assumed to combine internal and external factors, will mediate the effects. This type of connection is without precedent in previous versions of structural realism, so no example can be provided for translation into the terms favored by elaborated structural realism.

Elaborated structural realism's model of state behavior will be consistent with the basic sense of Waltz (1979) but will take a more developed form. For Waltz the system is populated by units that wish to survive. Under anarchy this is translated into a concern with relative capabilities. Yet that concept could be measured in a great many ways, and treatment of it so far remains dyadic (Grieco 1988, 1993b; Powell 1993; Snidal 1993a and b; James 1993b). For a system-level theory this is inadequate. A model of state behavior that takes into account positional standing in multilateral terms is needed. Furthermore, this model will allow for both external and internal factors, as would be anticipated on the basis of rational choice.

Macro and micro processes complete the cycle of effects by feeding back into system structure. Actions and events across the respective units of analysis are deemed capable of altering one or more elements. Effects could be dramatic: for example, the outcome of a war might eliminate one or more great powers or alliances, which in turn might have major effects on multiple elements at all four levels of structure. The impact of micro and macro processes also could be gradual and cumulative: if, for instance, a state was subjected to an effective economic boycott or suffered self-inflicted damage through bad macroeconomic policies, then it might gradually decline and fall out of the set of great powers.

Figure 5.1 does not include substantive content. The periodic table of elements, intrastructural effects, model of state behavior, direct connection of

Figure 5.1
Elaborated Structural Realism and World Politics

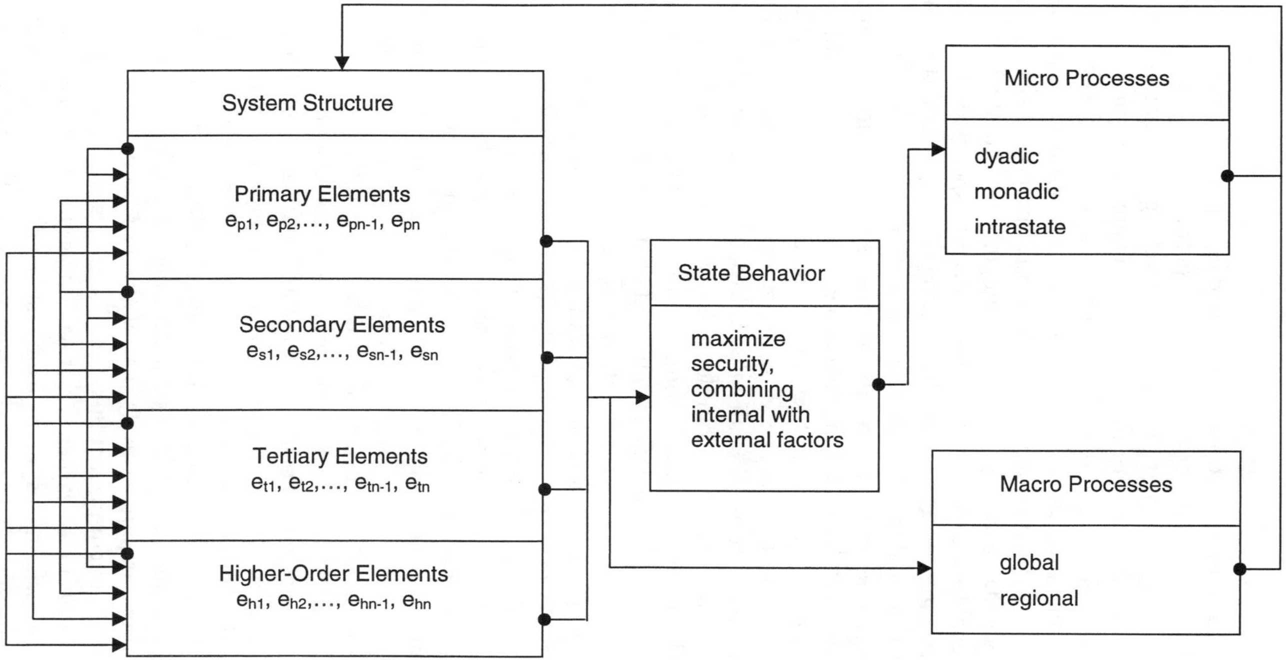

elements to macro processes, mediated linkages of elements to micro processes, and feedback from micro and macro processes to system structure are developed at length as part of a future research agenda that includes empirical testing (James 2002a). For the moment, it is useful to sum up the major intended contributions of elaborated structural realism as conveyed by the figure and preceding discussion. First, elaborated structural realism offers an inclusive vision of system structure, which creates the potential to pursue connections with a wide range of processes. Second, intrastructural effects are included, and that enables elaborated structural realism to specify how structure may evolve due to forces based on the distribution of capabilities rather than in response to processes alone. The third intended contribution is a model of state behavior that is based on structural realism's vision of security seeking but goes a step beyond to include both internal and external factors. Fourth, elements of structure are linked to a full set of macro and micro processes, with the latter connections being mediated by the model of state behavior. Fifth, and finally, elaborated structural realism acknowledges that processes accumulate and affect structure, which completes the cycle of cause and effect.

This is an appropriate point to reintroduce the framework from figure 3.2, which focused on marginal empirical content as a function of axioms for ideal types of scientific research enterprises. Trade-offs varied in that figure, making some trajectories more desirable than others. An authoritative application of the framework from this figure must await empirical testing of elaborated structural realism, but it is possible to offer a tentative assessment of the trajectory of structural realism as a scientific research enterprise.

On the basis of the argument presented in chapter 3, it will continue to be assumed that marginal empirical content increases in proportion to problems addressed and solved, along with anomalies. Since elaborated structural realism as T_3 within the sequence initiated by Waltz (i.e., T_0) has yet to be fully developed and tested, it seems appropriate to focus on empirical problems *addressed* as a subcategory. (Problems solved and anomalies, in other words, would be specified after at least one initial round of empirical testing has occurred.) How, then, does structural realism look in such terms? The basic conclusion is positive. As covered in chapter 4, versions T_0 through T_2 moved forward in terms of their potential to address a wider range of empirical problems. T_1 (i.e., Gilpin 1981) in comparison to T_0 (i.e., Waltz 1979), for example, created the possibility of micro-macro linkages. T_3 represents a *qualitative* leap forward because, as noted earlier in this section, it includes all four of the basic kinds of linkages within a system, from macro-macro through micro-micro. This is made possible by several characteristics of elaborated structural realism noted earlier: developing an inclusive vision of structure, allowing for intrastructural effects, incorporating a model of state behavior, linking elements of structure to both micro and macro processes, and recognizing that such processes accumulate and affect structure.

Without development and testing of specific connections in the form of hypotheses, it is impossible to know how the trade-off for elaborated structural realism in terms of content versus complexity—the former assessed on the basis of empirical problems addressed and solved, along with anomalies, and the latter measured in terms of the number of axioms—might look. Thus the appraisal of elaborated structural realism as T_3 is based at this point on intuition related to its schematic representation in figure 5.1. Creation of the potential to look at all four basic kinds of linkages, two of which—macro-micro and micro-micro—have not as yet been pursued in prior structural realist theories, makes for a greater likelihood of a favorable trade-off in content versus complexity for elaborated structural realism as understood in the terms represented by figure 3.2 (i.e., the scenario leading to [A, C] in the figure). The reason is that initial, general propositions introduced into the "virgin lands" of structural realism, such as micro-micro connections related to conflict, crisis, and war, are likely to be qualitatively more expansive and interesting because they are different in *kind* from hypotheses put forward before development of elaborated structural realism as T_3. Thus the intuition is that a great deal could be gained at the next stage of development for structural realism as a scientific research enterprise in terms of problem articulation and solving in return for a relatively modest increment in complexity in terms of additional axioms.

All of the preceding arguments about the progressiveness of structural realism, and especially elaborated structural realism as T_3, are of necessity exceedingly abstract. Consider, by contrast, the concreteness and finality of the critiques of structural realism reviewed in chapter 2. These would-be refutations must now be met with greater skepticism. The *possibility* that structural realism is, and can be, progressive as a scientific research enterprise must be acknowledged as a result of (a) the track record of theorizing, which comes through already to some extent in comparing previous theories (i.e., T_0, T_1, and T_2) to each other; and (b) the qualitative increase in the potential range of description, explanation, and prediction represented by elaborated structural realism as T_3.

6. Conclusions

This chapter has offered a preliminary assessment of the basic components of structural realism as a scientific research enterprise. The hard core and positive heuristic have been assessed in order to derive priorities for elaborated structural realism as T_3. Structural realism's hard core passes the test of consistency but will require further work to ensure that the assumptions of rationality and pursuit of security do not combine to produce inconsistencies. The positive heuristic features a series of just three theories prior to elaborated structural realism, which is somewhat surprising given the overall amount of attention that structural realism has received within international relations. Within this limited set of theories it is possible to point to progressiveness, given the potential to address a wider range of empirical problems from one instance to the next. The research findings of the positive heuristic, however, are problematic, especially in terms of finding expression as some kind of integrated whole.

Priorities for elaborated structural realism as T_3 are derived as a result of the difficulties that exist at both theoretical and empirical levels within structural realism. Among the most important needs are a more inclusive treatment of structure and incorporation of a model of state behavior. A schematic presentation of elaborated structural realism includes these and other features and appears to be relatively promising in terms of the standards derived for scientific progress put forward in chapter 3.

Part 3, which consists of chapter 6, will sum up what has been accomplished so far. This chapter also will include some priorities for future research.

Part 3

Conclusions and Implications

War, which used to be cruel and magnificent, has now become cruel and squalid. In fact, it has been completely spoilt. It is all the fault of Democracy and Science. From the moment that either of these meddlers and muddlers was allowed to take part in actual fighting, the doom of War was sealed. Instead of a small number of well-trained professionals championing their country's cause with ancient weapons and a beautiful intricacy of archaic manouevre, sustained at every moment by the applause of their nation, we now have entire populations, including even women and children, pitted against one another in brutish mutual extermination, and only a set of blear-eyed clerks left to add up the butcher's bill. From the moment Democracy was admitted to, or rather forced itself upon the battlefield, War ceased to be a gentleman's game.

—Winston Churchill, *My Early Life*

CHAPTER SIX

Toward Elaborated Structural Realism

1. Introduction

With appropriate revisions, structural realist theory can compete effectively in the new millennium and even reclaim its primacy in the field of international relations. Introduced near the outset of chapter 1, this is the book's central argument. The next section will review the various stages of that argument as put forward in preceding chapters and render a judgment on it. Section 3 will cover implications for future research, with subsections on development and testing of elaborated structural realism. Thus the two substantive sections of this brief chapter focus, respectively, on the main findings and development and testing of elaborated structural realism. A fourth and last section includes some final thoughts about international relations. This speculative concluding section will address the themes raised by Churchill in the epigraph to part 3, so the book will end, as it began, with a discussion of systems, change, and realism.

2. Is Structural Realism Worth the Effort?

This question can be answered in a word, "yes." A review of the main findings from each of the preceding chapters will point toward that conclusion.

Chapter 1 started with an overview of the realist tradition. Realist theorizing is both time-honored in international relations as a discipline and well connected to the practice of interstate politics. These points alone do not justify a continuing adherence to one or more schools within realism, but caution in casting aside this worldview is suggested as a result of its very longevity. From a philosophically conservative point of view, a flawed realism may be seen as having more potential for resurrection than competing approaches that lack any history beyond the last few decades. This theme is developed in later chapters.

Rapid change and complexity are the other subjects addressed at length by chapter 1. It is argued in some detail that an actor-oriented approach, paradoxically, may be at an increasing disadvantage when it comes to theorizing about the twentieth century and beyond. As actors proliferate and change, so must theories cast at the dyadic, monadic, or intrastate levels if they are to keep pace. System-level theory, by contrast, focuses on overall patterns at the global or regional levels and may be able to weather the storm more effectively. Factors such as unit-level complexity, asymmetry of impact, range of effects, and durability of impact combine to argue in favor of a renewed focus on system-level theory. Theory-building principles, such as economy of explana-tion, reinforce that conclusion. So too does the potentially exaggerated empha-sis on dyadic findings in empirical research on international cooperation and conflict over recent decades.

Chapter 2 builds on the introduction of realism and system-oriented theory in several specific ways. A unifying concept for theorizing, namely, systemism, is introduced. Systemism differs from holism and individualism in its require-ment that a theory take into account all four logically possible kinds of link-ages: macro-macro (i.e., holistic) and micro-micro (i.e., individualistic), along with micro-macro and macro-micro (i.e., hybrid). A theory specified in such terms will not be subject to the arbitrary directions that may be pursued by rivals that emerge from the tradition of puzzle solving within the social sci-ences, most notably international relations.

Chapter 2 also defines the international system in terms of actors, structure, process, issue, context, and environment. These components are sufficient as required by systemism in that composition, environment, and structure all are included. With this definition in hand, a theory of international relations based on systemism can be tested within a well-defined domain. Structure, a crucial concept within system-oriented realism, also is defined in chapter 2. Structure corresponds to the distribution of capabilities as assessed in terms of four mutu-ally exclusive and exhaustive types of elements: primary, secondary, tertiary, and higher order. This more inclusive definition of structure creates the poten-tial for a wider range of description, explanation, and prediction of empirical problems for a realist theory based on systemism. Regardless of their precise nature, all elements of structure are based on how capabilities are dispersed among states, which is consistent with a realist frame of reference.

Chapter 2 also defines polar points within the array of theories claiming sta-tus as realist, along with structural realism. This gives some sense of the expan-siveness, and even incoherence, of realist thinking, but it shows that identifica-tion of axioms for competing and complementary variants also is possible. It is possible to bring some degree of order to the vast welter of ideas held within realism: contingent and deterministic realism are identified as polar points among the approaches that emphasize the actor level in theorizing. Contingent realism assumes state centrism, rational choice, and security seeking, while deterministic realism posits the evil of human nature, power seeking, and an inability to change either of the preceding basic characteristics of the world. Structural realism incorporates the assumptions of contingent realism at the actor level and adds the axioms of anarchy, nondifferentiation of states by func-tion, and assessment of structure in terms of the distribution of capabilities.

Chapter 2 concludes with definitions of conflict, crisis, and war, the would-be empirical "home field" for a renewed structural realism. (These categories also are natural for reassessment of structural realist theory and research as car-ried out in chapters 4 and 5.) War is identified as a subset of crisis, which in turn exists as a subset of international conflict. A review of concept formation reveals that much more agreement exists on the meaning of these terms than on their presumed causes and effects.

Chapter 3 develops the concept of a scientific research enterprise, which permits assessment of progress in international relations. Salient points along a continuum of aggregation, including worldview, ontology, paradigm, theory, and hypothesis, are identified. These concepts range from most general and normatively focused (i.e., worldview) to most specific and positively oriented (i.e., hypothesis). The polar points of worldview and hypothesis are found to be too extreme to permit effective dialogue leading to agreement on the amount of progress in evidence. Thus three kinds of progress, each one corresponding to an intermediate point along the continuum, are identified: pragmatic, revolutionary, and evolutionary for ontology, paradigm, and theory, respectively. The first of the three types of progress, which is expected to be assessed naturally in society as a whole, lies beyond the scope of the present study.

Chapter 3 also includes an attempt to improve the standard apparatus from the philosophy of science that is used to assess progress in revolutionary terms: that is, at the paradigmatic level. A review of the basic rival concepts, referring to research program and tradition, produces a synthesis. The focal point shifts from a mechanistic pursuit of ever-expanding empirical content to a more practical and realistic emphasis on empirical problems addressed and solved, along with anomalies, understood in terms of the multiple dimensions of description, explanation, and prediction of actions and events.

Chapter 3 continues by identifying criteria for evaluation of the components of a theory: that is, it provides specific ideas about how to assess evolutionary progress as noted above. The hard core of a theory, represented by its fundamental axioms, is evaluated in terms of consistency and efficiency. The negative heuristic, which enumerates theorizing that is ruled out of order, must be precise. The positive heuristic—put simply, propositions derived from the theory and evidence from testing—is assessed in terms of the empirical problems that have been addressed and solved, along with anomalies identified, which collectively are assumed to correlate in an overall sense with empirical content.

Developed in terms of the preceding components, chapter 3 can be summed up in the concept of a scientific research enterprise: within a given worldview and ontology, a scientific research enterprise consists of (a) a set of assumptions with parametric status known as the hard core; (b) rules that prohibit certain kinds of theorizing, labeled as the negative heuristic; and (c) a positive heuristic, meaning a series of theories for which the solved and unsolved empirical problems (along with anomalies), which focus on the description, explanation, and prediction of actions and events, continue to accumulate. Defined in these terms, the scientific research enterprise is put forward as an accurate and operationally useful means toward assessment of progress in international relations. The concept represents a synthesis and extension of the standard frameworks borrowed from the philosophy of science, namely, the research program and tradition (Lakatos 1970; Laudan 1977).

Chapters 1 through 3 make up part 1, which focuses on the major issues related to theorizing about international relations. The preceding chapters introduce the tradition of political realism and the idea of system-level theory; identify key concepts such as systemism, international system, and structure; provide an exegesis of structural realism; and produce criteria for assessment of scientific progress. Taken together, these accomplishments set the stage for part 2, which applies the respective concepts and criteria to structural realism as a scientific research enterprise.

Chapter 4 focuses on the foundation and evolution of structural realism as a scientific research enterprise. The chapter begins by identifying the hard core, expressed as a set of axioms. These axioms combine contingent realism, as identified in chapter 2, with system-level thinking about international relations. Six assumptions are identified with structural realism: the most important actors in world politics are territorially organized entities (city-states and modern states); state behavior is rational; states seek security and calculate their interests in terms of relative standing within the international system; anarchy is the ordering principle of international structure; states, the units of the international system, are undifferentiated by function; and structure is defined by the distribution of capabilities among states. The preceding axioms are sufficient, from the standpoint of systemism, to facilitate a full range of macro and micro linkages in theorizing about international relations. The negative heuristic of structural realism is straightforward: it prohibits pure individualism (i.e., reductionism) and strategic altruism. These restrictions follow logically from structural realism's system- and actor-level axioms as presented a moment ago.

Chapter 4 also presents the positive heuristic of structural realism. Theories within the paradigm and research findings connected to it (at least implicitly) are reviewed.

Surprisingly, only three full-fledged structural realist theories can be identified.[1] Considering the amount of time and energy devoted to structural realism over the last two decades—measured at least in terms of scholarly criticism—this brief sequence is puzzling to behold. Theorizing started with macro-macro connections, such as balance of power and recurrence of war in the international system (i.e., T_0). Later variants (i.e., T_1 and T_2, as put forward by Gilpin [1981] and Buzan, Jones, and Little [1993], respectively) include micro-macro linkages (such as interstate war producing a new distribution of capabilities) and an expanded range of macro-macro propositions (which entail interaction capacity as a determinant of cooperation and conflict in the system).

Empirical research based on elements of structure is extensive, so the inferences that appear in chapter 4 are based strictly on the still-vast quantitative literature on conflict, crisis, and war. The focus on data-based findings, of course, also facilitates comparison. Hypothesis testing based on primary, secondary, tertiary, and higher-order elements of structure can be summarized as follows: the results are usually bivariate; connections hold in many instances and for all four kinds of elements (but generally not with great strength); interaction effects between elements generally have not been incorporated; testing of propositions normally assumes a linear functional form; and war is the overwhelming focus as opposed to conflict or crisis. Perhaps the most important and obvious general observation to be made is that the wide range of quantitative testing of propositions based on elements of structure shows no obvious connection to structural realism's hard core. (Given that the vast majority of all the quantitative testing that has been carried out by non- and even antirealists, this outcome should not be surprising.) In other words, collectively speaking, the propositions about war are not derived in any obvious and systematic way from the six axioms that are fundamental to structural realism. This point, in turn, raises questions about the overall significance of the findings and how they might contribute to knowledge about international relations.

Finally, chapter 4 includes a more in-depth review of aggregate research on the most central among the empirical problems addressed by structural realism: that is, the causes of war. Findings on actions and events related to war, including initiation and participation, along with frequency and intensity, are compiled. (Once again, and for the same reasons, the summary is restricted to data-based testing.) A wide range of elements among all four categories of structure appear, and a sizable number show connections to one or more aspects of the causes of war as noted a moment ago. The dyad emerges as the preeminent unit of analysis. Measurement practices are remarkably uniform, and general agreement exists that the post-Napoleonic period is most suitable for this type of research because of the inclusiveness of the Correlates of War (COW) data set. As in the earlier set of findings from chapter 4 about conflict, crisis, and war collectively, propositions often are confirmed, but the results just as frequently are modest in terms of the degree of explanation achieved for a given dependent variable.

On the basis of the approach identified in chapter 3, chapter 5 offers a tentative assessment of structural realism. This includes an appraisal of the hard core and various aspects of the positive heuristic of structural realism as presented in chapter 4.

When checked for consistency, the hard core stands up relatively well when its axioms are compared to each other on a pairwise basis. Four traits are identified for the axioms in the hard core, collectively speaking: each is related to at least one other; each is independent of at least one other; no pair is redundant; and one pair is potentially problematic. The final characteristic among those just noted, which refers to rational choice and pursuit of security in relation to each other, reinforces the need to develop a model of state behavior within structural realism.

Structural realism's positive heuristic begins with the series of theories starting with Waltz (1979), or T_0. From many vantage points, this initial variant of structural realism is regarded as deterministic, static, lacking in detail with respect to explanation and prediction, and mistaken in its assertion that the distribution of capabilities can serve as a general explanation for international politics. Some of these points of criticism are addressed by versions T_1 and T_2 (Gilpin 1981; Buzan, Jones, and Little 1993), which followed in the next two decades. For example, T_1 is able to address the issue of political change, which ameliorates the problem of determinism. Other difficulties, however, such as the limited range of explanation and prediction associated with structural realism, continue to challenge the paradigm.

Quantitative research findings about conflict, crisis, and war, when seen as part of the positive heuristic, tell a mixed story. The basic characteristics of the results, which have been compiled over several decades, can be summed up as follows: auxiliary assumptions vary across research designs; the overwhelming focus is on war; necessary rather than sufficient conditions are identified; and results are subject to revision when intervening factors and multivariate effects are considered. Key measurement issues, as yet undecided, may have major implications for how well existing results stand up, at least in some areas. To cite one prominent example, the meaning of "alliances" as a concept, most notably the proper subset of these agreements for inclusion in empirical analysis of conflict, crisis, and war, is more open to question than perhaps ever before.

Chapter 5 concludes with priorities for development of T_3 within the structural realist paradigm and a schematic presentation of such a theory, labeled elaborated structural realism. A model of state behavior to facilitate micro-macro and macro-micro linkages and an inclusive treatment of structure emerge as the central priorities for elaborated structural realism as T_3. The diagrammatic presentation of elaborated structural realism begins with primary, secondary, tertiary, and higher-order elements of structure. The possibility and even likelihood of intrastructural effects is acknowledged. A model of state behavior, consistent with rational choice, also appears. Elements of structure are anticipated to affect macro processes (i.e., in the global and regional systems) directly and micro processes (i.e., in the dyadic, monadic, and intrastate systems) indirectly. The latter set of linkages, of course, would be mediated by the model of state behavior. All of these processes, in turn, would feed back into the structure of the system.

Given the preceding characteristics, elaborated structural realism is regarded as a theory with the potential to address and solve more empirical problems, understood in terms of description, explanation, and prediction of actions and events in relation to conflict, crisis, and war, than earlier variants within the structural realist paradigm. It also fulfills the requirement for comprehensive theorizing, imposed by systemism, that all four basic linkages—macro-macro, macro-micro, micro-macro, and micro-micro—can be addressed. For such reasons elaborated structural realism is regarded as tentatively progressive within structural realism and, when fully developed, a potentially formidable challenger to the "best and the brightest" of theories from other paradigms.

Chapters 4 and 5 make up part 2, which focuses on structural realism as a scientific research enterprise. Taken together, these chapters present and evaluate the components of structural realism, which include its hard core, negative heuristic, and positive heuristic. The conclusion is that structural realism, cast at the system level and following in the realist tradition, can be revised and improved toward the goal of regaining its preeminent position within international relations. As noted in chapter 1 and at the outset of this chapter as well, reaching that conclusion is the overall purpose of the present book. Perhaps, in the words a formal theorist might use, the effort could be described as a lengthy "existence theorem." The point is to show that a theory such as elaborated structural realism can be created, and, it is hoped, that now is established. A natural and final question thus concerns what to do next.

Development and testing of elaborated structural realism as T_3 within the structural realist paradigm follows logically as a priority from the assessment of theory and research carried out so far. Figure 5.1 offered a schematic representation of elaborated structural realism but included neither variables nor linkages between and among them. The basic issues related to development and testing of elaborated structural realism will be covered in turn.

3. Implications for Future Research

3.1 Development of Elaborated Structural Realism as T_3

Development of elaborated structural realism will require answers to five basic questions:

1. What are the contents of the so-called "periodic table" of elements? This question focuses on relationships between and among structural elements. The vast array of capability-based variables with some potential connections to actions and events as related to conflict, crisis, and war will need to be organized into a coherent whole. Creation of a typology, ranging from primary to higher-order elements, is just the *beginning* of this process. In particular, logical consistency must be maintained in putting forward multielement propositions about micro and macro processes of conflict, crisis, and war. Furthermore, it is a priority to explore interaction effects between and among elements, so this creates wide vistas for exploration. Thus it will be important to work out priorities among the many possible combinations of elements or "compounds" that might be tried in developing explanations and predictions.

2. Do intrastructural effects exist? This question is important because very little is known or understood about how elements of structure might affect each other. If such linkages exist, then these are prior, in a sense, to any connections with processes that might be discovered. The discussion in chapter 5 established that the structure of the international system should be regarded as relatively stable yet still capable of evolution and even occasional transformation. Thus linkages between and among elements within and across the categories of structure, from primary through higher order, should be explored systematically.

Moreover, this work must not take place in a purely inductive way. Instead, another demand is imposed on elaborated structural realism, namely, that the theory must provide logical arguments for either independence or linkages among elements, as appropriate. Thus a network of anticipated effects between and among elements would need to be specified before empirical study.

3. What will the model of state behavior look like? Some ideas exist already. The model will need to incorporate both internal and external components for security, seen from the point of view of a state's national leadership. (Walker [1987: 73] refers to this as the "national security proposition.") From a structural realist standpoint, leaders are assumed to seek security in an international system of anarchy. In the context of rational choice, however, that is not everything; a self-interested leader is expected to attend to internal security as well. Thus the meaning of, and trade-off between, security at the internal and external levels becomes the focus for development of a model of state behavior. The strategic approach provides an obvious starting point in creating a functional representation of security (Bueno de Mesquita 1988, 1993; Simon and Starr 2000). An expression for a state's security in terms of expected value calculated at both the domestic and international levels becomes a priority for elaborated structural realism.

4. What are the macro and micro linkages between elements of structure and process? The answer to this question will require further theorizing that connects individual and multiple elements of structure to actions and events related to conflict, crisis, and war. Consistent with systemism, elaborated structural realism also will specify and justify a functional form in each instance.[2] It will aim for propositions about a full range of (a) actions, like initiation or participation by states in an international conflict, crisis or war; and (b) events, assessed in terms of frequency and intensity. Propositions will be formulated about trends, breakpoints, cycles, and other patterns, at both macro and micro levels. Theorizing eventually will extend beyond causes of actions and events to include consequences as well. Thus the goal of elaborated structural realism is to address and solve the widest possible range of empirical problems about conflict, crisis, and war. Although there is no such thing as a complete theory (Gödel [1931] 1988), elaborated structural realism will develop in a way that will eschew the self-limiting tendencies inherent in previous incarnations of structural realism.

5. How do processes feed back into structure? This is the most difficult question to address because, as pointed out during the discussion of figure 5.1, structural realism so far is very limited in its treatment of this issue. One structural realist theory (i.e., T_1) regards war as the basic cause of structural change, but no specific propositions are put forward about when that would be expected to occur. The impact of micro and macro processes of conflict, crisis, and

war on structure, understood in terms of the typology of elements, remains unknown. This subject is expected to be challenging and, if addressed successfully, highly informative about how the international system operates. Incorporation of feedback from process to structure does the most to establish elaborated structural realism as a theory that is consistent with the principles of systemism.

If and when they are answered, the preceding five questions would fulfill the mission of elaborated structural realism as a theory within the structural realist paradigm. The theory would surpass each of its predecessors by a wide margin in terms of the range of empirical problems addressed. Testing, the next subject, will establish whether elaborated structural realism is worth so much effort to produce.

3.2 Testing Elaborated Structural Realism

This subsection will cover two subjects related to testing. One concerns priorities for research, while the other focuses on the meta-issues related to evaluation of elaborated structural realism in terms of scientific progress.

Systemism helps to set priorities for empirical testing of a fully formulated elaborated structural realism. The goal is to test propositions that link elements of structure to macro and micro processes, so international and foreign policy crises emerge naturally as the initial testing grounds. The reason is simple: concept formation about crisis, due to a large-scale project in the area that includes both theory and evidence, is the most advanced among all of the events in the conflict domain. Specifically, international crisis and foreign policy crisis have been defined rigorously, as noted in chapter 2, and that makes it feasible to test hypotheses in both macro *and* micro terms. Propositions about crises both in the aggregate and on an individual basis can be tested (Brecher 1993; Brecher and Wilkenfeld 1997, 2000). Moreover, the existence of a data set on foreign policy crises allows testing to extend all the way down to the intrastate level. No other class of conflict events is amenable to testing in such complete terms, so crisis becomes the natural focal point for elaborated structural realism's initial rounds of deriving and testing propositions.[3]

While assessment of specific propositions must await the development of elaborated structural realism (James 2002a), the range of testing can be identified in preliminary terms. A taxonomy of processes is needed to get things started. The first and most obvious dimension is macro versus micro, but others require consideration as well, such as synchronic versus diachronic, event versus action, and discrete versus aggregate. As discussed in chapter 3, the range of empirical problems addressed and solved, in addition to sheer number, is worth considering when a theory is evaluated. The initial variant of structural realism is very restricted when viewed in that context: T_0's propositions deal strictly with synchronic events considered in aggregate terms. Thus elaborated structural realism must develop and test a wider range of propositions in order to move significantly beyond the empirical achievements of structural realism so far.

Another form of testing focuses on whether a theory as a whole is progressive or degenerative. Chapter 5 made a tentative assessment of structural realism as a scientific research enterprise but also explicitly noted that some items from the framework developed in chapter 3 would be more appropriate for application once elaborated structural realism had been fully articulated and subjected to empirical testing. Thus a systematic assessment of the performance of elaborated structural realism in terms of description, explanation, and prediction and an appraisal of marginal costs from greater complexity in theorizing become high priorities for future research. As noted in chapter 5, two specific aspects of evaluation also can be carried out more effectively at a later stage: assessment of (a) the hard core in terms of efficiency, because development of a wide range of propositions will help to isolate which, if any, of the axioms are not playing significant roles in explanation and prediction; and (b) the negative heuristic with respect to precision, since the ability to identify anomalies without ambiguity is the key indicator and that entails a compilation of research findings for review.

More general tasks related to evaluation also become appropriate once testing moves forward. A decisive judgment about whether one theory is superior to another can be rendered after empirical testing begins to provide tentative confirmation or refutation across a range of hypotheses. The newer variant, after all, could offer a vast array of propositions—at least in comparison to the older one—and yet come away empty from the process of testing. Empirical evaluation also will help to identify prospects for revolutionary as well as evolutionary change as defined in chapter 3. Specifically, is $T_3 > Q_i$ understood in terms of an expanding positive heuristic where, using the notation from chapter 3, Q_i represents the most advanced theory within some alternative paradigm? Questions such as this one can be answered only after elaborated structural realism is fully articulated and experiences empirical testing.

Finally, what about pragmatic assessment of scientific systemism as an ontology? Even empirical testing of elaborated structural realism, of course, is not enough to facilitate an answer to this question. Recall from chapter 3 that pragmatic assessment is regarded as a naturally occurring process within society as a whole. The time line on something like this is assumed, all other things being equal, to be decades, as the intellectual products of elaborated structural realism and successor theories either prove to have practical value or fail to make headway with society as a whole.

4. Some Final Thoughts about International Relations

This book began with observations about the twentieth century and beyond as a time of rapid, even fantastic change. For such reasons, scholars and practitioners of international relations might be persuaded to move away from theories that emphasize continuity and the immanence of power politics. The epigraph from part 3, however, shows that even prescient observers have a tendency to infer that their era is one of unprecedented change. Churchill's words, from a book published in 1930, actually refer to a change he perceived in *1895*. In spite of the rhetorical flourish, as would be expected from that author, it is clear that he had perceived the major changes in world politics around him and described them in terms that suggested they would be important and in place for some time. *Democracy* refers to the rise of massive, conscription-based armies that became the norm throughout the practice of twentieth-century international politics, while *Science* focuses on the advent of weapons of mass destruction and resulting high casualties. Thus, in the language of systemism, Churchill describes new macro-level causes and effects operating in international relations, most notably in the practice of war—which for him had become a sordid affair. In spite of these changes, war continued as part of the practice of politics among nations, in Morgenthau's terms, and the system of states continues to endure even to this day.

Churchill's observations about life and death over a century ago, which drew attention to important changes in world politics, are useful to bear in mind when deliberating on paths toward theory and even greater understanding. A system-level approach, such as structural realism, still has much to offer precisely because it *does* take into account the important continuities of world politics. To improve upon structural realism, it may be best to seek a variant of the theory that is grounded in a scientific approach toward international relations. This has been the deeper purpose of the present study and it is hoped that at least some progress has been made in that direction.

Comparing Rival Paradigms

When P is progressive and exceeds Q in problem solving, it retains status as the paradigm of choice. In other words, $P_i > P_k$ for all k (where $k < i$) and $P_i > Q_j$, where P_i and Q_j represent the best available theories in their respective paradigms. (The symbol ">" means that the problem-solving effectiveness of one theory is greater than the other.) It should be noted that the preceding decision rule conceivably could have the disadvantage of delaying implementation of a more dynamic and ultimately superior option. Suppose that comparison of current theories in each paradigm yields $P_2 > Q_0$ but that P later becomes at least temporarily degenerative and eventually $Q_2 > P_5$, with Q still progressive (i.e., $Q_2 > Q_1 > Q_0$). Although Q ultimately might prove better than P, the more conservative decision rule taken here ensures that (a) each paradigm is applied until its full potential is approximated and (b) "false alarms" are minimized, meaning that a paradigm is replaced only when the superiority of an alternative is well established rather than merely identified as a possibility.

When P is progressive but Q already is superior in terms of problem-solving ability, or $P_i > P_k$ for all $k < i$, and $Q_j > P_i$, a more difficult situation arises. Although P is performing well at the internal level, it would seem to be surpassed and even falsified by the more dynamic Q. Since decisions about paradigmatic affiliation are not instantaneous, this situation may be less troublesome in practice. Adherents of P can be expected to redouble efforts toward improvement as Q surpasses it, which creates ideal conditions for the former of the two paradigms to reassert its position, if possible, over the latter. Put differently, some lag is anticipated for paradigmatic shift, and that is functional in the world of applied science. In some instances the more established paradigm may reestablish superiority after a competitor's performance stimulates its improvement.

When P is degenerative but still ahead of Q, it is not falsified but clearly occupies a vulnerable position. Suppose that $P_6 > P_7 > Q_2$, meaning that the latest version of P is at best equal to or even inferior to its immediate predecessor yet still superior to the state-of-the-art theory for Q (i.e., Q_2). Advocates of P may be able to reverse its course, with $P_8 > P_6$ and all other previous versions, but interest in Q and other alternatives is likely to rise if the more established approach remains stalled. Falsification may even take an incremental form, with P failing to regain its progressiveness and Q eventually putting forward a superior alternative.

When P is degenerative and Q already is superior in problem solving, or $P_i > P_{i+1}$ and $Q_j > P_i$, this is the most obvious instance of falsification. Efficiency dictates the choice of Q, even while it remains possible that P might somehow be resurrected. In this scenario, however, P is further along than Q in terms of iterations: that is, $i > j$. Thus the risk of discarding P too early is minimized because the "trend line" in its development already is relatively visible and inferior to that of the new challenger. The probability of P returning to the lead after being replaced by the nascent Q becomes small enough that a possible error in neglecting P becomes an acceptable risk to assume.

APPENDIX A-2

Description, Explanation, and Prediction

Figure A-2.1 conveys a vision of how description, explanation, and prediction are anticipated to vary as a function of the number of axioms included in a theory. While the curves in the figure might possess wider relevance, they are intended for application to international relations. The horizontal axis represents the number of axioms for a theory, from zero to infinity. Along the vertical axis, the performance of a theory is measured in proportional terms for description, explanation, and prediction, with a range from none at all (0%) to perfection (100%). Each of the functional forms is monotonically increasing but different from the others. The exact shape of the curves is less important than how they look in relation to each other. (The equations used to generate the respective curves appear in appendix A-3.) Each will be described in turn, followed by a comparative analysis.

Description increases as a function of axioms but at a steadily diminishing rate of increase. It is straightforward to assume that more assumptions mean a greater ability to describe the world, but less obvious that diminishing returns should be expected. The reason is that any theory can be expected to begin with a description of the general properties of international relations and move on to more specific aspects in its later variants. At some point the contributions of further axioms are anticipated to approach an upper boundary, which appears as d* in the figure.

Explanation also follows a monotonically increasing path, but the functional form is different. The first issue to address is that, like description, explanation is subject to an upper limit. By Gödel's ([1931] 1988) incompleteness theorem, no set of axioms, regardless of how detailed, will be sufficient to generate all true statements.[1] This means that efforts to explain international relations through development and testing of hypotheses derived from a theory will converge toward some maximum point. This process is expected to continue until a theory approaches the upper limit of explanation depicted in the figure, e*.

Another aspect that needs to be accounted for is the s-shaped curve that appears for explanation. It increases slowly, then rapidly, and finally approaches its upper limit of e* asymptotically. This is a product of the way in which axioms are combined to produce explanations. If a theory is based on a given number of axioms, then the number of explanations that can be derived from it increases geometrically as more are added in later versions. Some hypotheses will depend on only one axiom, while others will combine two or more. Thus the rate of change upward is expected to increase more quickly as axioms are added, but only up to a certain point. Diminishing returns eventually take over

217

Figure A-2.1
Description, Explanation, and Prediction for Theories of International
Relations

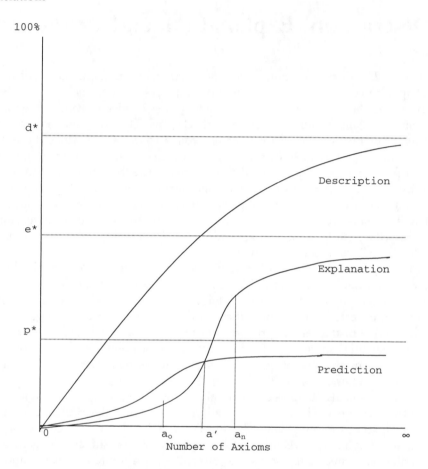

because of limits inherent within any set of axioms, no matter how expansive.

Prediction's functional form resembles that of explanation. The upper boundary of p^* is approached but never reached because of reasons familiar to social scientists in general and scholars of international relations in particular. The limits of observation alone are sufficient to ensure that this will happen. Since descriptive ability is expected to fall short of d^*, the ideal point (i.e., the idea of limits on observation), which in turn affects the ability to predict, already is built into this analysis.

Comparative analysis of the curves in the figure involves two tasks. One is to explain the hierarchy among the three ideal points on the vertical axis. The other is to account for anticipated differences in experiences with increasing and diminishing returns along the horizontal axis.

Each of the curves approaches a different upper limit (i.e., d^*, e^*, and p^*) in the figure. This variation can be explained in two stages: description relative to the other objectives and then the latter two goals in comparison to each other.

First, description is a task prior to either explanation or prediction. At any given point along the horizontal axis, assumptions are used to generate descriptive statements. The axioms, however, must be *combined* in some way to generate either valid explanations or accurate predictions. This introduces a further level of difficulty and ensures some degradation in performance for explanation and prediction relative to description.

Second, the relationship involving explanation and prediction with each other changes as the number of axioms increases. Prediction can occur without explanation when axioms are few, but a reversal is expected to occur at later stages of elaboration. The reasoning here would seem to apply regardless of discipline. At the most rudimentary stage of theorizing—that is, with a small number of axioms and possibly very little integration among them into an explicit framework that includes propositions—prediction occurs by intuition and runs ahead of explanation. For example, "[W]e need not know any astronomy to forecast that day will follow night, or any economics to forecast that mass unemployment will erode savings" (Bunge 1996: 159; see also Blaug 1980: 4). As a theory is elaborated, however, a threshold is reached at the point a' along the horizontal axis in the figure. From that point onward, the curve for explanation is found above the one for prediction. The reason for the reversal at point a' is that the ability to combine axioms, which produces explanations that experience corroboration, will begin to show appreciable returns within some range of development for a series of theories. (The width of the interval from a_0 to a_n and the height of explanation reached—that is, e^*—will depend on the series of theories involved.) At a_n theorizing enters a stage of diminishing returns, where further axioms generate marginal rather than geometric increments with regard to explanation.[2]

Viewed along the horizontal axis, the curves for explanation and prediction also are shaped somewhat differently. The change from a slow to a rapid ascent and back again is anticipated to occur more dramatically for explanation in comparison to prediction. The inductive process of predictions accumulating in response to an increasing number of axioms is expected to occur without a step-level component, which in turn produces a less pronounced s-shaped curve. As noted a moment ago, at a certain point during the rapid ascent for explanation, a', the curves cross each other. When a series of theories progresses, more complex, multivariate explanations are expected to become the norm. As the range of processes in a system are more fully understood, from macro-macro through micro-micro, additional increments in prediction nevertheless may become marginal. Revolutions, wars, and other events frequently can be explained after the fact by complex theories, but forecasting is another story.

Perhaps the best way to bring out the shift in relative achievement between prediction and explanation is to return to the basic principle, endorsed already, of probabilistic linkages between variables. With respect to conflict, crisis, and war, for example, it is possible to isolate many associations with a wide range of macro- and micro-variables (James 1993b; Brecher and Wilkenfeld 1997; Geller and Singer 1998; Vasquez 1998; Leng 1999). Yet these connections, more than a few of which reach statistical (and even substantive) significance and are robust with respect to alternative research designs, cannot simply be merged to produce "point predictions" for aspects of conflict, crisis, and war from onset through legacy. Instead, it would be more accurate to say that, as explanatory statements accumulate, predictive ability also improves but at a comparatively diminished rate.

Notes for Appendix A-2

1. The more subtle point about the theorem is that "for every formal system there is a mathematical proposition which can be expressed within the system but cannot be decided from the axioms of the system" (Gödel, quoted in Shanker 1988: 232). This property creates further complications for the notion of an overall amount of empirical content because additional axioms always would need to be added for decisions about (as yet) undecided propositions, with no conceivable end to that process.

2. Darwinian evolution might be raised as an extreme example here, where a' is reached almost at the outset, with virtually no further increase in prediction while, at least in comparison, explanation picks up dramatically.

Equations for Curves Corresponding to Description, Explanation, and Prediction

The curves for description (D), explanation (E), and prediction (P) that appear in figure A-2.1 are generated by the following equations:

(A.1) $\quad D = \ln_e (a + 1)$

(A.2) $\quad E = \dfrac{b_0}{1 + b_1 b_2{}^a}$ where $b_0 > 0, b_1 > 0, 0 < b_2 < 1$

(A.3) $\quad P = b_0 b_1{}^{b_2{}^a}$ where $b_0 > 0, 0 < b_1 < 1, 0 < b_2 < 1$

Equation A.1 expresses description (D) as the natural logarithmic function of the number of axioms in a theory (a). In equation A.2, explanation (E) takes the form of a logistic function, in which the presence of "a" as an exponent in the denominator produces the pronounced s-shape in the figure, with the constants b_0, b_1, and b_2 in the designated ranges of values. Finally, equation A.3 shows prediction (P) as a Gompertz function of "a." The curve in the figure is produced when the product of the two constants is raised to the exponent of another, which in turn has "a" as its exponent, with the constants falling in the noted range of values.

NOTES

Notes for Chapter 1

1. Thompson (1980, 1994), Schmidt (1994), Knutsen (1997), Guzzini (1998), Holsti (1998), and Liska (1998) provide comprehensive introductions to the evolution of international political theory, with special attention to the realist tradition. Postmodernists and some other critics, however, dispute the presumed continuity from ancient to modern times; for examples of dissenting interpretations of Thucydides and Machiavelli as exponents of realism (for which the terms *power politics* and *realpolitik,* among others, also commonly are used in the literature), consult Garst (1989) and Walker (1989). Further contending examples that focus on other major theorists appear in various volumes of the *Review of International Studies.* An overview of political realism appears later in this chapter.

2. *Structural realism* and *neorealism* will be used interchangeably throughout the rest of this book. Each of these terms refers in a general way to the theorizing initiated by Waltz (1979) that focuses on the structure of the international system (understood in terms of the distribution of capabilities among states) as the basic conditioning factor for processes at the aggregate level, most notably war and peace. (The differences between capabilities and the more familiar concept of power will be clarified during the overview, later in this chapter, of international politics in the twentieth century.) The preceding usage of *structural realism* is consistent with Waltz (1988: 40) and the prominent review by Keohane (1986b), although other expositions, such as Buzan, Jones, and Little (1993: 9), have reserved this term and *neorealism,* respectively, for different purposes.

3. Throughout this book, *international politics* will be used interchangeably with *world politics, global politics,* and other common designations for the study of international relations as a discipline (Brecher 1999: 214). Although it is understood that some of these variants are used in other contexts to convey particular outlooks or approaches toward the subject matter, such nuances are not addressed here.

4. Crisis occupies a crucial position as the most salient breakpoint between peace and war (Brecher 1977; Lebow 1981). Unlike the militarized interstate dispute (MID) or other nomenclature from the systematic study of international processes, crisis is virtually unique in being both intelligible and of interest at a more general level. With 895 foreign policy crises on record from late 1918 to 1994 (Brecher and Wilkenfeld 1997, 2000), this type of event emerges as common enough to permit either case- or database-based analysis while also remaining special among the variegated aspects of world politics that are available for study.

5. Summaries of major works from prominent scholars identified with twentieth-century realism are available in Dougherty and Pfaltzgraff (1971, 1990, 1996, 2001) and Thompson (1980). It should be noted that the scholars listed here also produced insightful critiques of realism—Carr, in that regard, stands out the most.

6. Holsti (1991b) identifies issues inductively through "statements by the parties involved, as reported in standard historical accounts" (19). The most prominent deductively derived framework, which focuses on a range of components from objectives to positions, appears in Mansbach and Vasquez (1981).

7. For example, Holsti (1985b; see also 1985a) dismisses the "necrologists" of inter-

national relations (most notably, postmodernists) and presents a compelling argument that the "classical" approach, with its focus on the struggle for war and peace, still offers the best hope for future advancement of knowledge.

8. A more recent essay (Holsti 1998: 44), however, identifies progress in a wide range of areas, from greater theoretical awareness to development of the concept of power in multifaceted ways, which suggests continuing support for mainstream research in spite of its known shortcomings. This type of mixed and fluctuating assessment of the field is consistent with the effects anticipated from rapidly changing events.

9. Mansbach and Vasquez (1981) and Buzan and Jones (1981) represent early attacks on perceived incrementalism; the latter, for instance, claim that "established theoretical approaches to the field have over-emphasized continuity at the expense of change" (2).

10. Even sudden and apparently incomprehensible transformations can be assessed in these terms; see, for example, Nicholson's (1989) exegesis of chaos and catastrophe theory.

11. For general introductions to rational choice and its central assumption of goal-directed behavior (normally in pursuit of self-interest, but also allowing for maximization of other ends, including altruism), consult Riker and Ordeshook (1973), Frohlich and Oppenheimer (1978), McLean (1987), Mueller (1979, 1989), and Booth, James, and Meadwell (1993); prominent critics include Green and Shapiro (1994) and Bunge (1996). Implications from the debate over rational choice will occupy a central place in the development of a model of state behavior in James (2002a).

12. For an important and effective warning against deterministic explanation in the social sciences that highlights the pervasive role of uncertainty, see Cioffi-Revilla (1998).

13. From the classical realist point of view, this dichotomy usually is articulated as the state versus the international system (Singer 1961). It is understood that, given more recent theoretical developments, explanations at the unit level also could include transnational and subnational actors (Keohane and Nye 1977, 1987, 1989; Baldwin 1993a, 1993b) and even the relationship of individuals to a group understood in ideational terms (Adler 1997).

14. Examples in this tradition include Snyder, Bruck, and Sapin ([1954] 1962), Allison (1971), George and Smoke (1974), Janis and Mann (1977), Snyder and Diesing (1977), Brecher (1980), George (1980), Stein and Tanter (1980), Jervis, Lebow, and Stein (1985), Hermann, Kegley, and Rosenau (1987), Vertzberger (1990, 1998), Leng (1993), Hermann and Kegley (1995), and James (2000a, 2000b). For an excellent introduction to comparative foreign policy analysis, consult Hook (2002).

15. Rosenau's (1966) pretheory of foreign policy generally is credited with stimulating the analysis of national attributes such as size, level of development, and type of government; for a comprehensive model of interstate behavior that includes factors from within and beyond national boundaries and serves as a point of culmination for the "events data" movement, see Wilkenfeld et al. (1980). More recent cross-national studies that link internal factors (most notably type of government [i.e., the democratic peace thesis] within the recent wave of research) to foreign policy outcomes include Maoz and Abdolali (1989), Russett (1990, 1993), Bueno de Mesquita, Jackman, and Siverson (1991), James and Oneal (1991a, 1991b), Bremer (1992, 1993), Morgan and Campbell (1992), Maoz and Russett (1993), Dixon (1993, 1994), James and Hristoulas (1994a, 1994b), Hermann and Kegley (1995), Hewitt and Wilkenfeld (1996), Oneal et al. (1996), Chan (1997), Oneal and Russett (1997, 2000), Enterline (1998a, 1998b), and Gartzke (1998, 2000).

16. Examples in this tradition, which appears to be less in favor now than perhaps at any other time, include Kaplan (1957), Wallerstein (1974, 1980), Bull (1977), Young (1978), Waltz (1979, 1993, 1995), Wayman (1984, 1985), Modelski (1987), Midlarsky (1988), Brecher, James, and Wilkenfeld (1990), and Harrison (2002). For a classic, albeit skeptical, introduction to system-level theory as applied to politics in general terms, see Young (1967b).

17. Disillusionment with system-level theory is a by-product of the general dissatisfaction with structural realism; the two sentiments appear virtually symbiotic at this point. Goldmann (1996) observes that the "social scientific equivalent of political correctness has been to dissociate oneself from *Theory of International Politics*" (403).

18. For an alternative viewpoint on the outset of the modern great-power system, consult Levy (1983), who argues convincingly that it dates back to the very late years of the fifteenth century.

19. The assumption of discrete boundaries between issues in economics and politics also is open to challenge. Consider as just one example the significant involvement of multinational corporations and international institutions (most notably the World Bank and International Monetary Fund) in the politics of host states, which sometimes can spill over into security issues (Lipson 1985; James and Mitchell 1995).

20. For a dissenting ontology, which asserts that "the exclusive bet of IR on stability and continuity may require serious rethinking," see Albert and Lapid (1997: 409; also Lapid 1996).

21. For a detailed analysis of the end of the Cold War as a major anomaly for realism, see Vasquez (1998: 317–68).

22. Of course, an arbitrary element exists in this choice because components also might be looked at as systems, depending on the scope of the analysis. A state, for example, constitutes a multifaceted system (Bunge 1996) in its own right.

23. For an alternative position, which emphasizes that stable balances of power are rare in comparison to stable unipolar systems, see Wilkinson (1999).

24. Structure conditions interactions in different ways across systems. For example, in some systems rulers may interact by sending each other gifts that help to preserve the status quo and avert costly wars, as in the Amarna Age of the Middle East and much of nineteenth-century Europe. In other systems, by contrast, breakdowns into war are very nearly continuous, as in the post-Armana Middle East during the rise of Assyria and sixteenth-century Europe.

25. Throughout this exposition it will be the practice to use *capabilities* to denote an attribute and *power* in reference to a relation in the classic sense identified by Dahl (1963; see also Cantori and Spiegel 1970: 13; James 1988); power includes "more than material capabilities, comprising the ability to exercise influence and resist the attempts of others" (Geller and Singer 1998: 57).

26. Some crises escalate to war and therefore might appear on both of the preceding lists. The more complex notion of an intrawar crisis, or a crisis for adversaries involved in an ongoing war, is explained in Brecher and Wilkenfeld (1997: 6–7).

27. Gilpin (1981: 40) identifies three types of international change in order to prevent this kind of confusion. The types are systems change (i.e., nature of actors), systemic change (i.e., governance of system), and interaction change (i.e., interstate processes). Thus, in Gilpin's terms, the shift at the end of the 1980s would correspond to systemic change as opposed to more fundamental systems change.

28. Parallel changes in the sociological aspects of the discipline of international relations, especially in the subfield of conflict processes, reflect Kuhn's (1962) description of

a shifting paradigm. Dyadic research designs appear to be emerging as the norm for articles published in mainstream journals and papers listed for presentation on conference programs (American Political Science Association 1998, 1999, 2000; International Studies Association 1999, 2000, 2001).

29. The ascendancy of the dyad may be traced most directly to Axelrod (1984), a prominent work that relied on simulated Prisoner's Dilemma games to "develop a theory of cooperation that can be used to discover what is necessary for cooperation to emerge" (6). The research design of that study, which focused on the relative effectiveness of strategies played within a series of simulated pairwise interactions, produced a startling verdict in favor of simple reciprocity. This result undoubtedly had the effect of shifting interest toward dyadic analysis, with the most sustained impact on the field of international relations.

30. While this discussion appears to focus exclusively on aggregate data analysis, the implications are much more encompassing. The centrality of dyadic research designs and the apparent success of models using that approach have forced even the critics of respective reductionist hypotheses to enter debate on such terms. The controversy over the democratic peace is probably the best example of that phenomenon; for an illustration, see the ongoing debate between Oneal et al. (1996) and Oneal and Russett (2000) on the one hand and James, Solberg, and Wolfson (1999, 2000; see also Wolfson, James, and Solberg 1998) on the other.

31. At the very least it builds in problems of inference related to the independence of events; for more details on this problem, consult Wolfson, James, and Soldberg (1998) and James, Soldberg, and Wolfson (1999, 2000).

32. For an extended argument that the end of the USSR poses as an anomaly for structural realism in particular, see Koslowski and Kratochwil (1994). The most complete explanation available for the demise of the USSR, founded on systemism (see n. 35 for a definition of this term) and derived on the basis of developments from four subsystems (i.e., biological, economic, political, and cultural), appears in Bunge (1998: 205–10).

33. For a compelling demonstration of how rivalry and conflict persist in the Asia-Pacific region during the post–Cold War era, with important connections between and among apparently disparate cases, see Hara (2000).

34. Mintz (1985) and Mintz and Huang (1990) provide compelling cross-national evidence about the harmful indirect effects of military spending on economic growth. In the case of the United States, for example, which also experienced pressure from the Cold War rivalry, the negative impact of military spending occurred "mainly as a result of its crowding-out effect on investment on the one hand and its inability to contribute positively to economic growth on the other" (Mintz and Huang 1990: 1289).

35. The underlying issue here is the superiority of "systemism" as an alternative to "individualism" or "holism" (Bunge 1996: 264). Systemism, which argues that both individual agency and social structure must be incorporated into any compelling system-level theory, is introduced in more detail during chapter 2 as a principle that underlies further development of structural realism.

36. A prominent example of unit-system linkage in the crisis domain is Brecher's (1993: 360–61) unified model of interstate crisis, which includes feedback from the impact of a given case to the attributes that would be in place at the potential outset of another.

37. This description refers to Waltz (1979) and Gilpin (1981), texts that have reached the status of orthodoxy within system-level realist theory.

38. Keohane and Nye (1989: 258) rely on Krasner's (1982b) widely accepted conception of an international regime: "sets of implicit or explicit principles, rules, norms and procedures around which actors' expectations converge in a given area of international relations" (186). See Young (1986: 29–30) for the most stimulating presentation of a research agenda on international regimes.

Notes for Chapter 2

1. For example, Russett (1993) speculates on the properties of a system "composed substantially of democratic states" on the final page of a prominent study of the democratic peace (138). Russett suggests that such a system "might reflect very different behavior than did the previous one composed predominantly of autocracies" (138). An initial overview of the system level in Kantian terms is provided by Huntley's (1996) analysis of the advantages derived by Western states from "their liberal governments and societies" (67). One recent attempt to incorporate system-level variables in a model of conflict between dyads appears in Oneal and Russett (1999: 17–20).

2. This is true of both the institutional and cultural variants of the theory, which emphasize, respectively, constraints on processes of decision making and the impact of norms and identities on policy formation and implementation. The monadic version is described in the example that follows to simplify the exposition, but the argument would apply equally to the more prominent dyadic specification because the latter also is cast at the micro level. The nuances of theory and evidence about democracy and peace are covered by Russett (1993) and Ray (1995). More complete assessments of system-level effects can be found in philosophical treatments of Kantianism and international relations; see Gates, Knutsen, and Moses (1996).

3. This example is developed at greater length, and in a different context, by Dessler (2002).

4. The use of the terms *micro* and *macro* in this exposition is different from that of Waltz (1979) and should be made clear for further reference. Waltz (1979) claims that structural realism is analogous to a "microeconomic theory" that "shows how the actions and interactions of the units form and affect the market and how the market in turn affects them" (110). In other words, from Waltz's point of view, structural realism might just as easily be labeled "microeconomic realism." By contrast, a "macrotheory is a theory about the national economy built on supply, income, and demand as systemwide aggregates" (Waltz 1979: 110). The position that will be taken here, however, is that Waltz's structural realism should be regarded as a *macrotheory* because the causal relations on which it focuses pertain to entities at the level of the international system itself, namely, structure and overall propensity among units toward destructive conflict. The point of origin for this theory—an application of the microeconomic explanation of behavior among firms in an oligopolistic market—is a different issue.

5. As a final note about this achievement, it is clear for at least three reasons that Even-Zohar's introduction of the idea of the literary system into the interdisciplinary fields of comparative literature and communication had an important and lasting impact: (a) devotion of an entire issue of *Poetics Today*, the leading journal in the field, to republication (with commentaries by the author) of the series of articles on "polysystem theory" (Even-Zohar 1990a, 1990b, 1990c, and several other articles not cited here); (b) evidence of cross-national impact for polysystem studies (Lambert 1997; Even-Zohar 1997); and (c) appearance of constructive criticism that is intended to facilitate further applied work (Lambert 1997).

6. It is interesting to note that the definitions in this table appear prior to the 1990s. This implicit shift in priorities related to concept formation away from the level of the system complements the dramatic movement toward dyadic analysis noted earlier. Definitions in the last decade for concepts beyond the dyadic level focus on aggregations below the international system as a whole: examples include Maoz (1997) on the politically relevant international environment (PRIE) for a state and Kacowicz (1998: 8) on regions. Even in such instances an important dyadic interest usually can be detected; one purpose of Maoz's PRIE, for example, is to facilitate pairwise aggregation within the most appropriate boundaries.

7. The presence in this list of Kaplan and Bull, participants in one of the most bitter arguments in the history of the field over methods of inquiry (Bull 1966; Kaplan 1966), serves as a further reminder of the different (if not orthogonal) nature of these issues in comparison to those of theory. In other words, it is entirely feasible and even desirable to see agreement over methods coupled with disagreement about theory, and vice versa.

8. The exception is the limiting case of the global system, for which the environment exists but effects remain hypothetical and within the domain of science fiction rather than international relations.

9. For a recent review of research on interstate conflict cast at the regional level, with an emphasis on war, consult Geller and Singer (1998).

10. The general definition is taken from sociology, the discipline in which structural-functional analysis originally developed (Parsons 1937, 1951). Johnson (1985) observed that the units "of any social system, including a society, may be either subcollectivities of it or social roles" (787) and that these sociological variables are linked to the continued functioning of the system.

11. The list of sources overlaps considerably with that of table 2.1, which covered definitions of international system. The lists are not identical because some sources define either system or structure but not both.

12. The third dimension of structure, which is the specification of functions for units, is held constant by Waltz. States under anarchy are considered to be undifferentiated by function (Waltz 1979: 101). Similar treatments of structure in otherwise diverse expositions include Bueno de Mesquita (1988: 2), Nogee and Donaldson (1988: 10), Keohane and Nye (1989: 260), and Rosenau (1990: 269). Numerous other discussions of structure also focus on the distribution of capabilities under conditions of anarchy; for detailed reviews consult James (1990a, 1995).

13. The origins of regime analysis can be traced to the neofunctionalists, notably Mitrany (1943) and Haas (1958). Their concept formation provided the foundations for regional integration theory, which generated considerable interest among students of European politics in particular during the 1960s but became dormant and virtually forgotten as a result of discouraging developments on that continent and elsewhere in the 1970s (Haas 1976). Research in the same tradition re-emerged with the theoretical treatments of social choice, compliance, and other key concepts by Young (1978, 1979) and took explicit form in a collective effort to define and study international regimes (Krasner 1982a, 1982b). Applications of regime analysis to a wide range of issue areas appear frequently in the journal *International Organization* from the early 1980s onward and play a key role in the debate between neorealists and neoliberals (see Baldwin 1993a, 1993b).

14. *Structure*, to be more precise, refers to the set of relations among the system's components, and among these and environmental items. Thus, in the language of systemism, the four kinds of elements combine to form *endostructure* as opposed to *exostructure* (Bunge 1996).

15. Garnham's (1985: 7) taxonomy also produces four categories of capability-based indicators—size of the system (often referring more exclusively to the number of great powers), concentration of capabilities within the system, extent of alliance commitments, and characteristics of those linkages—but the current designation is more complete for at least two reasons. One is that it arises in the context of theorizing rather than out of an inductively generated mapping of research already carried out. The other somewhat related reason is that the categories are not only mutually exclusive but also exhaustive: concentration, for example, covers only one set of potentially significant elements at the secondary level.

16. The following discussion of realist paradigms and theories differs from Rosenau (1997: 31) by including a wider range of examples than would appear to have been suggested by Waltz (1979) or other closely related, system-oriented realist expositions such as Gilpin (1981).

17. In chapter 3 the framework of a scientific research enterprise supersedes the concept of a paradigm; it approaches the intended purpose of evaluation with a more precise designation of operational criteria for progressive theorizing.

18. Kegley (1995) refers to his list as "ten assumptions and realist propositions" (5), but even when these items are divided explicitly into three assumptions and seven propositions, the former set is significantly different from those that appear in the other studies just noted.

19. The sources used by Keohane (1989) are included in the previously cited and authoritative reviews, *Masters of International Thought* and *Fathers of International Thought*, by Thompson (1980, 1994).

It should be acknowledged that, as Keohane (1989) observes of his review of realist theory, the scope of what follows in this section of the chapter also is "restricted to work published in English, principally in the United States" (67). While it is beyond the scope of this study to pursue an exhaustive gathering of sources on either structural realism or realism writ large, the analysis should retain general relevance for at least two reasons. First, classic works in other languages, such as *Kautilya's Arthasastra* ([c. 321–300 B.C.] 1951), generally become available in English. Second, some of the journals in English, such as *Cooperation and Conflict, European Journal of International Relations,* and *Journal of Peace Research,* publish a high percentage of articles by scholars from countries that use other languages. The general availability of research in English-language books and journals is a by-product of the leading status enjoyed by Great Britain and the United States as world powers in the last two centuries, which might be viewed as an ironic legacy of the practice of power politics in that era.

20. Among the many other sources that identify state centrism as an assumption of realism are Mansbach and Vasquez (1981: 5), Morgenthau and Thompson (1985: 4–14), Keohane (1986b: 7), Booth (1987: 41), Mastanduno, Lake, and Ikenberry (1989: 459), Couloumbis and Wolfe (1990: 48), Dougherty and Pfaltzgraff (1990: 81), Haglund and Hawes (1990: 4), Buzan, Jones, and Little (1993: 11), James (1993b), Grieco (1997: 164–66), and Mastanduno (1999: 21).

21. This assumption is attributed to realism by many scholars, including Morgenthau and Thompson (1985: 4–14), Keohane (1986b: 7), Dessler (1989: 465), Mastanduno, Lake, and Ikenberry (1989: 459), Couloumbis and Wolfe (1990: 6–7), Dougherty and Pfaltzgraff (1990: 126, 1996), Wesson (1990: 6), James (1993a), Grieco (1997: 164–66), and Mastanduno (1999: 21). A standard definition of rational choice is provided by Riker and Ordeshook (1973), with transitivity and completeness as the principal conditions: If X p Y and Y p Z, where X, Y, and Z are alternatives and "p"

means "is preferred to," then transitivity requires X p Z. Completeness means that either X p Y, Y p X, or X i Y, where "i" designates "is indifferent to," must be true.

22. Grieco (1988, 1990) deserves recognition for articulating the notion of interstate rivalry and concerns over relative gains in a rigorous way. The intense debate over this axiom is addressed in Snidal (1993a, 1993b), Powell (1993, 1994), Keohane (1993), Grieco (1993a, 1993b, 1993c), and Mastanduno (1999).

23. This term is used here in a way somewhat similar to that of Glaser (1995: 379), who sees "contingent realism" as more optimistic than structural realism on the subject of avoiding war. While Glaser's focus is on substantive issues related to interstate cooperation versus conflict, the present usage is meant to convey that contingent realism coincides with a relatively autonomous sense of what decision makers can do in meeting security-based needs.

24. *Choice* and *learning* in a realist context refer to the ability to pursue interests more effectively through experience, but the objectives continue to revolve around security as measured in terms of relative standing among states. So it might be said that *contingent realism* refers more to means than to ends pursued within the states system.

25. The other seven items listed by Kegley (1995) appear to be derived from the first three assumptions: for example, "4. Under such conditions international politics is, as the English [seventeenth]-century philosopher Thomas Hobbes [1990] put it, a struggle for power, 'a war of all against all'" (5).

26. Maximization of *power* is noted as a basic tenet of traditional realism by Mansbach and Vasquez (1981: 5), Morgenthau and Thompson (1985: 4–14), Keohane (1986b: 7), Blacker (1987: 7), Booth (1987: 41), Mastanduno, Lake, and Ikenberry (1989: 459), Niou, Ordeshook, and Rose (1989: 2), Couloumbis and Wolfe (1990: 6–7), Dougherty and Pfaltzgraff (1990: 81), Grieco (1988: 498), Haglund and Hawes (1990: 4), Wesson (1990: 6), Legro and Moravcsik (1998), Mastanduno (1999: 21), and a host of others.

27. Diehl and Wayman (1994), in summing up a study produced by a team of scholars, offer similar observations: "[R]ealist predictions are sometimes nonfalsifiable and contradictory and have innumerable auxiliary propositions" (262; see also Wayman and Diehl 1994). The exchange between Vasquez (1997) and several critics in a recent symposium, which focuses on the viability of realism in terms of criteria from the philosophy of science, is more appropriately discussed in chapter 5.

28. Gilpin (1981), for example, asserts that "the fundamental nature of international relations has not changed over the millennia"; it continues to be a "recurring struggle for wealth and power among independent units in a state of anarchy" (7; see also Grieco 1988: 488). The central role of anarchy in structural realist interpretations is identified by, among others, Blacker (1987: 6), Kennedy (1988: 440), Mastanduno, Lake, and Ikenberry (1989: 459), Niou, Ordeshook, and Rose (1989: 2), Couloumbis and Wolfe (1990: 48), Dougherty and Pfaltzgraff (1990: 81), Haglund and Hawes (1990: 4), Wesson (1990: 6), Grieco (1990, 1993a, 1993b, 1993c, 1997), and James (1993b).

29. This assumption tends to remain implicit within subsequent expositions based on structural realism. As Ruggie (1986) points out, however, it places strict limitations on the explanatory power of the theory.

30. Waltz (1993, 1995, 1997) and all other analyses based on structural realism continue to use this axiom as the principal means of generating hypotheses about processes ranging from war to trade (James 1993b).

31. Gurr notes that the first three conditions were identified previously by Mack and

Snyder (1957: 218). It should be noted that the third condition, concerning behavior, can be satisfied by any one of the intentions noted. In other words, destruction and injury do not have to occur; thus conflict can form part of a search for accommodation.

32. Kriesberg's (1985: 147) later definition of *social* conflict shows important parallels with Gurr's concept formation, including groups that take each other into account, group consciousness, perception of at least partially incompatible goals, and a series of exchanges or encounters. Blalock (1989) defines social conflict as "the intentional mutual exchange of negative sanctions, or punitive behaviors, by two or more parties, which may be individuals, corporate actors, or more loosely knit quasi-groups" (7). This definition is somewhat different from Kriesberg's in that it treats group consciousness as a variable rather than a constant, although both treatments maintain general consistency with the ideas disseminated widely by Gurr (1980).

33. This definition of international conflict shows some convergence with Kriesberg's and Blalock's in terms of the important roles played by group formation and interaction.

34. This definition is derived from Young's (1978) description of "social choice."

35. Subsequent definitions focusing on interstate crises seem to be consistent with the concerns evident in the concept formation pursued by Brecher et al. (1988), although none is so well developed. Two examples are summarized here. First, for Leng and Singer (1988), a military interstate crisis begins with a "specific precipitant event" having one or more of the following properties: "(1) an explicit threat, display, or use of force; (2) a challenge to the vital interests of the target, that is, its territorial integrity, political independence, or any foreign possessions or rights; or (3) a serious affront to the dignity or prestige of the target state" (160). The crisis terminates with either war, settlement, or nonsettlement (i.e., stalemate). Although finite time for response by the target state is not incorporated explicitly, it is implied by the intensity of the three categories related to force. The second example of a definition of crisis is from Lalman (1988): a "condition" where inaction no longer is feasible to at least one party (593). By building in time limitation directly, Lalman implies seriousness of threat, although there is no clear reference to potential military engagement.

36. The discussion of definitions that follows is based primarily on Brecher (1993: 20–25).

37. In an authoritative analysis of case studies and aggregate data from the ICB Project, Brecher (1993) concludes in favor of rational choice as a general property of decision making in crisis; this finding is reinforced by Harvey's (1997, 1998) compelling evidence in favor of rational deterrence theory. The substantive meaning of rational choice in the crisis domain is identified during discussion of the model of state behavior in James (2002a).

38. The evolution of concept formation about crises in foreign policy is traced with great insight by Brecher (1993: 15–20). Elements such as event origins, time pressure, surprise, conflicting objectives, stress, and perceived likelihood of war appear in a series of definitions developed by Robinson (1962, 1968, 1972), Hermann (1963, 1969, 1972), Morse (1972), Hazlewood, Hayes, and Brownell (1977), Snyder and Diesing (1977), and Stein and Tanter (1980). For a recent effort that revisits the relevance of surprise as a condition, see Robinson (1996: 16).

39. The nuances linking foreign policy and international crisis, such as the ability of a participant to experience more than one foreign policy crisis in a given international crisis, are explained during the presentation of data in James (2002a).

40. One obvious source of interstate conflict is ethnic nationalism, which remains a

powerful force in the new Europe. Both separatism and irredentism could produce major strife, most notably in the rapidly changing eastern regions, which already have experienced violent international crises (Brecher and Wilkenfeld 1997; Carment and James 1997, 1998; Kaufman 2001; Saideman 2001).

41. Furthermore, most of the world still lives in substandard conditions and under governments of uneven quality, so it is possible to point to an unintended ethnocentric strand to the argument that the reasons for intense international conflict are fading away.

42. Both Ray (1989) and Mueller (1988) have argued that war as a social institution is evolving toward obsolescence. The most compelling historical parallel is with slavery, which virtually disappeared in spite of a long history of general acceptance (Ray 1989).

43. The exception is the Western Hemisphere, which contains only one dyad with marginal significance, Guyana/Venezuela, with a long-standing conflict over Essequibo. From a realist standpoint, the hegemonic role of the United States provides a straightforward explanation for the absence of high-risk pairings in the Western Hemisphere; an alternative, Grotian analysis of South America as a zone of peace appears in Kacowicz (1998).

44. Sandler (1997) conceives of China as a "global challenge" (207), with properties that resemble those that economists attribute to a public good: that is, joint supply and nonexcludability. The most important problems posed by China, largely as a function of its sheer size and recent increase in activity, are environmental risk and potentially aggressive actions toward other states. Threats to Taiwan in 1995, 1998, and 2000, along with the airplane-related incident involving the United States in 2001, point to a high probability of recurrent crises between Beijing and Taipeh in the South China Sea in the years ahead.

45. Most and Starr (1989: 92–96) also provide an appendix that lists prominent signposts in the effort to define war and other forms of international conflict. See also Levy (1983: 51ff.) for a discussion of prior definitions.

46. This definition remains the standard among ongoing large-scale efforts to monitor international conflict events; recent and prominent examples would include Wallensteen and Sollenberg (1995, 1996). For a useful typology of interstate wars as "limited" (partial mobilization of disposable resources and willingness of at least one combatant to accept defeat), "total" (full mobilization of disposable resources and an unwillingness on the part of any combatant to accept defeat), or "major" (an intense struggle with the potential to affect the territory of great powers and leadership of the international order), see Kugler (1990).

Notes for Chapter 3

1. Those acquainted with the classic works of Lakatos (1970, 1971) and Laudan (1977, 1981, 1996) will see familiar terminology in this definition. As will become apparent, however, the scientific research enterprise as defined here represents a synthesis and step beyond the concepts of the research program and research tradition found in Lakatos and Laudan, respectively.

2. This issue, which reappears over half a century, is addressed by Guetzkow (1950), Waltz (1959), Gilpin (1981), Blalock (1989), Rosenau (1990, 1995, 1997), Rosenau and Durfee (1995), Goldmann (1996), Holsti (1998), and Vasquez (1998). The concept of a middle-range theory is introduced explicitly by Merton (1957).

3. This debate, which continues into the present, took form when general systems theory became prominent in the social sciences during the 1960s; see Singer (1961), McClelland (1966), Young (1968a), Waltz (1979, 1986, 1988, 1991, 1993, 1995, 1997), Gilpin (1981), Morrow (1988), Holsti (1991a), Wolfson, Puri, and Martelli (1992), and James (1993b).

4. Studies covering some or all of these issues in relation to intellectual progress include Wright (1942), Kaplan (1957, 1966, 1979), Hoffmann (1959, 1960, 1977), Bull (1966), Russett (1969), Young (1969), Phillips (1974), Bueno de Mesquita (1980b, 1985a, 1985b, 1988, 1993), Zinnes (1980a, 1980b), Gilpin (1984), Ashley (1984, 1986), Jervis (1985), Krasner (1985), Wendt (1987), Achen and Snidal (1989), Nicholson (1989), Simowitz and Price (1990, 1991), Morrow (1991), Puchala (1991), Brecher (1993, 1999), Onuf (1995), Adler (1997), Elshtain (1997), and Vasquez (2002).

5. As Brecher (1999) observes, the "paucity of serious attempts at synthesis, or at least complementarity, among contending paradigms is an indicator of deep malaise" (235). Constructive reviews, which incorporate at least some effort toward synthesis, include Guetzkow (1950), Wright (1957), McCloskey (1962), Dougherty and Pfaltzgraff (1971, 1990, 1996), Waltz (1975), Sullivan (1976, 1990), Biersteker (1989), George (1989), Holsti (1991a), Lapid (1989), Most and Starr (1989), Kugler (1991, 1993a), Bobrow (1996), Smith (1996), Albert and Lapid (1997), Kahler (1997), Lamborn (1997), Brecher (1999), Leng (1999), Wendt (1999), and Vasquez (2002).

6. Arguments in favor of realism (both generically and in respective variants since its inception) as the path to greater understanding include Morgenthau (1946, 1948), Aron (1957, 1966), Buzan (1981), Buzan and Jones (1981), Jones (1981), Frankel (1988), Grieco (1988, 1990, 1993a, 1993b, 1993c, 1997), Mastanduno, Lake, and Ikenberry (1989), Haggard (1991), Baldwin (1993a, 1993b), Buzan, Jones, and Little (1993), James (1993b, 1995), Powell (1993, 1994), Diehl and Wayman (1994), Layne (1994), Glaser (1995), Little (1995), Wohlforth (1995), Buzan and Little (1996), Levy (1996), Little and Buzan (1996), Sanders (1996), Christensen and Snyder (1997), Elman and Elman (1997), Schweller (1997), Walt (1997), Waltz (1997), Donnelly (1998), Halliday and Rosenberg (1998), Jervis (1998), Kagan (1998), Rose (1998), Mastanduno and Kapstein (1999), and Schweller (2002).

7. A selection of these critics would include Keohane and Nye (1972, 1977, 1987, 1989), Mansbach and Vasquez (1981), Vasquez (1983, 1997, 1998), Keohane (1986b, 1989, 1993), Ferguson and Mansbach (1989, 1991, 1996), Lapid (1989), Howe (1991), Katzenstein (1989), Kegley (1995), Ray (1995, 1999), Mansbach (1996), Guzzini (1998), Legro and Moravcsik (1998), Liska (1998), Freyberg-Inan (1999), Wendt (1999), and Harrison (2000). Further critiques are noted in Mastanduno and Kapstein (1999: 23, n. 1).

8. For reactions to Lapid, which generally agreed with his cautious optimism about the potential contributions of postpositivism and the need for pluralism in theorizing, see Biersteker (1989), George (1989), and Holsti (1991a).

9. Examples from the vast literature with either direct or indirect application to the social sciences, each of which finds at least partial usage in the present or following chapters, include Popper ([1935] 1959, 1969, 1981), Sheldon (1951), Quine (1953), Merton (1957), Brodbeck (1962), Kuhn (1962, 1970, 1971, 1977, 1981), Hempel (1965), Buchdal (1969), Lakatos (1970, 1971), Lakatos and Musgrave (1970), Giedmiyin (1971), Gillies (1971), Jeffrey (1971), Koertge (1971), Martin (1971), Smart (1972), Barbour (1974), Gellner (1975), Lakatos and Zahar (1975), Lave and March (1975), Toulmin (1975), Ball (1976, 1987), Grünbaum (1976), Duhem (1977), Laudan

(1977, 1981, 1996), Dacey (1978), McMullin (1978), Radnitzky and Andersson (1978), Urbach (1978), Watkins (1978), Blaug (1980), Feyerabend (1981), Hacking (1981), Putnam (1981), Shapere (1981), Fiorina and Shepsle (1982), Elster (1983), Glymour (1983, 1985), Zahar (1983), Churchland and Hooker (1985), Ellis (1985), Gutting (1985), Simon (1985), van Fraasen (1985), Wagner and Berger (1985), Coleman (1986), Dryzek (1986), Rosenberg (1986), Glymour et al. (1987), Nickles (1987), Nola (1987), Almond (1990), Caldwell (1991), Berger and Zelditch (1993), Lawler and Ford (1993), Bunge (1996), and Couvalis (1997).

10. As noted in chapter 1, linkages between and among variables are anticipated to be probabilistic.

11. The balance between normative and positive character for concepts along the continuum is virtually certain to remain beyond the scope of precise measurement. However, identifying inequalities in that balance between salient points on the continuum should be sufficient to bring out qualitative differences. Debates will tend to focus more on normative (positive) issues as the degree of aggregation approaches worldview (hypothesis) because viability is assessed differently at respective points. At one extreme, a worldview must offer a cognitively satisfying integration of observation and personal judgment, while at the other, a hypothesis needs to survive in confrontation with potentially falsifying evidence gathered in the context of one or more theories.

Consider the Malthusian worldview, which continues to influence, at least implicitly, arguments over public policy ranging from those of ideological liberals such as environmentalists to conservative advocates of family planning. The specific hypothesis about "crowding and combat," however, finds little or no support from systematic research so far in international relations; neither objective nor subjective indicators of population density are correlated with the war proneness of European states from 1816 to 1965 (Bremer, Singer, and Luterbacher 1979).

12. This point differs from the one made by Quine (1953) about the inability of a sentence to communicate an observation directly. All such statements are embedded in a prior context of theorizing. The choice among contexts for communication of a hypothesis, however, need not entail allegiance to any particular normative position. For example, an observer steeped in theories of international relations might say that the leaders of the United States, Canada, and Mexico signed the North American Free Trade Agreement (NAFTA) in anticipation of absolute gains. An observation like this one, as pointed out by Quine, requires the use of theory-laden terms such as *leader* and *absolute gains*. The statement is state centric and also relies on language from the debate between realists and liberals over why cooperation sometimes occurs at the international level (Baldwin 1993b), but it does not entail a judgment about the appropriateness of pursuing either absolute or relative gains through NAFTA.

13. A full explanation of the scientific approach is beyond the scope of this exposition, but the following points from Bunge (1996: 79) cover the main components: (a) relevant scientific knowledge and its underlying philosophy; (b) a set of cognitive problems; (c) gaining objective knowledge about a domain of facts; and (d) the scientific method plus a collection of special, scrutable techniques. A prominent dissenting view on the utility of a commitment to scientific research appears in Feyerabend (1981).

14. An impressionistic survey of journals and book-length expositions in the field during the 1990s suggests that social constructivism is very far along in supplanting postmodernism within "rejectionist" theorizing about international relations, defined as expositions that claim status fully outside of the contemporary mainstream of realism or liberalism. From the standpoint of scientific systemism, the correlated rise of con-

structivism and decline of postmodernism within rejectionist theorizing is explained by (a) postmodernism's ongoing creation of neologisms and alternative meanings for existing concepts, which seem intended to shield it from contact with "alien" worldviews (intentionally and unintentionally illustrated by Sokal [1996] and Der Derian [1997], respectively); and (b) constructivism's efforts to (i) use preexisting concepts to highlight potential oversimplification; (ii) suggest the value of a frame of reference that privileges the generation and dissemination of ideas as crucial in creating reality; and (iii) influence thinking within other worldviews through direct dialogue (effectively demonstrated by Adler [1997], with evidence of such engagement already available in Buzan, Jones, and Little [1993]; Copeland 2000b; and Hall and Jönsson 2001). For a critical view of "constructionism," with a general connection to constructivism and the pernicious effects of fad following, see Bauerlein (2001).

15. Some diversity of opinion on these points, however, seems to be developing among those self-identified as constructivists within international relations. As an illustration, Wendt (1999: 37) asserts that "ontology-talk is necessary" but needs to be translated into empirical propositions about international politics. For example, a constructivist might argue that Chinese nuclear capabilities are perceived as a "threat" by the United States in a way that the larger British arsenal is not because of intersubjective understanding rather than the material traits of the weapons.

16. In spite of this fundamental difference, it is interesting to note that at least one recent exposition of constructivism claims to reject, as does systemism, the extremes of both individualism and holism (Wendt 1999: 245). This assertion, however, seems to suggest some inconsistency with the placement of constructivism within the holist/idealist sociology of structure at an earlier point in the same study (Wendt 1999: 23–31).

17. Bobrow's (1996) observations make it clear that *reminder* is the right term to use in this context: "A century ago William James (*The Principles of Psychology,* 1950) observed the importance of what comes out of our mind, not just what comes through our senses, and the intensified reality to us of what we select and emphasize based on established thoughts" (440).

18. The term *linkage politics* is traced to Rosenau (1969) with respect to the connection between any two political systems.

19. Texts in phenomenology make this point clearly: the perspective held by the observer factors into how intentions are attributed to the actor(s) being observed (Bernstein 1976: 117–69; see also Schutz [1932] 1967). Thus variation in worldview is likely to produce parallel differences in ontologies, which in turn create the potential for attributing varying intentions to those observed.

20. This discussion highlights an advantage of using the definition of an international system from Brecher and Ben Yehuda (1985). Its components, such as actors, boundaries, and issues (which chapter 2 described in more detail), facilitate discussion at a wide range of points along the continuum of aggregation.

21. Baldwin's (1993b) collection encompasses the most recent iterations of this debate, in which neorealism and neoliberal institutionalism are labeled (depending upon the author) as either competing or complementary ways of thinking. For expressions of the most graphic differences, see Keohane (1993) and Grieco (1993c), with Powell (1993) representing an effort toward a synthesis at the level of strategic interaction.

22. Lamborn (1997) makes this point in a different way through analysis of seemingly disparate areas of literature within the field of international relations. The basic problem he identifies is that few expositions "explicitly evaluate the implications of their underlying metatheoretical assumptions about politics" (212–13). In some instances,

pointless arguments occur because, to use the language developed in this chapter, antagonists fail to recognize that they begin with different parameter settings but share beliefs about politics at the level of ontology. The ongoing debate between liberals and realists would seem to be a prominent example of this problem in action.

23. Alternative concept formation about theory, some of which is consistent with the definition put forward here, includes Popper ([1935] 1959), Merton (1957), Kuhn (1962), Hempel (1965), Lakatos (1970), Barbour (1974), Duhem (1977), Laudan (1977), Waltz (1979), Wagner and Berger (1985), Coleman (1986), Brecher (1993), and Bunge (1996).

24. Recall that P_1 through P_6 refer to the axioms of structural realism as presented in chapter 2: P_1—the most important actors in world politics are territorially organized entities (city-states and modern states); P_2—state behavior is rational; P_3—states seek security and calculate their interests in terms of relative standing within the international system; P_4—anarchy is the ordering principle of international structure; P_5—states are undifferentiated by function; P_6—structure is defined by the distribution of capabilities among states.

25. Waltz (1979), in the fundamental exposition of structural realism, disagrees with the use of concentration of capabilities to explain the occurrence of war (the usual measurement of instability) because no such theory exists "that in fact employs such a variable" (15). Theory C, however, can be created easily without contradicting the assumptions of structural realism as identified in chapter 2. Concentration is an alternative indicator of the distribution of capabilities within the system and cannot be dismissed from the effort to use structural analysis to account for processes. The ability to define structure in a more inclusive way is crucial for the elaboration of structural realism that begins in chapter 5.

26. For a more encompassing treatment of feedback and similar issues in system-level theory, see Jervis (1997).

27. Of course, nothing would prevent an alternative specification that includes the opposite hypothesis. Bipolarity might encourage greater (and successful) efforts among other states to improve their relative standing, which in turn (depending on the way in which redistribution occurred) would reduce concentration. This intrastructural dynamic might continue with an additional causal arrow from concentration to bipolarity: that is, declining concentration producing movement toward multipolarity.

28. Waltz (1995) acknowledges bidirectional cause and effect, from structure to process and the reverse, but is careful to point out that the latter means that "some causes of international outcomes are located at the level of the interacting units" (78). In other words, the distribution of capabilities (among other things) might be altered as a result of unit-level interactions, but structure is preserved in an *overall sense*. This commitment to unidirectional cause and effect at the system level creates for neorealism the problem of how to explain change in structure, about which the most insightful discussion appears in Buzan, Jones, and Little. (1993). The more general issue of whether theories such as that of Buzan, Jones, and Little should be regarded as paradigmatically different from Waltz's (1979) variant is addressed in chapter 4.

29. Adams (1999: 2) observes that normative critics of structural realism have received primarily theoretical and empirical replies. This unproductive dialogue suggests that structural realism might be more completely equipped for such discussions if it included a model that addressed state-society relations. Thus a theoretical improvement might produce an enhanced ability to compete at the normative level. This point is made in a somewhat different way by Kaufman (1999), who associates realism's inability to

explain international change—and therefore achieve greater practical relevance—with its self-imposed neglect of economics.

30. While it by no means includes all of those who might be regarded as experts in the field of international relations, the existence of the International Studies Association (ISA) as a global organization with thousands of members lends general support to the relevance of the comparison being developed here. The presence of the ISA as an organization points toward some degree of collective consciousness regarding international relations as a field of study. Even before the establishment of the ISA, Wright (1957: 23) noted that use of the term *discipline* implied some consciousness among scholars that there existed a subject with some kind of unity; a more recent observer describes international relations, in spite of ambiguities, as possessing "a distinct professional academic identity with an identifiable discourse" (Schmidt 1994: 365).

31. Kaplan (1979) makes this point about research communities as a whole because, at any given time, new entrants make up only a small percentage of those active: "Accepted theories will tend to come under challenge in the absence of falsification only when [a] lack of fit becomes apparent. Until then, even apparent direct falsifications will tend to be rejected or reinterpreted. New theories will tend to be accepted more easily the less they tend to challenge the general realm of scientific knowledge. And the greater the fit between such theories and the general realm of scientific knowledge, the more ready the scientific community will be to accept apparently confirming evidence for these theories or disconfirming evidence for rivals that are less satisfying in this respect" (109–10).

32. Of course, it is possible to observe that a jury's deliberation is not a random process and that bias—it would be hoped, in the direction of greater justice—is a certainty. This line of reasoning, which would move the discussion into the complex and inherently philosophical issue of the meaning of justice, will not be pursued further here.

33. A more interesting variant on this reasoning is that self-interest may intervene to affect beliefs (Cox 1986). For example, citizens of wealthy and poor states, respectively, might be disposed toward neoclassical versus dependency-oriented arguments. This question and others like it are beyond the scope of the present exposition, except to say that such bias might be expected to affect the pace with which arguments take hold rather than the ultimate outcome of public debate.

34. Kaplan (1979) leans in this direction during an assessment of "professionalism" in international theory. A public process of "communication among informed and literate minds with respect to the structure of the real world may produce a consensus" (110). This becomes more likely to occur when the subject matter is relatively straightforward and "research programs" are more complete. Thus effective paradigmatic competition among research *specialists* is the best way to develop knowledge that, in turn, can be transmitted in applied form to permit assessment in terms of pragmatic value by the mass public as a *generalist*.

35. The nonviability of astrology as a science, with an emphasis on its inherent inability to create research puzzles for practitioners, is addressed by Kuhn (1977: 276–77). Astrology's continuing appeal in terms of entertainment value is a subject beyond the scope of this study.

36. Further potential complications, such as whether (a) scholarly "fads" tend to follow public preferences (over at least the short term) or (b) information overload is likely to outrun improvement in filtering within one or more societies, also are not addressed.

37. All-encompassing treatments of the discipline tend toward nihilism and provide

little direction toward alternatives. Prominent examples, which share little other than a disdain for the discipline of international relations writ large, include Hoffmann (1959, 1977), Bull (1966), and Ashley (1984). For an indictment of the behavioral revolution as applied to the discipline of international relations, see Puchala (1991).

38. Aside from one direct debate between advocates of research programs and traditions for international relations (Simowitz and Price 1990, 1991; Morrow 1991; see also Simowitz 2002), criticism of the former (and more established) concept tends toward an implicit endorsement of an outlook based on Kuhnian incommensurability (Krasner 1985; Jervis 1985). However, what this would mean in operational terms for comparison at either paradigmatic or more specific degrees of aggregation (as that terminology is used here) is unknown.

39. For a full range of opinions about sophisticated methodological falsificationism as applied to the field of international relations, which covers issues ranging from the incommensurability of theories to the meaning of falsifiability, consult the symposium including Bueno de Mesquita (1985a, 1985b), Krasner (1985: 140), and Jervis (1985). Simon (1985: 291) offers a critique at a more general level within the social sciences.

40. Popper's falsificationism is represented most directly in recent and contemporary thought by the ideas of Lakatos (1970, 1971), those who have built on his framework (e.g., Lakatos and Zahar 1975; McMullin 1978), and, as the following discussion will make clear, to a lesser degree by Laudan (1977) as well. Nickles (1987: 181, 205) points out that the framework developed by Lakatos is consistent with Popper but, to use the language developed in the present exposition, is cast at a higher degree of aggregation: that is, for a series of theories rather than any individual hypothesis.

41. Kuhn (1981: 25) sees "thought experiments" as playing an important role in resolving crises at varying points in the history of science. The timing and degree of success for such efforts in relation to "incongruous experience" can be expected to vary throughout the history of a discipline for any number of reasons.

42. This treatment gives more of an operational meaning to the initial definition of the positive heuristic, which had equated it with a plan to improve a program's explanatory models (Lakatos 1970; Koertge 1971). The present exposition refers specifically to what results from the plan and is generally consistent with Lakatos's (1971) final attempt at definition: the positive heuristic "defines problems, outlines the construction of a belt of auxiliary hypotheses, foresees anomalies and turns them victoriously into examples, all according to a preconceived plan" (99).

43. Lakatos (1971) implicitly acknowledged that empirical research outside the formal evolution of a program will occur and that at least some of it may have implications for progress: "I distinguish three types of *ad hoc* auxiliary hypotheses: those which have no excess empirical content over their predecessors ('*ad hoc$_1$*'), those which do have such excess content but none of it is corroborated ('*ad hoc$_2$*') and finally those which are not *ad hoc* in these two senses but do not form an integral part of the positive heuristic ('*ad hoc$_3$*')" (125). As will become apparent in part 2, from the vantage point of structural realism, a plethora of ad hoc$_3$ hypotheses can be identified in research on international relations. This property is predicted for the social sciences in general by Lakatos (125).

44. Quoted in Kuhn 1970: 239. See also Barbour (1974: 102). Kuhn (1970) noted other points of continuity as well: while terminology varied, the "analytical apparatus is as close to mine as need be: hard core [of assumptions], work in the protective belt [of propositions], and degenerate phase [in explanatory power] are close parallels for my paradigms, normal science, and crisis" (256). The literature on Lakatos, especially in relation to Kuhn, is vast. The collection of essays in Lakatos and Musgrave (1970)

remains the most effective introduction to the debate, and Hacking (1981) provides an authoritative treatment of the evolving nature of Lakatos's thought; the *British Journal for the Philosophy of Science* and *Minnesota Studies in the Philosophy of Science* contain many further explorations of the issues that crystallized in the above-noted collection. Most of the issues involved, however, are at some distance from application to a social science such as international relations and will not be covered here.

45. Ripley (1990) offers a preliminary application of Lakatos's framework in order to present foreign policy decision making in a way that would have the potential to create a program of research independent from neorealism. This study, however, does not offer the degree of detail needed for inclusion in the table.

46. For a pointed exchange over the application of Laudan's framework to expected utility as an area of research about international conflict, see Simowitz and Price (1990, 1991) and Morrow (1991). This debate focuses on the performance of expected utility theory rather than the strengths and weaknesses of the research program and research tradition as applied frameworks, so it will not be addressed here.

47. Popper (1981) eventually modified his views on replacement, claiming that a certain amount of "dogmatism" is needed in defending old theories so that new ones can "show their mettle" (98). For assessments of Popper's greater and ongoing willingness to relax standards of falsification for the social sciences, see Caldwell (1991: 97–98) and Hands (1991: 111–16).

48. Jeffrey (1971: 40, 45), for example, tries to develop a measure of explanatory power. However, after a complex exposition consisting of formal logic, he concludes that "there is no clear, simple, useful intuitive notion of explanatory power to be explicated" (45).

49. Ball (1976) refers to "research programs" rather than theories in this context, but the point remains the same.

50. Consider Duhem's (1977) admonition about interpreting events in the physical sciences: "[I]f the predicted phenomenon is not produced, not only is the proposition questioned at fault, but so is the whole intellectual scaffolding. . . . The only thing the experiment teaches us is that among propositions used to predict the phenomena and to establish whether it would be produced, there is at least one error; but where this error lies is just what it does not tell us. . . . [L]ogic does not determine with strict precision the time when an inadequate hypothesis should give way to a more fruitful assumption" (185; see also Bunge 1996: 180). This advice should carry even more weight in the social sciences, where intuition alone is enough to know that errors can take place at many stages and in various ways from the outset of theorizing through analysis of data.

51. The description of the series of COW-based studies on arms races and war follows Geller and Singer (1998: 79–81).

52. Treatments in the philosophy of science include Jeffrey (1971), Barbour (1974), Kuhn (1977), Watkins (1978), Wagner and Berger (1985), Berger and Zelditch (1993), and Bunge (1996); for international theory in particular see Hoffmann (1960), McClelland (1966), Young (1968b), Phillips (1974), Booth (1987), Haggard (1991), Puchala (1991), Thompson (1994), Levy (1996), and Brecher (1999).

53. No consensus exists, independent of academic discipline and the context within it, about the value of the preceding goals in relation to each other. Arguments for and against the utility of prediction in comparison to explanation appear, without any ultimate resolution, in the classic exchange between Lakatos and Zahar (1975) and Toulmin (1975).

54. Even the apparently simple case of preventing disasters in the earlier example of

meteorology might include unseen complications. What if these events contribute in some way to preserving the ecosystem as whole? Then the issue of trading off short-term gains for long-term danger would have to be addressed within one or more worldviews. The indeterminate nature of such decision making is borne out in the range of options that developed in the forecasting of alternative futures at the global level, which gained and receded from prominence in the course of little more than a decade (Forrester 1971; Herrera et al. 1976; Hughes 1985, 1993).

55. Consistent with scientific systemism's belief in rationality and progress, all learning is assumed to be desirable in a long-term context. The balance between positive and negative applications for pure research is assumed to become favorable with time. Although important aberrations can be expected, such as the initial use and subsequent testing of nuclear weapons, the pursuit of knowledge for its own sake is regarded as at least a benign activity.

56. Perhaps Ray (1999) sums up the view from international relations most effectively: "[I]t is troublesome that the categories, criteria and concepts supplied to us by contemporary philosophy of science seem to be so imprecise and utterly un-operational" (6). For an especially revealing instance, consult the compilation from Radnitzky and Andersson (1978).

57. To be more precise, Shanker (1988) conveyed this as a summary of Wittgenstein's views on the nature of a mathematical system.

58. This creates the possibility of step-level and discontinuous change with respect to the impact of adding assumptions to create a more elaborate theory. A series of theories might be progressive in an overall sense, yet later versions could be less prolific than some of those that appeared earlier. This likely scenario is built into the curvilinear function for explanation in figure A-2.1 from appendix A-2, where the rate of return from further axioms steadily diminishes.

59. What about the other side of the question about ontology: that is, the concern that additional points along the continuum, either between ontology and worldview, or ontology and paradigm, might be worth exploring? An example of an intermediate point on the continuum that is close to ontology but that shifts somewhat further in the direction of specificity is metatheory. Metatheories "define the substantive problems of theoretical interest, dictate how these problems should be investigated, and establish boundaries for the sort of theoretical solutions that are deemed satisfactory" (Lawler and Ford 1993: 174). Thus metatheories focus on identification of issues, methods, and suitable theorizing but do not reach down to the designation of parameters, which defines paradigmlike entities. An example of a metatheory from international relations would be Waltz's (1959) classic *Man, the State and War*. This exposition focuses on war as the basic substantive problem, investigates its causes through analysis of human nature and the states system, and operates on a de facto "rule" that theoretical solutions have to build a bridge between the preceding sets of factors.

However, it is not clear that adding metatheory as an intermediate point along the continuum can be justified by its one noteworthy step beyond the existing components of ontology: that is, introduction of method as a concern beyond theorizing. The same might be said of other potential intermediate points on either side of ontology. At this stage the burden of proof would seem to rest on the argument that the continuum is missing inherently important components and needs to become more detailed than at present.

Worldview and *hypothesis* are defined in ways that limit the need for further discussion of possible intermediate points. Hypotheses are defined as basic "if-then" statements and are combined to form theories. Given the respective definitions for *hypothesis* and *theory,* no meaningful intermediate point would seem to exist between them. At the other extreme, *worldview* is defined in a holistic way. Thus ontology, which focuses on how the world is experienced, is the natural next step in the direction of specificity.

60. This path is consistent with intuition based on figure A-2.1 in appendix A-2. Returns from increasing the number of axioms increase monotonically for description, explanation, and prediction, and each reaches a maximum—d^*, e^*, and p^*, respectively—in that figure. Thus a curve resembling the one that appears in figure 3.2 would be expected regardless of the specific way in which the benefits from description, explanation, and prediction might be aggregated.

61. Although each of these curves also crosses the marginal empirical content curve at an earlier point, the later intersection point is preferred because of the much higher level attained for empirical content.

Notes for Chapter 4

1. A parameter conventionally refers to an empirical constant. In this context the axioms might be regarded as parameters with a value of 1 (i.e., yes = 1, no = 0).

2. For a contrary view, see Kuhn (1971), in which rational reconstruction (especially as practiced by Lakatos) is equated with "philosophy fabricating examples" (143).

3. While generally consistent with table 4.1, the other attempts to provide a description of the "neorealist hard core," by Grieco (1995: 27) and Elman and Elman (1997: 924), are incomplete. Grieco includes P_1, P_2, and P_4 explicitly and implies P_3 (through mentioning substantive rationality) but leaves out P_5 and P_6. Elman and Elman appear to omit P_6, which defines structure in terms of the distribution of capabilities among states. This axiom may be implicit in the final component listed by Elman and Elman, which asserts that states will "weigh options and make decisions based on their strategic situation and an assessment of the external environment" (924).

4. One other candidate for the list of empirical problems addressed by the initial variant of structural realism, namely, persistence of the international system as one of anarchy rather than hierarchy, is not granted that status. Two compelling, interrelated reasons justify this exclusion. First, persistence of a system of some kind cannot be regarded as an empirical problem unless that occurs in relation to something else. Thus it is reasonable to ask, for example, whether one distribution of capabilities can be expected to last longer than another but not why an anarchical structure persists. The second reason directly concerns anarchy's role as one of the parametric settings of structural realism. Anarchy, as a component of the hard core, is accepted as a valid assumption and is used in generating hypotheses rather than being evaluated itself for empirical accuracy.

5. Boyer (1993) provides evidence of comparative advantage in practice throughout his compelling treatment of burden sharing in NATO. Financial contributions generally vary in proportion to size (which supports the conventional economic hypothesis about cost sharing), but the *substantive* nature of functions among members also varies. For an authoritative review of burden sharing in NATO, see Sandler and Hartley (1999).

6. Neither theory A nor theory B, however, will be placed in the sequence of structural realist theories that starts with T_0. The reason derives from Kuhn's (1971) earlier point about carrying rational reconstruction to a potentially fraudulent extreme; since neither theory A nor theory B has been developed with an explicit foundation in the axioms of structural realism until the previous chapter of the present volume, it would be inappropriate to include either in the sequence from T_0 onward.

7. The first two types of ad hoc hypotheses refer to a lack of excess empirical content on the one hand and absence of corroboration on the other (Lakatos 1971: 125). Since no attempt is made to assess content directly for structural realism as a scientific research enterprise, neither ad hoc$_1$ nor ad hoc$_2$ will be considered further. This position also is adopted by Elman and Elman's (2002b) authoritative review of research programs in international relations.

8. It should be acknowledged that factors prominent within neotraditional realism, such as the offense-defense balance and nuclear weapons, are excluded from this review, which focuses on elements of structure within the system as opposed to components of a unit-oriented approach toward realism.

9. The review focuses on elements and combinations of them that already have been "discovered." It would be possible to enumerate other elements and explore potential linkages between them and conflict processes, but that work is carried out more appropriately in James (2002a), where an elaborated structural realism is presented in full and is subjected to both bivariate and multivariate testing.

10. It will become apparent that the linkages and results for primary elements (and especially the number of poles) are presented in greater detail than those for elements at the other levels. Two reasons account for the diminishing details across levels. One is that some connections for elements at different levels will call upon parallel explanations. The other is that several studies reappear throughout the discussion, so it becomes redundant in such instances to provide details about time frame for analysis and like matters.

11. Geller and Singer (1998: 57) review the limited findings on great-power status and international conflict prior to the COW Project and find connections involving some forms of interstate behavior, such as verbal foreign conflict.

12. A survey of the early treatments of centers of capability and alliances confirms this impression. One example is Kaplan's (1957) characterization of loose bipolarity, with the leading actor in each bloc representing a "pole of the system" (36). Another instance is Liska's (1962) description of poles in the post-1945 system: "NATO makes up the Western pole and the Sino-Soviet alliance plus the Warsaw pact make up the Eastern pole" (161).

13. Other advocates of bipolarity in the early stages of the debate include Riker (1962), Zoppo (1966), and Spiegel (1970). For a more extensive review of the literature supporting a system of two principal powers, see Brecher and James (1989).

14. While it became obvious years later that the United States had at least twice the economic strength of the Soviet Union, it is the available information at the time of events that determines polar designation. For such reasons the Cold War era is labeled one of bipolarity—measurements widely available then pointed to near-equality between the two giants.

15. The Soviet situation relative to an increasingly hostile and worrisome China should be noted at this point as an example of how actor-level specifics can affect system-level results. Although Chinese defection from the Soviet coalition did not produce a "systemic" or "systems" change in Gilpin's (1981) terms, it did affect the USSR's efforts in a tactical context. The Soviet Union had to build up massive forces and deploy half of the SS-20 intermediate-range ballistic missile force on the Chinese border. Thus an actor-level characteristic—referring to the very different border situations faced by the United States and the USSR, respectively—contributed significantly to the substantive outcome of their rivalry.

16. Midlarsky (1988: 49) provides a detailed numerical example of the difference

between two systems, one of which has twelve times the amount of resources as the other. The system with scarce resources can be expected to produce more extreme differences in distribution when random processes are used to generate outcomes.

17. Among the supporters of multipolarity in the early stages of the debate are Aron (1966) and Hoffmann (1968). A detailed review of the literature advocating a system with more than two leading powers is available in Brecher and James (1989).

18. In spite of this logic, historical counterexamples abound: the Thirty Years' War, the wars of Louis XIV, Austrian Succession, the Seven Years' War, and the French Revolutionary/Napoleonic Wars featured virtually all of Europe lined up on one side or the other. This reality points further to the need for an overall assessment of elements of structure on the basis of a comprehensive body of evidence.

19. Some of the other arguments related to conflict as a function of the number of poles either are specific to certain historical periods or do not rely on capability-based factors. For example, Copper (1975) notes multipolarity's presumably lower level of ideological confrontation. Similarly, Gaddis (1986, 1987) and Powell (1989) cite the stabilizing effects of nuclear weapons in support of bipolarity, although each describes the role played by the arsenals in a different way. These and other arguments outside the boundaries of capability-based indicators (e.g., Mearsheimer 1990) will not be pursued further in this review.

20. At the dyadic level, expected value calculations show a superior capacity to assist in predicting the outbreak of war.

21. Brecher (1993: 76) compares the same three systems over a slightly longer time frame (through 1988) and finds polycentrism to be by far the most unstable when measured by the frequency of both international and foreign policy crises. Bipolarity had a somewhat higher average annual frequency than multipolarity. None of the measurements, of course, can appraise *subjective* but nevertheless important considerations such as the likelihood of nuclear war. Even crisis-based indicators with perceptual elements cannot assess the qualitative leap in danger that might be associated with individual events such as the Cuban Missile Crisis.

22. As in the case of other elements, but perhaps more obviously in this instance, the number of states is not taken to be exogenous. Events such as previous wars, for example, affect how many states are present in the system at a given time. Thus a more compelling vision of structural realism must allow for the impact of processes on structures as well as the reverse (see chapter 6).

23. Concentration also appears in a multivariate analysis by Bueno de Mesquita and Lalman (1988). It reveals a marginal connection with the occurrence of war among major powers from 1815 to 1965.

24. Although Schroeder's analysis has already been granted near-classic status, questions about its accuracy are posed in a compelling way by Kagan (1997/1998: 56). According to Kagan, the standard account of the Concert of Europe conveyed by Schroeder and others may reflect an undue attention to diplomatic discourse rather than practice.

25. Many correlations result from the experiences of all independent states (subject to constraints on data) and the subset involved in the central European subsystem. Singer and Small also subdivide the data by century, with findings reported for the periods 1815–1899 and 1900–1945, respectively.

26. A later study that focuses on the frequency of war, however, fails to produce a connection with alliance pervasiveness (Singer and Small 1979).

27. They measure the independent variables with a Network Density Index (NDI),

which computes the actual number of internodal connections (alliance commitments) as a proportion of all possible internodal connections. Thompson, Rassler, and Li assess the amount of war in the system in two ways: (a) the number of wars ongoing and (b) nation-months of wars in progress.

28. The size variable, of course, also might be spurious in its implications: larger alliances have more members and therefore a greater number of dyads and resultant opportunities for warring pairs outside their membership.

29. The implications for these results of Gibler's (1996, 1997, 1999b) important work on alliance characteristics will be covered in chapter 5.

30. Several of the studies included in the tables do not appear in the review of propositions and testing in the preceding section. One or both of two reasons explain this discrepancy. In some instances the studies are unique and include relatively arcane variables that would require considerable time and effort to explain. The other reason for exclusion is that some studies focus very directly on replication, once again making it opportune to keep things brief in the previous section by not engaging in repetition about research design and like matters. The series of notes to the tables cover the more subtle points that come up regarding technical matters about the data that are included and differences from standard approaches to measurement.

Notes for Chapter 5

1. Efficiency, the second of the two criteria developed for the hard core, can be evaluated with greater accuracy once an elaborated structural realism is in place because T_3 will include a much wider range of propositions than any previous version of structural realism. This, in turn, creates more of an opportunity to isolate which, if any, of the axioms in the hard core have failed to play a viable role in generating explanations and predictions. Evaluation of the negative heuristic with respect to precision could be carried out for structural realism as it exists now, but that would not contribute to the basic agenda of the current chapter, which is to identify priorities for an elaborated structural realism. Furthermore, assessment of the negative heuristic's precision will be more complete once such a theory is in place, so this task naturally awaits fulfillment in the future (James 2002a).

2. The relative lack of attention to this point within the field of international relations is noted by Siverson (1996: 114). Published fifty years apart, Viner's (1948) classic analysis of mercantilism and Alagappa's (1998a, 1998b) assessment of governing groups who are willing to put state-level interests at risk to serve their own purposes are just two convincing reminders that the meaning of "security" can shift from one context to another.

3. It is beyond the scope of this investigation to deal with critiques that have a primarily normative basis: that is, with a focus above and beyond the paradigmatic degree of aggregation. Ashley (1986), for example, questions the ethical value of realist theory writ large, citing (among other things) its implicit endorsement of the status quo in world politics. For an especially insightful critique in terms of ontology, which emphasizes realism's lack of focus on "the boundaries for constituting meaning and value," consult Shapiro (1989: 12). Later normative assessments of realism and structural realism tend to follow the direction suggested by one or the other of the two expositions just noted.

4. Milner (1993), for example, reinforces this point in drawing attention to the potential contradictions that arise from complexities embedded in the market imagery: "It is unclear how Waltz intends to reconcile anarchy with its metaphor of a decentral-

ized, perfectly competitive market and hierarchy established through the distribution of capabilities with its metaphor of an oligopolistic market. As the conflicting metaphors reveal, the two structural principles work against one another, and their impact on one another and their causal priority are unclear" (156). The general lack of attention to the state as a concept in theories of international relations is discussed effectively by Motyl (1999: 38); see also Robinson (1994: 413) on the crisis-oriented literature in particular.

5. An authoritative study of 244 legal treaties reveals that the validity of the assumptions underlying each side in the argument will vary with time. It is interesting to note the particular importance of two elements of structure in changing conditions related to coalitions; the "greater the concentration of military capabilities and the greater the degree of alliance polarization, the greater the support for binding alliance commitments" (Kegley and Raymond 1990: 170).

6. These elements might be cross-referenced as "vertical" or "horizontal" (Ray 1980: 39; Singer 1989: 4), defined respectively as hierarchy and linkages among states. The existence of such concepts shows that a sense already exists of the need to obtain a greater degree of integration among capability-based indicators.

7. Institutions and networks, which are the products of rational choice by individuals, can introduce structure to any social system (Coleman 1986: 184–85).

8. Even the market analogy may be subject to this modification. In a given market "there is more structure than is assumed in neo-classical economic theory" (Coleman 1986: 184). For example, social institutions and networks reflect rational choices by individuals and also can be quite durable (185).

9. Of course, the purpose of Waltz's (1979) theory as developed initially is *not* to produce specific assertions about conflict, crisis, and war. Instead, the focus resembles that of Rousseau's and others' classic expositions on the subject of why wars *recur*. Thus systems theories explain how the organization of a realm acts as a constraining and disposing force on its interacting units (Waltz 1979). The theory must be extended, however, to go beyond designation of this relatively limited set of macro-macro connections.

10. Among the European structures that Vincent (1983: 28–58, 109–18) identifies are the Organization for Economic Cooperation and Development, the North Atlantic Treaty Organization, the European Coal and Steel Community, the Nordic Council, the European Economic Community, the Council for Mutual Economic Assistance, and the Warsaw Treaty Organization. He also notes analogous structures for other regions and points to others of an ex-colonial and worldwide nature.

11. Bueno de Mesquita (1981b) provides evidence from aggregate data analysis that favors treatment of alliances as relatively stable attributes of the system. From 1816 to 1965, alliances made an important difference in the configuration of actors observed in warfare: "Looking only at those nations that were attacked, thereby excluding war initiators and thus duplicating the principal contingent condition of most alliances, 76 percent of the allied nations received fighting support from some of their allies, while only 17 percent of the nonallied states found anyone fighting alongside them. This relationship would occur by chance less than once in a thousand times, given the number of nations involved" (112–13). This finding is reinforced by the research of Leeds, Long, and Mitchell (2000).

12. In a study focusing on especially intense wars over the last few centuries, Midlarsky (1988) finds that more equal distribution of capabilities within an alliance is linked to the onset of world war.

13. The few examples include Liska (1962: 261), with global loose bipolarity leading to regional multipolarity; and Aron (1966: 136) and Gilpin (1981: 88, 89; 1988:

596–97) seeing bipolarity as likely to produce bipolarization (with Gilpin then concluding that war is more likely to follow).

Notes for Chapter 6

1. This does not include attempts to modify and (or) test propositions derived from T_0. Two examples will be used to illustrate this type of work. One is Ruggie's (1989) call for a conception of structure that is "more space/time contingent" and therefore capable of accounting for system transformation (22; see also Ruggie 1986). Ruggie (1989) cites the rise of the Westphalian state system as a transforming series of events that occurred because "the institutional context for the exercise of power was changing" (28). Another example is Walt's (1990; see also 1988 on Southwest Asia) comparison of Waltzian power balancing with "threat" balancing as a way of accounting for the origins of alliances in the Middle East. While efforts such as those of Ruggie, Walt, and others contribute to structural realism's record of achievement, these studies neither individually nor collectively constitute iterations in the series of theories starting with T_0; instead, this research focuses on modification or evaluation of existing individual propositions, such as the balance of power, or the explanation of anomalies, like inability to cope with system transformation.

2. Nonlinear hypotheses rarely are put forward or tested in international relations; the few exceptions include Pudaite and Hower (1989: 81), Most and Starr (1989: 48), and Moul (1993).

3. Another advantage to crisis-based testing is the existence of the unified model of crisis, which appears in Brecher (1993). Linkages within the model, as relevant, can be compared with propositions derived from elaborated structural realism as a test for the latter's consistency with a large-scale, state-of-the-art theoretical and empirical investigation of crisis. No comparable model exists, as yet, for either conflict or war.

BIBLIOGRAPHY

Achen, Christopher H. 1989. "When Is a State with Bureaucratic Politics Representable as a Unitary Rational Actor?" Paper presented at the Annual Meeting of the International Studies Association, March–April, London, England.

Achen, Christopher H., and Duncan Snidal. 1989. "Rational Deterrence Theory and Comparative Case Studies." *World Politics* 41: 143–69.

Adams, Karen Ruth. 1999. "The Norms and Relevance of Structural-Realist Theory." Paper presented at the Annual Meeting of the International Studies Association, February, Washington, D.C.

Adler, Emanuel. 1997. "Seizing the Middle Ground: Constructivism in World Politics." *European Journal of International Relations* 3: 319–63.

Alagappa, Muthiah. 1998a. "Rethinking Security: A Critical Review and Appraisal of the Debate." In Muthiah Alagappa, ed., *Asian Security Practice: Material and Ideational Influences.* Stanford, Calif.: Stanford University Press.

———. 1998b. "Conceptualizing Security: Hierarchy and Conceptual Traveling." In Muthiah Alagappa, ed., *Asian Security Practice: Material and Ideational Influences.* Stanford, Calif.: Stanford University Press.

Albert, Mathias, and Yosef Lapid. 1997. "On Dialectic and IR Theory: Hazards of a Proposed Marriage." *Millennium* 26: 403–15.

Allison, Graham T. 1971. *Essence of Decision: Explaining the Cuban Missile Crisis.* Boston: Little, Brown.

Almond, Gabriel A. 1990. *A Discipline Divided: Schools and Sects in Political Science.* Newbury Park, Calif.: Sage.

American Political Science Association. 2000. *Annual Conference Program.* Washington, D.C.: APSA.

———. 1999. *Annual Conference Program.* Atlanta: APSA.

———. 1998. *Annual Conference Program.* Boston: APSA.

Anderson, Paul A., and Timothy J. McKeown. 1987. "Changing Aspirations, Limited Attention, and War." *World Politics* 40: 1–29.

Aron, Raymond. 1966. *Peace and War.* 2nd ed. Garden City, N.Y.: Doubleday.

———. 1957. *Peace and War.* Garden City, N.Y.: Doubleday.

Arrow, Kenneth J. 1987. "Rationality of Self and Others in an Economic System." In Robin M. Hogarth and Melvin Reder, eds., *Rational Choice: The Contrast between Economics and Psychology.* Chicago: University of Chicago Press.

Ashley, Richard K. 1986. "The Poverty of Neorealism." In Robert O. Keohane, ed., *Neorealism and Its Critics.* New York: Columbia University Press.

———. 1984. "The Poverty of Neorealism." *International Organization* 38: 225–86.

Axelrod, Robert. 1984. *The Evolution of Cooperation.* New York: Basic Books.

Ayoob, Mohammed. 1995. *The Third World Security Predicament: State Making, Regional Conflict, and the International System.* Boulder, Colo.: Lynne Rienner.

Azar, Edward E. 1972. "Conflict Escalation and Conflict Reduction in an International Crisis: Suez, 1956." *Journal of Conflict Resolution* 16: 183–201.

Azar, Edward E., Paul Jureidini, and Robert McLaurin. 1978. "Protracted Social Conflict: Theory and Practice in the Middle East." *Journal of Palestine Studies* 8: 41–60.

Bailey, Kenneth D. 1994. *Typologies and Taxonomies: An Introduction to Classification Techniques.* Thousand Oaks, Calif.: Sage.

Baldwin, David A. 1993a. "Neoliberalism, Neorealism, and World Politics." In David A. Baldwin, ed., *Neorealism and Neoliberalism: The Contemporary Debate*. New York: Columbia University Press.

———, ed. 1993b. *Neorealism and Neoliberalism: The Contemporary Debate*. New York: Columbia University Press.

Ball, Terrence. 1987. "Is There Progress in Political Science?" In Terrence Ball, ed., *Idioms of Inquiry: Critique and Renewal in Political Science*. Albany: State University of New York Press.

———. 1976. "From Paradigms to Research Programs: Toward a Post-Kuhnian Political Science." *American Journal of Political Science* 20: 151–77.

Barbour, Ian G. 1974. *Myths, Models and Paradigms: A Comparative Study in Science and Religion*. New York: HarperCollins.

Barnett, Michael N., and Jack S. Levy. 1991. "Domestic Sources of Alliances and Alignments: The Case of Egypt, 1962–1973." *International Organization* 45: 369–95.

Bartlett, John. 1980. *Familiar Quotations*. 15th ed. Emily Morison Beck, ed. Boston: Little, Brown.

Bauerlein, Mark. 2001. "Social Constructionism: Philosophy for the Academic Workplace." *Partisan Review* 68: 228–40.

Beck, Nathaniel, Gary King, and Langhe Zeng. 2000. "Improving Quantitative Studies of International Conflict: A Conjecture." *American Political Science Review* 94: 21–35.

Becker, Gary S. 1976. *The Economic Approach toward Human Behavior*. Chicago: University of Chicago Press.

Beer, Francis A. 1981. *Peace against War: The Ecology of International Violence*. San Francisco: W. H. Freeman.

Bennett, Andrew. 2002. "A Lakatosian Reading of Lakatos: What Can We Salvage from the Hard Core?" In Colin Elman and Miriam Fendius Elman, eds., *Progress in International Relations Theory: Metrics and Methods of Scientific Change*. Cambridge, Mass.: MIT Press.

Bennett, Jonathan. 1989. *Rationality: An Essay towards an Analysis*. Indianapolis, Ind.: Hackett.

Benson, Michelle, and Jacek Kugler. 1998. "Power Parity, Democracy, and the Severity of Internal Violence." *Journal of Conflict Resolution* 42: 196–209.

Berger, Joseph, and Morris Zelditch, Jr. 1993. "Orienting Strategies and Theory Growth." In Joseph Berger and Morris Zelditch, Jr., eds., *Theoretical Research Programs: Studies in the Growth of Theory*. Stanford, Calif.: Stanford University Press.

Bernstein, Richard J. 1976. *The Restructuring of Social and Political Theory*. New York: Harcourt Brace Jovanovich.

Biersteker, Thomas J. 1989. "Critical Reflections on Post-Positivism in International Relations." *International Studies Quarterly* 33: 263–67.

Blacker, Coit D. 1987. *Reluctant Warriors: The United States, the Soviet Union and Arms Control*. New York: W. H. Freeman.

Blainey, Geoffrey. 1973. *The Causes of War*. New York: Free Press.

Blalock, Hubert M., Jr. 1989. *Power and Conflict: Toward a General Theory*. Newbury Park, Calif.: Sage.

Blaug, Mark. 1980. *The Methodology of Economics*. New York: Cambridge University Press.

Blight, James G. 1990. *The Shattered Crystal Ball: Fear and Learning in the Cuban Missile Crisis*. Savage, Md.: Rowman and Littlefield.

Bobrow, Davis B. 1996. "Complex Insecurity: Implications of a Sobering Metaphor." *International Studies Quarterly* 40: 435–50.

Booth, Ken. 1987. "New Challenges and Old Mind-Sets: Ten Rules for Empirical Realists." In Carl G. Jacobsen, ed., *The Uncertain Course: New Weapons, Strategies and Mind-Sets*. New York: Oxford University Press.

Booth, William James, Patrick James, and Hudson Meadwell, eds. 1993. *Politics and Rationality*. New York: Cambridge University Press.

Boulding, Kenneth. 1962. *Conflict and Defense: A General Theory*. New York: Harper and Brothers.

Boyer, Mark A. 1993. *International Cooperation and Public Goods: Opportunities for the Western Alliance*. Baltimore: Johns Hopkins University Press.

Branaman, Ann. 1997. "Goffman's Social Theory." In Charles Lemert and Ann Branaman, eds., *The Goffman Reader*. Oxford, England: Blackwell.

Brawley, Mark R. 1999. *Afterglow or Adjustment? Domestic Institutions and Responses to Overstretch*. New York: Columbia University Press.

———. 1993. *Liberal Leadership: Great Powers and Their Challengers in Peace and War*. Ithaca, N.Y.: Cornell University Press.

Brecher, Michael. 1999. "International Studies in the Twentieth Century and Beyond: Flawed Dichotomies, Synthesis, Cumulation." *International Studies Quarterly* 43: 213–64.

———. 1994. "International Crises: Reflections on the Future." *Security Studies* 3: 650–77.

———. 1993. *Crises in World Politics*. New York: Pergamon.

———. 1989. "Toward a Theory of Crisis in World Politics." In Michael Brecher and Jonathan Wilkenfeld, eds., *Crisis, Conflict and Instability*. New York: Pergamon.

———. 1980. *Decisions in Crisis: Israel, 1967 and 1973*. Berkeley: University of California Press.

———. 1977. "Toward a Theory of International Crisis Behavior." *International Studies Quarterly* 21: 39–74.

Brecher, Michael, and Hemda Ben Yehuda. 1985. "System and Crisis in International Politics." *Review of International Studies* 11: 17–36.

Brecher, Michael, and Patrick James. 1989. "Polarity, Stability, Crisis: The Debate over Structure and Conflict Twenty-Five Years Later. I. State of the Art and New Directions." In Michael Brecher and Jonathan Wilkenfeld, eds., *Crisis, Conflict and Instability*. New York: Pergamon.

———. 1986. *Crisis and Change in World Politics*. Boulder, Colo.: Westview.

Brecher, Michael, Patrick James, and Jonathan Wilkenfeld. 1990. "Polarity and Stability: New Concepts, Indicators and Evidence." *International Interactions* 16: 69–100.

Brecher, Michael, and Jonathan Wilkenfeld. 2000. *A Study of Crisis*. Ann Arbor: University of Michigan Press. CD-ROM.

———. 1997. *A Study of Crisis*. Ann Arbor: University of Michigan Press.

———. 1989. *Crisis, Conflict and Instability*. New York: Pergamon.

Brecher, Michael, and Jonathan Wilkenfeld, et al. 1988. *Crises in the Twentieth Century, Volume I: Handbook of International Crises*. Oxford and New York: Pergamon Press.

Brecher, Michael, Jonathan Wilkenfeld, and Patrick James. 1989. "Polarity, Stability, Crisis: The Debate over Structure and Conflict Twenty-Five Years Later. II. Weighing the Evidence." In Michael Brecher and Jonathan Wilkenfeld, eds., *Crisis, Conflict and Instability*. New York: Pergamon Press.

Bremer, Stuart A. 1993. "Democracy and Militarized Interstate Conflict, 1816–1965." *International Interactions* 18: 231–49.

———. 1992. "Dangerous Dyads: Conditions Affecting the Likelihood of Interstate War, 1816–1965." *Journal of Conflict Resolution* 36: 309–41.

———. 1980. "National Capabilities and War Proneness." In J. David Singer, ed., *The Correlates of War II: Testing Some Realpolitik Models*. New York: Free Press.

Bremer, Stuart A., J. David Singer, and Urs Luterbacher. 1979. "The Population Density and War Proneness of European Nations, 1816–1965." In J. David Singer and Associates, eds., *Explaining War*. Beverly Hills, Calif.: Sage.

Brodbeck, Mary. 1962. "Explanation, Prediction and 'Imperfect' Knowledge." In Herbert Feigl and Grover Maxwell, eds., *Minnesota Studies in the Philosophy of Science. Vol. 3, Scientific Explanation, Space, and Time*. Minneapolis: University of Minnesota Press.

Brown, Seyom. 1991. "Explaining the Transformation of World Politics." *International Journal* 46: 207–19.

———. 1988. *New Forces, Old Forces, and the Future of World Politics*. Glenview, Ill.: Scott, Foresman.

Buchdal, Gerd. 1969. *Metaphysics and the Philosophy of Science: The Classical Origins, Descartes to Kant*. Oxford, England: Basil Blackwell.

Bueno de Mesquita, Bruce. 1998. "The End of the Cold War: Predicting an Emergent Property." *Journal of Conflict Resolution* 42: 131–55.

———. 1993. "The Game of Conflict Interactions: A Research Program." In Joseph Berger and Morris Zelditch, Jr., eds., *Theoretical Research Programs: Studies in the Growth of Theory*. Stanford, Calif.: Stanford University Press.

———. 1988. "The Contribution of Expected Utility Theory to the Study of International Conflict." In Robert I. Rotberg and Theodore K. Rabb, eds., *The Origin and Prevention of Major Wars*. New York: Cambridge University Press.

———. 1985a. "Reply to Stephen Krasner and Robert Jervis." *International Studies Quarterly* 29: 151–54.

———. 1985b. "Toward a Scientific Understanding of International Conflict: A Personal View." *International Studies Quarterly* 29: 121–36.

———. 1985c. "The War Trap Revisited: A Revised Expected Utility Model." *American Political Science Review* 79: 156–77.

———. 1984. "A Critique of 'A Critique of the War Trap.'" *Journal of Conflict Resolution* 28: 341–60.

———. 1981a. "Risk, Power Distributions, and the Likelihood of War." *International Studies Quarterly* 25: 541–68.

———. 1981b. *The War Trap*. New Haven, Conn.: Yale University Press.

———. 1980a. "An Expected Utility Theory of International Conflict." *American Political Science Review* 74: 917–32.

———. 1980b. "Theories of International Conflict: An Analysis and an Appraisal." In Ted Robert Gurr, ed., *Handbook of Political Conflict: Theory and Research*. New York: Free Press.

———. 1979. "Systemic Polarization and the Occurrence and Duration of War." In J. David Singer and Associates, eds., *Explaining War*. Beverly Hills, Calif.: Sage.

———. 1978. "Systemic Polarization and the Occurrence and Duration of War." *Journal of Conflict Resolution* 22: 241–67.

Bueno de Mesquita, Bruce, Robert W. Jackman, and Randolph M. Siverson. 1991. "Introduction." *Journal of Conflict Resolution* 35: 181–86.

Bueno de Mesquita, Bruce, and David Lalman. 1992. *War and Reason*. New Haven, Conn.: Yale University Press.

———. 1989. "Dyadic Power, Expectations, and War." In Richard J. Stoll and Michael D. Ward, eds., *Power in World Politics*. Boulder, Colo.: Lynne Rienner.

———. 1988. "Empirical Support for Systemic and Dyadic Explanations of International Conflict." *World Politics* 41: 1–20.

———. 1986. "Reason and War." *American Political Science Review* 80: 1113–29.

Bueno de Mesquita, Bruce, David Lalman, and James D. Morrow. 1999. "Sorting through the Wealth of Nations." *International Security* 24: 56–73.

Bull, Hedley. 1977. *The Anarchical Society: A Study of Order in World Politics*. New York: Macmillan.

———. 1966. "International Theory: The Case for a Classical Approach." *World Politics* 18: 361–77.

Bull, Hedley, and Adam Watson. 1984. "Conclusion." In Hedley Bull and Adam Watson, eds., *The Expansion of International Society*. Oxford, England: Clarendon.

Bunge, Mario. 1998. *Social Science under Debate: A Philosophical Perspective*. Toronto: University of Toronto Press.

———. 1996. *Finding Philosophy in Social Science*. New Haven, Conn.: Yale University Press.

Burgess, Philip M., and David W. Moore. 1972. "Inter-Nation Alliances: An Inventory and Appraisal of Propositions." In James A. Robinson, ed., *Political Science Annual: An International Review*, vol. 3. Indianapolis, Ind.: Bobbs-Merrill.

Butterfield, Herbert. 1952. *History and Human Relations*. New York: Macmillan.

Buzan, Barry. 1991. *People, States and Fear: An Agenda for International Security Studies in the Post–Cold War Era*. 2nd ed. New York: Harvester Wheatsheaf.

———. 1981. "Change and Insecurity: A Critique of Strategic Studies." In Barry Buzan and R. J. Barry Jones, eds., *Change and the Study of International Relations: The Evaded Dimension*. London: Frances Pinter.

Buzan, Barry, R.J. Barry Jones, and Richard Little. 1993. *The Logic of Anarchy: Neorealism to Structural Realism*. New York: Columbia University Press.

Buzan, Barry, and R. J. Barry Jones, eds. 1981. *Change and the Study of International Relations: The Evaded Dimension*. London: Frances Pinter.

Buzan, Barry, and Richard Little. 1996. "Reconceptualizing Anarchy: Structural Realism Meets World History." *European Journal of International Relations* 2: 403–38.

Caldwell, Bruce J. 1991. "The Methodology of Scientific Research Programmes in Economics: Criticisms and Conjectures." In G. K. Shaw, ed., *Economics, Culture and Education: Essays in Honour of Mark Blaug*. Aldershot, England: Edward Elgar.

Call, Steven T., and William L. Holahan. 1983. *Microeconomics*. 2nd ed. Belmont, Calif.: Wadsworth.

Cameron, Maxwell A., and Brian W. Tomlin. 2000. *The Making of NAFTA: How the Deal Was Done*. Ithaca, N.Y.: Cornell University Press.

Cannizzo, Cynthia. 1978. "Capability Distribution and Major-Power War Experience, 1816–1965." *Orbis* 21: 947–57.

Cantori, Louis J., and Steven L. Spiegel. 1970. *The International Politics of Regions: A Comparative Approach*. Englewood Cliffs, N.J.: Prentice Hall.

Carlsnaes, W. 1992. "The Agency-Structure Problem in Foreign Policy Analysis." *International Studies Quarterly* 36: 245–70.

Carment, David, and Patrick James, eds. 1998. *Peace in the Midst of Wars.* Columbia: University of South Carolina Press.

———, eds. 1997. *Wars in the Midst of Peace.* Pittsburgh, Pa.: University of Pittsburgh Press.

Carr, Edward Hallett. [1940] 2001. *The Twenty Years' Crisis, 1919–1939: An Introduction to the Study of International Relations.* New York: Palgrave.

Cederman, Lars-Erik. 1994. "Emergent Polarity: Analyzing State-Formation and Power Politics." *International Studies Quarterly* 38: 501–33.

Chan, Steve. 1997. "In Search of Democratic Peace: Problems and Prospects." *Mershon International Studies Review* 41: 59–91.

Chan, Steve, and Davis B. Bobrow. 1981. "Horse Races, Security Markets and Foreign Relations: Some Implications and Evidence for Crisis Participation." *Journal of Conflict Resolution* 25: 187–236.

Choucri, Nazli, and Robert C. North. 1975. *Nations in Conflict.* San Francisco: W. H. Freeman.

Christensen, Thomas J., and Jack Snyder. 1997. "Progressive Research on Degenerate Alliances." *American Political Science Review* 91: 919–22.

Churchill, Winston S. 1958 [1930]. *My Early Life.* Andrew Scotland, ed. London: Odhams.

Churchland, Paul M., and Clifford A. Hooker, eds. 1985. *Images of Science: Essays on Realism and Empiricism, with a Reply from Bas C. van Fraasen.* Chicago: University of Chicago Press.

Cioffi-Revilla, Claudio. 1998. *Politics and Uncertainty: Theory, Models and Applications.* New York: Cambridge University Press.

Cioffi-Revilla, Claudio, and Harvey Starr. 1995. "Opportunity, Willingness and Political Uncertainty." *Journal of Theoretical Politics* 7: 447–76.

Clark, Ian. 1997. *Globalization and Fragmentation: International Relations in the Twentieth Century.* New York: Oxford University Press.

Claude, Inis L., Jr. 1962. *Power and International Relations.* New York: Random House.

Coase, Ronald H. 1960. "The Problem of Social Cost." *Journal of Law and Economics* 3: 1–44.

Coleman, James S. 1986. "Psychological Structure and Social Structure in Economic Models." In Robin M. Hogarth and Melvin W. Reder, eds., *Rational Choice: The Contrast between Economics and Psychology.* Chicago: University of Chicago Press.

Cook, Thomas D., and Donald T. Campbell. 1979. *Quasi-Experimentation: Design and Analysis: Issues for Field Settings.* Chicago: Rand McNally.

Copeland, Dale C. 2000a. *The Origins of Major War.* Ithaca, N.Y.: Cornell University Press.

———. 2000b. "The Constructivist Challenge to Structural Realism: A Review Essay." *International Security* 25: 187–212.

———. 1997. "From Structural Realism to Dynamic Realism." Paper presented at the Annual Meeting of the International Studies Association, March, Toronto, Canada.

Copper, J. F. 1975. "The Advantages of a Multipolar International System: An Analysis of Theory and Practice." *International Studies* 14: 397–415.

Couloumbis, Theodore A., and James H. Wolfe. 1990. *Introduction to International Relations: Power and Justice.* 4th ed. Englewood Cliffs, N.J.: Prentice Hall.

Couvalis, George. 1997. *The Philosophy of Science: Science and Objectivity.* Thousand Oaks, Calif.: Sage.

Cox, Robert W. 1986. "Social Forces, States and World Order: Beyond International Relations Theory." In Robert O. Keohane, ed., *Neorealism and Its Critics*. New York: Columbia University Press.

Crawford, Beverly. 1991. "Toward a Theory of Progress in International Relations." In Emanuel Adler and Beverly Crawford, eds., *Progress in Postwar International Relations*. New York: Columbia University Press.

Cusack, Thomas R. 1989. "The Management of Power in a Warring State System: An Evaluation of Balancing, Collective Security, and Laissez-Faire Policies." In Richard J. Stoll and Michael D. Ward, eds., *Power in World Politics*. Boulder, Colo.: Lynne Rienner.

———. 1985. "The Evolution of Power, Threat, and Security: Past and Potential Developments." *International Interactions* 12: 151–98.

Cusack, Thomas R., and Richard J. Stoll. 1990. *Exploring Realpolitik: Probing International Relations Theory with Computer Simulation*. Boulder, Colo.: Lynne Rienner.

Dacey, Raymond. 1978. "A Theory of Conclusions." *Philosophy of Science* 45: 563–74.

Dahl, Robert A. 1963. *Modern Political Analysis*. Englewood Cliffs, N.J.: Prentice Hall.

David, Steven R. 1991. *Choosing Sides: Alignment and Realignment in the Third World*. Baltimore: Johns Hopkins University Press.

Davies, James Chowning. 1973. "Aggression, Violence, Revolution, and War." In Jeanne N. Knutson, ed., *Handbook of Political Psychology*. San Francisco: Jossey-Bass.

De Soysa, Indra, John Oneal, and Yong-Hee Park. 1997. "Testing Power-Transition Theory Using Alternative Measures of National Capabilities." *Journal of Conflict Resolution* 41: 509–28.

Der Derian, James. 1997. "Post-Theory: The Eternal Return of Ethics in International Relations." In Michael W. Doyle and G. John Ikenberry, eds., *New Thinking in International Relations Theory*. Boulder, Colo.: Westview.

Desch, Michael C. 1993. *When the Third World Matters: Latin America and United States Grand Strategy*. Baltimore, Md.: Johns Hopkins University Press.

Dessler, David. 2002. "Explanation and Scientific Progress." In Colin Elman and Miriam Fendius Elman, eds., *Progress in International Relations Theory: Metrics and Methods of Scientific Change*. Cambridge, Mass.: MIT Press.

———. 1989. "What's at Stake in the Agent-Structure Debate?" *International Organization* 43: 441–73.

Deutsch, Karl W. 1988. *The Analysis of International Relations*. 3rd ed. Englewood Cliffs, N.J.: Prentice Hall.

Deutsch, Karl W., and J. David Singer. 1964. "Multipolar Power Systems and International Stability." *World Politics* 16: 390–406.

DiCicco, Jonathan M., and Jack S. Levy. 2002. "The Power Transition Research Program: Theoretical Development, Empirical Corroboration, and Metatheoretical Implications." In Colin Elman and Miriam Fendius Elman, eds., *Progress in International Relations Theory: Metrics and Methods of Scientific Change*. Cambridge, Mass.: MIT Press.

———. 1999. "Power Shifts and Problem Shifts: The Evolution of the Power Transition Research Program." *Journal of Conflict Resolution* 43: 675–704.

Diehl, Paul F., and Gary Goertz. 2000. *War and Peace in International Rivalry*. Ann Arbor: University of Michigan Press.

Diehl, Paul F., and Frank W. Wayman. 1994. "Realpolitik: Dead End, Detour or Road

Map?" In Frank W. Wayman and Paul F. Diehl, eds., *Reconstructing Realpolitik*. Ann Arbor: University of Michigan Press.

Dixon, William J. 1994. "Democracy and the Peaceful Settlement of International Conflicts." *American Political Science Review* 88: 14–32.

———. 1993. "Democracy and the Management of International Conflict." *Journal of Conflict Resolution* 37: 42–68.

Domke, William K. 1989. "Power, Political Capacity, and Security in the Global System." In Richard J. Stoll and Michael D. Ward, eds., *Power in World Politics*. Boulder, Colo.: Lynne Rienner.

———. 1988. *War and the Changing Global System*. New Haven, Conn.: Yale University Press.

Donnelly, Jack. 1998. "Realism: Roots and Renewal." *Review of International Studies* 24: 399–405.

Doran, Charles F. 1991. *Systems in Crisis: New Imperatives of High Politics at Century's End*. New York: Cambridge University Press.

———. 1989a. "Power Cycle Theory of Systems Structure and Stability: Commonalities and Complementarities." In Manus I. Midlarsky, ed., *Handbook of War Studies*. Boston: Unwin Hyman.

———. 1989b. "Systemic Disequilibrium, Foreign Policy Role, and the Power Cycle." *Journal of Conflict Resolution* 33: 371–401.

———. 1985. "Power Cycle Theory and Systems Stability." In Paul M. Johnson and William R. Thompson, eds., *Rhythms in Politics and Economics*. New York: Praeger.

Doran, Charles F., and Alvin Paul Drischler, eds. 1996. *A New North America: Cooperation and Enhanced Interdependence*. Westport, Calif.: Praeger.

Doran, Charles F., and Wes Parsons. 1980. "War and the Cycle of Relative Power." *American Political Science Review* 74: 947–65.

Dougherty, James E., and Robert L. Pfaltzgraff, Jr. 2001. *Contending Theories of International Relations: A Comprehansive Survey*. 5th ed. New York: Longman.

———. 1996. *Contending Theories of International Relations: A Comprehensive Survey*. 4th ed. New York: Harper and Row.

———. 1990. *Contending Theories of International Relations: A Comprehensive Survey*. 3rd ed. New York: Harper and Row.

———. *Contending Theories of International Relations: A Comprehensive Survey*. New York: Harper and Row.

Dryzek, John S. 1986. "The Progress of Political Science." *Journal of Politics* 48: 301–20.

Duhem, Pierre. 1977. *The Aim and Structure of Physical Theory*. Philip P. Wiener, trans. New York: Atheneum.

East, Maurice A., Stephen A. Salmore, and Charles F. Hermann, eds. 1978. *Why Nations Act: Theoretical Perspectives for Comparative Foreign Policy Studies*. Beverly Hills, Calif.: Sage.

Eberwein, Wolf-Dieter. 1982. "The Seduction of Power: Serious International Disputes and the Power Status of Nations, 1900–1976." *International Interactions* 9: 57–74.

Einstein, Albert. 1996. *Einstein's 1912 Manuscript on the Special Theory of Relativity: A Facsimile*. New York: George Braziller.

Ellis, Brian. 1985. "What Science Aims to Do." In Paul M. Churchland and Clifford A. Hooker, eds., *Images of Science: Essays on Realism and Empiricism, with a Reply from Bas C. van Fraasen*. Chicago: University of Chicago Press.

Elman, Colin, and Miriam Fendius Elman. 2002a. "Introduction: Appraising Progress in International Relations Theory." In Colin Elman and Miriam Fendius Elman, eds., *Progress in International Relations Theory: Metrics and Methods of Scientific Change.* Cambridge, Mass.: MIT Press.

———. 2002b. "Lessons from Lakatos." In Colin Elman and Miriam Fendius Elman, eds., *Progress in International Relations Theory: Metrics and Methods of Scientific Change.* Cambridge, Mass.: MIT Press.

———, eds. 2002c. *Progress in International Relations Theory: Metrics and Methods of Scientific Change.* Cambridge, Mass.: MIT Press.

———. 1997. "Lakatos and Neorealism: A Reply to Vasquez." *American Political Science Review* 91: 923–26.

Elshtain, Jean Bethke. 1997. "Feminist Inquiry and International Relations." In Michael W. Doyle and G. John Ikenberry, eds., *New Thinking in International Relations Theory.* Boulder, Colo.: Westview Press.

Elster, Jon. 1983. *Explaining Technical Change: A Case Study in the Philosophy of Science.* New York: Cambridge University Press.

Enterline, Andrew J. 1998a. "Regime Changes and Interstate Conflict, 1816–1992." *Political Research Quarterly* 51: 385–409.

———. 1998b. "Regime Changes, Neighborhoods, and International Conflict, 1816–1992." *Journal of Conflict Resolution* 42: 804–29.

Even-Zohar, Itamar. 1997. "Polysystem Theory." Revised version. <http://www.tau.ac.il/~itamarez/papers/ps-th-r.htm>.

———. 1990a. "Introduction." *Poetics Today* 11: 1–8.

———. 1990b. "The 'Literary System'." *Poetics Today* 11: 27–44.

———. 1990c. "Polysystem Theory." *Poetics Today* 11: 9–26.

Ferguson, Yale H., and Richard W. Mansbach. 1996. *Polities: Authority, Identities, and Change.* Columbia: University of South Carolina Press.

———. 1991. "Between Celebration and Despair: Constructive Suggestions for Future International Theory." *International Studies Quarterly* 35: 363–86.

———. 1989. *The State, Conceptual Chaos and the Future of International Relations Theory.* Boulder, Colo.: Lynne Rienner.

Feyerabend, Paul K. 1981. "How to Defend Society against Science." In Ian Hacking, ed., *Scientific Revolutions.* New York: Oxford University Press.

———. 1970. "Consolations for the Specialist." In Imre Lakatos and Alan Musgrave, eds., *Criticism and the Growth of Knowledge.* New York: Cambridge University Press.

Fiorina, Morris P., and Kenneth A. Shepsle. 1982. "Equilibrium, Disequilibrium, and the General Possibility of a Science of Politics." In Peter C. Ordeshook and Kenneth A. Shepsle, eds., *Political Equilibrium.* Boston: Kluwer-Nijhoff.

Fischer, Markus. 1992. "Feudal Europe, 800–1300: Communal Discourse and Conflictual Practices." *International Organization* 46: 427–66.

Forrester, Jay W. 1971. *World Dynamics.* Cambridge, Mass.: Wright-Allen.

Fox, Jonathan. 2000a. "The Effects of Religious Discrimination on Ethno-Religious Protest and Rebellion." *Journal of Conflict Studies* 20: 16–43.

———. 2000b. "The Ethnic-Religious Nexus: The Impact of Religion on Ethnic Conflict." *Civil Wars* 3: 1–22.

———. 2000c. "Is Islam More Conflict Prone Than Other Religions? A Cross-Sectional Study of Ethnoreligious Conflict." *Nationalism and Ethnic Politics* 6: 1–24.

Frankel, Joseph. 1988. *International Relations in a Changing World.* 4th ed. New York: Oxford University Press.

———. 1981. "Perspectives on Change." In Barry Buzan and R. J. Barry Jones, eds., *Change and the Study of International Relations: The Evaded Dimension*. London: Frances Pinter.

Freeman, John R., and Brian L. Job. 1979. "Scientific Forecasts in International Relations: Problems of Definition and Epistemology." *International Studies Quarterly* 23: 113–43.

Freyberg-Inan, Annette. 2002. *What Moves Man: The Realist Theory of International Relations and Its Judgment of Human Nature*. Forthcoming.

———. 1999. "Human Nature in International Relations Theory: An Analysis and Critique of Realist Assumptions about Motivation." Paper presented at the Annual Meeting of the International Studies Association, February, Washington, D.C.

Frohlich, Norman, and Joe A. Oppenheimer. 1978. *Modern Political Economy*. Englewood Cliffs, N.J.: Prentice Hall.

Gaddis, John Lewis. 1997. *We Now Know: Rethinking Cold War History*. Oxford, England: Clarendon.

———. 1987. *The Long Peace: Inquiries into the History of the Cold War*. New York: Oxford University Press.

———. 1986. "The Long Peace: Elements of Stability in the Postwar International System." *International Security* 10: 99–142.

Galtung, Johan. 1964. "A Structural Theory of Aggression." *Journal of Peace Research* 1: 95–119.

Garnham, David. 1985. "The Causes of War: Systemic Findings." In A. Ned Sabrosky, ed., *Polarity and War: The Changing Structure of International Conflict*. Boulder, Colo.: Westview.

———. 1976. "Power Parity and Lethal International Violence, 1969–1973." *Journal of Conflict Resolution* 20: 379–94.

Garst, Daniel. 1989. "Thucydides and Neorealism." *International Studies Quarterly* 33: 3–27.

Gartzke, Erik. 2000. "Preferences and the Democratic Peace." *International Studies Quarterly* 44: 191–210.

———. 1998. "Kant We All Just Get Along? Opportunity, Willingness, and the Origins of the Democratic Peace." *American Journal of Political Science* 42: 1–27.

Gates, Scott, Torbjørn L. Knutsen, and Jonathon W. Moses. 1996. "Democracy and Peace: A More Sceptical View." *Journal of Peace Research* 33: 1–10.

Geller, Daniel S. 1993. "Power Differentials and War in Rival Dyads." *International Studies Quarterly* 37: 173–93.

———. 1992a. "Capability Concentration, Power Transition, and War." *International Interactions* 17: 269–84.

———. 1992b. "Power Transition and Conflict Initiation." *Conflict Management and Peace Science* 12: 1–16.

———. 1988. "Power System Membership and Patterns of War." *International Political Science Review* 9: 365–79.

Geller, Daniel S., and J. David Singer. 1998. *Nations at War: A Scientific Study of International Conflict*. New York: Cambridge University Press.

Gellner, Ernest. 1975. "Beyond Truth and Falsehood." *British Journal for the Philosophy of Science* 26: 331–42.

George, Alexander L. 1993. *Bridging the Gap: Theory and Practice in Foreign Policy*. Washington, D.C.: USIP Press.

———. 1988a. "U.S.-Soviet Efforts to Cooperate in Crisis Management and Crisis

Avoidance." In Alexander L. George, Philip J. Farley, and Alexander Dallin, eds., *U.S.-Soviet Security Cooperation: Achievements, Failures, Lessons.* New York: Oxford University Press.

———. 1988b. "Incentives for U.S.-Soviet Security Cooperation and Mutual Adjustment." In Alexander L. George, Philip J. Farley, and Alexander Dallin, eds., *U.S.-Soviet Security Cooperation: Achievements, Failures, Lessons.* New York: Oxford University Press.

———. 1988c. "Epilogue: Perspectives." In Alexander L. George, Philip J. Farley, and Alexander Dallin, eds., *U.S.-Soviet Security Cooperation: Achievements, Failures, Lessons.* New York: Oxford University Press.

———. 1980. *Presidential Decisionmaking in Foreign Policy: The Effective Use of Information and Advice.* Boulder, Colo.: Westview.

George, Alexander L., and Richard Smoke. 1974. *Deterrence in American Foreign Policy.* New York: Columbia University Press.

George, Jim. 1989. "International Relations and the Search for Thinking Space: Another View of the Third Debate." *International Studies Quarterly* 33: 269–79.

Gibler, Douglas M. 1999a. "Alliance Systems." In *Encyclopedia of Violence, Peace and Conflict,* vol. 1. New York: Academic Press.

———. 1999b. "An Extension of the Correlates of War Formal Alliance Data Set, 1648–1815." *International Interactions* 25: 1–28.

———. 1997. "Control the Issues, Control the Conflict: The Effects of Alliances That Settle Territorial Issues on Interstate Rivalries." *International Interactions* 22: 341–68.

———. 1996. "Alliances That Never Balance: The Territorial Settlement Treaty." *Conflict Management and Peace Science* 15: 75–97.

Gibler, Douglas M., and John A. Vasquez. 1998. "Uncovering the Dangerous Alliances, 1495–1980." *International Studies Quarterly* 42: 785–807.

Giedymin, Jerzy. 1971. "Consolations for the Irrationalist?" *British Journal for the Philosophy of Science* 22: 39–53.

Gillies, Donald A. 1971. "Falsifying Rule for Probability Statements." *British Journal for the Philosophy of Science* 22: 231–61.

Gilpin, Robert. 1988. "The Theory of Hegemonic War." *Journal of Interdisciplinary History* 18: 591–614.

———. 1987. *The Political Economy of International Relations.* Princeton, N.J.: Princeton University Press.

———. 1984. "The Rich Tradition of Political Realism." *International Organization* 38: 287–304.

———. 1981. *War and Change in World Politics.* New York: Cambridge University Press.

Glaser, Charles L. 1995. "Realists as Opportunists: Cooperation as Self-Help." In Michael E. Brown, Sean M. Lynn-Jones, and Steven E. Miller, eds., *The Perils of Anarchy: Contemporary Realism and International Security.* Cambridge, Mass.: MIT Press.

Gleditsch, Kristian S., and Michael D. Ward. 2000. "War and Peace in Space and Time: The Role of Democratization." *International Studies Quarterly* 44: 1–29.

Gleditsch, Nils Petter, Håvard Strand, Mikael Erikson, Margareta Sollenberg, and Peter Wallensteen. 2001. "Armed Conflict 1945–99: A New Dataset." Paper presented at the Annual Meeting of the International Studies Association, February, Chicago.

Glymour, Clark. 1985. "Explanation and Realism." In Paul M. Churchland and

Clifford A. Hooker, eds., *Images of Science: Essays on Realism and Empiricism, with a Reply from Bas C. van Fraasen.* Chicago: University of Chicago Press.

———. 1983. "On Testing and Evidence." In John Earman, ed., *Testing Scientific Theories.* Minneapolis: University of Minnesota Press.

Glymour, Clark, Richard Scheines, Peter Spirtes, and Kevin Kelly. 1987. *Discovering Causal Structure.* New York: Academic Press.

Gochman, Charles S. 1980. "Status, Capabilities, and Major Power Conflict." In J. David Singer, ed., *The Correlates of War: II. Testing Some Realpolitik Models.* New York: Free Press.

Gochman, Charles S., and Aaron M. Hoffman. 1996. "Peace in the Balance? A Matter of Design." *International Studies Notes* 21, no. 2: 20–25.

Gochman, Charles S., and Zeev Maoz. 1984. "Militarized Interstate Disputes, 1816–1976: Procedures, Patterns, and Insights." *Journal of Conflict Resolution* 28: 585–615.

Gödel, Kurt. [1931] 1988. "On Formally Undecidable Propositions of *Principia Mathematica* and Related Systems I." In S. G. Shanker, ed., *Gödel's Theorem in Focus.* New York: Croom Helm.

Goertz, Gary, and Paul F. Diehl. 1993. "Enduring Rivalries: Theoretical Constructs and Empirical Patterns." *International Studies Quarterly* 37: 145–71.

———. 1992. "The Empirical Importance of Enduring Rivalries." *International Interactions* 18: 151–63.

Goffman, Erving. 1997. "Frame Analysis." In Charles Lemert and Ann Branaman, eds., *The Goffman Reader.* Oxford, England: Blackwell.

Goldmann, Kjell. 1996. "International Relations: An Overview." In Robert E. Goodin and Hans-Dieter Klingemann, eds., *A New Handbook of Political Science.* New York: Oxford University Press.

———. 1981. "The International System: A Note from a Conceptual Prison." *Cooperation and Conflict* 16: 119–26.

———. 1974. *Tension and Detente in Bipolar Europe.* Stockholm, Sweden: Scandinavian University Books.

Green, Donald P., and Ian Shapiro. 1994. *Pathologies of Rational Choice Theory: A Critique of Applications in Political Science.* New Haven, Conn.: Yale University Press.

Grieco, Joseph M. 1997. "Realist International Theory and the Study of World Politics." In Michael W. Doyle and G. John Ikenberry, eds., *New Thinking in International Relations Theory.* Boulder, Colo.: Westview.

———. 1995. "The Maastricht Treaty, Economic and Monetary Union and the Neo-Realist Research Program." *Review of International Studies* 21: 21–40.

———. 1993a. "Anarchy and the Limits of Cooperation: A Realist Critique of the Newest Liberal Institutionalism." In David A. Baldwin, ed., *Neorealism and Neoliberalism: The Contemporary Debate.* New York: Columbia University Press.

———. 1993b. "The Relative Gains Problem for International Cooperation: Comment." *American Political Science Review* 87: 729–43.

———. 1993c. "Understanding the Problems of International Cooperation: The Limits of Neoliberal Institutionalism and the Future of Realist Theory." In David A. Baldwin, ed., *Neorealism and Neoliberalism: The Contemporary Debate.* New York: Columbia University Press.

———. 1990. *Cooperation among Nations: Europe, America, and Non-Tariff Barriers to Trade.* Ithaca, N.Y.: Cornell University Press.

———. 1988. "Anarchy and the Limits of Cooperation: A Realist Critique of the

Newest Liberal Institutionalism." *International Organization* 42: 485–507.

Grünbaum, Adolf. 1976. "Is the Method of Bold Conjectures and Attempted Refutations *Justifiably* the Method of Science?" *British Journal for the Philosophy of Science* 27: 105–36.

Gueztkow, Harold. 1950. "Long Range Research in International Relations." *American Perspective* 4: 421–40.

Guilmartin, John F., Jr. 1988. "Ideology and Conflict: The Wars of the Ottoman Empire, 1453–1606." In Robert I. Rotberg and Theodore K. Rabb, eds., *The Origin and Prevention of Major Wars*. New York: Cambridge University Press.

Gulick, Edward. 1955. *Europe's Classical Balance of Power*. Ithaca, N.Y.: Cornell University Press.

Gurr, Ted Robert. 2000. *People versus States: Minorities at Risk in the New Century*. Washington, D.C.: United States Institute of Peace Press.

———. 1993. *Minorities at Risk: A Global View of Ethnopolitical Conflicts*. Washington, D.C.: United States Institute of Peace.

———. 1980. "Introduction." In Ted Robert Gurr, ed., *Handbook of Political Conflict: Theory and Research*. New York: Free Press.

Gutting, Gary. 1985. "Scientific Realism versus Constructive Empiricism: A Dialogue." In Paul M. Churchland and Clifford A. Hooker, eds., *Images of Science: Essays on Realism and Empiricism, with a Reply from Bas C. van Fraasen*. Chicago: University of Chicago Press.

Guzzini, Stefano. 1998. *Realism in International Relations and International Political Economy: The Continuing Story of a Death Foretold*. New York: Routledge.

Haas, Ernst. 1976. "Turbulent Fields and the Theory of Regional Integration." *International Organization* 28: 173–212.

———. 1964. *Beyond the Nation-State: Functionalism in International Organization*. Stanford, Calif.: Stanford University Press.

———. 1958. *The Uniting of Europe: Political, Social, and Economic Forces, 1950–1957*. Stanford, Calif.: Stanford University Press.

———. 1953. "The Balance of Power: Prescription, Concept, or Propaganda?" *World Politics* 5: 442–77.

Haas, Michael. 1970a. *International Conflict*. Indianapolis, Ind.: Bobbs-Merrill.

———. 1970b. "International Subsystems: Stability and Polarity." *American Political Science Review* 64: 98–123.

Habermas, Jurgen. 1975. *Legitimation Crisis*. Thomas McCarthy, trans. Boston: Beacon.

Hacking, Ian. 1981. "Lakatos's Philosophy of Science." In Ian Hacking, ed., *Scientific Revolutions*. New York: Oxford University Press.

Haggard, Stephan. 1991. "Structuralism and Its Critics: Recent Progress in International Relations Theory." In Emanuel Adler and Beverly Crawford, eds., *Progress in Postwar International Relations*. New York: Columbia University Press.

Haglund, David G., and Michael K. Hawes. 1990. "Introduction: Contemporary Issues and Approaches." In David G. Haglund and Michael K. Hawes, eds., *World Politics: Power, Interdependence and Dependence*. Toronto: Harcourt Brace Jovanovich.

Hall, Martin, and Christer Jönsson. 2001. "The Reproduction of International Society: A View from Comparative History." Lund, Sweden: Lund University Working Paper.

Halliday, Fred, and Justin Rosenberg. 1998. "Interview with Ken Waltz." *Review of International Studies* 24: 371–86.

Handel, Michael I. 1992. *Masters of War: Sun Tzu, Clausewitz and Jomini.* Portland, Ore.: Frank Cass.

Hands, D. Wade. 1991. "Popper, the Rationality Principle and Economic Explanation." In G. K. Shaw, ed., *Economics, Culture and Education: Essays in Honor of Mark Blaug.* Brookfield, Vt.: Edward Elgar.

Hara, Kimie. 2000. "Rethinking the 'Cold War' in the Asia-Pacific." *Pacific Review* 12: 515–36.

Hardin, Garrett. 1977. "The Tragedy of the Commons." In Garrett Hardin and John Baden, eds., *Managing the Commons.* San Francisco: W. H. Freeman.

Hardin, Russell. 1987. "Rational Choice Theories." In Terence Ball, ed., *Idioms of Inquiry: Critique and Renewal in Political Science.* Albany: State University of New York Press.

Harrison, Ewan. 2002. "Waltz, Kant and Systemic Approaches to International Relations." *Review of International Studies* 28: 143–62.

———. 2000. "Contemporary Realism and Post Cold War State Strategies." Unpublished manuscript.

Hart, Jeffrey A. 1985. "Power and Polarity." In Alan Ned Sabrosky, ed., *Polarity and War.* Boulder, Colo.: Westview.

Harvey, Frank P. 1998. "Rigor Mortis or Rigor, More Tests: Necessity, Sufficiency, and Deterrence Logic." *International Studies Quarterly* 42: 675–707.

———. 1997. *The Future's Back: Nuclear Rivalry, Deterrence Theory, and Crisis Stability after the Cold War.* Montreal: McGill-Queen's University Press.

Harvey, Frank, and Ben Mor, eds. 1997. *Conflict in World Politics: Advances in the Study of Crisis, War and Peace.* London: Macmillan.

Hazlewood, Leo, John J. Hayes, and James R. Brownell, Jr. 1977. "Planning for Problems in Crisis Management: An Analysis of Post-1945 Behavior in the U.S. Department of Defense." *International Studies Quarterly* 21: 75–106.

Hebron, Lui, and Patrick James. 1997. "Great Powers, Cycles of Relative Capability and Crises in World Politics." *International Interactions* 23: 145–73.

Hempel, Carl G. 1965. *Aspects of Scientific Explanation.* New York: Free Press.

Hermann, Charles F., ed. 1972. *International Crises: Insights from Behavioral Research.* New York: Free Press.

———. 1969. *Crises in Foreign Policy: A Simulation Analysis.* Indianapolis, Ind.: Bobbs-Merrill.

———. 1963. "Some Consequences of Crisis Which Limit the Viability of Organizations." *Administrative Science Quarterly* 8: 61–82.

Hermann, Charles F., Charles W. Kegley, Jr., and James N. Rosenau, eds. 1987. *New Directions in the Study of Foreign Policy.* Boston: Allen and Unwin.

Hermann, Margaret G., and Charles W. Kegley, Jr. 1995. "Rethinking Democracy and International Peace: Perspectives from Political Psychology." *International Studies Quarterly* 29: 511–33.

Herrera, Amílcar O., et al. 1976. *Catastrophe or New Society? A Latin American World Model.* Ottawa, Canada: International Development Research Centre.

Herz, John H. 1951. *Political Realism and Political Idealism: A Study in Theories and Realities.* Chicago: University of Chicago Press.

———. 1950. "Idealist Internationalism and the Security Dilemma." *World Politics* 20: 157–80.

Hewitt, J. Joseph, and Jonathan Wilkenfeld. 1996. "Democracy and International Crisis." *International Interactions* 22: 123–42.

Hinsley, F. H. 1963. *Power and the Pursuit of Peace*. New York: Cambridge University Press.

Hirschman, Albert O. 1970. *Exit, Voice, and Loyalty: Responses to Decline in Firms, Organizations, and States*. Cambridge, Mass.: Harvard University Press.

Hobbes, Thomas. 1990. "Of the Naturall Condition of Mankind, as Concerning Their Felicity and Misery." In John A. Vasquez, ed., *Classics of International Relations*. 2nd ed. Englewood Cliffs, N.J.: Prentice Hall.

Hoffmann, Stanley. 1977. "An American Social Science: International Relations." *Daedalus* 106, 3: 41–60.

———. 1968. *Gulliver's Troubles, or the Setting of American Foreign Policy*. New York: McGraw-Hill.

———, ed. 1960. *Contemporary Theory in International Relations*. Englewood Cliffs, N.J.: Prentice Hall.

———. 1959. "International Relations: The Long Road to Theory." *World Politics* 11: 346–77.

Holsti, K. J. 1998. "Scholarship in an Era of Anxiety: The Study of International Politics during the Cold War." *Review of International Studies* 24: 17–46.

———. 1996. *The State, War, and the State of War*. New York: Cambridge University Press.

———. 1991a. "Mirror, Mirror on the Wall, Which Are the Fairest Theories of All?" *International Studies Quarterly* 33: 255–61.

———. 1991b. *Peace and War: Armed Conflicts and International Order, 1648–1989*. New York: Cambridge University Press.

———. 1988. *International Politics: A Framework for Analysis*. 5th ed. Englewood Cliffs, N.J.: Prentice Hall.

———. 1985a. *The Dividing Discipline: Hegemony and Diversity in International Theory*. Boston: Allen and Unwin.

———. 1985b. "The Necrologists of International Relations." *Canadian Journal of Political Science* 18: 675–95.

Holsti, Ole R. 1995. "Theories of International Relations and Foreign Policy: Realism and Its Challenges." In Charles W. Kegley, Jr., ed., *Controversies in International Relations: Realism and the Neoliberal Challenge*. New York: St. Martin's.

———. 1972. *Crisis, Escalation, War*. Montreal: McGill-Queen's University Press.

Holsti, Ole R., P. Terrence Hopmann, and John D. Sullivan. 1973. *Unity and Disintegration in International Alliances: Comparative Studies*. New York: John Wiley.

Hook, Steven W., ed. 2002. *Comparative Foreign Policy: Adaptation Strategies of the Great and Emerging Powers*. Upper Saddle River, N.J.: Prentice Hall.

Hopf, Ted. 1993. "Polarity and International Stability: Response." *American Political Science Review* 87: 177–80.

———. 1991. "Polarity, the Offense-Defense Balance, and War." *American Political Science Review* 85: 475–93.

Horwich, Paul. 1983. "Explanations of Irrelevance." In John Earman, ed., *Testing Scientific Theories*. Minneapolis: University of Minnesota Press.

Howe, Paul. 1991. "Neorealism Revisited: The Neorealist Landscape Surveyed Through Nationalist Spectacles." *International Journal* 46: 326–51.

Hughes, Barry B. 1993. *International Futures: Choices in the Creation of a New World Order*. Boulder, Colo.: Westview.

———. 1985. *World Futures: A Critical Analysis of Alternatives*. Baltimore: Johns Hopkins University Press.

Huntley, Wade L. 1996. "Kant's Third Image: Systemic Sources of the Liberal Peace." *International Studies Quarterly* 40: 45–76.

Huth, Paul K. 1996. *Standing Your Ground: Territorial Disputes and International Conflict.* Ann Arbor: University of Michigan Press.

Huth, Paul K., Christopher Gelpi, and D. Scott Bennett. 1993. "The Escalation of Great Power Militarized Disputes: Testing Rational Deterrence Theory and Structural Realism." *American Political Science Review* 87: 609–23.

International Studies Association. 2001. *Annual Conference Program.* Tucson, Ariz.: ISA.

———. 2000. *Annual Conference Program.* Tucson, Ariz.: ISA.

———. 1999. *Annual Conference Program.* Tucson, Ariz.: ISA.

Jackson, W. D. 1977. "Polarity in International Systems: A Conceptual Note." *International Interactions* 4: 87–96.

Jacobson, Harold K. 1984. *Networks of Interdependence: International Organizations and the Global Political System.* 2nd ed. New York: Alfred A. Knopf.

———. 1978. *Networks of Interdependence: International Organizations and the Global Political System.* New York: Alfred A. Knopf.

James, Carolyn C. 2000a. "Iran and Iraq as Rational Crisis Actors: Dangers and Dynamics of Successful Nuclear War." *Journal of Strategic Studies* 23: 72–73.

———. 2000b. "Nuclear Arsenal Games: Coping with Proliferation in a World of Changing Rivalries." *Canadian Journal of Political Science* 33: 723–46.

James, Patrick. 2002a. *Elaborated Structural Realism and Crises in World Politics.* Columbus: Ohio State University Press, in progress.

———. 2002b. "Systemism and International Relations: Toward a Reassessment of Realism." In Michael Brecher and Frank Harvey, eds., *Millennial Reflections on International Relations.* Ann Arbor: University of Michigan Press, forthcoming.

———. 1995. "Structural Realism and the Causes of War." *Mershon International Studies Review* 39: 181–208.

———. 1993a. "The Great Powers and Crisis-Generated Instability: Preliminary Findings." *Journal of International Studies* 30: 1–25.

———. 1993b. "Neorealism as a Scientific Research Enterprise: Toward Elaborated Structural Realism." *International Political Science Review* 14: 123–48.

———. 1990a. "The Causes of War: How Does the Structure of the System Affect International Conflict?" In David G. Haglund and Michael K. Hawes, eds., *World Politics: Power, Interdependence and Dependence.* Toronto: Harcourt Brace Jovanovich.

———. 1990b. "International Crises: A View from the South." *Pacific Focus* 5: 5–18.

———. 1989. "Structure et conflit en politique internationale: Une analyse sequentielle des crises internationales 1929–1979." *Etudes Internationales* 20: 791–815.

———. 1988. *Crisis and War.* Montreal: McGill-Queen's University Press.

James, Patrick, and Michael Brecher. 1988. "Stability and Polarity: New Paths for Inquiry." *Journal of Peace Research* 25: 31–42.

James, Patrick, and Athanasios Hristoulas. 1994a. "Accounting for Crises in World Politics: Realpolitik versus Internal Processes." In Frank W. Wayman and Paul F. Diehl, eds., *Reconstructing Realpolitik.* Ann Arbor: University of Michigan Press.

———. 1994b. "Domestic Politics and Foreign Policy: Evaluating a Model of Crisis Activity for the United States." *Journal of Politics* 56: 327–48.

James, Patrick, and Glenn E. Mitchell II. 1995. "Targets of Covert Pressure: The Hidden Victims of the Democratic Peace." *International Interactions* 21: 85–107.

James, Patrick, and John R. Oneal. 1991a. "The Influence of Domestic and International Politics on the President's Use of Force." *Journal of Conflict Resolution* 35: 307–32.

———. 1991b. "The President and the Political Use of Force." Paper presented at the Annual Meeting of the International Studies Association, March, Vancouver, Canada.

James, Patrick, Eric Solberg, and Murray Wolfson. 2000. "A Reply to Oneal and Russett." *Defence and Peace Economics* 11: 215–29.

———. 1999. "An Identified Systemic Model of the Democracy-Peace Nexus." *Defence and Peace Economics* 10: 1–37.

James, Patrick, and Jonathan Wilkenfeld. 1984. "Structural Factors and International Crisis Behavior." *Conflict Management and Peace Science* 7: 33–53.

Janis, Irving L. 1972. *Victims of Groupthink: A Psychological Study of Foreign Policy Decisions and Fiascos.* Boston: Houghton Mifflin.

Janis, Irving L., and Leon Mann. 1977. *Decision-Making.* New York: Free Press.

Jeffrey, Richard C. 1971. "Remarks on Explanatory Power." In Roger C. Buck and Robert S. Cohen, eds., *Philosophy of Science Association 1970: In Memory of Rudolf Carnap.* Dordrecht, The Netherlands: D. Reidel.

Jervis, Robert. 1998. "Realism in the Study of World Politics." *International Organization* 52: 971–91.

———. 1997. *System Effects: Complexity in Political and Social Life.* Princeton, N.J.: Princeton University Press.

———. 1991. "Models and Cases in the Study of International Conflict." In Robert L. Rothstein, ed., *The Evolution of Theory in International Relations.* Columbia: University of South Carolina Press.

———. 1989. "Rational Deterrence: Theory and Evidence." *World Politics* 41: 183–207.

———. 1985. "Pluralistic Rigor: A Comment on Bueno de Mesquita." *International Studies Quarterly* 29: 145–49.

———. 1982. "Security Regimes." *International Organization* 36: 357–78.

———. 1979. "Systems Theories and Diplomatic History." In Paul Gordon Lauren, ed., *Diplomacy: New Approaches in History, Theory, and Policy.* New York: Free Press.

Jervis, Robert, Richard N. Lebow, and Janice G. Stein. 1985. *Psychology and Deterrence.* Baltimore, Md.: Johns Hopkins University Press.

Johnson, Harry M. 1985. "Social Structure." In A. Kuper and J. Kuper, eds., *The Social Science Encyclopedia.* Boston: Routledge and Kegan Paul.

Jones, Daniel M., Stuart A. Bremer, and J. David Singer. 1996. "Militarized Interstate Disputes, 1816–1992: Rationale, Coding Rules, and Empirical Patterns." *Conflict Management and Peace Science* 15: 163–213.

Jones, R. J. Barry. 1981. "Concepts and Models of Change in International Relations." In Barry Buzan and R. J. Barry Jones, eds., *Change and the Study of International Relations: The Evaded Dimension.* London: Frances Pinter.

Kacowicz, Arie M. 1998. *Zones of Peace in the Third World: South America and West Africa in Comparative Perspective.* Albany: State University of New York Press.

Kadera, Kelly M. 2001. *The Power-Conflict Story: A Dynamic Model of Interstate Rivalry.* Ann Arbor: University of Michigan Press.

———. 1998. "Transmission, Barriers, and Constraints: A Dynamic Model of the Spread of War." *Journal of Conflict Resolution* 42: 367–87.

Kagan, Korina. 1998. "The Failure of the Great Powers to Coerce Small States in the

Balkans, 1875–1877 and 1914: Situational versus Tactical Explanations." In Lawrence Freedman, ed., *Strategic Coercion: Concepts and Cases*. New York: Oxford University Press.

———. 1997/1998. "The Myth of the European Concert: The Realist-Institutionalist Debate and Great Power Behavior in the Eastern Question, 1821–41." *Security Studies* 7: 1–57.

Kahler, Miles. 1998. "Rationality in International Relations." *International Organization* 52: 919–41.

———. 1997. "Inventing International Relations: International Relations Theory after 1945." In Michael W. Doyle and G. John Ikenberry, eds., *New Thinking in International Relations Theory*. Boulder, Colo.: Westview.

Kaplan, Morton A. 1979. *Towards Professionalism in International Relations Theory: Macrosystem Analysis*. New York: Free Press.

———. 1966. "The New Great Debate: Traditionalism vs. Science in International Relations." *World Politics* 19: 1–20.

———. 1957. *System and Process in International Politics*. New York: John Wiley.

Katzenstein, Peter J. 1989. "International Relations and the Analysis of Change." In O. Czempiel and J. N. Rosenau, eds., *Global Changes and Theoretical Challenges: Approaches to World Politics for the 1990s*. Lexington, Mass.: Lexington.

Kaufman, Stuart J. 2001. *Modern Hatreds: The Symbolic Politics of Ethnic War*. Ithaca, N.Y.: Cornell University Press.

———. 1999. "Approaches to Global Politics in the Twenty-first Century: A Review Essay." *International Studies Review* 1: 193–221.

———. 1997. "The Fragmentation and Consolidation of International Systems." *International Organization* 51: 173–208.

Kautilya. [321–300 B.C.] 1951. *Kautilya's Arthasastra*. 4th. ed.. Mysore, India: Sri Raghuveer.

Keating, Tom. 1990. "The State and International Relations." In David G. Haglund and Michael K. Hawes, eds., *World Politics: Power, Interdependence and Dependence*. Toronto: Harcourt Brace Jovanovich.

Kegley, Charles W., Jr. 1995. "The Neoliberal Challenge to Realist Theories of World Politics: An Introduction." In Charles W. Kegley, Jr., ed., *Controversies in International Relations Theory: Realism and the Neoliberal Challenge*. New York: St. Martin's.

———. 1994. "Redirecting Realism: A Rejoinder to Riggs." *International Studies Notes* 19, 1: 7–9.

Kegley, Charles W., Jr., and Margaret G. Hermann. 1996. "How Democracies Use Intervention: A Neglected Dimension in Studies of the Democratic Peace." *Journal of Peace Research* 33: 309–22.

Kegley, Charles W., Jr., and Gregory A. Raymond. 1992. "Must We Fear a Post–Cold War Multipolar System?" *Journal of Conflict Resolution* 36: 573–85.

———. 1994. *A Multipolar Peace? Great Power Politics in the Twenty-first Century*. New York: St. Martin's.

———. 1991. "Alliances and the Preservation of the Postwar Peace: Weighing the Contribution." In Charles W. Kegley, Jr., ed., *The Long Postwar Peace: Contending Explanations and Projections*. New York: HarperCollins.

———. 1990. *When Trust Breaks Down: Alliance Norms and World Politics*. Columbia: University of South Carolina Press.

Kennedy, Paul. 1988. *The Rise and Fall of the Great Powers: Economic Change and*

Military Conflict from 1500 to 2000. London: Unwin Hyman.

Keohane, Robert O. 1993. "Institutional Theory and the Realist Challenge: After the Cold War." In David A. Baldwin, ed., *Neorealism and Neoliberalism: The Contemporary Debate.* New York: Columbia University Press.

———. 1989. *International Institutions and State Power: Essays in International Relations Theory.* Boulder, Colo.: Westview.

———, ed. 1986a. *Neorealism and Its Critics.* New York: Columbia University Press.

———. 1986b. "Realism, Neorealism and the Study of World Politics." In Robert O. Keohane, ed., *Neorealism and Its Critics.* New York: Columbia University Press.

———. 1984. *After Hegemony.* Princeton, N.J.: Princeton University Press.

———. 1982. "The Demand for International Regimes." *International Organization* 36: 325–56.

Keohane, Robert O., and Lisa L. Martin. 2002. "Institutional Theory as a Research Program." In Colin Elman and Miriam Fendius Elman, eds., *Progress in International Relations Theory: Metrics and Methods of Scientific Change.* Cambridge, Mass.: MIT Press.

Keohane, Robert O., and Joseph S. Nye. 2000a. "Globalization: What's New? What's Now? (And So What?)" *Foreign Policy* 118: 104–19.

———. 2000b. *Power and Interdependence.* 3rd ed. New York: Longman.

———. 1989. *Power and Interdependence.* 2nd ed. Boston: Little, Brown.

———. 1987. "*Power and Interdependence* Revisited." *International Organization* 41: 725–53.

———. 1977. *Power and Interdependence.* Boston: Little, Brown.

———. 1972. *Transnational Relations and World Politics.* Cambridge, Mass.: Harvard University Press.

Kim, Woosang. 1996. "Power Parity, Alliance, and War from 1648 to 1975." In Jacek Kugler and Douglas Lemke, eds., *Parity and War.* Ann Arbor: University of Michigan Press.

———. 1991. "Alliance Transitions and Great Power War." *American Journal of Political Science* 35: 833–50.

———. 1989. "Power, Alliance, and Major Wars, 1816–1975." *Journal of Conflict Resolution* 33: 255–73.

Kim, Woosang, and Bruce Bueno de Mesquita. 1995. "How Perceptions Influence the Risk of War." *International Studies Quarterly* 39: 51–65.

Kim, Woosang, and James D. Morrow. 1992. "When Do Power Shifts Lead to War?" *American Journal of Political Science* 36: 896–922.

Kindleberger, Charles P. 1977. "U.S. Foreign Economic Policy, 1776–1976." In William P. Bundy, ed., *Two Hundred Years of American Foreign Policy.* New York: New York University Press.

———. 1973. *The World in Depression, 1929–1939.* Berkeley: University of California Press.

———. 1959. "United States Economic Foreign Policy: Research Requirements for 1965." *World Politics* 11: 588–613.

Kirshner, Jonathan. 1999. "The Political Economy of Realism." In Ethan B. Kapstein and Michael Mastanduno, eds., *Unipolar Politics: Realism and State Strategies after the Cold War.* New York: Columbia University Press.

Klingberg, Frank L. 1970. "Historical Periods, Trends, and Cycles in International Relations." *Journal of Conflict Resolution* 14: 505–11.

Knutsen, Torbjørn. 1997. *A History of International Relations Theory.* 2nd ed. New

York: Manchester University Press.

Koertge, Noretta. 1971. "Inter-Theoretic Criticism and the Growth of Science." In Roger C. Buck and Robert S. Cohen, eds., *Philosophy of Science Association 1970: In Memory of Rudolf Carnap*. Dordrecht, The Netherlands: D. Reidel.

Köhler, Gernot. 1975. "Imperialism as a Level of Analysis in Correlates of War Research." *Journal of Conflict Resolution* 19: 48–62.

Koslowski, Rey, and Friedrich V. Kratochwil. 1994. "Understanding Change in International Politics: The Soviet Empire's Demise and the International System." *International Organization* 48: 215–47.

Krasner, Stephen D. 1988. "Sovereignty: An Institutional Perspective." *Comparative Political Studies* 21: 66–94.

———. 1985. "Toward Understanding in International Relations." *International Studies Quarterly* 29: 137–44.

———. 1982a. "Regimes and the Limits of Realism: Regimes as Autonomous Variables." *International Organization* 36: 497–510.

———. 1982b. "Structural Causes and Regime Consequences: Regimes as Intervening Variables." *International Organization* 36: 185–205.

———. 1978. *Defending the National Interest: Raw Materials Investments and U.S. Foreign Policy*. Princeton, N.J.: Princeton University Press.

Krathwohl, David R. 1987. *Social and Behavioral Science Research*. San Francisco: Jossey-Bass.

Kriesberg, Louis. 1985. "Social Conflict." In Adam Kuper and Jessica Kuper, eds., *The Social Science Encyclopedia*. Boston: Routledge and Kegan Paul.

Kugler, Jacek. 1993a. "Political Conflict, War, and Peace." In Ada W. Finifter, ed., *Political Science: The State of the Discipline II*. Washington, D.C.: American Political Science Association.

———. 1993b. "War." In Joel Krieger et al., eds., *The Oxford Companion to Politics of the World*. New York: Oxford University Press.

———. 1991. "The Study of War and Peace: Quo Vadis?" In William Crotty, ed., *Political Science: Looking to the Future. Vol. 2, Comparative Politics, Policy, and International Relations*. Evanston, Ill.: Northwestern University Press.

———. 1990. "The War Phenomenon: A Working Distinction." *International Interactions* 16: 201–13.

Kugler, Jacek, and Marina Arbetman. 1989. "Choosing among Measures of Power: A Review of the Empirical Record." In Richard J. Stoll and Michael D. Ward, eds., *Power in World Politics*. Boulder, Colo.: Lynne Rienner.

Kugler, Jacek, and Douglas Lemke, eds. 1996. *Parity and War*. Ann Arbor: University of Michigan Press.

Kugler, Jacek, and A. F. K. Organski. 1989. "The Power Transition: A Retrospective and Prospective Evaluation." In Manus I. Midlarsky, ed., *Handbook of War Studies*. Boston: Unwin Hyman.

Kuhn, Thomas S. 1981. "A Function for Thought Experiments." In Ian Hacking, ed., *Scientific Revolutions*. New York: Oxford University Press.

———. 1977. *The Essential Tension: Selected Studies in Scientific Tradition and Change*. Chicago: University of Chicago Press.

———. 1971. "Notes on Lakatos." In Roger C. Buck and Robert S. Cohen, eds., *Philosophy of Science Association 1970: In Memory of Rudolf Carnap*. Dordrecht, The Netherlands: D. Reidel.

———. 1970. "Logic of Discovery or Psychology of Research: Reflections on My

Critics." In Imre Lakatos and Alan Musgrave, eds., *Criticism and the Growth of Knowledge*. New York: Cambridge University Press.

———. 1962. *The Structure of Scientific Revolutions*. Chicago: University of Chicago Press.

Kukla, Andre. 1997. "Review of *Beyond Positivism and Relativism*." *British Journal for the Philosophy of Science* 48: 447–54.

Lakatos, Imre. 1971. "History of Science and Its Rational Reconstructions." In Roger C. Buck and Robert S. Cohen, eds., *Philosophy of Science Association 1970: In Memory of Rudolf Carnap*. Dordrecht, The Netherlands: D. Reidel.

———. 1970. "Falsification and the Methodology of Scientific Research Programmes." In Imre Lakatos and Alan Musgrave, eds., *Criticism and the Growth of Knowledge*. New York: Cambridge University Press.

Lakatos, Imre, and Alan Musgrave, eds. 1970. *Criticism and the Growth of Knowledge*. New York: Cambridge University Press.

Lakatos, Imre, and Elie Zahar. 1975. "Why Did Copernicus' Research Program Supersede Ptolemy's?" In Robert S. Westman, ed., *The Copernican Achievement*. Berkeley: University of California Press.

Lake, David A., and Robert Powell. 1999. "International Relations: A Strategic-Choice Approach." In David A. Lake and Robert Powell, eds., *Strategic Choice and International Relations*. Princeton, N.J.: Princeton University Press.

Lalman, David. 1988. "Conflict Resolution and Peace." *American Journal of Political Science* 32: 590–615.

Lambert, José. 1997. "Itamar Even-Zohar's Polysystem Studies: An Interdisciplinary Perspective on Culture Research." *Canadian Review of Comparative Literature* 24: 8–14.

Lamborn, Alan C. 1997. "Theory and the Politics in World Politics." *International Studies Quarterly* 41: 187–214.

Langhorne, Richard. 2001. *The Coming of Globalization: Its Evolution and Contemporary Consequences*. New York: Palgrave.

Lapid, Yosef. 1996. "Culture's Ship: Returns and Departures in International Relations Theory." In Yosef Lapid and Friedrich Kratochwil, eds., *The Return of Culture and Identity in International Relations Theory*. Boulder, Colo.: Lynne Rienner.

———. 1989. "The Third Debate: On the Prospects of International Theory in a Post-Positivist Era." *International Studies Quarterly* 33: 235–54.

Laudan, Larry. 1996. *Beyond Positivism and Relativism*. Boulder, Colo.: Westview.

———. 1981. "A Problem-Solving Approach to Scientific Progress." In Ian Hacking, ed., *Scientific Revolutions*. New York: Oxford University Press.

———. 1977. *Progress and Its Problems: Towards a Theory of Scientific Growth*. Berkeley: University of California Press.

Lave, Charles A., and James G. March. 1975. *An Introduction to Models in the Social Sciences*. New York: Harper and Row.

Lawler, Edward J., and Rebecca Ford. 1993. "Metatheory and Friendly Competition in Theory Growth: The Case of Power Processes in Bargaining." In Joseph Berger and Morris Zelditch, eds., *Theoretical Research Programs: Studies in the Growth of Theory*. Stanford, Calif.: Stanford University Press.

Layne, Christopher. 1995. "The Unipolar Illusion: Why New Great Powers Will Rise." In Michael E. Brown, Sean M. Lynn-Jones, and Steven E. Miller, eds., *The Perils of Anarchy: Contemporary Realism and International Security*. Cambridge, Mass.: MIT Press.

———. 1994. "Kant or Cant: The Myth of the Democratic Peace." *International Security* 19: 5–49.

Lebow, Richard Ned. 1981. *Between Peace and War: The Nature of International Crisis.* Baltimore: Johns Hopkins University Press.

Lebow, Richard Ned, and Janice Gross Stein. 1989. "Rational Deterrence Theory: I Think, Therefore I Deter." *World Politics* 41: 208–24.

Leeds, Brett Ashley, Andrew G. Long, and Sara McLaughlin Mitchell. 2000. "Reevaluating Alliance Reliability: Specific Threats, Specific Promises." *Journal of Conflict Resolution* 44: 686–99.

Legro, Jeffrey W., and Andrew Moravcsik. 1999. "Is Anybody Still a Realist?" *International Security* 24: 5–55.

———. 1998. *Is Anybody Still a Realist?* Cambridge, Mass.: Weatherhead Center for International Affairs, Harvard University.

Leng, Russell J. 1999. "Cumulation in QIP [Quantitative International Politics]: Twenty-Five Years after Ojai." *Conflict Management and Peace Science* 17: 133–47.

———. 1993. *Interstate Crisis Behavior, 1816–1980: Realism versus Reciprocity.* Cambridge, Mass.: Cambridge University Press.

Leng, Russell J., and J. David Singer. 1988. "Militarized Interstate Crisis: The BCOW Typology and Its Application." *International Studies Quarterly* 32: 155–73.

Levy, Jack S. 1998. "The Causes of War and the Conditions of Peace." *Annual Review of Political Science* 1: 139–65.

———. 1996. "Loss Aversion, Framing, and Bargaining: The Implications of Prospect Theory for International Conflict." *International Political Science Review* 17: 179–95.

———. 1995. "On the Evolution of Militarized Interstate Conflicts." In Stuart A. Bremer and Thomas R. Cusack, eds., *The Process of War: Advancing the Scientific Study of War.* Luxembourg: Gordon and Breach.

———. 1989. "The Diversionary Theory of War." In Manus I. Midlarsky, ed., *Handbook of War Studies.* Boston: Unwin Hyman.

———. 1988. "Domestic Politics and War." *Journal of Interdisciplinary History* 18: 653–73.

———. 1984. "Size and Stability in the Modern Great Power System." *International Interactions* 10: 341–58.

———. 1983. *War in the Modern Great Power System, 1495-1975.* Lexington: University Press of Kentucky.

———. 1981. "Alliance Formation and War Behavior: An Analysis of the Great Powers, 1495–1975." *Journal of Conflict Resolution* 25: 581–614.

Levy, Jack S., and T. Clifton Morgan. 1984. "The Frequency and Seriousness of War: An Inverse Relationship?" *Journal of Conflict Resolution* 28: 731–49.

Levy, Jack S., Thomas C. Walker, and Martin S. Edwards. 2001. "Continuity and Change in the Evolution of Warfare." In Zeev Maoz and Azar Gat, eds., *War in a Changing World.* Ann Arbor: University of Michigan Press.

Lider, Julian. 1977. *On the Nature of War.* Aldershot, England: Gower.

Lipson, Charles. 1985. *Standing Guard: Protecting Foreign Capital in the Nineteenth and Twentieth Centuries.* Berkeley: University of California Press.

———. 1984. "International Cooperation in Economic and Security Affairs." *World Politics* 37: 1–23.

Liska, George. 1998. *In Search of Poetry in the Politics of Power: Perspectives on Expanding Realism.* New York: Lexington.

————. 1962. *Nations in Alliance: The Limits of Interdependence.* Baltimore: Johns Hopkins University Press.

Little, Richard. 1995. "Neorealism and the English School: A Methodological, Ontological and Theoretical Reassessment." *European Journal of International Relations* 1: 9–34.

Little, Richard, and Barry Buzan. 1996. "Reconceptualizing Anarchy: Structural Realism Meets World History." *European Journal of International Relations* 2: 403–38.

Lusztig, Michael. 1996. *Risking Free Trade: The Politics of Free Trade in Britain, Canada, Mexico, and the United States.* Pittsburgh, Pa.: University of Pittsburgh Press.

Lynn-Jones, Sean M., and Steven E. Miller. 1995. "Preface." In Michael E. Brown, Sean M. Lynn-Jones, and Steven E. Miller, eds., *The Perils of Anarchy: Contemporary Realism and International Security.* Cambridge, Mass.: MIT Press.

Mack, R. W., and R. C. Snyder. 1957. "The Analysis of Social Conflict: Toward an Overview and Synthesis." *Journal of Conflict Resolution* 1: 212–48.

Malinowski, Bronislaw. [1941] 1968. "An Anthropological Analysis of War." In Leon Bramson and George W. Goethals, eds., *War: Studies from Psychology, Sociology, Anthropology.* Rev. ed. New York: Basic Books.

Mandel, Robert. 1980. "Roots of the Modern Interstate Border Dispute." *Journal of Conflict Resolution* 24: 427–54.

Mansbach, Richard W. 1996. "Neo-This and Neo-That: Or, 'Play It Sam' (Again and Again)." *Mershon International Studies Review* 40: 90–95.

Mansbach, Richard W., and John A. Vasquez. 1981. *In Search of Theory: A New Paradigm for Global Politics.* New York: Columbia University Press.

Mansfield, Edward D. 1992. "The Concentration of Capabilities and the Onset of War." *Journal of Conflict Resolution* 36: 3–24.

————. 1988. "Distributions of War over Time." *World Politics* 41: 21–51.

Maoz, Zeev. 1997. "Domestic Political Change and Strategic Response: The Impact of Domestic Conflict on State Behavior, 1816–1986." In David Carment and Patrick James, eds., *Wars in the Midst of Peace: The International Politics of Ethnic Conflict.* Pittsburgh, Pa.: University of Pittsburgh Press.

————. 1990. *Paradoxes of War.* Boston: Unwin Hyman.

Maoz, Zeev, and Nasrin Abdolali. 1989. "Regime Types and International Conflict, 1816–1976." *Journal of Conflict Resolution* 33: 3–35.

Maoz, Zeev, and Bruce Russett. 1993. "Normative and Structural Causes of Democratic Peace, 1946–1986." *American Political Science Review* 87: 624–38.

Marshall, Monty G. 1999. *Third World War: System, Process, and Conflict Dynamics.* New York: Rowman and Littlefield.

Martin, Lisa L. 2000. *Democratic Commitments: Legislatures and International Cooperation.* Princeton, N.J.: Princeton University Press.

————. 1999. "The Contributions of Rational Choice: A Defense of Pluralism." *International Security* 24: 74–83.

————. 1993. *Coercive Cooperation: Explaining Multilateral Economic Sanctions.* Princeton, N.J.: Princeton University Press.

Martin, Michael. 1971. "The Referential Variance and Scientific Objectivity." *British Journal for the Philosophy of Science* 22: 17–26.

Mastanduno, Michael. 1999. "Preserving the Unipolar Moment: Realist Theories and U.S. Grand Strategy after the Cold War." In Ethan B. Kapstein and Michael

Mastanduno, eds., *Unipolar Politics: Realism and State Strategies after the Cold War*. New York: Columbia University Press.

Mastanduno, Michael, and Ethan B. Kapstein. 1999. "Realism and State Strategies after the Cold War." In Ethan B. Kapstein and Michael Mastanduno, eds., *Unipolar Politics: Realism and State Strategies after the Cold War*. New York: Columbia University Press.

Mastanduno, Michael, David A. Lake, and G. John Ikenberry. 1989. "Toward a Realist Theory of State Action." *International Studies Quarterly* 33: 457–74.

Masterman, Margaret. 1970. "The Nature of a Paradigm." In Imre Lakatos and Alan Musgrave, eds., *Criticism and the Growth of Knowledge*. New York: Cambridge University Press.

Mattingly, Garrett. 1959. *The Armada*. Boston: Houghton Mifflin.

McLean, Iain. 1987. *Public Choice: An Introduction*. Oxford, England: Basil Blackwell.

McCleary, Richard, and Richard A. Hay, Jr. 1980. *Applied Time Series Analysis for the Social Sciences*. Beverly Hills, Calif.: Sage.

McClelland, Charles A. 1972. "The Beginning, Duration, and Abatement of International Crises: Comparisons in Two Conflict Arenas." In Charles F. Hermann, ed., *International Crises: Insights from Behavioral Research*. New York: Free Press.

———. 1968. "Access to Berlin: The Quantity and Variety of Events, 1948–1963." In J. David Singer, ed., *Quantitative International Politics: Insights and Evidence*. New York: Free Press.

———. 1966. *Theory and the International System*. New York: Macmillan.

———. 1961. "The Acute International Crisis." In Klaus Knorr and Sidney Verba, eds., *The International System: Theoretical Essays*. Princeton, N.J.: Princeton University Press.

McClosky, Herbert. 1962. "Concerning Strategies for a Science of International Politics." In Richard C. Snyder, H. W. Bruck, and Burton Sapin, eds., *Foreign Policy Decision-Making: An Approach to the Study of International Politics*. New York: Free Press.

McMullin, Ernan. 1978. "Philosophy of Science and Its Rational Reconstructions." In Gerard Radnitzky and Gunnar Andersson, eds., *Progress and Rationality in Science*. Boston: D. Reidel.

Mearsheimer, John J. 1990. "Back to the Future: Instability in Europe after the Cold War." *International Security* 15: 5–56.

Merton, Robert K. 1957. *Social Theory and Social Structure*. Rev. ed. New York: Free Press.

Mickolus, Edward F., Todd Sandler, and Jean M. Murdock. 1989. *International Terrorism in the 1980s: A Chronology of Events, 1968–1979*. Ames: Iowa State University Press.

Midlarsky, Manus I, ed. 2000. *Handbook of War Studies II*. Ann Arbor: University of Michigan Press.

———. 1993. "Polarity and International Stability: Comment." *American Political Science Review* 87: 173–77.

———. 1991. "International Structure and the Learning of Cooperation: The Postwar Experience." In Charles W. Kegley, Jr., ed., *The Long Postwar Peace: Contending Explanations and Projections*. New York: HarperCollins.

———. 1989. "Hierarchical Equilibria and the Long-Run Instability of Multipolar Systems." In Manus I. Midlarsky, ed., *Handbook of War Studies*. Boston: Unwin Hyman.

———. 1988. *The Onset of World War.* Boston: Unwin Hyman.

Mihalka, Michael. 1976. "Hostilities in the European State System, 1816–1970." *Peace Science Society Papers* 26: 100–116.

Miller, Benjamin. 1998. "The Logic of US Military Intervention in the Post–Cold War Era." *Contemporary Security Policy* 19: 72–109.

———. 1995. *When Opponents Cooperate: Great Power Conflict and Cooperation in World Politics.* Ann Arbor: University of Michigan Press.

———. 1994. "Explaining the Emergence of Great Power Concerts." *Review of International Studies* 20: 327–48.

Milner, Helen. 1993. "The Assumption of Anarchy in International Relations Theory: A Critique." In David A. Baldwin, ed., *Neorealism and Neoliberalism: The Contemporary Debate.* New York: Columbia University Press.

Mintz, Alex. 1985. "Military-Industrial Linkages in Israel." *Armed Forces and Society* 12: 9–27.

Mintz, Alex, and Chia Huang. 1990. "Defense Expenditures, Economic Growth, and the 'Peace Dividend.'" *American Political Science Review* 84: 1283–93.

Mitchell, C. R. 1981. *The Structure of International Conflict.* New York: Macmillan.

Mitrany, David. 1943. *A Working Peace System.* London: Royal Institute of International Affairs.

Modelski, George. 1987. *Long Cycles in World Politics.* Seattle: University of Washington Press.

Moravcsik, Andrew. 2002. "Liberal International Relations Theory: A Scientific Assessment." In Colin Elman and Miriam Fendius Elman, eds., *Progress in International Relations Theory: Metrics and Methods of Scientific Change.* Cambridge, Mass.: MIT Press.

Morgan, T. Clifton, and Sally Howard Campbell. 1992. "Domestic Structure, Decisional Constraints, and War." *Journal of Conflict Resolution* 35: 187–211.

Morgan, T. Clifton, and Jack S. Levy. 1990. "Base Stealers versus Power Hitters: A Nation-State Level Analysis of the Frequency and Seriousness of War." In Charles S. Gochman and Alan Ned Sabrosky, eds., *Prisoners of War? Nation-States in the Modern Era.* Lexington, Mass.: Lexington.

Morgenthau, Hans J. 1948. *Politics among Nations: The Struggle for Power and Peace.* New York: Alfred A. Knopf.

———. 1946. *Scientific Man versus Power Politics.* Chicago: University of Chicago Press.

Morgenthau, Hans J., and Kenneth W. Thompson. 1985. *Politics among Nations: The Struggle for Power and Peace.* 6th ed. New York: Alfred A. Knopf.

Morrow, James D. 1993. "Arms versus Allies: Trade-offs in the Search for Security." *International Organization* 47: 207–33.

———. 1991. "Conceptual Problems in Theorizing about International Conflict." *American Political Science Review* 85: 923–29.

———. 1988. "Social Choice and System Structure in World Politics." *World Politics* 41: 75–97.

———. 1985. "A Continuous-Outcome Expected Utility Theory of War." *Journal of Conflict Resolution* 29: 473–502.

Morse, Edward L. 1972. "Crisis Diplomacy, Interdependence, and the Politics of International Economic Relations." In Raymond Tanter and Richard H. Ullman, eds., *Theory and Policy in International Relations.* Princeton, N.J.: Princeton University Press.

Most, Benjamin A., and Harvey Starr. 1989. *Inquiry, Logic and International Politics.* Columbia: University of South Carolina Press.

———. 1987. "Polarity, Preponderance and Power Parity in the Generation of International Conflict." *International Interactions* 13: 255–62.

Motyl, Alexander J. 1999. *Revolutions, Nations, Empires: Conceptual Limits and Theoretical Possibilities.* New York: Columbia University Press.

Moul, William B. 1993. "Polarization, Polynomials, and War." *Journal of Conflict Resolution* 37: 735–48.

———. 1988. "Balance of Power and the Escalation of Serious Disputes among European Great Powers, 1815–1939: Some Evidence." *American Journal of Political Science* 32: 241–75.

Mueller, Dennis C. 1989. *Public Choice II.* New York: Cambridge University Press.

———. 1979. *Public Choice.* New York: Cambridge University Press.

Mueller, John. 1988. *Retreat from Doomsday: The Obsolescence of Major War.* New York: Basic Books.

Nicholson, Michael. 1989. *Formal Theories in International Relations.* New York: Cambridge University Press.

———. 1981. "Co-operation, Anarchy and 'Random' Change." In Barry Buzan and R. J. Barry Jones, eds., *Change and the Study of International Relations: The Evaded Dimension.* London: Frances Pinter.

Nickles, Thomas. 1987. "Lakatosian Heuristics and Epistemic Support." *British Journal for the Philosophy of Science* 38: 181–205.

Niou, Emerson M. S., and Peter C. Ordeshook. 1999. "Return of the Luddites." *International Security* 24: 84–96.

Niou, Emerson M. S., Peter C. Ordeshook, and Gregory F. Rose. 1989. *The Balance of Power: Stability in International Systems.* New York: Cambridge University Press.

Nogee, Joseph L., and Robert H. Donaldson. 1988. *Soviet Foreign Policy since World War II.* 3rd ed. New York: Pergamon.

Nola, Robert. 1987. "The Status of Popper's Theory of Scientific Method." *British Journal for the Philosophy of Science* 38: 441–80.

Olson, Mancur. 1982. *The Rise and Decline of Nations: Economic Growth, Stagflation and Social Rigidities.* New Haven, Conn.: Yale University Press.

———. 1965. *The Logic of Collective Action.* Cambridge, Mass.: Harvard University Press.

O'Meara, Patrick, Howard D. Mehlinger, and Matthew Krain, eds. 2000. *Globalization and the Challenges of a New Century.* Bloomington: Indiana University Press.

Oneal, John R. 1988. "The Rationality of Decision Making During International Crises." *Polity* 20: 598–622.

———. 1982. *Foreign Policy Making in Times of Crisis.* Columbus: Ohio State University Press.

Oneal, John R., Frances H. Oneal, Zeev Maoz, and Bruce M. Russett. 1996. "The Liberal Peace: Interdependence, Democracy, and International Conflict, 1950–1985." *Journal of Peace Research* 33: 11–28.

Oneal, John, and Bruce M. Russett. 2000. "Why 'An Identified Systemic Model of the Democracy-Peace Nexus' Fails to Persuade." *Defence and Peace Economics* 11: 197–214.

———. 1999. "The Kantian Peace: The Pacific Benefits of Democracy, Interdependence, and Internatinal Organizations, 1885–1992." *World Politics* 52: 1–37.

———. 1997. "The Classical Liberals Were Right: Democracy, Interdependence, and

Conflict, 1950–1985." *International Studies Quarterly* 41: 267–94.

Onuf, Nicholas. 1995. "Levels." *European Journal of International Relations* 1: 35–58.

Oren, Ido. 1990. "The War Proneness of Alliances." *Journal of Conflict Resolution* 34: 208–33.

Organski, A. F. K. 1958. *World Politics*. New York: Alfred A. Knopf.

Organski, A. F. K., and Jacek Kugler. 1980. *The War Ledger*. Chicago: University of Chicago Press.

O'Reilly, Marc J. 1998. "Omanibalancing: Oman Confronts an Uncertain Future." *Middle East Journal* 52: 70–84.

Osgood, Robert, and Robert Tucker. 1967. *Force, Order and Justice*. Baltimore: Johns Hopkins University Press.

Østergaard, Clemens Stubbe. 1983. "Multipolarity and Modernization: Sources of China's Foreign Policy in the 1980's." *Cooperation and Conflict* 18: 245–67.

Ostrom, Charles W., Jr., and John H. Aldrich. 1978. "The Relationship between Size and Stability in the Major Power International System." *American Journal of Political Science* 22: 743–71.

Ostrom, Charles W., Jr., and Francis W. Hoole. 1978. "Alliances and Wars Revisited: A Research Note." *International Studies Quarterly* 22: 215–36.

Palan, Ronen. 1992. "The Second Structuralist Theories of International Relations: A Research Note." *International Studies Notes* 17, 3: 22–29.

Parsons, Talcott. 1951. *The Social System*. Glencoe, Ill.: Free Press.

———. 1937. *Structure of Social Action*. New York: McGraw-Hill.

Phillips, Warren R. 1974. "Where Have All the Theories Gone?" *World Politics* 26: 155–88.

Popper, Sir Karl R. 1981. "The Rationality of Scientific Revolutions." In Ian Hacking, ed., *Scientific Revolutions*. New York: Oxford University Press.

———. 1974. *The Poverty of Historicism*. 2nd ed. New York: Routledge and Kegan Paul.

———. 1969. *Conjectures and Refutations: The Growth of Scientific Knowledge*. 3rd ed. New York: Routledge and Kegan Paul.

———. [1935] 1959. *The Logic of Scientific Discovery*. New York: Harper.

Pouncy, Hillard. 1988. "Terms of Agreement: Evaluating the Theory of Symbolic Politics' Impact on the Pluralist Research Program." *American Journal of Political Science* 32: 781–95.

Powell, Robert. 1999. "The Modeling Enterprise and Security Studies." *International Security* 24: 97–106.

———. 1994. "Anarchy in International Relations Theory: The Neorealist-Neoliberal Debate." *International Organization* 48: 313–44.

———. 1993. "Absolute and Relative Gains in International Relations Theory." In David A. Baldwin, ed., *Neorealism and Neoliberalism: The Contemporary Debate*. New York: Columbia University Press.

———. 1989. "Crisis Stability in the Nuclear Age." *American Political Science Review* 83: 61–76.

Puchala, Donald J. 1991. "Woe to the Orphans of the Scientific Revolution." In Robert L. Rothstein, ed., *The Evolution of Theory in International Relations: Essays in Honor of William T. R. Fox*. Columbia: University of South Carolina Press.

Pudaite, Paul R., and Gretchen Hower. 1989. "National Capability and Conflict Outcome: An Application of Indicator Building in the Social Sciences." In Richard J. Stoll and Michael D. Ward, eds., *Power in World Politics*. Boulder, Colo.: Lynne Rienner.

Putnam, Hilary. 1981. "The 'Corroboration' of Theories." In Ian Hacking, ed., *Scientific Revolutions*. New York: Oxford University Press.

Putnam, Robert D. 1988. "Diplomacy and Domestic Politics: The Logic of Two-Level Games." *International Organization* 42: 427–60.

Quattrone, George A., and Amos Tversky. 1988. "Contrasting Rational and Psychological Analyses of Political Choice." *American Political Science Review* 82: 719–36.

Quine, Willard Van Orman. 1953. *From a Logical Point of View*. Cambridge, Mass.: Harvard University Press.

Radnitzky, Gerard, and Gunnar Andersson. 1978. "Objective Criteria of Scientific Progress? Inductivism, Falsificationism, and Relativism." In Gerard Radnitzky and Gunnar Andersson, eds., *Progress and Rationality in Science*. Boston: D. Reidel.

Rafferty, Kirsten L. 2001. "Alliances as Institutions: Persistence and Disintegration in Security Cooperation." Unpublished manuscript.

Rapkin, David P., and William R. Thompson. 1980. "A Comparative Note on Two Alternative Indexes of Bipolarization." *International Interactions* 6: 377–86.

Rapoport, Anatol. 1960. *Fights, Games, and Debates*. Ann Arbor: University of Michigan Press.

Rasler, Karen A., and William R. Thompson. 1994. *The Great Powers and Global Struggle, 1490–1990*. Lexington: University of Kentucky Press.

Ray, James Lee. 2002. "A Lakatosian View of the Democratic Peace Research Program: Does It Falsify Realism (or Neorealism)?" In Colin Elman and Miriam Fendius Elman, eds., *Progress in International Relations Theory: Metrics and Methods of Scientific Change*. Cambridge, Mass.: MIT Press.

———. 1999. "A Lakatosian View of the Democratic Peace Research Programme: Does It Falsify Realism (or Neorealism)?" Paper presented at the Conference on Progress in International Relations Theory, Scottsdale, Arizona.

———. 1995. "Promise or Peril? Neorealism, Neoliberalism and the Future of International Politics." In Charles W. Kegley, Jr., ed., *Controversies in International Relations Theory: Realism and the Neoliberal Challenge*. Columbia: University of South Carolina Press.

———. 1989. "The Abolition of Slavery and the End of International War." *International Organization* 43: 405–39.

———. 1980. "The Measurement of System Structure." In J. David Singer and Paul F. Diehl, eds., *Measuring the Correlates of War*. Ann Arbor: University of Michigan Press.

Ray, James Lee, and J. David Singer. 1973. "Measuring the Concentration of Power in the International System." *Sociological Methods and Research* 1: 403–37.

Richardson, J. L. 1990. "Informal Theories of Rationality." *Working Paper 1990/8, Department of International Relations*. Canberra, Australia: Australian National University.

———. 1988. "New Insights on International Crises." *Review of International Studies* 14: 309–16.

Richardson, Lewis F. 1960. *Arms and Insecurity*. Pittsburgh, Pa.: Boxwood.

Riggs, Fred W. 1994. "Thoughts about Neoidealism vs. Realism: Reflections on Charles Kegley's ISA Presidential Address, March 25, 1993." *International Studies Notes* 19, no. 1: 1–6.

Riker, William H. 1962. *The Theory of Political Coalitions*. New Haven, Conn.: Yale University Press.

Riker, William H., and Peter C. Ordeshook. 1973. *An Introduction to Positive Political Theory.* Englewood Cliffs, N.J.: Prentice Hall.

Ripley, Brian. 1990. "A Lakatosian Appraisal of Foreign Policy Decision-Making." Paper presented at the Annual Meeting of the International Studies Association, April, Washington, D.C.

Robinson, James A. 1972. "Crisis: An Appraisal of Concepts and Theories." In Charles F. Hermann, ed., *International Crises: Insights from Behavioral Research.* New York: Free Press.

———. 1968. "Crisis." In David L. Sills, ed., *International Encyclopedia of the Social Sciences.* New York: Collier-Macmillan.

———. 1962. *The Concept of Crisis in Decision-Making.* Symposia Study Series No. 11. Washington, D.C.: National Institute of Social and Behavioral Science.

Robinson, P. Stuart. 1996. *The Politics of International Crisis Escalation: Decision-Making under Pressure.* New York: Tauris Academic Studies.

———. 1994. "Reason, Meaning, and the Institutional Context of Foreign Policy Decision-Making." *International Journal* 44: 408–33.

Rogowski, Ronald. 1999. "Institutions as Constraints on Strategic Choice." In David A. Lake and Robert Powell, eds., *Strategic Choice and International Relations.* Princeton, N.J.: Princeton University Press.

Rose, Gideon. 1998. "Neoclassical Realism and Theories of Foreign Policy." *World Politics* 51: 144–72.

Rosecrance, Richard N. 1966. "Bipolarity, Multipolarity, and the Future." *Journal of Conflict Resolution* 10: 314–27.

———. 1963. *Action and Reaction in World Politics: International Systems in Perspective.* Westport, Conn.: Greenwood.

Rosenau, James N. 1997. *Along the Domestic-Foreign Frontier: Explaining Governance in a Turbulent World.* New York: Cambridge University Press.

———. 1995. "Signals, Signposts and Symptoms: Interpreting Change and Anomalies in World Politics." *European Journal of International Relations* 1: 113–22.

———. 1990. *Turbulence in World Politics: A Theory of Change and Continuity.* Princeton, N.J.: Princeton University Press.

———. 1988. "Patterned Chaos in Global Life: Structure and Process in the Two Worlds of World Politics." *International Political Science Review* 9: 327–64.

———, ed. 1969. *Linkage Politics.* New York: Free Press.

———. 1966. "Pre-theories and Theories of Foreign Policy." In R. Barry Farrel, ed., *Approaches to Comparative and International Politics.* Evanston, Ill.: Northwestern University Press.

Rosenau, James N., and Mary Durfee. 1995. *Thinking Theory Thoroughly: Coherent Approaches to an Incoherent World.* Boulder, Colo.: Westview.

Rosenberg, Alexander. 1986. "Lakatosian Consolations for Economics." *Economics and Philosophy* 2: 127–39.

Roskin, Michael, and Nicholas Berry. 1990. *An Introduction to International Relations.* Englewood Cliffs, N.J.: Prentice Hall.

Rourke, John T. 1990. *Making Foreign Policy: United States, Soviet Union, China.* Pacific Grove, Calif.: Brooks/Cole.

Ruggie, John Gerard. 1989. "International Structure and International Transformation: Space, Time, and Method." In Ernst-Otto Cziempel and James N. Rosenau, eds., *Global Changes and Theoretical Challenges: Approaches to World Politics for the 1990s.* Lexington, Mass.: Lexington.

————. 1986. "Continuity and Transformation in the World Polity: Toward a Neorealist Synthesis." In Robert O. Keohane, ed., *Neorealism and Its Critics*. New York: Columbia University Press.

Rummel, R. J. 1975–1981. *Understanding Conflict and War*. 5 vols. Beverly Hills, Calif.: Sage.

Russett, Bruce M. 1993. *Grasping the Democratic Peace: Principles for a Post–Cold War World*. Princeton, N.J.: Princeton University Press.

————. 1990. "Economic Decline, Electoral Pressure, and the Initiation of Interstate Conflict." In Charles S. Gochman and Alan Ned Sabrosky, eds., *Prisoners of War? Nation-States in the Modern Era*. Lexington, Mass.: Lexington.

————, ed. 1972. *Peace, War, and Numbers*. Beverly Hills, Calif.: Sage.

————. 1969. "The Young Science of International Politics." *World Politics* 22: 87–94.

Ryan, Alan. 1987. "Introduction." In Alan Ryan, ed., *Utilitarianism and Other Essays: J. S. Mill and Jeremy Bentham*. New York: Penguin.

Sabrosky, Alan Ned, ed. 1985. *Polarity and War: The Changing Structure of International Conflict*. Boulder, Colo.: Westview.

Saideman, Stephen M. 2001. *The Ties That Divide: Ethnic Politics, Foreign Policy, and International Conflict*. New York: Columbia University Press.

Sanders, David. 1996. "International Relations: Neo-Realism and Neo-Liberalism." In Robert Goodin and Hans-Dieter Klingmann, eds., *A New Handbook of Political Science*. New York: Oxford University Press.

Sandler, Todd. 1997. *Global Challenges*. New York: Cambridge University Press.

————. 1992. *Collective Action: Theory and Applications*. Ann Arbor: University of Michigan Press.

Sandler, Todd, and Keith Hartley. 1999. *The Political Economy of NATO: Past, Present, and into the 21st Century*. Cambridge, Mass.: Cambridge University Press.

Saperstein, Alvin M. 1991. "The 'Long Peace': Result of a Bipolar Competitive World?" *Journal of Conflict Resolution* 35: 68–79.

Sayer, Andrew. 1984. *Method in Social Science: A Realist Approach*. London: Hutchinson.

Scarborough, Grace Iusi. 1988. "Polarity, Power, and Risk in International Disputes." *Journal of Conflict Resolution* 32: 511–33.

Schelling, Thomas C. 1978. *Micromotives and Macrobehavior*. New York: W. W. Norton.

————. 1966. *Arms and Influence*. New Haven, Conn.: Yale University Press.

————. 1960. *The Strategy of Conflict*. Cambridge, Mass.: Harvard University Press.

Schmidt, Brian C. 1994. "The Historiography of Academic International Relations." *Review of International Studies* 20: 349–67.

Schroeder, Paul W. 1986. "The 19th-Century System: Changes in the Structure." *World Politics* 39: 1–26.

Schütz, A. [1932] 1967. *The Phenomenology of the Social World*. Evanston, Ill.: Northwestern University Press.

Schweller, Randall. 2002. "The Progressive Nature of Neoclassical Realism." In Colin Elman and Miriam Fendius Elman, eds., *Progress in International Relations Theory: Metrics and Methods of Scientific Change*. Cambridge, Mass.: MIT Press.

————. 1997. "New Realist Research on Alliances: Refining, Not Refuting, Waltz's Balancing Proposition." *American Political Science Review* 91: 927–30.

Schweller, Randall L., and David Priess. 1997. "A Tale of Two Realisms: Expanding the Institutions Debate." *Mershon International Studies Review* 41, 1: 1–32.

Shanker, S. G. 1988. "Wittgenstein's Remarks on the Significance of Gödel's Second Theorem." In S. G. Shanker, ed., *Gödel's Theorem in Focus*. New York: Croom Helm.

Shapere, Dudley. 1981. "Meaning and Scientific Change." In Ian Hacking, ed., *Scientific Revolutions*. New York: Oxford University Press.

Shapiro, Michael J. 1989. "Textualizing Global Politics." In James Der Derian and Michael J. Shapiro, eds., *International/Intertextual Relations*. Lexington, Mass.: Lexington.

Sheldon, Richard C. 1951. "Some Observations on Theory in Social Science." In Talcott Parsons and Edward A. Shils, eds., *Toward a General Theory of Action*. Cambridge, Mass.: Harvard University Press.

Simon, Herbert A. 1985. "Quantification of Theoretical Terms and the Falsifiability of Theories." *British Journal for the Philosophy of Science* 36: 291–98.

Simon, Marc V., and Harvey Starr. 2000. "Two-Level Security Management and the Prospects for New Democracies: A Simulation Analysis." *International Studies Quarterly* 44: 391–422.

———. 1996. "Extraction, Allocation and the Rise and Decline of States: A Simulation Analysis of Two-Level Security Management." *Journal of Conflict Resolution* 40: 272–97.

Simowitz, Roslyn. 2002. "Applying Lakatos to International Relations: What Do We Learn from DiCicco and Levy, and Snyder?" In Colin Elman and Miriam Fendius Elman, eds., *Progress in International Relations Theory: Metrics and Methods of Scientific Change*. Cambridge, Mass.: MIT Press.

Simowitz, Roslyn, and Barry L. Price. 1991. "Conceptual Problems in Theorizing about International Conflict." *American Political Science Review* 85: 929–39.

———. 1990. "The Expected Utility Theory of Conflict: Measuring Theoretical Progress." *American Political Science Review* 84: 439–60.

Singer, J. David. 1989. "System Structure, Decision Processes, and the Incidence of International War." In Manus I. Midlarsky, ed., *Handbook of War Studies*. Boston: Unwin Hyman.

———. 1982. "Confrontational Behavior and Escalation to War 1816–1980: A Research Plan." *Journal of Peace Research* 19: 37–48.

———. 1961. "The Level-of-Analysis Problem in International Relations." *World Politics* 14: 77–92.

Singer, J. David, and Sandra B. Bouxsein. 1975. "Structural Clarity and International War: Some Tentative Findings." In Thomas Murray, ed., *Interdisciplinary Aspects of General Systems Theory*. Washington, D.C.: Society for General Systems Research.

Singer, J. David, Stuart A. Bremer, and John Stuckey. 1979. "Capability Distribution, Uncertainty, and Major Power War, 1820–1965." In J. David Singer and Associates, eds., *Explaining War*. Beverly Hills, Calif.: Sage.

———. 1972. "Capability Distribution, Uncertainty, and Major Power War, 1820–1965." In Bruce M. Russett, ed., *Peace, War and Numbers*. Beverly Hills, Calif.: Sage.

Singer, J. David, and Melvin Small. 1979. "Alliance Aggregation and the Onset of War, 1815–1945." In J. David Singer, ed. *The Correlates of War: I. Research Origins and Rationale*. New York: Free Press.

———. 1972. *The Wages of War, 1816–1965: A Statistical Handbook*. New York: John Wiley.

———. 1968. "Alliance Aggregation and the Onset of War, 1815–1945." In J. David

Singer, ed., *Quantitative International Politics*. New York: Free Press.

———. 1966. "National Alliance Commitments and War Involvement, 1815–1945." *Peace Research Society (International) Papers* 5: 109–40.

Sislin, John, and Frederic S. Pearson. 2001. *Arms and Ethnic Conflict*. Lanham, Md.: Rowman and Littlefield.

Siverson, Randolph M. 1996. "Thinking about Puzzles in the Study of International War." *Conflict Management and Peace Science* 15: 113–32.

Siverson, Randolph M., and Harvey Starr. 1989. "Alliance and Border Effects on the War Behavior of States: Refining the Interaction Opportunity Model." *Conflict Management and Peace Science* 10: 21–46.

Siverson, Randolph M., and Michael P. Sullivan. 1984. "Alliances and War: A New Examination of an Old Problem." *Conflict Management and Peace Science* 8: 1–15.

———. 1983. "The Distribution of Power and the Onset of War." *Journal of Conflict Resolution* 27: 473–97.

Siverson, Randolph M., and Michael R. Tennefoss. 1984. "Power, Alliance, and the Escalation of International Conflict, 1815–1965, " *American Political Science Review* 78: 1057–69.

Small, Melvin, and J. David Singer. 1982. *Resort to Arms: International and Civil Wars, 1816–1980*. Beverly Hills, Calif.: Sage.

———. 1970. "Patterns in International Warfare, 1816–1965." *Annals of the American Academy of Political and Social Science* 391: 145–55.

Smart, J. J. C. 1972. "Science, History and Methodology." *British Journal for the Philosophy of Science* 23: 266–74.

Smith, Dan. 1996. "The Field of Study in International Relations." *European Journal of International Relations* 2: 259–69.

Snidal, Duncan. 1993a. "Relative Gains and the Pattern of International Cooperation." In David A. Baldwin, ed., *Neorealism and Neoliberalism: The Contemporary Debate*. New York: Columbia University Press.

———. 1993b. "The Relative Gains Problem for International Cooperation: Response." *American Political Science Review* 87: 729–43.

———. 1991. "International Cooperation among Relative Gains Maximizers." *International Studies Quarterly* 35: 387–402.

Snyder, Glenn H. 1991. "Alliance Theory: A Neorealist First Cut." In Robert L. Rothstein, ed., *The Evolution of Theory in International Relations: Essays in Honor of William T. R. Fox*. Columbia: University of South Carolina Press.

———. 1984. "The Security Dilemma in Alliance Politics." *World Politics* 36: 461–95.

Snyder, Glenn H., and Paul Diesing. 1989. "System Structure." In Robert O. Matthews, Arthur G. Rubinoff, and Janice Gross Stein, eds., *International Conflict and Conflict Management: Readings in World Politics*. 2nd ed. Scarborough, Canada: Prentice Hall.

———. 1977. *Conflict among Nations: Bargaining, Decision Making and System Structure in International Crises*. Princeton, N.J.: Princeton University Press.

Snyder, Jack. 2002. "'Is' and 'Ought': Evaluating Aspects of Normative Research." In Colin Elman and Miriam Fendius Elman, eds., *Progress in International Relations Theory: Metrics and Methods of Scientific Change*. Cambridge, Mass.: MIT Press.

Snyder, Richard C., H. W. Bruck, and Burton Sapin, eds. [1954] 1962. *Foreign Policy Decision-Making: An Approach to the Study of International Politics*. New York: Free Press.

Sokal, Alan D. 1996. "Transgressing the Boundaries: Toward a Transformative

Hermeneutics of Quantum Gravity." *Social Text* 14: 217–52.

Solingen, Etel. 1998. *Regional Orders at Century's Dawn: Global and Domestic Influences on Grand Strategy*. Princeton, N.J.: Princeton University Press.

Sorokin, Gerald L. 1994. "Alliance Formation and General Deterrence: A Game-Theoretic Model and the Case of Israel." *Journal of Conflict Resolution* 38: 298–325.

Sorokin, Pitirim A. 1937. *Social and Cultural Dynamics. Vol. 3, Fluctuation of Social Relationships, War, and Revolution*. New York: American Book Company.

Spiegel, Steven L. 1970. "Bimodality and the International Order: Paradox of Parity." *Public Policy* 18: 383–412.

Spiezio, K. Edward. 1990. "British Hegemony and Major Power War, 1815–1939: An Empirical Test of Gilpin's Model of Hegemonic Governance." *International Studies Quarterly* 34: 165–81.

Stack, John, ed. 1986. *The Primordial Challenge: Ethnicity in the Contemporary World*. Westport, Conn.: Greenwood.

———, ed. 1981. *Ethnic Identities in a Transnational World*. Westport, Conn.: Greenwood.

Stein, Arthur A. 1999. "The Limits of Strategic Choice: Constrained Rationality and Incomplete Information." In David A. Lake and Robert Powell, eds., *Strategic Choice and International Relations*. Princeton, N.J.: Princeton University Press.

Stein, Janice G., and Raymond Tanter. 1980. *Rational Decision-Making: Israel's Security Choices, 1967*. Columbus: Ohio State University Press.

Steinbruner, John D. 1974. *The Cybernetic Theory of Decision: New Dimensions of Political Analysis*. Princeton, N.J.: Princeton University Press.

Stephens, Jerome. 1972. "An Appraisal of Some Systems Approaches in the Study of International Systems." *International Studies Quarterly* 16: 321–49.

Stoll, Richard J. 1989. "State Power, World Views, and the Major Powers." In Richard J. Stoll and Michael D. Ward, eds., *Power in World Politics*. Boulder, Colo.: Lynne Rienner.

———. 1987. "System and State in International Politics: Computer Simulation of Balancing in an Anarchic World." *International Studies Quarterly* 31: 387–402.

Stoll, Richard J., and Michael Champion. 1985. "Capability Concentration, Alliance Bonding and Conflict among the Major Powers." In A. Ned Sabrosky, ed., *Polarity and War*. Boulder, Colo.: Westview.

Sullivan, Michael P. 1990. *Power in Contemporary International Politics*. Columbia: University of South Carolina Press.

———. 1976. *International Relations: Theories and Evidence*. Englewood Cliffs, N.J.: Prentice Hall.

Taagepera, Rein, and James Lee Ray. 1977. "A Generalized Index of Concentration." *Sociological Methods and Research* 5: 367–84.

Tammen, Ronald L., Jacek Kugler, Douglas Lemke, Allan C. Stam III, Mark Abdollahian, Carole Asharabati, Brian Efird, and A. F. K. Organski. 2000. *Power Transitions: Strategies for the 21st Century*. New York: Chatham House.

Teschke, Benno. 1998. "Geopolitical Relations in the European Middle Ages: History and Theory." *International Organization* 52: 325–58.

Tellis, Ashley. 1996. "Reconstructing Political Realism: The Long March to Scientific Theory." In Benjamin Frankel, ed., *Roots of Realism*. London: Frank Cass.

Thompson, Kenneth W. 1994. *Fathers of International Thought: The Legacy of Political Theory*. Baton Rouge: Louisiana State University Press.

———. 1980. *Masters of International Thought: Major Twentieth Century Theorists and the World Crisis.* Baton Rouge: Louisiana State University Press.

Thompson, William R. 1986. "Polarity, the Long Cycle, and Global Power Warfare." *Journal of Conflict Resolution* 30: 587–615.

Thompson, William R., Karen A. Rasler, and R. P. Y. Li. 1980. "Systemic Interaction Opportunities and War Behavior." *International Interactions* 7: 57–85.

Tickner, J. Ann. 1992. *Gender in International Relations: Feminist Perspectives on Achieving Global Society.* New York: Columbia University Press.

Tillema, Herbert K. 1991. *International Armed Conflict Since 1945: A Bibliographic Handbook of Wars and Military Interventions.* Boulder, Colo.: Westview Press.

Toulmin, Stephen E. 1975. "Commentary." In Robert S. Westman, ed., *The Copernican Achievement.* Berkeley: University of California Press.

Tsebelis, George. 1990. *Nested Games: Rational Choice in Comparative Politics.* Berkeley: University of California Press.

Urbach, Peter. 1978. "The Objective Promise of a Research Programme." In Gerard Radnitzky and Gunnar Andersson, eds., *Progress and Rationality in Science.* Boston: D. Reidel.

van Fraasen, Bas C. 1985. "Empiricism in the Philosophy of Science." In Paul M. Churchland and Clifford A. Hooker, eds., *Images of Science: Essays on Realism and Empiricism, with a Reply from Bas C. van Fraasen.* Chicago: University of Chicago Press.

Vasquez, John A. 2002. "Kuhn vs. Lakatos? The Case for Multiple Frames in Appraising IR Theory." In Colin Elman and Miriam Fendius Elman, eds., *Progress in International Relations Theory: Metrics and Methods of Scientific Change.* Cambridge, Mass.: MIT Press.

———. 2000a. "Reexamining the Steps to War." In Manus I. Midlarsky, ed., *Handbook of War Studies II.* Ann Arbor: University of Michigan Press.

———, ed. 2000b. *What Do We Know about War?* New York: Rowman and Littlefield.

———. 1998. *The Power of Power Politics.* 2nd ed. New Brunswick, N.J.: Rutgers University Press.

———. 1997. "The Realist Paradigm and Degenerative versus Progressive Research Programs: An Appraisal of Neotraditional Research on Waltz's Balancing Proposition." *American Political Science Review* 91: 899–912.

———. 1993. *The War Puzzle.* New York: Cambridge University Press.

———. 1987. "The Steps to War: Toward a Scientific Explanation of Correlates of War Findings." *World Politics* 40: 108–145.

———. 1986. "Capability, Types of War, Peace." *Western Political Quarterly* 39: 313–27.

———. 1983. *The Power of Power Politics.* New Brunswick, N.J.: Rutgers University Press.

Veblen, Thorstein. 1912. *The Theory of the Leisure Class: An Economic Study of Institutions.* 2nd ed. London: Macmillan.

Vernon, Raymond. 1977. *Storm over the Multinationals: The Real Issues.* Cambridge, Mass.: Harvard University Press.

Vertzberger, Yaacov Y. I. 1998. *Risk-Taking and Decisionmaking: Foreign Military Intervention Decisions.* Stanford, Calif.: Stanford University Press.

———. 1990. *The World in Their Minds: Information Processing, Cognition and Perception in Foreign Policy Decisionmaking.* Stanford, Calif.: Stanford University Press.

Vincent, Jack E. 1983. *International Relations. Vol. 2, Structures.* Lanham, Md.: University Press of America.

Viner, Jacob. 1948. "Power Versus Plenty as Objectives of Foreign Policy in the Seventeenth and Eighteenth Centuries." *World Politics* 1: 1–29.

Voltaire, Jean François Marie Arouet de. [1759] 1929. *Candide.* New York: Literary Guild.

Wagner, David B., and Joseph Berger. 1985. "Do Sociological Theories Grow?" *American Journal of Sociology* 90: 697–728.

Wagner, R. Harrison. 1994. "Peace, War, and the Balance of Power." *American Political Science Review* 88: 593–607.

———. 1984. "War and Expected Utility Theory." *World Politics* 6: 407–23.

Walker, R. B. J. 1989. "*The Prince* and "The Pauper": Tradition, Modernity, and Practice in the Theory of International Relations." In James Der Derian and Michael J. Shapiro, eds., *International/Intertextual Relations: Postmodern Readings of World Politics.* Lexington, Mass.: Lexington.

Walker, Stephen G. 2002. "A Cautionary Tale: Operational Code Analysis as a Scientific Research Program." In Colin Elman and Miriam Fendius Elman, eds., *Progress in International Relations Theory: Metrics and Methods of Scientific Change.* Cambridge, Mass.: MIT Press.

———. 1987. "Role Theory and the International System: A Postscript to Waltz's Theory of International Politics." In Stephen G. Walker, ed., *Role Theory and Foreign Policy Analysis.* Durham, N.C.: Duke University Press.

Wallace, Michael D. 1979a. "Arms Races and Escalation: Some New Evidence." *Journal of Conflict Resolution* 23: 3–16.

———. 1979b. "Alliance Polarization, Cross-Cutting, and International War, 1815–1964: A Measurement Procedure and Some Preliminary Evidence." In J. David Singer and Associates, eds., *Explaining War: Selected Papers from the Correlates of War Project.* Beverly Hills, Calif.: Sage.

———. 1973. "Alliance Polarization, Cross-Cutting, and International War, 1815–1964." *Journal of Conflict Resolution* 17: 575–604.

Wallensteen, Peter, and Margareta Sollenberg. 1996. "The End of International War? Armed Conflict 1989–95." *Journal of Peace Research* 33: 353–70.

———. 1995. "After the Cold War: Emerging Patterns of Armed Conflict 1989–94." *Journal of Peace Research* 32: 345–60.

Wallerstein, Immanuel. 1980. *The Modern World System II.* New York: Academic Press.

———. 1974. *The Modern World System.* New York: Academic Press.

Walt, Stephen M. 1999a. "Rigor or Rigor Mortis? Rational Choice and Security Studies." *International Security* 23: 5–48.

———. 1999b. "A Model Disagreement." *International Security* 24: 115–30.

———. 1997. "The Progressive Power of Realism." *American Political Science Review* 91: 931–35.

———. 1995. "Alliance Formation and the Balance of World Power." In Michael E. Brown, Sean M. Lynn-Jones, and Steven E. Miller, eds., *The Perils of Anarchy: Contemporary Realism and International Security.* Cambridge, Mass.: MIT Press.

———. 1990. *The Origins of Alliances.* Ithaca, N.Y.: Cornell University Press.

———. 1989. "Alliances in Theory and Practice: What Lies Ahead?" *Journal of International Affairs* 43: 1–18.

———. 1988. "Testing Theories of Alliances: The Case of Southwest Asia." *International Organization* 42: 275–316.

Waltz, Kenneth M. 2000. "Structural Realism after the Cold War." *International Security* 25: 5–41.

———. 1997. "Evaluating Theories." *American Political Science Review* 91: 913–17.

———. 1995. "Realist Thought and Neorealist Theory." In Charles W. Kegley, Jr., ed., *Controversies in International Relations Theory: Realism and the Neoliberal Challenge.* New York: St. Martin's.

———. 1993. "The Emerging Structure of International Politics." *International Security* 18: 44–79.

———. 1991. "Realist Thought and Neorealist Theory." In Robert L. Rothstein, ed., *The Evolution of Theory in International Relations: Essays in Honor of William T. R. Fox.* Columbia: University of South Carolina Press.

———. 1988. "The Origins of War in Neorealist Theory." In Robert I. Rotberg and Theodore K. Rabb, eds., *The Origin and Prevention of Major Wars.* New York: Cambridge University Press.

———. 1986. "Reflections on *Theory of International Politics*: A Response to My Critics." In Robert O. Keohane, ed., *Neorealism and Its Critics.* New York: Columbia University Press.

———. 1979. *Theory of International Politics.* Reading, Mass.: Addison-Wesley.

———. 1975. "Theory of International Relations." In Fred Greenstein and Nelson Polsby, eds., *The Handbook of Political Science.* Reading, Mass.: Addison-Wesley.

———. 1967. "International Structure, National Force, and the Balance of World Power." *Journal of International Affairs* 21: 215–31.

———. 1964. "The Stability of a Bipolar World." *Daedalus* 93: 881–909.

———. 1959. *Man, the State and War.* New York: Columbia University Press.

Ward, Michael D. 1989. "Power in the International System: Behavioral Salience and Material Capabilities." In Richard J. Stoll and Michael D. Ward, eds., *Power in World Politics.* Boulder, Colo.: Lynne Rienner.

Watkins, John. 1978. "Corroboration and the Problem of Content-Comparison." In Gerard Radnitzky and Gunnar Andersson, eds., *Progress and Rationality in Science.* Boston: D. Reidel.

Watson, Adam. 1992. *The Evolution of International Society: A Comparative Historical Analysis.* New York: Routledge.

Wayman, Frank Whelon. 1985. "Bipolarity, Multipolarity and the Threat of War." In A. Ned Sabrosky, ed., *Polarity and War.* Boulder, Colo.: Westview.

———. 1984. "Bipolarity and War: The Role of Capability Concentration and Alliance Patterns among Major Powers, 1816–1965." *Journal of Peace Research* 21: 61–78.

Wayman, Frank Whelon, and Paul F. Diehl. 1994. "Realism Reconsidered: The Realpolitik Framework and Its Basic Propositions." In Frank Whelon Wayman and Paul F. Diehl, eds., *Reconstructing Realpolitik.* Ann Arbor: University of Michigan Press.

Wayman, Frank Whelon, and T. Clifton Morgan. 1990. "Measuring Polarity in the International System." In J. David Singer and Paul F. Diehl, eds., *Measuring the Correlates of War.* Ann Arbor: University of Michigan Press.

Weber, Max. 1949. *The Methodology of the Social Sciences.* Edward A. Shils and Henry A. Finch, trans. Glencoe, Ill.: Free Press.

Weede, Erich. 1976. "Overwhelming Preponderance as a Pacifying Condition among Contiguous Asian Dyads, 1950–1969." *Journal of Conflict Resolution* 20: 395–411.

Wendt, Alexander E. 1999. *Social Theory of International Politics.* New York:

Cambridge University Press.

———. 1992. "Anarchy Is What States Make of It: The Social Construction of Power Politics." *International Organization* 46: 391–425.

———. 1987. "The Agent-Structure Problem in International Relations Theory." *International Organization* 41: 335–70.

Wesson, Robert. 1990. *International Relations in Transition.* Englewood Cliffs, N.J.: Prentice Hall.

Wight, Martin. 1986. *Power Politics.* 2nd ed. Middlesex, England: Penguin.

Wilkenfeld, Jonathan, ed. 1973. *Conflict Behavior and Linkage Politics.* New York: David McKay.

Wilkenfeld, Jonathan, Michael Brecher, and Sheila Moser. 1988. *Crises in the Twentieth Century. Vol 2, Handbook of Foreign Policy Crises.* New York: Pergamon.

Wilkenfeld, Jonathan, Gerald W. Hopple, Paul J. Rossa, and Stephen J. Andriole. 1980. *Foreign Policy Behavior: The Interstate Behavior Analysis Model.* Bevery Hills, Calif.: Sage.

Wilkinson, David. 1999. "Unipolarity without Hegemony." *International Studies Review* 1: 141–72.

Wilson, E. O. 1998. "Back from Chaos." *Atlantic Monthly,* March, 41–62.

Wohlforth, William C. 1998. "Reality Check: Revising Theories of International Politics in Response to the End of the Cold War." *World Politics* 50: 650–80.

———. 1995. "Realism and the End of the Cold War." In Michael E. Brown, Sean M. Lynn-Jones, and Steven E. Miller, eds., *The Perils of Anarchy: Contemporary Realism and International Security.* Cambridge, Mass.: MIT Press.

———. 1993. *The Elusive Balance: Power and Perceptions During the Cold War.* Ithaca, N.Y.: Cornell University Press.

Wolfers, Arnold. 1962. *Discord and Collaboration: Essays on International Politics.* Baltimore: Johns Hopkins University Press.

Wolfson, Murray, ed. 1998. *The Political Economy of War and Peace.* Boston: Kluwer Academic Publishers.

———. 1995. "A House Divided against Itself Cannot Stand." *Conflict Management and Peace Science* 14: 115–41.

Wolfson, Murray, Patrick James, and Eric Solberg. 1998. "In a World of Cannibals Everyone Votes for War: Democracy and Peace Reconsidered." In Murray Wolfson, ed., *The Political Economy of War and Peace.* Boston: Kluwer Academic Publishers.

Wolfson, Murray, Anil Puri, and Mario Martelli. 1992. "The Non-Linear Dynamics of International Conflict." *Journal of Conflict Resolution* 36: 119–49.

Wright, Quincy. 1957. *The Study of International Relations.* New York: Irvington.

———. 1942. *A Study of War.* Chicago: University of Chicago Press.

Yergin, Daniel. 1990. *Shattered Peace: The Origins of the Cold War.* New York: Penguin.

Young, Oran R. 1999. *Governance in World Affairs.* Ithaca, N.Y.: Cornell University Press.

———. 1986. "International Regimes: Toward a New Theory of Institutions." *World Politics* 39: 104–122.

———. 1979. *Compliance and Public Authority.* Baltimore: Johns Hopkins University Press.

———. 1978. "Anarchy and Social Choice: Reflections on the International Polity." *World Politics* 30: 241–63.

———. 1969. "Professor Russett: Industrious Tailor to a Naked Emperor." *World Politics* 21: 486–511.

———. 1968a. *The Politics of Force: Bargaining During International Crises.* Princeton, N.J.: Princeton University Press.

———. 1968b. *A Systemic Approach to International Politics.* Center of International Studies, Research Monograph no. 33. Princeton, N.J.: Woodrow Wilson School of Public and International Affairs, Princeton University.

———. 1967a. *The Intermediaries: Third Parties in International Crises.* Princeton, N.J.: Princeton University Press.

———. 1967b. *Systems of Political Science.* Englewood Cliffs, N.J.: Prentice Hall.

Zagare, Frank C. "All Mortis, No Rigor." 1999. *International Security* 24: 107–14.

Zahar, E. G. 1983. "The Popper-Lakatos Controversy in the Light of 'Die beiden Grundprobleme der Erkenntnisteorie.'" *British Journal for the Philosophy of Science* 34: 149–71.

Zinnes, Dina A. 1980a. "Three Puzzles in Search of a Researcher: Presidential Address." *International Studies Quarterly* 24: 315–342.

———. 1980b. "Why War? Evidence on the Outbreak of International Conflict." In Ted Robert Gurr, ed., *Handbook of Political Conflict: Theory and Research.* New York: Free Press.

Zoppo, Ciro E. 1966. "Nuclear Technology, Multipolarity and International Stability." *World Politics* 18: 579–606.

Index

Achen, Christopher H., 177
Adams, Karen Ruth, 236 n. 29
ad hoc hypotheses, 119, 126, 132,
    181, 185, 238 n. 43, 242 n. 7
Adler, Emanuel, 235 n. 14
Afghan War (2001), 64
Africa, 9, 54
aggregation of concepts: and assess-
    ing scientific progress, 81–82;
    comparison of degrees of,
    82–110; continuum of, 68–70,
    110–12, 240 n. 59. *See also*
    hypotheses; ontologies; para-
    digms; theories; worldviews
Alagappa, Muthiah, 244 n. 2
Aldrich, John H., 143
alliances: balancing capabilities in,
    126, 158; distribution of capabili-
    ties in, 158; in elaborated struc-
    tural realism, 190–94; measure-
    ment issues regarding, 187–88,
    208; polarization in, 48, 135,
    136–37, 155–58; stability of, 245
    n. 11; as tertiary element of struc-
    ture, 48, 135, 151–55; and war,
    151–55, 161, 182, 188
altruism, strategic and tactical, 124
American Revolution, 8
anarchy: in axioms of structural real-
    ism, 53, 54, 121, 122, 174, 175,
    230 n. 28, 241 n. 4; and balance
    of power, 17; Buzan, Jones, and
    Little on, 128, 129; fatalistic
    implications of, 178; and war, 126

Anglo-Dutch Wars, 8
anomalies, 91, 92–94, 103–4, 106,
    108
Arab world, 56
arms races, 104–5, 123, 148
Aron, Raymond, 6, 185
Art of War, The (Sun Tzu), 5
Ashley, Richard K., 238 n. 37, 244 n.
    3
Asia: Central Asia, 61; China, 40, 60,
    62, 141, 157, 232 n. 44, 242 n.
    15; European institutions adopted
    in, 9; India, 24; Japan, 58, 141,
    157; Pakistan, 24; Southeast Asia,
    179; Vietnam, 40
astrology, 87, 237 n. 35
auxiliary assumptions, 182–85
Axelrod, Robert, 226 n. 29
axioms: in hard core of a research
    program, 91–92; of realism,
    49–52; in scientific research enter-
    prises, 113–16; of structural real-
    ism, 53–55, 94, 121–22, 174–77
Azar, Edward E., 57–58

balance of interests, 73, 185
balance of power: alliances for
    achieving, 151; bipolarity and,
    139; cooperation and, 126; in
    dyadic research models, 21; gen-
    erality of predictions from, 179,
    192; systems apparently resisting
    hegemony, 17
balance of threat, 73, 92, 185,

285